AN IDIOM BOOK
OF
NEW TESTAMENT GREEK

BY

C. F. D. MOULE

Lady Margaret's Professor of Divinity in the
University of Cambridge

SECOND EDITION

CAMBRIDGE
AT THE UNIVERSITY PRESS
1971

Published by the Syndics of the Cambridge University Press
Bentley House, 200 Euston Road, London NW1 2DB
American Branch: 32 East 57th Street, New York, N.Y.10022

ISBN
0 521 05774 4 clothbound
0 521 09237 X paperback

First Edition 1953
Second Edition 1959
Reprinted 1960 1963 1968 1971

Printed in Great Britain at the University Printing House, Cambridge
(Brooke Crutchley, University Printer)

CONTENTS

NOTE

The symbol † in the text refers the reader to the
Notes and Corrections on pp. 202 ff.

PREFACE

This book is an attempt to provide a syntactical companion to the interpretation of the New Testament: that is to say, it does not set out to be a systematic syntax, although the main sections of such a work are represented in it; but it aims rather at providing sufficient material to enable a student who is already reasonably well acquainted with the language to form some opinion on matters of exegesis which involve syntax. A fair number of passages of this type are discussed under the headings appropriate to their syntactical nature, and it is hoped that these are sufficiently representative to provide a pointer to the treatment of other similar problems.

It is true that I began the collection of material, in response to an invitation by the late Professor J. M. Creed, with a view to compiling a full grammar or syntax; but many delays and distractions have combined with a natural preference for the study of idiom to reduce what is here offered to the reader to something far less pretentious. Instead of a systematic introduction to syntax or an exhaustive catalogue, it is an obviously incomplete idiom-book—an amateur's collection of specimens. My only hope is that even with such limitations it may yet prove useful as a companion and supplement to the many already existing commentaries. It is surprising, when one attempts to produce an exact and idiomatic translation or paraphrase of the New Testament, how many problems present themselves which cry out for more than what is provided in many of the commentaries in the way of discussion of the subtle nuances and idioms of the elusive and sometimes highly individual style of St Paul, St Luke, or one of the others; surprising, too, how much research still remains to be done into the thorny but fascinating problem of the degree to which the Greek of the New Testament writers can be distinguished from that of their contemporaries represented by the papyri and other non-biblical Greek writings.

If the present compilation makes any claim upon the attention of students, it will simply be as the work of a fellow-student who has seen something of what needs to be done but has not gone far towards the achievement.

No attempt has been made to treat the idioms of the Apocalypse systematically. That is a study in itself, and R. H. Charles's edition (*International Critical Commentary*) has gone far to supply the need.

The text used, except where otherwise stated, is the eclectic one of Eberhard Nestle (4th edition, published by the British and Foreign Bible Society in 1904).

My indebtedness to those who have already written upon these matters is great, although not so great as it would have been if I had been a faster and more diligent reader. In particular I am conscious of having done all too little reading of secular writings of the period, both literary and non-literary. But I here record my gratitude for so much of the work of others as I have had the capacity to receive.

Among many who have helped me by personal friendship and encouragement, I must first mention the late Doctor J. W. Hunkin, whose sudden death has been a great grief to his multitudes of friends. I believe that he more than once surreptitiously put my name forward in one matter or another, and I suspect that I owe it to him that Professor J. M. Creed ever thought of inviting me to undertake a grammatical work. My particular gratitude is due also to Professor Creed himself, who consistently encouraged me in the work until he, like Dr Hunkin more recently, was unexpectedly taken from us, to our grievous loss; and to the committee who with him patiently read and discussed my first drafts—Dr C. H. Dodd, Dr R. N. Flew, and the Reverend H. Burnaby. In the latter stages, since the committee work lapsed, Dr Dodd in particular has been often consulted and has given much patient assistance.

I am sincerely grateful also for the skill, patience, and unfailing courtesy with which a peculiarly exacting and exasperating piece of work has been handled at the University Press; and I wish to express my thanks to all who are concerned.

But most of all I must thank my Father, the Reverend H. W. Moule, Vicar of Damerham,[1] not only for instilling into me my earliest interest in Classics, nor only for holding up an example of exact scholarship which has always been inspiring if unattainable, but also for constant advice and encouragement in this particular piece of work, and for devoting hours of toil and eye-strain to copying the manuscript and verifying the references.

C. F. D. MOULE

CLARE COLLEGE
October 1952

---

[1] He retired in December 1952, and died on 8 April 1953.

PREFACE TO THE SECOND EDITION

From this edition a few mistakes have been eliminated and a considerable body of notes and corrections added to the few already printed in the first edition. But substantially it remains the same: to make of it a scientific treatise would have required not trimming but re-writing—and that by a trained philologist. Neither has any attempt been made to furnish it with a bibliography. Recently, English-reading students have been greatly enriched by the translation and adaptation of Bauer's *Wörterbuch* (fourth edition) by Arndt and Gingrich, by the Bible Society's new Greek Testament, and by E. G. Jay's *New Testament Greek*; while, for those who read German, there is the new Debrunner-Blass and now the splendid fifth edition of Bauer. In these will be found ample pointers to further reading; and in any case those who need it will mostly have gone beyond the need of this book.

I am greatly indebted to the criticism and help of reviewers and others, and, once again, to all in the Cambridge University Press who have so skilfully achieved this revision and adaptation.

C.F.D.M.

CLARE COLLEGE
November 1958

LIST OF ABBREVIATIONS

It is hoped that most abbreviations will be sufficiently obvious. The following are some that may need definition.

B.S. = G. Adolf Deissmann, *Bible Studies* (English translation by A. Grieve, 2nd edit., T. and T. Clark, 1909.)

Beg. = *The Beginnings of Christianity*, ed. F. J. Foakes-Jackson and Kirsopp Lake (Macmillan, 5 vols., 1920–33).

D.-B. = Friedrich Blass's *Grammatik des neutestamentlichen Griechisch* bearbeitet von Albert Debrunner (Vandenhoeck und Ruprecht, Göttingen, 9th edit., 1954).

E.T. = *The Expository Times*, founded by J. Hastings (T. and T. Clark).

Giles, *Manual* = P. Giles, *A Short Manual of Comparative Philology* (Macmillan, 1901).

Goodwin = W. W. Goodwin, *A Greek Grammar* (Macmillan, 1916).

Grimm-Thayer = Grimm's lexicon based on Wilke's *Clavis Novi Testamenti*, translated, revised, and enlarged by J. H. Thayer (T. and T. Clark, 1886).

I.C.C. = *International Critical Commentary*, ed. S. R. Driver, A. Plummer, C. A. Briggs (T. and T. Clark).

J.B.L. = *Journal of Biblical Literature* (the Society of Biblical Literature and Exegesis, U.S.A.).

J.T.S. = *Journal of Theological Studies* (Oxford University Press).

M.-H. = J. H. Moulton and W. F. Howard, *A Grammar of New Testament Greek*, vol. II (T. and T. Clark, 1929). Cf. *Proleg.* below.

M.M. = J. H. Moulton and G. Milligan, *The Vocabulary of the Greek Testament* (Hodder and Stoughton, 1930).

M.T. = E. de W. Burton, *Syntax of the Moods and Tenses in New Testament Greek* (T. and T. Clark, 1894).

Proleg. = J. H. Moulton, *A Grammar of New Testament Greek*, vol. I, *Prolegomena* (3rd edit., T. and T. Clark, 1908). Cf. M.-H. above.

Rad. = L. Radermacher, *Neutestamentliche Grammatik* (J. C. B. Mohr, Tübingen, 2nd edit., 1925).

Rob. = A. T. Robertson, *A Grammar of the Greek New Testament in the Light of Historical Research* (Hodder and Stoughton, n.d.; preface dated 1914).

Rob. and Davis = A. T. Robertson and W. H. Davis, *A New Short Grammar of the Greek Testament* (S.P.C.K., 1931).

Ryl. Bull. = *The Bulletin of the John Rylands Library, Manchester.*

S. and H. = W. Sanday and A. C. Headlam, *The Epistle to the Romans* (*I.C.C.*).

T.-B. = Friedrich Blass, *Grammar of New Testament Greek*, trans. H. St J. Thackeray (Macmillan, 2nd edit., 1905).

T.W.N.T. = *Theologisches Wörterbuch zum Neuen Testament*, begun under the editorship of Gerhard Kittel, continued, on his death, under the editorship of Gerhard Friedrich (Kohlhammer, Stuttgart, 1933–).

I

THE LANGUAGE OF THE
NEW TESTAMENT

Without using intolerably cumbrous and pedantic methods, it is nearly
impossible to define a particular phase of some language with strict
accuracy. Consider, for instance, the many types and intermerging
gradations of dialect current in England alone. The difficulty of reaching
precision in such cases makes careful writers hesitant about the use
of such labels as 'Hellenistic' and κοινή (short for κοινὴ διάλεκτος,
i.e. *a language in common or widespread use*). But, broadly speaking,
both these labels are habitually applied to the new language whose
establishment came with the rise of Alexander of Macedon, otherwise
Alexander the Great (who reigned from 336 to 323 B.C.). To call it
a new language serves to emphasize the fact that it is not simply
Classical Greek growing senile and going into a decline—a mistake
which it is easy for anybody to make who comes straight from
a Classical education to the study of the New Testament. Κοινή is
not, as it were, pure gold accidentally contaminated, but something
more like a new and serviceable alloy. The dominant component is the
Attic dialect—not because it was the most widely spoken dialect at
the time, but apparently because it had a certain vitality which asserted
itself: in fact (as D.-B. § 2 puts it) Hellenistic Greek is a compromise
between the rights of the stronger minority (i.e. Attic) and the weaker
majority (other dialects).[1]
The fact that, roughly speaking, a single alloy did emerge was due,
it is said, to the unifying power of Alexander's conquests. Colonies
in earlier Greek history had been more or less uniform: by definition,
they were the budding-off from some one species of city—Ionic,
Attic, etc. But Alexander's colonies were not monochrome but mixed;
and this must have been a new and powerful factor in blending the dialects: probably the most powerful, in fact, until the advent of printing.[2]

---

[1] Of these, the opinion of Thumb (as presented in *Beg.* II, 32) specifies Ionic:
'...the κοινή in its nascent stage was formed by a dominant influence of Attic
crossed by an Ionic counter-current.'
[2] I owe this observation to Mr N. G. L. Hammond, of Clare College, although
he is not responsible for the form in which it is expressed.

Besides this, the very scope of Alexander's empire must have accelerated the formation of a κοινή διάλεκτος: '...in the days of Macedonian ascendancy the old boundary lines grew fainter: soldiers of fortune, diplomatists and traders freely moved from place to place, and lost their fineness of ear for purity of speech, while some sort of official language was required for the uses of government and the intercourse of educated men.'[1] In our own day broadcasting must be 'ironing out', for better or for worse, some of the local varieties of speech; and, undoubtedly for the worse, certain types of 'cinema' film are certainly breeding a barbarous vocabulary. The Macedonian dialect itself does not appear to have constituted more than a negligible component in the new alloy. What counted in the growth of the language was not the origin of the impulse to unity, but the respective degrees of assertiveness in its components.

But to speak in general terms about the establishment of this new lingua franca, known as Hellenistic Greek or κοινή, is, of course, not to deny that it, too, varied considerably at different times and places, or according to the idiosyncrasies of individuals even at the same time and in the same region. Polybius the historian (who died *c.* 128 B.C.) is usually claimed as its earliest representative; and there are many gradations of style and quality from his time onwards, including the extremely colloquial character of some of the papyri. Indeed, at any period the literary style was probably very different from the colloquial (see *Beg.* II, 31); and although the genius of Christianity made at least some of the New Testament writers into creators of great literature (cf. Milligan in M.M. xix, xx), still Josephus (for example) writes in a markedly more literary style than that of his near contemporary St Luke, with the exception of comparatively few passages from the latter.

Within the general field, therefore, of Hellenistic Greek as a whole, there is a wide and fascinating range of variety; and it is the style of the New Testament writers in particular which here claims our attention; while they, in their turn, vary among themselves. St Luke (probably a Gentile and perhaps the only one among the writers of the New Testament) is usually claimed as the most accomplished of them in respect of style. But it needs to be said that his Gospel and the Acts (which is by many scholars regarded as substantially his work also) are so uneven in style that it is probable that he used sources

[1] W. W. Capes, *The History of the Achaean League as contained in the Remains of Polybius* (1888), xv.

(oral or written) and often incorporated them; and it may be also that he deliberately varied his style, making it more and less Semitic according to the setting of the scene. At any rate St Luke is less uniformly elegant than the anonymous writer to the Hebrews, who has a considerable sense of the rhetorical and the poetic, and a style which has glitter if not warmth. At the other end of the scale is the author of the Apocalypse, who writes like a person who, nurtured in a Semitic speech, is only just learning to write in Greek. He is capable of horrifying grammatical blunders and patently Semitic idioms, but is not thereby prevented from achieving extraordinary power and sometimes a quite unearthly beauty. Few can now believe that the John of the Apocalypse is the same as the author (or authors) of what are commonly called the Johannine writings—the Gospel and the three Epistles. These are in a very simple, 'paratactic' style (sometimes, at least, with a Semitic tinge), but are mostly free from grammatical mistakes. In an utterly different style, St Paul's Epistles surge along with the fervid heat of a very agile mind and a highly-strung temperament, thinking and feeling as an Aramaean, but thoroughly familiar with the vocabulary of the Greek world.

The arrival of papyrus fragments from Egypt upon the philologists' desks marks a new era in the study of New Testament Greek. Till then, despite shrewd forecasts from some great men, most of the scholars—even the finest—had allowed their exegesis to be dominated (perhaps half unconsciously) by two misleading ideas: one was that Classical standards could be applied to the language; and the other was that, if Biblical Greek differed from Classical Greek, it was also quite distinct from contemporary 'secular' Greek. But the discovery and editing of piles of documents from the waste paper dumps of ancient Egypt (the only place with a climate and conditions such that so fragile a material could survive)† revolutionized Biblical scholarship; and A. Deissmann and J. H. Moulton, among others, revealed a large number of words and idioms which, while previously classed as belonging exclusively to 'Biblical' Greek, could in fact be demonstrated by the papyrus scraps to have been part of the 'secular' currency.

A fresh chapter is thus opened in the story of New Testament interpretation. But one word of caution is perhaps necessary. The pendulum has swung rather too far in the direction of equating Biblical with 'secular' Greek; and we must not allow these fascinating discoveries to blind us to the fact that Biblical Greek still does retain certain peculiarities, due in part to Semitic influence[1] (which must be far stronger in the New Testament than in an equivalent bulk of colloquial or literary 'secular' Greek, even allowing for the permeation of society by Jewish settlements), and in part to the moulding influence of the Christian experience, which did in some measure create an idiom and a vocabulary of its own.[2]

[1] W. F. Howard (M.-H. 414 n. 1) aptly quotes Père Lagrange (*S. Luc*, xcvi): 'Il n'en est pas moins vrai que lorsqu'un helléniste ouvre le NT, en particulier les évangiles, il se trouve transporté dans les tentes de Sem. L'exagération de quelques hellénistes a été, reconnaissant chaque objet comme déjà vu dans le domaine de Japhet, de prétendre qu'il en venait toujours.'

[2] For a valuable review of various features of the language, see L. Radermacher's *Koine* (Akademie der Wissenschaft in Wien, 1947).

II

THE TENSES

A. 'Aktionsart'†

The *ethos* of English verbs concentrates attention mainly on the *time* to which an event is referred—past, present, or future. In Greek, on the other hand, this is probably not the most fundamental question; and the interpretation of many N.T. passages depends not a little on the recognition that, to the Greek mind, another consideration appears to have presented itself first—namely the *nature* of the event, or (to use a German word which has become a technical term of grammarians) the *Aktionsart* ('the kind of action'). Generally speaking, the first question that the Greek writer seems to ask himself is not 'When did (or will) this happen?' but 'Am I conceiving of it as protracted or as virtually instantaneous?' Moulton has represented this pictorially by popularizing the terms 'linear' and 'punctiliar' to denote the two chief contrasted types of action—protracted like a line and focused into a point.[1]

In English the idea of protracted action can as a rule only be conveyed by the use of some auxiliary word or words; e.g. 'to be releasing' is a 'linear' phrase, while 'to release' is (or at least may be) 'punctiliar'; 'he was releasing' is 'linear', but 'he released' is definitely 'punctiliar'. Greek, however, expresses this distinction more neatly by altering the form of a single word; e.g. βάλλειν (Present Infinitive) is 'to be throwing', while βαλεῖν (Aorist Infinitive) is simply 'to throw'; βάλλειν is 'linear', but βαλεῖν is 'punctiliar'. Thus, the first question to ask about a Greek verb stem is whether it expresses 'linear' or 'punctiliar' *Aktionsart*.

It ought to be added that both in Greek and English there are some verbs which, owing to their very meaning, can only be *either* 'linear' *or* 'punctiliar' (not both). Thus, 'to snatch' is necessarily 'punctiliar', and the Imperfect, 'he was snatching a few moments of sleep', can, in the nature of the case, only refer in reality to the protracted *result* of a 'punctiliar' act—'he was *enjoying* the rest which he snatched' (at a given moment—'punctiliar'). And conversely, 'to enjoy' is, for obvious reasons, necessarily 'linear'. So in Greek (as Moulton, *Proleg.*

[1] See, especially, *Proleg.* 109 and n.

110, points out) 'the root of ἐνεγκεῖν, like our *bring*, is essentially a "point" word' and has no Present stem; whereas 'that of φέρω... *bear*, on the other hand, is essentially durative or "linear", and therefore forms no Aorist stem'.[1] Similarly λέγω, *say*, has an Imperfect ἔλεγον but no Aorist; while εἶπον, *said*, has no Present or Imperfect (though it is a question whether the durative nature of the stem λεγ- can be pressed. See *M.T.* § 57).

Many fascinating exceptions and modifications will present themselves in due course, but meanwhile it may make for clear thinking if we add the next step, namely—*Time of Action*. When the Greek does proceed to what, as I have suggested, is for the English mind the prior consideration—namely the question 'When?'—he indicates this by taking his stem—whether linear or punctiliar—and adding the appropriate termination and, if necessary, prefix.

The process may be represented in tabular form:

1. Pres. Indic. Act.   βάλλω, I am throwing ('linear' event in the present).
2. Imperf. Indic. Act.   ἔβαλλον, I was throwing ('linear' event in the past).
3. Fut. Indic. Act.   βαλῶ, I shall throw (mostly 'punctiliar' event in the future).
4. Aor. Indic. Act.   ἔβαλον, I threw ('punctiliar' event in the past).
5. Perf. Indic. Act.   βέβληκα, I have thrown ('punctiliar' event in the past, related in its effects to the present).
6. Pluperf. Indic. Act. ἐβεβλήκειν, I had thrown ('punctiliar' event in the past, related in its effects to a time itself now past).

It will be seen that, whereas the stem of the verb indicates the *Aktionsart* (the *kind* of action—whether 'linear' or 'punctiliar') the *time* of the occurrence is expressed by termination and prefix.

The tenses will now be reviewed, chiefly with reference to the Indicative mood, but with allusions, where occasion seems to offer, to similar principles in other parts of the verb. The *Aktionsart* of participles is discussed separately.

[1] I have quoted this as an interesting and provocative point. But it seems to me questionable whether one can really argue that φέρω has no similar Aorist stem *because* it is essentially linear, and vice versa. Most present stems are essentially linear, but that does not necessarily prevent them from having a not dissimilar Aorist stem.

1. **The Present Indicative.** The Greek Present Indicative normally denotes 'linear' action in present time, and it is therefore wise, in any given instance, to start by seeing whether it can be translated by the English periphrastic Present (see below, p. 17); e.g. (*M.T.* § 8) Matt. xxv. 8 αἱ λαμπάδες ἡμῶν σβέννυνται, *Our lamps are going out.*

The English simple (i.e. not periphrastic) Present normally denotes not 'linear' but 'punctiliar', or at most repeated, action in present time; and, in consequence, the English simple Present is often equivalent to a Greek Aorist; e.g. *I approve* (i.e. *I am pleased with*— referring to an immediate reaction), εὐδόκησα (e.g. Matt. iii. 17); *I know what I will do,* ἔγνων τί ποιήσω (Luke xvi. 4).

At the same time, it is impossible to generalize. Here, for example, are some English simple Presents ('punctiliar') which correspond perfectly to Greek Presents: *I perceive,* θεωρῶ[1] (John iv. 19, Acts xvii. 22); *I regret,* μεταμέλομαι (II Cor. vii. 8); *we wish,* θέλομεν (e.g. Mark x. 35). Add (with *M.T.* § 13): *I command,* παραγγέλλω (e.g. Acts xvi. 18); *heals,* ἶᾶται[2] (Acts ix. 34); *it is now permissible,* ἐπιτρέπεται (Acts xxvi. 1); *I wish you to know,* γνωρίζω...ὑμῖν (Gal. i. 11); 'and the numerous instances of λέγω in the gospels'.

Further, there are the following more easily definable uses of the Present tense:

i. *Historical Present* (very frequent in Mark),† e.g. Mark i. 21, 30, Luke viii. 49, John xviii. 28: a familiar idiom also in English.

ii. *Present equivalent to the Future,* e.g. Matt. xxvi. 18 ποιῶ τὸ πάσχα, *I will celebrate the Passover*; xxvii. 63 ἐγείρομαι, *I shall rise*; Mark ix. 31 παραδίδοται (cf. Matt. xxvi. 2), *shall be betrayed*; Luke xiii. 32 ἐκβάλλω...ἀποτελῶ...τελειοῦμαι, *I shall cast out... perform...be perfected*; I Cor. xv. 32 ἀποθνήσκομεν, *we shall die*; xvi. 5 Μακεδονίαν γὰρ διέρχομαι, *I shall go through M.* (for cf. *v.* 8). Moulton (*Proleg.* 120) says that such Futural Presents differ from the Future tense 'mainly in the tone of assurance which is imparted'. All the above examples could be fairly translated by the idiom 'I am to celebrate', 'I am to rise', etc. In fact, a pure, cold statement 'I *shall* celebrate' would seem in the first example less than the Greek conveys. Cf. Matt. ii. 4 γεννᾶται, *is to be born.*

---

[1] But see below, under 'Miscellaneous Notes on Style' (6, p. 198): θεωρῶ may be used for no better reason than that there is no convenient Aorist of this particular verb.

[2] But H. J. Cadbury in *J.T.S.* XLIX, 193–4 (Jan.–April 1948) suggests accenting ἶαται and parsing as a deponent Perfect.

iii. *Conative Present.* The Present tense is sometimes used of action attempted, but not accomplished. Burton, *M.T.* § 11, adduces John x. 32 λιθάζετε, *try to stone*, Gal. v. 4 δικαιοῦσθε, *try to get 'justified'*, Rom. ii. 4 ἄγει, *is trying* or *tending to lead*.

iv. *Gnomic Present*—i.e. that used in a γνώμη, a maxim or generalization. This is equivalent to the English frequentative Present: *a good tree [always] bears good fruit*, πᾶν δένδρον ἀγαθὸν καρποὺς καλοὺς ποιεῖ, Matt. vii. 17; *God loves a cheerful giver*, ἱλαρὸν...δότην ἀγαπᾷ ὁ θεός, II Cor. ix. 7 (both quoted in *M.T.* § 12). Cf. several examples in Jas. i. 13–15.

v. *Present of Past Action Still in Progress* (*M.T.* § 17): e.g. Acts xv. 21 Μωϋσῆς γὰρ ἐκ γενεῶν ἀρχαίων κατὰ πόλιν τοὺς κηρύσσοντας αὐτὸν ἔχει, *for Moses from generations of old has had in every city them that preached him.* Cf. Luke ii. 48, xiii. 7, xv. 29, John v. 6, II Tim. iii. 15 (where οἶδας is equivalent to a present tense).

vi. For the *Present in Reported Speech*, see below (pp. 153 f.).

Notes. (*a*) In view of the fact that a 'punctiliar' Present is an obvious requisite, it is surprising that we do not find instances of a 'punctiliar' root in the Present side by side with a 'linear', durative root; as though, besides ἀγγέλλω, *I am announcing*, there were a Present ἀγγείλω (cf. Aorist ἤγγειλα), *I announce.* Blass (T.-B. § 56. 4) points out how, although ἀσπάζεται (Present), *sends greeting*, is the regular formula in a letter when the Indicative is used, the Imperative equivalent is the Aorist ἀσπάσασθε; which suggests that if there were a 'punctiliar' Present it would be used in preference to ἀσπάζεται. Perhaps the reason for the lack of such forms is the likelihood of their being confused with Aorists and Futures. III John 15 actually has ἀσπάζου (but ℵ ἄσπασαι).

(*b*) An interesting instance of the blurring of the *Aktionsart* in the Present *Infinitive* is in Acts ii. 1 συμπληροῦσθαι. See *Beg. in loc.*

2. **The Imperfect.** For the sake of clearness, we start with an elementary statement of the use, and then discuss more interesting nuances.

The Imperfect tense is used when referring to a 'linear' or protracted action in past time:

Pres. Indic. Act. βάλλω, *I am throwing.*
Imperf. Indic. Act. ἔβαλλον, *I was throwing.*

In sharp distinction to this, the Aorist Indicative denotes 'punctiliar', instantaneous action in past time: ἔβαλον, *I threw.*

But there are other, related ideas covered by the Imperfect tense:

i. ἐδίδασκεν (e.g. Mark i. 21), *he began to teach*—the Inceptive Imperfect. This is frequent in the N.T.

ii. ἐκωλύομεν αὐτόν, Mark ix. 38 (Luke ix. 49), probably *we tried to prevent him*—the Conative Imperfect. Cf. (with *M.T.* § 23) Matt. iii. 14, Luke i. 59, Acts vii. 26. Acts xxvi. 11, ἠνάγκαζον βλασφημεῖν (mentioned by Burton, *loc. cit.* and discussed by Moulton, *Proleg.* 129), seems open to doubt, but may be conative—*I tried to compel them to blaspheme*. Moulton (*loc. cit.*) adds Heb. xi. 17 and cf. Luke iv. 42.

iii. ηὐλίζετο, Luke xxi. 37, *he used to spend the night* (parallel to ἦν . . . διδάσκων, see on periphrastic tenses below, p. 17)—the *Iterative Imperfect*. Cf. Luke viii. 29

ἐδεσμεύετο . . . καὶ διαρήσσων τὰ δεσμὰ ἠλαύνετο . . . εἰς τὰς ἐρήμους,

he $\begin{Bmatrix} used\ to \\ would \end{Bmatrix}$ *be bound . . . and* $\begin{Bmatrix} used\ to \\ would \end{Bmatrix}$ *break the bonds and be driven . . . into the uninhabited parts.*

The dividing line between these uses of the Imperfect and what has been assumed above as the regular and primary use is obviously vague. The only value of classifying the two as different is to call attention to the need for a study of the context when translating.

iv. Ἐβουλόμην . . . ἀκοῦσαι, Acts xxv. 22, *I would like to listen*. This represents an idiomatic use of the Imperfect which might be called the *Desiderative Imperfect*, because it is chiefly used in expressing a wish. It seems to soften a remark, and make it more vague or more diffident or polite; as we might say 'I could almost do so-and-so'. Cf. ηὐχόμην γὰρ ἀνάθεμα εἶναι, Rom. ix. 3, *I could almost pray to be accursed*—the Imperfect softening the shock of the daring statement or expressing awe at the terrible thought. Burton, *M.T.* § 33, mentions Philem. 13 as illustrating this class of Imperfect, but the translation of ἐβουλόμην there is surely complicated by the possibility of its being an 'epistolary' tense (see below, p. 12). The same perhaps applies to his reference to ἤθελον παρεῖναι in Gal. iv. 20.†

v. For the Imperfect in conditional clauses, see some examples below, under 'Conditional Clauses', p. 151.

As with other tenses, the English equivalent varies with the context. E.g. whereas in Greek the Imperfect is used with reference to a continuous action in the past when no interval is contemplated between it and the time of speaking, the English equivalent is a periphrastic Perfect or Pluperfect; e.g. Luke viii. 29 παρήγγελλεν, *he had been commanding*, Mark vi. 18 ἔλεγεν γὰρ ὁ 'Ιωάνης, *for John had been saying.*†

3. The Future. The Future tense seems to be used chiefly to express 'punctiliar' action in the future. To express a 'linear' sense, the normal expedient is a periphrastic tense (see below, p. 18). Moulton's 'linear' futures (*Proleg.* 149, 150) do not all seem to be convincing, though admittedly there are some. E.g. φοβηθήσομαι in Heb. xiii. 6 (κύριος ἐμοὶ βοηθός, οὐ φοβηθήσομαι) does, as he says, look more like *be afraid* ('linear') than *become afraid* ('punctiliar'). Add, from *M.T.* § 60, χαρήσομαι, Phil. i. 18, *will [continue to] rejoice*, 3ήσομεν, Rom. vi. 2. His other examples, Phil. i. 6, Rev. ix. 6, seem less convincing. Similarly (as above) the stem represented by ἔχω (*possess*, 'linear', not *acquire*, 'punctiliar') seems to be necessarily 'linear', and the future ἕξω will be 'linear'—*I shall be possessing.* σχήσω would be the truly 'punctiliar' future of *to have*—*viz. I shall acquire*; but this is obsolete in κοινή.

4. The Aorist Indicative. It has already been said that the chief function of the Aorist tense is to indicate an action viewed as instantaneous (a 'punctiliar' *Aktionsart*), no matter whether present, future, or past.

The Aorist *Indicative*, however, with its prefixed augment, further defines the instantaneous or 'punctiliar' action as having taken place in the *past*. It is therefore roughly equivalent to the English simple past tense: ἐπάταξα αὐτόν, *I struck him.* Contrast the Imperfect, ἐπάτασσον αὐτόν, *I was* or *kept on striking* or *began to strike him.*

Moulton conveniently distinguishes certain meanings within the general scope of the Aorist. Particularly notable are what he terms (*Proleg.* 109) the *Ingressive* and (following German terminology) the *Constative* respectively. The Ingressive (Burton, *Inceptive*, see esp. *M.T.* §§ 54, 55) Aorist represents, as he says, 'the point of entrance'.[1] The following may be adduced as illustrations: Luke xv. 32 νεκρὸς ἦν καὶ ἔ3ησεν, perhaps *came to life* (cf. Rom. xiv. 9, Rev. ii. 8 ἐγένετο νεκρὸς καὶ ἔ3ησεν, and Rev. i. 18 ἐγενόμην νεκρὸς καὶ ἰδοὺ 3ῶν εἰμι), John iv. 52 κομψότερον ἔσχεν, *took a turn for the better*, Acts vii. 60

[1] Burton, *M.T.* § 41, points out that it is used with verbs 'whose Present denotes a state or condition'.

ἐκοιμήθη, *fell asleep*, I Cor. iv. 8 ἐβασιλεύσατε, *you have become kings*, II Cor. viii. 9 ἐπτώχευσεν, *he became poor* (in both of which cases the use of *to become* sufficiently represents the *ingressive* idea, and in the former of which English idiom demands a perfect). The *Constative* (or *Summary*) Aorist is, as Moulton ingeniously says, like 'a line reduced to a point by perspective': John ii. 20 τεσσεράκοντα καὶ ἒξ ἔτεσιν οἰκοδομήθη ὁ ναὸς οὗτος, *this temple took forty-six years to build* (my example—but it seems exactly of a class with Moulton's ἐποίησεν ὁ δεῖνα of a craftsman's signature, i.e. *this was made by so-and-so*).

Where a Greek Aorist Indicative has to be rendered, as already shown, by an English Perfect, this is due to the difference in English idiom, and does not usually prove any exception to the rule that the Aorist Indicative refers to a 'punctiliar' action in past time, the present continued results of which (if any) are not specially prominent to the writer's mind[1] (see examples under the 'Perfect Indicative', below, pp. 13 f.).

Again, since (*M.T.* § 48) 'the Aorist Indicative is frequently used in narrative passages of a past event which precedes another past event mentioned or implied in the context', there will be cases where the most natural translation is by an English Pluperfect (below, p. 16).

Other apparent exceptions can most of them be similarly analysed away; e.g. in the case of such Aorists (see 'Present Indicative', above, p. 7) as are most naturally rendered by an English 'punctiliar' Present, the Greek idiom really scores over the English in exactness: an instantaneous action is necessarily past before it can be fairly commented on, and we are less exact when we use a word describing a condition, and say 'I know what I'll do', than the Greek who goes back to the origin of that condition, and says ἔγνων τί ποιήσω (Luke xvi. 4), *I found out (a moment ago)*. Cf. Mark i. 11, etc. ἐν σοὶ εὐδόκησα; Luke xii. 32 εὐδόκησεν ὁ πατὴρ ὑμῶν δοῦναι ὑμῖν τὴν βασιλείαν. On the other hand, a certain number refuse to be so explained away: Matt. xxiii. 2 ἐπὶ τῆς Μωϋσέως καθέδρας ἐκάθισαν οἱ γραμματεῖς καὶ οἱ Φαρισαῖοι is one such, for Moulton's explanation, quoted in M.-H. ii, 458, is unconvincing. Is it (see G. C. Richards quoted *ibid.*) a Semitism?

[1] This should mean that the ἐγκατέλιπες of Matt. xxvii. 46, Mark xv. 34, Ps. xxi. 2 (LXX) refers to an event in the past, the *results* of which are not prominently contemplated by the writer. But, even if this is to be pressed here, it does not mean that the rendering by the English Perfect, *hast thou forsaken*, is incorrect.

The *Epistolary Aorist* is an understandable idiom—and a rather gracious one, though it causes more ambiguity than the English—whereby the writer courteously projects himself in imagination into the position of the reader, for whom actions contemporaneous with the time of writing will be past.[1] This is a familiar idiom in Latin also ('especially common in Latin, but also found in Greek').[2] Burton, *M.T.* § 44, quotes Eph. vi. 22 ὃν ἔπεμψα..., *whom I send...*; and refers to Acts xxiii. 30, I Cor. v. 11 [note the contrast in meaning with the identical word, ἔγραψα, in *v*. 9], Phil. ii. 28, Col. iv. 8, Philem. 12. See also II Cor. viii. 17, 18, 22, ix. 3, 5, and I John ii. 12–14, which latter is a notoriously problematic passage, in that a thrice-repeated γράφω is followed by a thrice-repeated ἔγραψα. Is it an instance of such absolute identity of meaning between the Present and the epistolary Aorist as to make the writer indifferent as to which he uses? Or are we to assume an interruption after the thrice-repeated γράφω, followed by a threefold retrospective Aorist;[3] or take the Aorists as referring back to the Gospel;[4] or assume displacement?[5] No really convincing explanation is known to me.

In I Pet. i. 24, Jas. i. 11 the Aorists represent the Hebrew Perfect (Isa. xl. 7), which (I suggest) is used not 'gnomically', as is sometimes claimed, but to emphasize the suddenness and completeness of the withering: the grass has withered and the flower has faded before you can look round, as it were. The same may be the explanation of the κατενόησεν and ἐπελάθετο of Jas. i. 24 (which are surprisingly interrupted by the Perfect ἀπελήλυθεν), where a fair translation might be *No sooner has he looked...than he has gone away and...forgotten....* In John xv. 6, ἐὰν μή τις μένῃ ἐν ἐμοί, ἐβλήθη ἔξω...καὶ ἐξηράνθη, the

---

[1] Gal. vi. 11 is a well-known instance of the difference which the due recognition of an epistolary aorist may make to exegesis: ἴδετε πηλίκοις ὑμῖν γράμμασιν ἔγραψα τῇ ἐμῇ χειρί appears in A.V. as *Ye see how large a letter I have written unto you with mine own hand*; R.V., with better understanding of πηλίκοις γράμμασιν, renders *See with how large letters I have written...*, but R.V. marg. substitutes *write* for *have written*, which means that the Apostle here takes the pen from the amanuensis and writes the closing paragraph himself in a notably larger hand. For speculations as to the reason for the large size of the letters, see W. M. Ramsay, *A Historical Commentary on St Paul's Epistle to the Galatians*, 464–6. Note, however, that the epistolary Aorist is not *de rigueur*: II Cor. xiii. 10 διὰ τοῦτο ταῦτα ἀπὼν γράφω....

[2] W. M. Ramsay, *op. cit.* 465.

[3] R. Law, *The Tests of Life*, 309.

[4] So Plummer, *Cambridge Greek Testament, in loc.*

[5] See C. C. Oke in *E.T.* li, no. 7 (April 1940), 349, 350.

Aorists may be similarly explained as dramatically suggesting immediacy: *he has forthwith been thrown out*....[1] In Matt. xiii. 44, 46, 48 I do not see any proof that the Aorists are not true Narrative (as opposed to generalizing Gnomic) Aorists. In Luke vii. 35 ἐδικαιώθη makes excellent sense if translated as a Gnomic Aorist, *Wisdom is [always] justified...*, but could nevertheless be a statement of a single past fact, *Wisdom received her justification....*[2]

The Aorist of verbs whose very sense seems to be essentially 'linear' (see above, pp. 5 f.) may perhaps be logically accounted for in Burton's words (*M.T.* § 39 (*b*)) as expressing 'an extended act or state, however prolonged in time, if viewed as constituting a single fact without reference to its progress'. He quotes Acts xxviii. 30 ἐνέμεινεν, Eph. ii. 4 ἠγάπησεν; one may add Luke xx. 26, Acts xv. 12 ἐσίγησαν (-σεν), i.e. *they relapsed into silence* (cf. Acts xi. 18 ἡσύχασαν), Acts xx. 25 διῆλθον. What of Luke ix. 32 διαγρηγορήσαντες? Does it mean *when they were thoroughly roused*, or *having kept awake all through* (in which case the δια- imparts a 'linear' sense not germane to the Aorist itself)?†

5. The Perfect. In the table above, the Perfect is described as expressing 'punctiliar event in the past, related in its effects to the present'. Therein it differs slightly from the English Perfect, which (*M.T.* § 52) 'is used of any past action between which and the time of speaking the speaker does not intend distinctly to interpose an interval'.[3] I.e. the Greek tense is concerned with *result*, while the English tense is concerned solely with the absence (from the immediate interests of the speaker) of an *interval*. Consequently, a Greek Aorist sometimes appears in English idiom as a Perfect, and vice versa, as the following examples show: I Cor. iv. 13 ὡς περικαθάρματα τοῦ κόσμου ἐγενήθημεν,...ἕως ἄρτι, literally *we became the filth of the world...until now*; but the *until now* (obliterating the interval between the fact and the time of speaking) demands an English Perfect, *we have become....*

---

[1] Cf. Ignatius, *Eph.* v, 3 ὁ οὖν μὴ ἐρχόμενος ἐπὶ τὸ αὐτὸ οὗτος...ἑαυτὸν διέκρινεν (i.e. forthwith *excommunicates himself*), with Lightfoot's note *in loc.*

[2] A very difficult exception to explain away is in Acts i. 21 where συνελθόντων and εἰσῆλθεν καὶ ἐξῆλθεν all undoubtedly refer to 'linear' actions (contrast Acts ix. 28; see also 'Participles', below, p. 99 n. 1). And what of John xviii. 20?

[3] Our idiom *I never knew such a rascal*, which seems identical in sense with *I have never known...*, is, on this showing, exceptional. See R. Law, *The Tests of Life*, 366. Conversely, an English idiom like 'Sir W. Ramsay has demonstrated that...' (p. 111 below) is an exception in the other direction.

Matt. xxvii. 8, διὸ ἐκλήθη ὁ ἀγρὸς ἐκεῖνος 'Αγρὸς αἵματος ἕως τῆς σήμερον, which looks like a downright exception to the above generalization, and is so recognized by Burton, *M.T.* § 18, is perhaps not really 'perfective' but is explicable rather by taking ἕως τῆς σήμερον as 'pregnant'—*was called* [*then*] *and has retained the name until today.* Cf. Matt. xxviii. 15 διεφημίσθη ὁ λόγος οὗτος . . . μέχρι τῆς σήμερον ἡμέρας; John i. 32 Τεθέαμαι τὸ πνεῦμα καταβαῖνον, literally *I have seen the Spirit descending,* but English idiom (contemplating an interval) demands *I saw* . . . (if not a clumsy paraphrase such as *I saw* . . . *and therefore I am now convinced,* to bring out the *result* which the Greek Perfect suggests).

On the other hand, in John xx. 25 'Εωράκαμεν τὸν κύριον, the Perfect† is natural in both languages: *We have seen the Lord,* though the Greek Perfect probably contemplates the result, whereas the English only suggests that the speakers are not deliberately emphasizing an interval between the fact and the time of speaking.

It must be recognized, however, that there are exceptions in the N.T. to the principles here enunciated, which cannot be explained away: e.g. II Cor. ii. 13 and vii. 5 (ἔσχηκα, ἔσχηκεν—both apparently used exactly like Aorists); II Cor. xi. 25 νυχθήμερον ἐν τῷ βυθῷ πεποίηκα; I John iv. 14 (ἀπέσταλκεν, evidently synonymous with the ἀπέστειλεν of *v.* 10);† Matt. xiii. 46 (πέπρακεν), xxv. 6 (γέγονεν).† Again, is Deissmann[1] right in maintaining that to preach χριστὸν ἐσταυρωμένον is different from preaching χριστὸν σταυρωθέντα?† And what is the force of Matt. v. 10 οἱ δεδιωγμένοι?[2]

A particularly interesting extension of the Greek Perfect usage is what might be styled the *Perfect of Allegory,* which appears several times in the N.T. when the O T. is being expounded. Heb. vii provides good specimens: in the Melchizedek allegory we get (*v.* 6) [Melchizedek] δεδεκάτωκεν 'Αβραάμ, καὶ . . . εὐλόγηκεν, and (*v.* 9) Λευεὶς . . . δεδεκάτωται. So in viii. 5 καθὼς κεχρημάτισται Μωϋσῆς. Noteworthy, too, are: John vi. 32 οὐ Μωϋσῆς δέδωκεν ὑμῖν τὸν ἄρτον . . . ;[3] Acts vii. 35 (Stephen's speech) τοῦτον [*sc.* Moses] ὁ θεὸς

---

[1] *Paul* (Eng. trans.[2] by W. E. Wilson, H. and S., 1926), 197f. He points out that the Aorist participle is never applied to Christ in the Pauline letters.

[2] See the important and interesting remarks on idiosyncrasies in the use of Perfects in *M.T.* § 88, to which reference is made under 'Miscellaneous Notes on Style', 9 (*c*), p. 200 below.

[3] John vii. 22, Μωϋσῆς δέδωκεν ὑμῖν τὴν περιτομήν, is not exactly parallel, since here the result of the giving really is still present.

καὶ ἄρχοντα καὶ λυτρωτὴν ἀπέσταλκεν; Gal. iii. 18 τῷ δὲ Ἀβραὰμ δι᾽ ἐπαγγελίας κεχάρισται ὁ θεός; iv. 23 ὁ μὲν ἐκ τῆς παιδίσκης κατὰ σάρκα γεγέννηται. In view of such instances, one is inclined to accept A. H. McNeile's statement, when, commenting on the Matthaean phrase, i. 22 (cf. xxi. 4, xxvi. 56) τοῦτο δὲ ὅλον γέγονεν ἵνα πληρωθῇ..., he writes: 'The perf.... denotes that the event stands recorded in the abiding Christian tradition', and adduces some of the above passages.†
It was as though this type of Christian interpretation viewed the O.T. narrative as 'contemporary', and could therefore say 'such-and-such an incident *has happened*'. It is, in fact, a logical extension of the Greek Perfect used of a past but still relevant event. This kind of Perfect does *not* appear in II Cor. iii, which is one of the great Pauline allegories; but the phrasing is such that perhaps there is no scope for it: the Aorist ἐγενήθη in *v.* 7 is strictly appropriate—of a glory which is *past*; and the perfect οὐ δεδόξασται in *v.* 10 is its strictly correct correlative—of a glory which *no longer exists* because it is superseded.

Reverting to Heb. vii, there are Perfects in *vv.* 13, 14 which at first look like 'allegorical' ones; but as they refer to the living Christ, it may be that they fall rather into the normal category of a past event which is still operative—not merely still relevant as 'standing recorded in the abiding Christian tradition'.

Perhaps a fair example of the true Greek Perfect is II Cor. xii. 9 καὶ εἴρηκέν μοι—i.e. *his answer to me has been*.... Moulton (*Proleg.* 137) instructively compares the Aorist ἠγέρθη of Mark xvi. 6 with the Perfect ἐγήγερται of I Cor. xv. 4. The latter 'sets forth with the utmost possible emphasis the abiding results of the event',[1] although the definite mark of time (τῇ ἡμέρᾳ τῇ τρίτῃ) makes it very difficult to find an idiomatic English translation which will do it justice.

Just as, in the introductory remarks, we noticed the existence of some verbs which, owing to their very meaning, are *either* 'linear' *or* 'punctiliar' but not both, so in connexion with the perfect it is worth noting (with *Proleg.* 110) that ἔχω (*I have*) really carries a perfect meaning, viz. *I enjoy the possession of something already obtained*. Thus Rom. v. 1 means (*loc. cit.*) '"let us enjoy the possession of peace": (δικαιωθέντες) ἔσχομεν εἰρήνην is the unexpressed antecedent premiss'. I.e. the present stem represented by ἔχω is, in meaning, essentially analogous to a Greek Perfect. Conversely, οἶδα, which in form is

---

[1] Note also that the other verbs in this context are Aorists (so R. H. Strachan, quoted by J. S. Stewart, *A Man in Christ*, 137).

a Perfect, and which strictly means *I have acquired the knowledge of,* can regularly be translated by an English Present: *I know* (i.e. *I am in the possession of previously acquired knowledge*). Cf. πέποιθα, *I believe,* ἤγγικα, *I am at hand* (lit. *I have drawn near*), εἴωθα, *it is my wont,* etc.

Note. It has been said that graphically Perfects can be described, some as a point followed by a line, and some as a line followed by a point, e.g. ἠγώνισμαι, II Tim. iv. 7. These would be the *Inceptive* (or *Ingressive*) and *Constative* categories respectively (see under 'Aorist', above, p. 10).

6. The Pluperfect. The remarks about the relationship between the English and Greek Perfects apply *mutatis mutandis* also to the Pluperfect; for whereas the English Pluperfect implies nothing more necessarily[1] than that the event 'preceded another past event indicated by the context' (*M.T.* § 52), 'The Greek Pluperfect is used to represent an action as standing complete, i.e. as having an existing result, at a point of past time indicated by the context' (*ibid.*).

Consequently, whereas the Greek Pluperfect will always be translated by an English Pluperfect (except in the case of verbs which are perfect in form but present in meaning, see above), there are also cases where even an Aorist in Greek demands a Pluperfect in English; e.g. (see *M.T.* § 48): John xix. 30 ὅτε οὖν ἔλαβεν τὸ ὄξος ὁ Ἰησοῦς εἶπεν, Τετέλεσται, *When therefore Jesus had received the vinegar, he said, It is finished*; Matt. xiv. 3 ὁ γὰρ Ἡρῴδης κρατήσας τὸν Ἰωάνην ἔδησεν, *for Herod had laid hold on John and had bound him.* Cf. Matt. xxvii. 31, Mark viii. 14, Luke viii. 27, John xii. 17, xiii. 12.

B. Periphrastic Tenses

These are tenses formed by a participle together with an auxiliary verb or verbs such as *to be* or *to have.* Greek is more sparing with them than English, but N.T. Greek (particularly when influenced by Aramaic (see *Proleg.* 226, 227)) yields plenty of instances.

---

[1] This is not to say that the English Pluperfect, any more than the English Perfect, necessarily *excludes* the conception of continued result such as is inherent in the Greek Perfect and Pluperfect, but merely that it does not necessarily *include* it.

In English the periphrastic tenses are absolutely necessary. There is no method of expressing 'linear' action in English except by periphrasis: 'I am (was, shall be, have been) releasing', etc. The Greek usage will be best analysed by taking the tenses one by one.

1. **The Present.** 'Linear' action in the present is normally represented by the simple Present Indicative. But there are rare instances of periphrasis: Burton (*M.T.* § 20) adduces II Cor. ii. 17 οὐ γάρ ἐσμεν ὡς οἱ πολλοὶ καπηλεύοντες τὸν λόγον τοῦ θεοῦ, *for we are not, like the majority, merely making merchandise of God's message*, and ix. 12 ἡ διακονία τῆς λειτουργίας ταύτης οὐ μόνον ἐστὶν προσαναπληροῦσα..., *the ministry of this service is not merely supplying....* It is difficult to see exactly how the sense would have been altered by the use of the simple Present here.[1] His other instances (Matt. i. 23, xxvii. 33, Mark v. 41) are all of εἰμί with the participle λεγόμενος or μεθερμηνευόμενος, and it is a question whether εἰμί should not there rather be regarded as standing on its own feet, with an explanatory participle: e.g. Matt. xxvii. 33 ὅ ἐστιν κρανίου τόπος λεγόμενος, *which means* (lit. *is, when said* or *translated*) *Skull Place* (instead of *which is being translated...*). So Jas. i. 17 ἄνωθέν ἐστιν καταβαῖνον may be translated (see J. B. Mayor *ad loc.*) *is from above, descending* (i.e. need not be periphrastic at all). Jas. iii. 15 οὐκ ἔστιν αὕτη ἡ σοφία ἄνωθεν κατερχομένη is translated by J. B. Mayor, *this wisdom is not one that descends from above.*

2. **The Imperfect.** Similarly, whereas the simple Imperfect, normally enough, is used to express 'linear' action in the past, there are cases where periphrasis is used, apparently to emphasize the durative nature of the action (or, sometimes, simply owing to Aramaic influence):[2] e.g. Luke i. 21 ἦν ὁ λαὸς προσδοκῶν, *the people were expecting*; Luke i. 10, 22, ii. 33, v. 16, 17, Gal. i. 22, 23. Again distinguish from this cases where the verb εἰμί stands on its own feet and not as an auxiliary; e.g. perhaps Luke ii. 8 ποιμένες ἦσαν...ἀγραυλοῦντες, *there were* (i.e. *existed*) *shepherds, staying in the fields* (not *shepherds were-staying...*). In II Cor. v. 19 it is debatable whether ἦν...καταλλάσσων

---

[1] Is it significant that in Luke ix one finds in succession, ἐν τῷ εἶναι αὐτὸν προσευχόμενον (*v.* 18) and ἐν τῷ προσεύχεσθαι αὐτόν (*v.* 29)—apparently identical in sense?

[2] See de Zwaan in *Beg.* II, 62.

is periphrastic or not. Note further Matt. xix. 22, John i. 28, iii. 23, x. 40, xiii. 23; possibly also xviii. 30, where the question arises whether κακὸν ποιῶν is not virtually a noun (*v.l.* κακοποιός): see, for example, Bernard *in loc.*

3. The Future. Here there is (sometimes, at least) a clear difference between the simple and the periphrastic tenses; for whereas the simple Future is normally 'punctiliar', the periphrastic is 'linear'; e.g. Luke i. 20 ἔσῃ σιωπῶν, *you shall be dumb* (not σιωπήσεις, *you shall become dumb*).[1] So Burton, *M.T.* § 71, quotes Luke v. 10, xxi. 24. Cf. Mark xiii. 25 (but note Matt. xxiv. 29 has πεσοῦνται, which W. F. Howard (M.-H. II, 451) regards as a correction of Mark's vernacular).

4. The Future Perfect. Curiously enough, there appears to be no N.T. instance of the Greek for such a sentence as 'I shall have finished' (*negative* sentences of this type are negotiated differently, e.g. Matt. x. 23, Mark ix. 1; see below, p. 156). The four passages adduced in *M.T.* § 94 are none of them quite parallel, for the participle in three cases is virtually an adjective, with little trace of the perfect sense still adhering; e.g. Matt. xvi. 19 ἔσται δεδεμένον seems more naturally to mean *shall be bound* than *shall have been bound* (though it might be stretched to mean *shall be found to be bound*); so xviii. 18, Luke xii. 52; and in the fourth case, Heb. ii. 13 ἔσομαι πεποιθώς, the participle is only perfect in form and not in meaning.

5. The Perfect. There are some periphrastic Perfects which are perfect in form more than in meaning: e.g. (see *M.T.* § 84) Luke xx. 6 πεπεισμένος γάρ ἐστιν, [*the people*] *are convinced.* Here πεπεισμένος is virtually an adjective (cf. the instances in the preceding section), with little or no reference to the time at which the convincing was done, and it would be misleading to translate *has been persuaded.* So with John ii. 17, Acts ii. 13, xxv. 10, II Cor. iv. 3.

As for those which are genuinely perfect, it is not always easy to see the force of the distinction between the simple and the periphrastic Perfect. E.g. would the sense have been altered if, for χάριτί ἐστε

---

[1] It is striking that there are so many periphrastic tenses within so few verses of Luke i: *vv.* 7, 10, 18 (?), 20, 21, 22; all the more so in view of Luke's avoidance of periphrasis in xvii. 27 (ἤσθιον, ἔπινον, ἐγάμουν, ἐγαμίζοντο) as against Matt. xxiv. 38 (ἤσαν...τρώγοντες κ.τ.λ.).

σεσωσμένοι (Eph. ii. 8), χάριτι σέσωσθε had been written?[1] Perhaps the answer is that this too is an instance where the participle has little or no time-significance and is practically adjectival—*as a result of free favour you are safe*; but nevertheless *you have been saved* [*and therefore enjoy your present status*] makes good sense.

6. The Pluperfect. Burton, *M.T.* § 91, analyses periphrastic Pluperfects into: (*a*) Those 'of existing state', e.g. Matt. xxvi. 43 ἦσαν γὰρ αὐτῶν οἱ ὀφθαλμοὶ βεβαρημένοι, *for their eyes were heavy* (lit. *were having been weighed down*). Here the participle is virtually an adjective, referring only to the existing result and not also to the time of weighing down. (*b*) Those 'denoting completed action, referring to the past act as well as the existing result', e.g. Luke ii. 26 καὶ ἦν αὐτῷ κεχρηματισμένον, *and it had been revealed to him*.

Now class (*a*) can really hardly be called Pluperfects except in form (cf. 'Future Perfect' and 'Perfect', above, p. 18). And in class (*b*) it is again difficult (as with the periphrastic Perfect) to see always wherein the periphrastic Pluperfect differs in meaning from the simple Pluperfect.

The use of the Aorist Participle with ἦν is regarded by Burton, *M.T.* § 20, as 'quite exceptional', the only N.T. instance being, apparently, Luke xxiii. 19 ἦν...βληθείς, *had been thrown*.[2]

[1] Moulton, *Proleg*, 127, says that it tells 'of a work which is finished on its Author's side, but progressively realized by its objects'. What are we to make of Acts xxvi. 26 οὐ γάρ ἐστιν ἐν γωνίᾳ πεπραγμένον τοῦτο?

[2] H. G. Meecham, *Journal of New Testament Studies* (C.U.P.), 1, no. 1 (Sept. 1954), 62 ff., compares Athanasius *De Incarn.* 23 κρύψας ἦν.

III

THE IMPERATIVE, SUBJUNCTIVE, AND OPTATIVE MOODS

We have seen how the nature of an action is defined in Greek by the stem of a verb, while statements as to the time of that action's taking place are made by the tenses of the Indicative mood. We come next to moods other than the Indicative. The *Indicative* mood is used for making simple statements of fact, while the *Imperative*, *Subjunctive* and *Optative* moods are all 'characterized by a common subjective element, representing an attitude of mind on the part of the speaker' (*Proleg.* 164). Leaving the Indicative mood with the illustrations of it already adduced, we look at these moods in turn.

1. The Imperative Mood. Logically, one would expect the remarks already made about *Aktionsart* to hold good for the tenses of the Imperative; i.e. an Aorist Imperative ought, one would think, to represent a command to do something instantly, or once for all; or to indicate simply indifference to the time-factor; whereas a Present Imperative ought to refer to repeated, or to protracted, or to attempted action.

Now, good illustrations can indeed be adduced for Aorists and Presents fitting perfectly into these respective categories; but it is far more difficult to demonstrate that this is not due to some chance, and there are exceptions which make one wonder whether the underlying *rationale* has yet been discovered.

Examples of the *Aktionsart* behaving, so to speak, as it should, are: (i) *Aorist Imperative*: δὸς ἐργασίαν, *give diligence* (Luke xii. 58), ἔξελθε, *come out* (Luke xiv. 23), ἑτοίμασον τί δειπνήσω, *make ready something for my supper* (Luke xvii. 8), λύσαντες αὐτὸν ἀγάγετε, *untie it and bring it* (Luke xix. 30). (ii) *Present Imperative*: περιζωσάμενος διακόνει μοι, *gird yourself and wait on me* (Luke xvii. 8—in interesting contrast to the Aorist quoted from the same sentence above).

Thus Burton, *M.T.* § 184, says that 'the distinction of force' between different tenses of the imperative is 'that of the tenses of the dependent moods in general'.

But, if so, it is curious that (*ibid.*) 'in prohibitions...the use of the Imperative is confined almost entirely to the Present tense'. Why is this?† There is no evidence that the tense is any less important as a factor in *prohibitions* than elsewhere, for the Aorist *Subjunctive* with μή is a perfectly normal way of expressing a prohibition: all we can say is that (perhaps unaccountably) usage came to dictate that an *Aorist* prohibition should be expressed by the Subjunctive (not an Imperative), while a *present* prohibition should be expressed by the Imperative.

There remain, further, instances (whether of commands or prohibitions) where the reason for the use of the tense is difficult to detect;[1] e.g. Mark xiii. 7, 21 μὴ θροεῖσθε, μὴ πιστεύετε, John xix. 21 μὴ γράφε, Eph. v. 18 μὴ μεθύσκεσθε οἴνῳ . . . ἀλλὰ πληροῦσθε ἐν πνεύματι, Col. iii. 9 μὴ ψεύδεσθε, Jas. v. 12 μὴ ὀμνύετε (whereas Matt. v. 34, 36 has μὴ ὀμόσαι (Aor. Inf.), μὴ ὀμόσῃς (Aor. Subj.)), I Pet. ii. 17 πάντας τιμήσατε, τὴν ἀδελφότητα ἀγαπᾶτε, τὸν θεὸν φοβεῖσθε, τὸν βασιλέα τιμᾶτε. With regard to this latter, James P. Wilson (*E.T.* LIV, no. 7 (April 1943), 193, 194) makes the very interesting suggestion that we should emend πάντας τιμήσατε into πάντα ποιήσατε, and take it with what precedes (. . . ὡς θεοῦ δοῦλοι πάντα ποιήσατε. τὴν ἀδελφότητα ἀγαπᾶτε . . .). In the course of the discussion, he remarks that πάντα ποιήσατε then 'has the impressiveness of a climax, the Aorist Imperative sharpening the edge of the exhortation in accordance with the tone of urgency which the writer constantly expresses in this way. By the succeeding Present Imperatives he is inculcating states of mind in a calmer tone.' Yet, what of II Cor. xiii. 11, 12 χαίρετε, καταρτίζεσθε, παρακαλεῖσθε, τὸ αὐτὸ φρονεῖτε, εἰρηνεύετε, . . . Ἀσπάσασθε ἀλλήλους . . . Ἀσπάζονται ὑμᾶς οἱ ἅγιοι πάντες? Has ἀσπάσασθε any significance in contrast to the Present Imperatives which precede it and the Present Indicative which follows it? See above, p. 8, *Notes.* (*a*).

Another passage where the *Aktionsart* of an Imperative might, if it could be certainly depended on, carry exegetical importance is the much debated I Cor. vii. 21 ἀλλ' εἰ καὶ δύνασαι ἐλεύθερος γενέσθαι, μᾶλλον χρῆσαι: does this mean *but if you can gain your freedom, choose to use* [*the opportunity to do so*]? Or does it mean *but even if you can* . . . , *choose instead to continue in your present employ?* In the latter case one would have expected a 'linear' (Present) Imperative; and, in fact, the former interpretation sounds, to judge by the context also, preferable.

2. **The Subjunctive Mood.** In the history of its development, this seems to be closely related to the Future tense: the two are mutually

---

[1] Moulton, *Proleg.* 122 (cf. 173, 174), attempts to maintain an *Aktionsart* distinction; but is he convincing?

exclusive—i.e. there is no separate *Subjunctive* Future—and are usually allied in form. This connexion is illustrated in some of the usages which are here tabulated.

i. The 2nd person Aorist Subjunctive with μή is common enough in *Prohibitions* (see above under 'The Imperative Mood', p. 21). For a prohibition in the Present tense, however, the Imperative is regular.

When the Subjunctive is used in a similar manner in the 1st person, it is usually classed as *Hortatory*: Luke ii. 15 διέλθωμεν δή, *let us go now*. This hortatory use is very rare in the 1st singular. It is found in Matt. vii. 4 and Luke vi. 42, preceded by ἄφες, *allow* or *let*.[1] In Acts vii. 34 an extraordinary Subjunctive appears (as it does also in Exod. iii. 10 (LXX), which is being quoted) where the future would be absolutely natural: for ἀποστείλω one would expect ἀποστελῶ.† Burton, *M.T.* § 161, classes this as hortatory.† There are claimed to be a few instances of a hortatory Subjunctive in the 3rd person singular. See (with *Proleg.* 178) I Cor. xvi. 11 μή τις...αὐτὸν ἐξουθενήσῃ, *let no one despise him*, II Cor. xi. 16, II Thess. ii. 3. But this merges insensibly into the *imperative* use—i.e. simple aorist Prohibitions.

The *Deliberative* Subjunctive is merely the hortatory turned into a question: the hortatory says *let me do so-and-so*, the deliberative says *am I to do...?* Mark xii. 14 δῶμεν ἢ μὴ δῶμεν; *are we to give or are we not to give?*

ii. *Future Negation* can be expressed by the Aorist Subjunctive with the double negative οὐ μή. About this, note: (*a*) that it illustrates the kinship between Future and Aorist to which reference has been made above; (*b*) that it is often regarded as a particularly *emphatic* negative; but Moulton, *Proleg.* 188ff., is inclined to question its *emphatic* nature in N.T. writings: it may, he suggests, be a survival of a formula which might once have been emphatic, but which had lost its stress by over-familiarity; (*c*) that its use in the N.T. may be influenced by LXX usage (see on 'μὴ and οὐ', pp. 156 f.); (*d*) that in Heb. xiii. 5 there is a *triple* (!) negative—οὐδ' οὐ μή σε ἐγκαταλίπω, which is not warranted by Deut. xxxi. 6, 8, Joshua i. 5, the LXX passages which appear to be in mind;† (*e*) that it is possible (see Moulton, *loc. cit.*) that the *origin* of the construction may be found in μή as = *perhaps*.

iii. The use of the Subjunctive in *Final* and in *Conditional* clauses is dealt with below under these headings.

---

[1] Add M.-H. ii. 420 for (?) Semitic co-ordinate Subjunctive after (*a*) an imperative (as ἄφες); (*b*) θέλειν.

iv. In Mark iv. 26 the Subjunctive is used in a *Comparison*: ὡς βάλῃ, *as though he might throw*. This has been claimed as unique; but Luke xi. 5, 6 looks uncommonly like the same usage (it might be called a *parabolic* Subjunctive): introduced in this case by τίς ἐξ ὑμῶν ἕξει φίλον, the construction passes over to this hypothetical Subjunctive, with a twice-repeated εἴπῃ.

Once more we are faced with the close kinship of Future and Subjunctive; for which we may now further call attention to the following: Luke xii. 58 μή ποτε κατασύρῃ...καί...παραδώσει; xiv. 10 ἵνα...ἐρεῖ; Rev. iii. 9 ἵνα ἥξουσιν...καί γνῶσιν. For ἵνα ἀναπαήσονται, Rev. xiv. 13, see under 'Remarks on ἵνα and ὥστε' p. 145, n. 1; but it is far from clear that this is not, so to speak, a 'subjunctive Future'. Similarly Moulton, *Proleg.* 204 n. 2, refers to the 'Hellenistic weakening of the Future infinitive, which in the papyri is very frequently used for aorist or even present'.†

3. The Optative Mood. This is rare in the N.T. 'No language but Greek', writes Moulton, *Proleg.* 165, 'has preserved both Subjunctive and Optative as separate and living elements in speech, and Hellenistic Greek took care to abolish this singularity in a fairly drastic way.' As compared with the Subjunctive, it might be said to be remoter, vaguer, less assured in tone; but inevitably the two domains overlap, and this may be why the weaker Optative has receded. Where it still remains, it either figures in certain types of temporal, conditional, or concessive clauses, or in indirect speech (for all of which see below), or to express a wish—a *wish*, one might say, as distinct from the more resolute *resolve* of the hortatory Subjunctive.

Grammarians adduce thirty-seven examples in the N.T. of the Optative expressing a wish, of which fifteen are the familiar μή γένοιτο. The only N.T. example of the 1st person Optative to express a wish is Philem. 20 ὀναίμην, *let me benefit!* All the others are in the 3rd person singular.

Examples: Luke i. 38 γένοιτό μοι; Acts viii. 20 τό ἀργύριόν σου σύν σοί εἴη εἰς ἀπώλειαν; I Thess. iii. 11 αὐτός δέ ὁ θεός...κατευθύναι....

4. The Infinitive Mood. See below, under 'Observations on Certain Uses of the Infinitive', pp. 126 ff. Note that the use o fthe Infinitive as a noun *qualifiable by an adjective* does not seem to occur in N.T. Greek, as it does, for example, in Ignatius (e.g. τό ἀληθινόν ζῆν, *Eph.* xi, with J. B. Lightfoot's note).

IV

THE VOICES

The Middle voice calls for comment first. Grammars sometimes describe the Middle as primarily reflexive. Whether or not this is true for certain periods,† it is manifestly not true of N.T. usage. Even the ἀπήγξατο of Matt. xxvii. 5 is not necessarily *he hanged himself*; it may be (as Moulton, *Proleg*. 155, suggests) nearer in meaning to 'the English intransitive *choke*'. Luke viii. 52 ἐκόπτοντο αὐτήν is admittedly *they beat their breasts for her*, but the word has practically crystallized into a colourless *they mourned for her*. It is safer to say (*ibid*. 153, following Brugmann) that the Middle (where a specific meaning can be detected) calls attention to the whole subject being concerned in the action: Acts xxvi. 2 ἀπολογεῖσθαι, *to make* my *defence* (cf. xxiv. 10 τὰ περὶ ἐμαυτοῦ ἀπολογοῦμαι). It may sometimes be analysed (*ibid*. 157) into an Active voice with a Dative: προσκαλοῦμαι, *I call* to myself (=προσκαλῶ ἐμαυτῷ)—though the προσ- by itself practically secures this. Moulton suggests that the *form* of the Middle, as contrasted with that of the Active, calls attention (in keeping with the above contention) to the pronominal element: Active τίθημι, but Middle τίθεμαι. He suggests (*ibid*. 152), along these lines, that in the Absolution in the Book of Common Prayer, alternative emphases could be represented respectively by Active and Middle in Greek: 'He *pardoneth* and *absolveth*...' would be Active; '*He* pardoneth and absolveth...' would be Middle.†

The above is an attempt to define where the difference may be looked for when difference there is. But the fact remains that the distinction has become blurred by the N.T. period,[1] and, as a rule, it is far from easy to come down from the fence with much decisiveness on either side in an exegetical problem if it depends on the voice.[2]

[1] E.g. W. C. Allen (*I.C.C. Matthew*, xxiii) gives the following instances of Middles in Mark changed to Actives in Matt.:

Mark	Matt.
x. 20 ἐφυλαξάμην	xix. 20 ἐφύλαξα†
xiv. 20 ἐμβαπτόμενος	xxvi. 23 ἐμβάψας
xiv. 47 σπασάμενος	xxvi. 51 ἀπέσπασεν

[2] A comparable ambiguity attaches to the *Niph'al* in Hebrew—notably in Gen. xii. 3, etc., where LXX (followed in Gal. iii. 8, etc.) has the passive,

There is the further problem, where the *form* of Middle and Passive is the same, of determining whether the verb is to be given a passive sense, or an active sense (like a Latin deponent), or a middle sense (as indicated above). The following are specimens of problematic passages.

i. Eph. i. 23 τὸ πλήρωμα τοῦ τὰ πάντα ἐν πᾶσιν πληρουμένου. Here A.V. and R.V. both take πληρουμένου as middle with active sense: *him that filleth all in all.* J. Armitage Robinson[1] takes it as passive: *him that all in all is being fulfilled* ('to St Paul's mind the Christ in a true sense still waited for completion, and would find that completion only in the Church'); W. L. Knox[2] also takes it as a Passive, but refers it to the 'filling' of Christ, not by the growth of his body, the Church, but by God: *him who is always being filled [by God].* Dibelius[3] questions whether the phrase may not imply both these latter senses. It is possible, though this is strenuously denied, e.g. by T. K. Abbott (*I.C.C. in loc.*), that τὸ πλήρωμα itself may be in apposition, not with *the Church*, but with *Christ*. It will then be right to take πληρουμένου as active in sense and as designating God, of whom Christ (as elsewhere in the Epistles) is spoken of as the πλήρωμα.[4]

ii. Eph. v. 13 πᾶν γὰρ τὸ φανερούμενον φῶς ἐστιν. Does this mean *whatever illuminates is light* (a not very illuminating remark!), or *whatever is illuminated becomes light* (which would embody the hopeful doctrine that the darkness of sin, once illuminated by the Gospel, may be converted into light)?

iii. Gal. iv. 18 καλὸν δὲ ζηλοῦσθαι ἐν καλῷ πάντοτε.... Here the context (with the Active ζηλοῦσιν ὑμᾶς οὐ καλῶς in the preceding verse) suggests that ζηλοῦσθαι is a true Passive: *they are zealously cultivating you...but it is good [for you] to be zealously cultivated....* Yet the issue is complicated by the phrase ἀλλὰ ἐκκλεῖσαι ὑμᾶς θέλουσιν, ἵνα αὐτοὺς ζηλοῦτε—where the same persons form the subject of the active ζηλοῦτε as of ζηλοῦσθαι, which might point to ζηλοῦσθαι

ἐνευλογηθήσονται, but the original probably meant not *shall be blessed* but *shall bless themselves* ('the name of Abram will pass into a formula of benediction'). See Skinner (*I.C.C. Genesis*) on Gen. xii. 3.

[1] *Ephesians*, 42, 44.

[2] *St Paul and the Church of the Gentiles*, 164, 186.

[3] In Lietzmann's *Handbuch z. N.T.*, *in loc.*

[4] See A. E. N. Hitchcock, *E.T.* xxii (1910–11), 91, and my note, *E.T.* lx (1948–9), 53. See also under 'Some Observations on the Cases', below, p. 35.

carrying an active sense. Amid much uncertainty the following paraphrastic interpretation may be suggested, making ζηλοῦσθαι Passive: The Judaizers are zealously cultivating you [—showing solicitous concern for you as evangelists over converts], but their motives are unworthy: they want to make you feel excluded whenever you do not come into their circle of élite ritualists, so that you may emulate them [a slightly different sense of ζηλόω from the first]. But [returning to the first sense, but in the passive] what is really good is to be zealously cultivated in a worthy cause; and that is the condition I want you to be in always, and not only while I am with you to keep you on the right lines. . . .

iv. Gal. v. 6 πίστις δι' ἀγάπης ἐνεργουμένη. This is a case where probability seems to lie strongly on the side of translating the participle not as a Passive (*faith operated by love*) but as an Active (*operating*) or some Middle nuance of the same.

v. Note also Jas. v. 16 πολὺ ἰσχύει δέησις δικαίου ἐνεργουμένη (perhaps *the prayer of an upright man is very powerful in its effect*), in which a transitive sense seems best. Eph. iii. 20 κατὰ τὴν δύναμιν τὴν ἐνεργουμένην ἐν ἡμῖν is, in itself, ambiguous.

vi. Whether one can find any substantial difference between Luke vii. 14 ἐγέρθητι (Passive form) and viii. 54 ἔγειρε (Active) is doubtful: they *appear* both to be simply intransitive in sense.† And a similar question may be asked with regard to references to the Resurrection: is the Passive verb with which it is usually, though not always, described, to be pressed as theologically significant—indicating the initiative of God Himself—or to be taken as a mere intransitive? That in this case the former is probable is suggested by the frequent use of a transitive with God as subject and Christ as object.

vii. Βαπτίζω is another instance. Is there any significance in the comparison between Acts ix. 18 ἀναστὰς ἐβαπτίσθη and xxii. 16 ἀναστὰς βάπτισαι καὶ ἀπόλουσαι τὰς ἁμαρτίας σου? Did a Christian in fact generally 'baptize himself', 'get himself baptized', or 'submit to baptism'?[1]

---

[1] See, for example, G. Dix, *The Theology of Confirmation in relation to Baptism*, 13 *sub fin.*

V

IMPERSONAL VERBS

The strictly 'Impersonal' use of verbs is that in which no definite subject can be mentally supplied, but only the vague *it* (or sometimes a periphrasis, *there is* . . ., will be required): e.g. Mark ii. 2 ὥστε μηκέτι χωρεῖν μηδὲ τὰ πρὸς τὴν θύραν, *so that there was no longer room, not even in the part near the door* (unless τὰ πρὸς τὴν θύραν is not an 'Accusative of Respect' but the subject of χωρεῖν); Luke xxiv. 21 τρίτην ταύτην ἡμέραν ἄγει, *this is the third day* (perhaps = *it is spending the third day*); Mark xiv. 41 ἀπέχει, *it is enough* (*enough of this!*).[1]

On the other hand the majority of the verbs commonly called impersonal have, in reality, an expressed or implied subject at least in the form of a substantival clause. This seems to be the case with ἀνένδεκτόν ἐστιν (Luke xvii. 1, where τοῦ τὰ σκάνδαλα μὴ ἐλθεῖν is perhaps a substantival clause comparable to ἵνα clauses of the same sort), δεῖ (e.g. in Acts xv. 5 περιτέμνειν αὐτούς is the subject), δέον (ἐστίν) (e.g. in I Pet. i. 6 an implied λυπηθῆναι ὑμᾶς would be the subject), δοκεῖ, ἔξεστιν, ἐξόν, λυσιτελεῖ (only Luke xvii. 2), πρέπει, πρέπον ἐστίν, συμφέρει, συνέβη, and the phrase, Acts vii. 23, ἀνέβη ἐπὶ τὴν καρδίαν αὐτοῦ, *it occurred to him* (where the subject of ἀνέβη is ἐπισκέψασθαι, *to visit*). In Matt. xii. 4 ὃ οὐκ ἐξὸν ἦν αὐτῷ φαγεῖν, there seems to be a mixed construction—the relative ὅ, which refers to the eating of the shewbread, being the subject of ἐξὸν ἦν, and then φαγεῖν appearing as a reiterated subject, as though the sentence had begun with ἀλλά or καίπερ instead of ὅ.[2]

The same applies to apparently impersonal Passives, where in reality the noun cognate to the verb can in most cases be supplied as subject: e.g. (μέτρον) μετρηθήσεται, Matt. vii. 2, etc., (δῶρον) δοθήσεται, Luke vi. 38, etc. But Rom. x. 10 πιστεύεται . . . ὁμολογεῖται—*one believes . . . one acknowledges*—is in a different class, and is striking.

[1] In Jas. v. 17 οὐκ ἔβρεξεν, *it did not rain*, a subject such as ὑετός—cf. Rev. xi. 6—or οὐρανός or ὁ θεός would be easy to supply. Cf. Matt. v. 45 (θεός), Luke xvii. 29 (θεός). Professor Dodd, in discussing this, alluded to a relief showing Zeus with hands outstretched, raining. The use of Zeus or Jupiter for 'the weather' is, of course, common enough.

[2] Some of these, e.g. ἔξεστιν and συμφέρει, are also found with such a straightforward subject as πάντα (e.g. I Cor. vi. 12).

Similarly subjects can be supplied for ἐγένετο, γέγραπται, etc. Cf. I Pet. ii. 6 περιέχει ἐν γραφῇ, *it is contained in Scripture*, which may have the quotation which follows it as its subject. There seems to be nothing in New Testament Greek exactly like the Latin *itur, concurritur*, etc., though even for these, cognate nouns could be mentally supplied.

The verb μέλει *it matters* will serve as an example of the connexion between the true impersonal and the quasi-impersonal. In Matt. xxii. 16, Mark xii. 14, John x. 13, xii. 6, and I Pet. v. 7 it is constructed like a pure impersonal, followed by περί with the genitive: *it matters to someone concerning....* But in I Cor. vii. 21 δοῦλος ἐκλήθης; μή σοι μελέτω, *were you called as a slave? let not that trouble you*, a clearly implied substantival clause is the subject: and in Mark iv. 38, Luke x. 40 there is a ὅτι-clause expressed. In Acts xviii. 17 οὐδὲν τούτων τῷ Γαλλίωνι ἔμελεν, *Gallio did not concern himself with any of these things*, we should have no doubt that οὐδέν was the subject, were it not that I Cor. ix. 9 μὴ τῶν βοῶν μέλει τῷ θεῷ; makes it evident that μέλει can be constructed impersonally with a plain Genitive of Reference (without περί), which makes it just possible that in the Gallio passage also ἔμελεν is impersonal, τούτων is a Genitive of Reference, and οὐδέν is an Accusative of Respect.

ὠφελεῖν, *to profit*, has not gone so far towards the impersonal, Mark viii. 36 τί γὰρ ὠφελεῖ ἄνθρωπον κερδῆσαι κ.τ.λ. being the only semblance of such a use; and even here (as with the other quasi-impersonals above) the real subject is the Infinitive-clause.

Here may be mentioned also the use of the 3rd person plural with a vague and unexpressed subject, 'they', as in our phrase 'they say', which is equivalent to a Passive, '*such-and-such a thing is said*' (cf. also English 'one', French *on*, German *man*). This usage seems to have been encouraged by the influence of Aramaic (D.-B. § 130).† See, for example, Luke xii. 20 τὴν ψυχήν σου ἀπαιτοῦσιν ἀπὸ σοῦ; xvi. 9 ἵνα...δέξωνται ὑμᾶς....¹

In Mark viii. 27 we have an intermediate stage, with the general subject, οἱ ἄνθρωποι, expressed: τίνα με λέγουσιν οἱ ἄνθρωποι εἶναι; but the subject is omitted in Matt. v. 15 (καίουσιν...τιθέασιν), Matt. vii. 16, Luke vi. 44 (συλλέγουσιν), Mark x. 13 (προσέφερον), Mark xv. 27 (σταυροῦσιν), Luke vi. 38 (δώσουσιν), xii. 20 (just quoted),

---

¹ See further under 'Semitisms' (below, pp. 180 f.). But in Luke xvi. 9 the subject may be οἱ φίλοι.

xiv. 35 (βάλλουσιν), xvii. 23 (ἐροῦσιν). So also John xv. 6, xx. 2, Acts iii. 2, I Cor. x. 20 (in the best text), Rev. xii. 6.[1]

A similar use of the 3rd person singular is noted by D.-B. (§ 130. 3) in II Cor. vi. 2, Gal. iii. 16, etc. (λέγει); I Cor. vi. 16, Heb. viii. 5 (φησίν); Heb. iv. 4 (εἴρηκεν). In II Cor. x. 10 he suggests that the φησίν (ℵ D, E, etc., φασίν B) is the idiom of the 'diatribe', and refers to a supposed objector; *someone will say*.

[1] Cf. Luke xii. 48, where in the first clause two Passives with their subjects are used, but in the parallel clause two 'impersonal' 3rd plurals: παντὶ δὲ ᾧ ἐδόθη πολύ, πολὺ ζητηθήσεται παρ' αὐτοῦ, καὶ ᾧ παρέθεντο πολύ, περισσότερον αἰτήσουσιν αὐτόν. Note the typically Semitic parallelism here, and the Semitic handling of the personal pronouns.

VI

SOME OBSERVATIONS ON THE CASES

The cases of the Greek noun extant in the N.T. period are here taken seriatim, and observations are offered under each heading. But first it may be well to note that there are still traces, in κοινή Greek, of cases no longer properly current, namely the Ablative and the Locative.

i. *Ablative.* Certain common N.T. words ending in -θεν and denoting *origin* are, although classed as adverbs, recognized (e.g. by M.-H. II, § 66) as 'quasi-ablative'; but the weakening of the case is evident, from the fact that supporting prepositions are sometimes used. Such words are: ἀλλαχόθεν, ἄνωθεν (ἀπὸ ἄνωθεν, ἐκ τῶν ἄνωθεν), ἐκεῖθεν, ἐκ παιδιόθεν, ἔμπροσθεν, ἔνθεν, ἐντεῦθεν, ἔξωθεν, ἔσωθεν, κυκλόθεν, μακρόθεν (ἀπὸ μακρόθεν), ὅθεν, οὐρανόθεν, πόρρωθεν. (In one or two instances the text is uncertain.)

ii. *Locative.* There seem also to be traces of a separate Locative case (as in Latin), denoting position (literal or metaphorical), although the endings of some of the adverbs here in question suggest that they may be 'crystallized' Genitives or Datives. E.g.: εἶτα, ἐνθάδε, ὧδε, ἐκτός, ἐντός, ἐκεῖ, ἔξω, ἔσω, ἀλλαχοῦ, αὐτοῦ, ὁμοῦ, ὅπου, οὗ, πανταχοῦ, πανταχῇ. (Again the reading is not always certain.) As for the termination -σε (ἐκεῖσε, ὁμόσε—the latter in Acts xx. 18 D), which, judging by classical usage, should indicate direction (a 'linear' Locative, so to speak), the N.T. instances (which, in any case, are not numerous) tend to express situation rather than direction—they tend, that is, to be 'punctiliar'.

A study of these 'fossilized' cases is germane to that of the prepositions; but neither can here be treated etymologically. We proceed to the extant cases.

1. Nominative. Here need only be noted some peculiar uses, which it is difficult to justify grammatically.

i. In reference to a person or thing which is in fact not the subject of the sentence: Matt. xii. 36 πᾶν ῥῆμα ἀργὸν ὃ λαλήσουσιν οἱ ἄνθρωποι, ἀποδώσουσιν περὶ αὐτοῦ λόγον (unless πᾶν κ.τ.λ. here is Accusative attracted to ὅ (see D.-B. § 466)); John vii. 38 ὁ πιστεύων εἰς ἐμέ,...ποταμοὶ ἐκ τῆς κοιλίας αὐτοῦ ῥεύσουσιν (unless here a full stop should be placed after ὁ πιστεύων εἰς ἐμέ, in which case it becomes the perfectly grammatical subject of the preceding πινέτω); Acts xix. 34 ἐπιγνόντες δὲ...φωνὴ ἐγένετο μία ἐκ πάντων...κράζοντες...; II Cor. ix. 11, 13 ἐν παντὶ πλουτιζόμενοι...δοξάζοντες τὸν θεόν (but here, as the grammarians remark, the participles may stand—perhaps by a Semitic idiom (see under 'Semitisms', pp. 179 f.)—for imperatives or indicatives).

Note also the following: II Cor. i. 7 καὶ ἡ ἐλπὶς ἡμῶν βεβαία ὑπὲρ ὑμῶν, εἰδότες...; Eph. iii. 17, 18 κατοικῆσαι τὸν χριστὸν διὰ τῆς πίστεως ἐν ταῖς καρδίαις ὑμῶν, ἐν ἀγάπῃ ἐρριζωμένοι καὶ τεθεμελιωμένοι, ἵνα ἐξισχύσητε... (where it is probably not the writer's intention—especially in view of the following examples—to make the Nominatives the subject of the ἵνα-clause: see commentators in loc.); iv. 1–3 παρακαλῶ οὖν ὑμᾶς...περιπατῆσαι...ἀνεχόμενοι ἀλλήλων... σπουδάζοντες...; Phil. i. 29, 30 ὑμῖν ἐχαρίσθη τὸ...πάσχειν... ἔχοντες...; Col. ii. 2 ἵνα παρακληθῶσιν αἱ καρδίαι αὐτῶν, συνβιβασθέντες...; iii. 16 ὁ λόγος τοῦ χριστοῦ ἐνοικείτω ἐν ὑμῖν...διδάσκοντες καὶ νουθετοῦντες ἑαυτούς,...ᾄδοντες...; iv. 11 οἱ ὄντες ἐκ περιτομῆς οὗτοι μόνοι... which (pace Lightfoot in loc.) must surely mean τῶν ὄντων ἐκ περιτομῆς, οὗτοι..., or οἵ, ὄντες ἐκ περιτομῆς, μόνοι...; Acts i. 21, 22 τῶν συνελθόντων ἡμῖν ἀνδρῶν ἐν παντὶ χρόνῳ... ἀρξάμενος ἀπὸ τοῦ βαπτίσματος Ἰωάνου may be due to a Semitic source. Note also John i. 29 ἴδε ὁ ἀμνὸς τοῦ θεοῦ; xix. 26, 27 ἴδε ὁ υἱός σου...ἴδε ἡ μήτηρ σου, etc. This seems exactly equivalent to ἰδού. See D.-B. § 144.[1]

ii. In a context where an Accusative of Duration would be natural: Matt. xv. 32 ἤδη ἡμέραι (v.l. -ρας) τρεῖς προσμένουσίν μοι (D.-B. § 144. Other N.T. instances are textually even more uncertain).[2]

iii. Used for the Vocative: see below.

2. Vocative. Although the true Vocative is found (with and without ὤ)—e.g. Rom. ii. 1, 3 ὦ ἄνθρωπε; Acts i. 1 ὦ Θεόφιλε; Luke i. 3

___

[1] Luke xxii. 20, τοῦτο τὸ ποτήριον ἡ καινὴ διαθήκη ἐν τῷ αἵματί μου, τὸ ὑπὲρ ὑμῶν ἐκχυννόμενον, looks uncommonly like a 'false concord'—as though τῷ...ἐκχυννομένῳ were the sense intended; but it might be argued that the participle is intended to refer to τὸ ποτήριον.

[2] Acts xxiv. 11 οὐ πλείους εἰσίν μοι ἡμέραι δώδεκα is startling enough, where a Genitive of Comparison (see below, p. 42) would be regular.† But it is an idiom of comparison (see under 'The Adjective', p. 98 n. 1) and not limited to the Nominative as such.

κράτιστε Θεόφιλε; Acts xxvi. 13 βασιλεῦ; Matt. xv. 28, Luke xxii. 57, John ii. 4, iv. 21, etc. ὦ γύναι or γύναι; Matt. xxvii. 46 θεέ (only here, and as translation of Ἠλει); Heb. i. 10 σύ...κύριε (from LXX); John xvii. 11 πάτερ ἅγιε (but ? text: cf. *vv.* 21, 24, 25), etc.—it is being supplanted by the Nominative: e.g. Luke viii. 54 ἡ παῖς, ἔγειρε; Mark v. 41 τὸ κοράσιον; Luke xviii. 11 ὁ θεός (Heb. i. 8, which looks similar, may conceivably be a true Nominative, construed so as to mean *Thy throne* is *God*; but see commentators *in loc.*); Matt. xi. 26 ὁ πατήρ; etc. Moulton (*Proleg.* 70) contrasts the harshness of the Classical ὁ παῖς ἀκολούθει, *You there! the lad, I mean*... with the obvious gentleness (though still decisiveness) of the N.T. usage (e.g. Luke viii. 54 above).

3. Accusative. Here we may use the familiar subheadings.

i. *The Cognate Accusative* or 'Accusative of Content' or 'of the Inner Object' (so T.-B.) is an Accusative repeating the content of the verb itself (where English idiom more often uses a preposition such as *with*, or else varies the verb): e.g. Matt. ii. 10 ἐχάρησαν χαρὰν μεγάλην σφόδρα, *they rejoiced with very great joy* [1] (but John iii. 29 χαρᾷ χαίρει— see under 'Semitisms', below, p. 178); Luke xi. 46 φορτίζετε τοὺς ἀνθρώπους φορτία, *you load people with burdens*; Eph. ii. 4 διὰ τὴν... ἀγάπην...ἣν ἠγάπησεν ἡμᾶς, *because of the...love with which he loved us*; I Pet. iii. 14 (quotation from LXX) τὸν δὲ φόβον αὐτῶν μὴ φοβηθῆτε, *do not be afraid with fear of them*; I John v. 16 ἁμαρτάνοντα ἁμαρτίαν, *committing a sin* (examples from D.-B. § 153). A slight extension of the same method is Jas. v. 12 μὴ ὀμνύετε, μήτε τὸν οὐρανὸν...μήτε ἄλλον τινὰ ὅρκον, *do not swear, either by heaven... or with any other oath*, for τὸν οὐρανόν is almost parallel to ὅρκον (so too Jas. v. 18 ἡ γῆ ἐβλάστησεν τὸν καρπὸν αὐτῆς, cf. Gen. i. 11, etc.). Possibly an example of the Cognate Accusative is also supplied by Luke iv. 35 μηδὲν βλάψαν αὐτόν (as though it were μηδεμίαν βλάβην κ.τ.λ.); but this might equally well be an 'Accusative of Respect' (see below, pp. 33 f.).

Note also the retention of the Accusative even with a Passive verb: I Cor. ix. 17 οἰκονομίαν πεπίστευμαι, *I have been entrusted with a stewardship* (where the Active would be πιστεύω οἰκονομίαν τινί); cf. I Thess. ii. 4 πιστευθῆναι τὸ εὐαγγέλιον; and note Luke xii. 47, 48

---

[1] Even the use of the preposition does not here make it into idiomatic English; we should probably turn it by a phrase such as *they were overjoyed*.

THE ACCUSATIVE 33

δαρήσεται πολλάς...ὀλίγας [πληγάς]. Very curious is John vi. 27 ἐργάζεσθε...τὴν βρῶσιν (Rob. 471 mentions it with ὀμνύειν with the Accusative).†

But note: κορέννυμι, *I satisfy, satiate*, is found with the *Genitive* of that which gives the satisfaction: Acts xxvii. 38 κορεσθέντες... τροφῆς. So χορτάζειν: Mark viii. 4 τούτους...χορτάσαι ἄρτων.

κρίνειν, which can take a Cognate Accusative (John vii. 24 τὴν δικαίαν κρίσιν), is also found with ἐν with the Dative of the judgment: Matt. vii. 2 ἐν ᾧ...κρίματι κρίνετε κριθήσεσθε, cf. ἐν ᾧ μέτρῳ μετρεῖτε (so Mark iv. 24; but in the Lucan parallel, Luke vi. 37, the phrase is by-passed altogether; and in *v.* 38 the plain Dative, ᾧ...μέτρῳ, takes the place of ἐν ᾧ κ.τ.λ.).

ii. *Double Accusative.* Certain verbs (often contrary to English idiom) take an Accusative of the *remoter* object as well as of the immediate object: e.g. Acts xxi. 21 ἀποστασίαν διδάσκεις...πάντας, *you teach everyone apostasy*; I Cor. iv. 17 ὑμᾶς ἀναμνήσει τὰς ὁδούς μου, *he will remind you of my ways*; Mark vi. 22 αἴτησόν με ὃ ἐὰν θέλῃς, *request of me whatever you like* (though αἰτεῖν παρ' ἐμοῦ also occurs, John iv. 9); Matt. xxi. 24 ἐρωτήσω ὑμᾶς...λόγον ἕνα, *I will ask you one thing*; Luke xii. 48 περισσότερον αἰτήσουσιν αὐτόν, Mark ix. 41 ὃς γὰρ ἂν ποτίσῃ ὑμᾶς ποτήριον ὕδατος, *for whoever gives you a cup of water to drink*; Luke xi. 46 (already quoted above for its Cognate Accusative) φορτίζετε τοὺς ἀνθρώπους φορτία, *you load men with burdens*; Heb. i. 9 (quotation from LXX) ἔχρισέν σε...ὁ θεός σου ἔλαιον, *thy God hath anointed thee with oil* (but in Acts x. 38 with a Dative, ἔχρισεν αὐτὸν ὁ θεὸς πνεύματι ἁγίῳ καὶ δυνάμει); even ἐξέδυσαν and ἐνέδυσαν, which, with such prepositions, might have been expected to take the Genitive and Dative respectively, are used with the Accusative in Matt. xxvii. 31 ἐξέδυσαν αὐτὸν τὴν χλαμύδα καὶ ἐνέδυσαν αὐτὸν τὰ ἱμάτια αὐτοῦ, *they stripped him of the cloak and put his own garments on him* (cf. Mark xv. 17, 20). Note also Luke viii. 52 ἐκόπτοντο αὐτήν, *they were beating their breasts for her* (but see above under 'The Voices', p. 24). Examples from D.-B. §§ 155, 148.†

iii. *Accusative of Respect or Reference*—denoting that in respect of which some statement is made: e.g. John vi. 10 τὸν ἀριθμὸν ὡς πεντακισχίλιοι, *about five thousand in number*; Heb. ii. 17 πιστὸς ἀρχιερεὺς τὰ πρὸς τὸν θεόν, *a faithful high priest in respect of things pertaining to God* (or perhaps *on the Godward side*);[1] Rom. xii. 18

[1] See A. Nairne, *Cambridge Greek Testament, in loc.*

τὸ ἐξ ὑμῶν, *for your part, so far as it is in your power.* This Accusative is practically adverbial, as appears from the following examples: Matt. xxiii. 37 ὃν τρόπον, *in the way in which*; I Pet. iii. 8 τὸ τέλος, *finally* (or perhaps *in short*); (τὸ) λοιπόν, *finally* or *henceforward* (I Cor. vii. 29, I Thess. iv. 1, Heb. x. 13, etc.); John viii. 25 τὴν ἀρχήν, *from the beginning* (or perhaps *at all, in the first instance*: ἀπ' ἀρχῆς is the phrase in I John for *from the beginning*) (see T.-B. § 34); Matt. xxvii. 44, Phil. ii. 18 τὸ δὲ αὐτό, *in the same way.* But some apparently adverbial uses might better be classed as 'cognate' (see (i.) above, p. 32), e.g. Phil. iv. 6 μηδὲν μεριμνᾶτε (as though it were μηδεμίαν μέριμναν μεριμνᾶτε); Luke iv. 35 μηδὲν βλάψαν; Rom. vi. 10 ὃ γὰρ ἀπέθανεν... ὃ δὲ ζῇ (though an adverbial interpretation, *whereas...whereas*, fits this latter well). As for II Cor. vi. 13 τὴν δὲ αὐτὴν ἀντιμισθίαν, this is possibly adverbial—*with the same recompense*, i.e. *by way of recompense in kind* (see D.-B. § 154)—but see below, under v. *Accusative in Apposition to a Sentence*, pp. 35 f. A desperately problematic passage is Luke xi. 41 πλὴν τὰ ἐνόντα δότε ἐλεημοσύνην. It could conceivably be interpreted *but as for what is inside, give alms,* in which case τὰ ἐνόντα is an Accusative of Respect. Alternatively, the τὰ ἐνόντα may be in apposition to ἐλεημοσύνην: *give, as alms, what is inside* (or, following a suggestion made verbally by Professor C. H. Dodd, *give, as alms, what you can* (*that which is within your power*)); or the passage may be corrupt or mistaken (see under 'Semitisms', below, p. 186).

The Accusative of Respect, as indicating *extent* (whether of space or time), is exemplified by: John xxi. 8 οὐ...μακρὰν ἀπὸ τῆς γῆς; Luke xxii. 41 ἀπεσπάσθη ἀπ' αὐτῶν ὡσεὶ λίθου βολήν; Luke xxiv. 13 ἀπέχουσαν σταδίους ἑξήκοντα ἀπὸ Ἰερουσαλήμ; Mark iv. 27, etc. νύκτα καὶ ἡμέραν; Matt. xxviii. 20 πάσας τὰς ἡμέρας (perhaps strictly = *the whole of every day*); Luke ii. 36 ζήσασα μετὰ ἀνδρὸς ἔτη ἑπτά (for the *Nominative* in this sense, see above, under 1. 'Nominative', p. 31). Strangely, an Accusative is also sometimes used to indicate not 'for how long' (duration, a 'linear' idea), but 'at what time' (a 'punctiliar' use): John iv. 52 ἐχθὲς ὥραν ἑβδόμην; Acts x. 30 ἤμην τὴν ἐνάτην προσευχόμενος (unless τὴν ἐνάτην conceivably means *the ninth-hour prayer*, and forms a Cognate Accusative to προσευχόμενος; in any case note v. 9 περὶ ὥραν ἕκτην); Rev. iii. 3 ποίαν ὥραν (contrast Matt. xxiv. 43 ποίᾳ φυλακῇ; v. 44 ᾗ οὐ δοκεῖτε ὥρᾳ, and Genitives as below). As for Matt. xx. 2 συμφωνήσας...ἐκ δηναρίου τὴν ἡμέραν, T.-B. Appendix, p. 311, says: 'the acc. is not "for the length of the day", but is based on a long-established idiomatic usage: κριθῶν πραθεισῶν ἐκ τριῶν δραχμῶν τὸν μέδιμνον ἕκαστον Corp. Inscr. Att. ii 834ᵇ ii 70.' The Accusative is also used to denote *number* or *frequency*: Luke v. 33 πυκνά; Mark ix. 26 πολλὰ σπαράξας (*fit after fit*—Weymouth); I Cor. x. 33, xi. 2, etc. πάντα, *in all respects*. Cf. phrases like Eph. i. 23 τὰ πάντα ἐν πᾶσιν.

iv. *The Accusative used Predicatively*, i.e. to 'predicate' something of a noun already in the Accusative, is common enough, and is not really a characteristic of the Accusative as such; the only distinctive feature of the Accusative so used being that it does not positively require a helping particle such as ὡς or a helping participle such as would almost always[1] be used with any other case (and is, in fact, frequently used with the Accusative): thus, Acts xiii. 5 εἶχον...'Ιωάνην ὑπηρέτην, *they had...John as an attendant* (but Matt. xxi. 26 ὡς προφήτην ἔχουσιν τὸν 'Ιωάνην; and *v.* 46 (in some MSS.) εἰς προφήτην); Jas. v. 10 ὑπόδειγμα λάβετε...τοὺς προφήτας, *take the prophets as an example*; John x. 35 ἐκείνους εἶπεν θεούς, *he called them gods*; Gal. ii. 18 παραβάτην ἐμαυτὸν συνιστάνω, *I constitute myself a transgressor*; Luke xi. 11 τίνα δὲ ἐξ ὑμῶν τὸν πατέρα αἰτήσει ὁ υἱός...; literally, *which of you shall the son ask as the father...?* I Pet. i. 17 εἰ πατέρα ἐπικαλεῖσθε τόν...κρίνοντα, *if you invoke as father the one who judges...*; Rom. iii. 25 ὃν προέθετο ὁ θεὸς ἱλαστήριον, *whom God set forth* [if that is the meaning[2]] *as expiation* [or perhaps *with expiatory effect*[2]]; Luke ix. 14 κατακλίνατε αὐτοὺς κλισίας, *make them recline in parties*. For another possible example from Eph. i. 23, see above, 'The Voices', p. 25. Less in keeping with English idiom, but presumably to be classified here, is Matt. xxvii. 22 τί οὖν ποιήσω 'Ιησοῦν; *what shall I do with Jesus?* (Cf. with D.-B. § 157, Acts xii. 18 τί...ὁ Πέτρος ἐγένετο, *what had become of Peter*.)

v. *Accusative in Apposition to a Sentence.* When a word or phrase is flung loosely into apposition with a whole sentence it is (or, where the form is ambiguous, may be assumed to be) in the Accusative.[3] Thus: Rom. viii. 3 τὸ γὰρ ἀδύνατον τοῦ νόμου...ὁ θεὸς τὸν ἑαυτοῦ υἱὸν πέμψας...κατέκρινεν τὴν ἁμαρτίαν..., *God, by sending his own Son...condemned sin...—a thing impossible for the law*; Rom. xii. 1

[1] Though note Jude 15 ...ὧν ἐλάλησαν κατ' αὐτοῦ ἁμαρτωλοὶ ἀσεβεῖς,... *godless as they are.*
[2] See T. W. Manson in *J.T.S.* XLVI (Jan.–April 1945), 181–2.
[3] See James Riddell's canons for Platonic usage, summarized in S. and H. 191.

παρακαλῶ οὖν ὑμᾶς... παραστῆσαι τὰ σώματα ὑμῶν... τὴν λογικὴν λατρείαν ὑμῶν, *I beg you therefore... to present yourselves...—[which is] your spiritual service*; II Cor. vi. 13 τὴν δὲ αὐτὴν ἀντιμισθίαν... πλατύνθητε καὶ ὑμεῖς may (with S. and H. *loc. cit.*) be classed here with more probability than under the *Accusative of Respect*, iii. above, *q.v.*). II Pet. ii. 12 f. φθαρήσονται, ἀδικούμενοι μισθὸν ἀδικίας might be similar: *they shall perish—which is the proper recompense for their wickedness, wicked that they are*, if only the Middle, ἀδικεῖσθαι, could be taken as transitive: but it is not so attested. (The *v.l.* κομιούμενοι of course smooths out the construction, but robs the sentence of some of its point.) Cf. Ignatius, *Eph.* xi ἤ... φοβηθῶμεν ἤ... ἀγαπήσωμεν, ἐν τῶν δύο, *Magn.* 1 τὸ δὲ κυριώτερον, *and what is more important*, with Lightfoot's notes.

vi. For the curious *Anticipatory Accusative* in II Cor. xii. 17 μή τινα... δι' αὐτοῦ ἐπλεονέκτησα, see under 'Semitisms', 11, iv (*b*), p. 176, though it is by no means certainly a 'Semitism'.

4. Accusative and Genitive—Disputed Territory.[1] The seemingly direct object of many verbs is in the *Genitive*: e.g. of verbs connected with a portion or share or with other ideas demanding a 'Partitive Genitive' (see below under '5. Genitive', pp. 42 f.): μεταλαμβάνειν (but Acc. in Acts xxiv. **25** καιρὸν... μεταλαβών), μετέχειν, γεύεσθαι (but John ii. 9 ἐγεύσατο... τὸ ὕδωρ. In Heb. vi. 5 καλὸν γευσαμένους θεοῦ ῥῆμα, the direct object of the verb is virtually a substantival clause (καλὸν θεοῦ ῥῆμα = καλὸν εἶναι θεοῦ ῥῆμα; cf. I Pet. ii. 3, with its ὅτι-clause)), and, sometimes, ἀκούειν, with regard to which the facts are obscure. The Classical rule is said to be 'Genitive of person, Accusative of thing'—i.e. one *listens to* a person (Gen.) but *hears* him say something (Acc.) (D.-B. § 173); but the N.T. usage varies in a way which defies classification; e.g. it seems to me (*pace Proleg.* 66) impossible to find a satisfactory distinction in meaning between the Gen. and Acc. in Acts ix. 7 (ἀκούοντες μὲν τῆς φωνῆς) and xxii. 9 (τὴν δὲ φωνὴν οὐκ ἤκουσαν).† In this class also are verbs connected with *laying hold of* or *touching*:[2] e.g. ἅπτεσθαι, καθάπτειν, θιγγάνειν, ἐπιλαμβάνεσθαι, κρατεῖν, ἔχεσθαι, ἀντέχεσθαι, ἀναλαμβάνεσθαι; verbs of *longing after*:

---

[1] See also under 'Dative' (below, pp. 43; 44 f., n.).

[2] With these there are exceptions, but the Genitive is the rule. Note the Acc. and Gen. in Acts iii. 7 καὶ πιάσας αὐτὸν τῆς δεξιᾶς χειρός, *grasping him by his right hand.*

e.g. ἐπιθυμεῖν, ὀρέγεσθαι, ὁμείρεσθαι (or ὁμ-); ἐπιτυγχάνειν, *to attain to* (but Acc. in Rom. xi. 7); ἐνπνεῖν (only in Acts ix. 1 ἐνπνέων ἀπειλῆς καὶ φόνου, *whose every breath was a threat of destruction*, Weymouth); μνημονεύειν (yet in II Tim. ii. 14 ταῦτα ὑπομίμνησκε, a verb of *re-minding* takes the Accusative of the thing to be remembered); ἀνέχεσθαι (*to bear with*); verbs of *caring for* or *despising*: e.g. ἐπιμελεῖσθαι, ἀμελεῖν, ὀλιγωρεῖν, προνοεῖσθαι, μεριμνᾶν (yet in Luke xxiii. 11 etc. ἐξουθενεῖν, *to set at nought*, takes an Acc.); verbs of *ruling over*: e.g. ἄρχειν, κυριεύειν, κατακυριεύειν, κατισχύειν, αὐθεντεῖν, ἡγεμονεύειν, τετραρχεῖν, ἀνθυπατεύειν, etc.

Compare further certain verbs (other than those specified above) compounded with κατα- and taking the Genitive, but such that in all probability a direct object in the form of a 'cognate' Accusative is lurking just beneath the writer's consciousness, so that the Genitive which follows is not strictly the direct object: καταγελᾶν, *to laugh at*, καταγινώσκειν, *to condemn*. Conversely, when the force of the verb itself outweighs the force of the preposition, and the simple verb is one which naturally takes the Acc., the Genitive which the preposition might have suggested is dropped in favour of an Acc.; e.g. καταδουλοῦν in II Cor. xi. 20, or καταγωνίζεσθαι in Heb. xi. 33. (Cf. English *they laughed at him* where the verb stands apart and the preposition is forceful, and *they laughed him down*, where the verb is dominant and the preposition virtually merges with it = *downlaughed*. Cf. also the distinction between German 'separable' and 'inseparable' prepositions.)[1]

5. Genitive. This is so immensely versatile and hard-worked a case that anything like an exhaustive catalogue of its uses would be only confusing and unnecessarily dull. But the following rough classification may serve as a reminder of what to watch for and as some guide to the translation of some of the more obscure and ambiguous uses. It should be remembered that the Greek Genitive includes within it much that in Latin is associated with the Ablative (e.g. the idea of separation and comparison, and the 'absolute' use).

i. *Genitive of Definition.* A large variety of uses is here included, because not much is gained by attaching distinguishing labels such as

---

[1] In Acts xxvi. 3 one might conceivably find another overlapping of Genitive and Accusative 'territory', for μάλιστα γνώστην ὄντα σε is in no simple or orthodox grammatical relation with the antecedent ἐπὶ σοῦ.

Possessive Genitive, Genitive of Origin, etc. The chief thing to remember is that the Genitive often practically does the duty of an adjective, distinguishing two otherwise similar things; e.g. 'to which of many men called James do you refer?' Answer: 'To the Zebedaean one—the James who was Zabdi's son': Matt. iv. 21 Ἰάκωβον τὸν τοῦ Ζεβεδαίου; cf. many other instances of a name in the Genitive indicating some relation (not always parent) or connexion which would serve to define the person, e.g. Mark xv. 47, John xix. 25, Rom. xvi. 10, 11. So with *possessive* or *adjectival* phrases such as I Cor. xv. 23 οἱ τοῦ χριστοῦ, *those who belong to Christ* (= χριστιανοί); Acts i. 7 οὐχ ὑμῶν ἐστιν γνῶναι, *it is not for you to know* (= οὐχ ὑμέτερον); Acts iv. 22 ἐτῶν... ἦν πλειόνων τεσσεράκοντα, *he was of more than forty years* (= *more than* τεσσερακονταετής; cf. also 'Genitive of Comparison', below, iv (*b*), p. 42). As in Attic prose, so in N.T. Greek, there is no 3rd singular possessive adjective (*his*, etc.), and here the Genitive alone is possible: Rom. viii. 9 οὐκ ἔστιν αὐτοῦ, *he is not his.* Is ἐγένετο γνώμης (= *he decided*), Acts xx. 3, to be classed as possessive, as though it meant *he became possessed of a decision?* An if possible even more strongly adjectival use is that which appears frequently in the N.T.: e.g. Luke xvi. 9 ὁ μαμωνᾶς τῆς ἀδικίας = *the dishonest Mammon*; Rom. vi. 6 τὸ σῶμα τῆς ἁμαρτίας, *the sin-possessed body* (cf. Rom. vii. 24 τοῦ σώματος τοῦ θανάτου τούτου, whereas in vi. 12, viii. 11 θνητός is used); Acts ix. 15 σκεῦος ἐκλογῆς, *a chosen instrument*; Matt. x. 5 εἰς ὁδὸν ἐθνῶν, *to Gentile parts*; Matt. i. 11, 12 ἡ μετοικεσία Βαβυλῶνος, *the Babylonian captivity.* Whether any of these usages is attributable to Semitic influence has been debated; see below, on 'Semitisms' (p. 175), where the matter is further considered, side by side with the acknowledged 'Semitism' by which *son of* = *belonging to*, *destined for*, etc.

In certain cases the Defining Genitive represents more than an adjective; it represents nothing less than a second noun in apposition to the first; e.g. Rom. iv. 11 σημεῖον ἔλαβεν περιτομῆς, *he received the sign of circumcision* (i.e. *received circumcision as a sign*, or *received a sign consisting of circumcision*). This is exactly equivalent to the English idiom 'the city of Manchester' (= 'the city Manchester'), which is indeed exactly represented (but only once for certain)† in the New Testament: II Pet. ii. 6 πόλεις Σοδόμων καὶ Γομόρρας (Luke ii. 4 ἐκ πόλεως Ναζαρέθ would be ambiguous even if Ναζαρέθ were declinable; Acts xvi. 14 πόλεως Θυατείρων is ambiguous; but xi. 5 has ἐν πόλει Ἰόππῃ, not Ἰόππης; and when Ἰορδάνης is used with ποταμός, it is in apposition). Cf. the English purists' controversy over the relative claims of 'The Book Genesis' and 'The Book of Genesis'.

ii. *Genitive of Time, Place, and Quantity.* Though these uses of the Genitive might logically be classified under section (i), they are sufficiently distinctive to be given a section to themselves. (*a*) Of Time (cf. the 'punctiliar' Accusative, under 3 (iii), above, p. 34): e.g. Matt. xxiv. 20, etc. χειμῶνος, *in winter*; Rev. xxi. 25 ἡμέρας, *by day*; Mark v. 5 διὰ παντὸς νυκτὸς καὶ ἡμέρας, *continually, night and day* (a phrase which invites a 'howler' from those who neglect their concords!); Luke xviii. 12 δὶς τοῦ σαββάτου, *twice each week*; Luke xxiv. 1 ὄρθρου βαθέως, *at early dawn.*[1] The adverbial expression τοῦ λοιποῦ, *henceforth, finally, for the rest*, Gal. vi. 17, Eph. vi. 10 (according to ℵ*A, B) is classed with the above by D.-B. (§ 186) with χρόνου understood. Compare the adverbial use of the Accusative, τὸ λοιπόν or λοιπόν ('Accusative', 1 (iii), above, p. 34). (*b*) Of Place. Luke v. 19 ποίας [*sc.* ὁδοῦ] εἰσενέγκωσιν αὐτόν, *by what way they might bring him in*; xix. 4 ἐκείνης ἤμελλεν διέρχεσθαι, *he was about to go through by that way.*

It is tempting to regard Acts xix. 26, οὐ μόνον Ἐφέσου ἀλλὰ σχεδὸν πάσης τῆς Ἀσίας, as a solitary example of the locative use of the Genitive of place names, Ἐφέσου then being an exact equivalent to the Latin idiom *Romæ, at Rome.* But it is possible that the Genitives are partitive (see below, pp. 42 f.) and depend on the ἱκανὸν ὄχλον which follows (though at a surprising distance): *a good crowd out of Ephesus*, etc. (see *Proleg.* 73). (*c*) Of Quantity. E.g. Matt. x. 29 ἀσσαρίου *for an* assarion; I Cor. vi. 20 ἠγοράσθητε. . .τιμῆς, *you were bought for a price* (cf. vii. 23); Matt. xx. 13 δηναρίου, *at a* denarius (though *v.* 2 ἐκ δηναρίου). Possibly Jude 11, μισθοῦ ἐξεχύθησαν (*they went headlong for a reward*), is to be classed here. Similar to this Genitive of Price may be one indicating the accusation with which a defendant is charged, if Acts xix. 40, ἐγκαλεῖσθαι στάσεως περὶ τῆς σήμερον, means *to be accused of riot concerning this day* (R.V. marg.) (but this would seem to be the solitary New Testament example (in Acts xxiii. 6, 29 περί with the Genitive is used), and it is very doubtful if it is to be so construed).†

iii. (*a*) *Subjective Genitive*, i.e. the Genitive indicating the subject from which the action, etc., originates and is separated, and (*b*) *Objective Genitive*, i.e. the Genitive indicating the object of the verb represented

---

[1] Cf. the Gen. Absolute: it makes little odds whether we say χειμῶνος simply, or χειμῶνος ἐνεστῶτος. See below, p. 43.

by the word which governs it. E.g. I John ii. 16 ἡ ἐπιθυμία τῆς σαρκός, *the lust of the flesh*, is subjective, being parallel to the sentence ἡ σάρξ ἐπιθυμεῖ, in which σάρξ is subject; while Rom. x. 2 ζῆλος θεοῦ, literally *zeal of God*, is objective, because it represents the idea ζηλοῦσιν θεόν, *they are zealous after God*, in which *God* is object. There is no formal distinction (as Moulton, *Proleg.* 72, points out) between these two uses, comparable to our frequent though not invariable distinction between the 'inflexional' Genitive and the 'prepositional' Genitive (e.g. *mankind's thoughts*, subjective = *the thoughts which mankind thinks*; and *thoughts of mankind*, objective = *the thoughts in which we ponder mankind*); consequently there are some ambiguities, in cases where the context or the known usage of the word elsewhere does not give a clear lead: e.g. whereas I Cor. ii. 13, οὐκ ἐν διδακτοῖς ἀνθρωπίνης σοφίας λόγοις, ἀλλ' ἐν διδακτοῖς πνεύματος, *not in words taught by human wisdom, but in words taught by the Spirit*, is a very bold[1] but quite unambiguous use of the Subjective Genitive after an adjective, the phrase quoted above, ζῆλος θεοῦ, depends entirely on its context for its interpretation *zeal towards God* (objective) rather than *zeal shown by God* (subjective). A similar problem of interpretation attaches to the composite adjective θεοστυγεῖς in Rom. i. 30: does the θεο- there represent a subjective θεοῦ (*hated by God*) or an objective θεοῦ (*haters of God*)? Again, in I Pet. iii. 14, τὸν δὲ φόβον αὐτῶν μὴ φοβηθῆτε could grammatically mean *do not be afraid as they are afraid* (subjective αὐτῶν); but the context makes it obvious that the Genitive is objective—*do not be afraid with fear of them*. Objective Genitives are very frequent and do not require further illustration; while the Subjective Genitive merges indistinguishably into the possessive Genitive. Thus ἡ σοφία τοῦ θεοῦ (I Cor. i. 21, etc.) might be classed as a subjective Genitive (parallel to ὁ θεὸς σοφός ἐστιν); but it might equally well (or better) be called possessive—*the wisdom which belongs to God*. See above under i. *Genitive of Definition*. An interesting Genitive is in Luke iv. 19 (from LXX) ἐνιαυτὸν κυρίου δεκτόν. It is presumably strictly a possessive—*the acceptable year belonging to the Lord*; but no doubt the κυρίου also combines in a special way with the idea behind δεκτόν, to convey the meaning that it is *the year when the Lord will accept man* (*M.T.* שְׁנַת־רָצוֹן לַיהוָה)—i.e. there is a tinge of 'subjective' in the Genitive.

---

[1] Somewhat rare but classical, according to G. G. Findlay (*Expositor's Greek Testament, in loc.*) who compares John vi. 45, Isa. liv. 13, and contrasts I Macc. iv. 7 διδακτοὶ πολέμου. (But see M.-H. II, 459.)

Notorious problems of interpretation in this connexion are ἡ ἀγάπη τοῦ θεοῦ (χριστοῦ, etc.)—is it exclusively *subjective*, e.g. in II Cor. v. 14? —and ἡ κοινωνία τοῦ ἁγίου πνεύματος (e.g. in II Cor. xiii. 13).† It seems to me that the latter is more probably *objective*. The *objective* is favoured with more or less confidence by Lightfoot (on Philem. 6), Vincent (*I.C.C.*, *ibid*), L. S. Thornton (*The Common Life in the Body of Christ*, 71 ff.), and Hauck in *T.W.N.T. s.v.* κοινωνία (as quoted by L. S. Thornton, *op. cit.* 450, 451).[1]

iv. *Genitive of Separation.* This is a 'Genitive' in form; but its meaning justifies its description by grammarians as Ablative. In other words, the definition of the Genitive as referring to the 'sphere in which' holds good for most uses; and this ablatival use can then be separated off for special study. Note, then:

(a) Although prepositions are often employed, the simple Genitive is also found to express the idea of separation, after such verbs as *to hinder from, to estrange from, to miss, to lack, to be distant from*, etc., and with corresponding adjectives and adverbs. E.g.: Acts xxvii. 43 ἐκώλυσεν αὐτοὺς τοῦ βουλήματος, *he hindered them from their plan* (though Luke vi. 29 uses a preposition, ἀπό); Eph. ii. 12 ἀπηλλοτριωμένοι τῆς πολιτείας τοῦ Ἰσραήλ, *estranged from the citizenship of Israel*; I Tim. i. 6 ὧν τινες ἀστοχήσαντες, *which things some having missed* (i.e. *failed to hit*); χρῄζειν, προσδεῖσθαι, *to need*, λείπεσθαι, *to be short of*, ὑστερεῖσθαι, *to fall short of* (Matt. vi. 32, Acts xvii. 25, Jas. i. 5, Rom. iii. 23); Acts xv. 29 ἀπέχεσθαι εἰδωλοθύτων, *to abstain from things sacrificed to idols*. So φείδεσθαι, *to spare* (i.e. *refrain from*) (e.g. Acts xx. 29), πεπαῦσθαι, *to have ceased from* (I Pet. iv. 1), ἀποστερεῖν, *to deprive of* (e.g. I Tim. vi. 5, though D* has ἀπό).

Compare the use of the simple Genitive with the adjective ξένος, *stranger to*, Eph. ii. 12. The adjectives ἀπείραστος, *untempted by* (?), Jas. i. 13; ἀκατάπαυστος, *that has never had enough of* (i.e. *that never ceases from*; but *v.l.* ἀκατάπαστος = perhaps *unfed, that cannot be satisfied with*), II Pet. ii. 14,[2] may owe their construction with the Genitive to the idea of separation; but in the case of ἀπείραστος it is

---

[1] For a discussion of this point, see V. Taylor, *Forgiveness and Reconciliation in the N.T.*, 132; and see the particularly important discussions of κοινωνία by J. Y. Campbell in *J.B.L.* LI (1932), 352–80, and A. R. George, *Communion with God* (Epworth Press, 1953).

[2] Very curious and hard to define is another Genitive in the same verse, καρδίαν γεγυμνασμένην πλεονεξίας (a better-supported reading than -ίαις), *a heart trained in extortion*.

easy to suppose that the corresponding noun (πεῖρα) was lying close to the surface of consciousness and reinforced the Genitive as though it were also a Genitive of apposition (above i. *sub fin.*): 'without temptation consisting of evil'. Cf. I Cor. ix. 21 ἄνομος θεοῦ...ἔννομος χριστοῦ, where the Genitives are clearly governed by the νόμος.

Compare also the quasi-prepositional adverbs which take a 'Genitive of Separation', e.g. ἐκτός, ἔξω, πέραν, ὑπερέκεινα, ἀντιπέρα. But it is only fair to add that the Genitive also follows such adverbs as ἐγγύς, πλησίον, meaning *near to*! It is difficult to see how such usages fit the general conception of the functions of the Genitive as derived from the majority of its usages; but, anomalous or not, they are undeniable.

(*b*) A further use which falls under the heading of 'separation', and in which the Genitive is comparable to the Latin Ablative, is in comparative clauses. The striking exceptions to this (cf. also above, under 'Nominative', p. 31 n. 2), and other ways of expressing comparison are discussed elsewhere ('The Adjective', p. 98 n.), but the following are examples of the use of the Genitive after a comparative adjective: Matt. v. 37 τὸ δὲ περισσὸν τούτων, *anything more than* (cf. *in excess of*) *these*; Acts iv. 22 ἐτῶν...ἦν πλειόνων τεσσεράκοντα, *he was of more than forty years* (where ἐτῶν, with its adjective πλειόνων, forms a Genitive of Definition, describing the man (above, i. p. 38), and τεσσεράκοντα, if it were declinable, would almost certainly be a Genitive of Comparison after πλειόνων); Luke vii. 28 μείζων...'Ιωάνου, *one greater than John.*

So with an *adverb* of comparison: Eph. iii. 20 ὑπερεκπερισσοῦ ὧν..., *exceedingly much more than....* (although here the preceding ὑπὲρ πάντα ποιῆσαι confuses the construction: is πάντα direct object of ποιῆσαι, and ὑπέρ an adverb, reiterated by ὑπερεκπερισσοῦ? Or is ὑπέρ a preposition governing πάντα, and ὧν a grammatical laxity for ἅ, perhaps partly suggested by the idea of comparison with its genitive associations?)

So also with a *verb* of comparison: Luke xii. 7 πολλῶν στρουθίων διαφέρετε, *you are of more value than many sparrows.*

Noteworthy also is the (unclassical) use with πρῶτος, as though it were the comparative πρότερος: John i. 15, 30 πρῶτός μου, *before me.* This is in keeping with the tendency in New Testament Greek to blur the degrees of comparison (see 'The Adjective', p. 97).

v. *Partitive Genitive.* The Genitive of *things of which a share is received*, etc., has been discussed above (under 4. 'Accusative and Genitive—Disputed Territory', p. 36). It remains to mention here the more strictly or obviously partitive uses, such as: after words denoting a part or fraction—εἶς, τίς, ἕκαστος, οἱ λοιποί, etc.; words used in reference to a group or a subdivision: Rom. xv. 26 τοὺς πτωχοὺς τῶν ἁγίων, *the poor among God's people*; I Tim. i. 20 ὧν ἐστιν Ὑμέναιος, *among whom is H.*; possibly Mark ii. 16 οἱ γραμματεῖς τῶν Φαρισαίων (*si vera lectio*—see commentators *in loc.*). In Luke xvi. 24 ἵνα βάψῃ τὸ ἄκρον τοῦ δακτύλου αὐτοῦ ὕδατος, the ὕδατος is perhaps virtually partitive.

vi. *Genitive Absolute*. This is familiar enough. All that need be noted here is the growing laxity of Greek of the N.T. period, as compared with the Classical. It countenances the use of a clumsy Genitive Absolute where a phrase in agreement with an already present (or implied) Nominative, Accusative, or Dative would be both correct and neat: e.g. Acts xxi. 34 μὴ δυναμένου δὲ αὐτοῦ γνῶναι τὸ ἀσφαλές (instead of μὴ δυνάμενος γνῶναι...); xxii. 17 ἐγένετο δέ μοι ὑποστρέψαντι εἰς Ἱερουσαλὴμ καὶ προσευχομένου μου (instead of καὶ προσευχομένῳ).†

6. **Dative**. Once more, all that is attempted here is to provide a rough classification of the chief functions performed by the case as a guide to the student.

i. We have already seen how the Greek *Genitive* performs many of the functions of the Latin *Ablative*; but the Greek *Dative* also, in some of its uses, expresses what in Latin would be expressed by the Ablative.[1] Among such 'ablatival' uses note, e.g.:

(*a*) *Temporal* uses: *Instantaneous or 'punctiliar'*: Luke viii. 29 πολλοῖς...χρόνοις συνηρπάκει αὐτόν seems most naturally translated *on many occasions* [the evil spirit] *had seized him*; Mark vi. 21 τοῖς γενεσίοις αὐτοῦ, *at his birthday feast*; Eph. iii. 5 ἑτέραις γενεαῖς, *in other generations*. But in Luke viii. 27 χρόνῳ ἱκανῷ οὐκ ἐνεδύσατο ἱμάτιον, the Dative is clearly *durative* or '*linear*', as it is in Luke i. 75 πάσαις ταῖς ἡμέραις ἡμῶν (contrast Matt. xxviii. 20 πάσας τὰς ἡμέρας which is, perhaps, more regular). Possibly the curious Dative in Rev. viii. 3, 4 ταῖς προσευχαῖς, meaning *simultaneously with the prayers*, might be

---

[1] The Dative and Accusative also overlap mysteriously. Under 3. iv. *The Accusative used Predicatively* above, p. 35, the phrase τί οὖν ποιήσω Ἰησοῦν; (Matt. xxvii. 22) was noted; but now compare Matt. xxi. 40 τί ποιήσει τοῖς γεωργοῖς ἐκείνοις; (Dative). So in Acts v. 3, 4 ψεύσασθαι is used first with Acc., then with Dat.; in Mark x. 17 γονυπετήσας takes Acc.

classed as temporal.[1] So in Rom. xi. 30, 31 it would certainly make good sense if τῇ τούτων ἀπειθείᾳ and τῷ ὑμετέρῳ ἐλέει were translated in a temporal sense, *at the time of their disbelief, at the time when pity is shown to you*; *v.* 20, on the other hand, τῇ ἀπιστίᾳ ἐξεκλάσθησαν, looks virtually instrumental (see (*c*) below). Note further: Luke xiii. 14, 15, 16 τῷ σαββάτῳ, τῇ ἡμέρᾳ τοῦ σαββάτου, but *v.* 10 ἐν τοῖς σάββασιν; Luke xiii. 32 τῇ τρίτῃ [ἡμέρᾳ] τελειοῦμαι; Luke xiii. 33 σήμερον καὶ αὔριον καὶ τῇ ἐχομένῃ.

(*b*) *Metaphorically Local* uses: I Pet. iv. 1 ὁ παθὼν σαρκί, *anyone who has suffered physically*; I Cor. xiv. 15 προσεύξομαι τῷ πνεύματι... τῷ νοΐ (or is this instrumental rather than local?); Rom. xiv. 1 τὸν δὲ ἀσθενοῦντα τῇ πίστει, *the one who is weak in his faith* (or should this come under iii (*b*) p. 46 below?). See the 'adverbial' uses at the end of ii. below, p. 46.

(*c*) *Instrumental* uses:† Rom. xiv. 15 μὴ τῷ βρώματί σου ἐκεῖνον ἀπόλλυε..., *do not by your food destroy him*...; I Pet. ii. 24 οὗ τῷ μώλωπι ἰάθητε (cf. Isa. liii. 5 LXX), *by whose bruises you have been healed*; Rom. i. 20 τὰ ἀόρατα αὐτοῦ...τοῖς ποιήμασιν νοούμενα, *his invisible qualities, perceived by means of his works* (?); Rom. v. 15, 17 τῷ...παραπτώματι, *by the transgression* (cf. *v.* 18 δι' ἑνὸς παραπτώματος); Rom. viii. 13 εἰ δὲ πνεύματι τὰς πράξεις τοῦ σώματος θανατοῦτε, ζήσεσθε, *if by the Spirit you put to death sensual activities, you shall live* (cf. also *v.* 14 and Gal. v. 5, 16, 18, 25 for πνεύματι similarly used); Rom. xii. 2 μεταμορφοῦσθε τῇ ἀνακαινώσει τοῦ νοός, *be transformed by the renewing of your attitude*; Eph. ii. 5 χάριτί ἐστε σεσωσμένοι, *by favour you are saved*; John xvii. 5 δόξασόν με...τῇ δόξῃ, *glorify me...with the glory* (but *v.* 17 ἐν τῇ ἀληθείᾳ); Rom. xi. 20 τῇ ἀπιστίᾳ, perhaps *because of unbelief* (cf. Rom. xi. 30, 31 under (*a*) above); II Cor. ii. 13 τῷ μὴ εὑρεῖν με, *because I failed to find* (which seems virtually instrumental).[2]

(*d*) *Of Measure*: Heb. x. 29 πόσῳ...χείρονος, *by how much... worse*; Rom. v. 17 πολλῷ μᾶλλον, etc.

(*e*) *An 'Absolute' use.* Among instances of the Dative used in a sense which would normally be expressed in Latin by an Ablative (and which may thus be said to have affinities with the use of the Greek Genitive) may be mentioned Matt. xiv. 6, where, according

[1] Moulton (*Proleg.* 75) regards it as 'probably to be taken as the sociative instrumental'.

[2] Gal. v. 1 τῇ ἐλευθερίᾳ...ἠλευθέρωσεν (if correct reading) seems to be an *emphatic* use, not strictly *instrumental*. (See under 'Semitisms' below, p. 178.)

to the best text, the Dative seems to be used exactly like the regular
Greek Genitive *Absolute* (or Latin Ablative Absolute): γενεσίοις δὲ
γενομένοις, *when his birthday celebrations had come.* There is no other
N.T. example,[1] unless the reading of 𝔓⁴⁵ in Mark ix. 28 is correct
(εἰσελθόντι αὐτῷ, where אBCDLWΘ famm. 1 and 13,700 have Gen.,
AEFGH, etc., ς, have Acc.). It may, however, be regarded as a combination of a *temporal* Dative—*at his birthday celebrations*—with
a participial construction belonging properly to another case.

ii. Harder to class are uses which do not correspond precisely to
the Latin use of any case; e.g. Acts xv. 1 ἐὰν μὴ περιτμηθῆτε τῷ ἔθει
τῷ Μωϋσέως, *unless you are circumcised* according to *the custom of
Moses* (where κατὰ τὸ ἔθος would be a commoner way of expressing it);
xxi. 21 τοῖς ἔθεσιν περιπατεῖν (contrast Luke i. 6 πορευόμενοι ἐν πάσαις
ταῖς ἐντολαῖς κ.τ.λ.); Col. ii. 14 τὸ...χειρόγραφον τοῖς δόγμασιν,
the document with *its decrees* (meaning, apparently, a document
containing, or *consisting of*, decrees;[2] cf. Eph. ii. 15 τὸν νόμον τῶν
ἐντολῶν ἐν δόγμασιν, where ἐν helps out the sense); Gal. ii. 5 οἷς
οὐδὲ πρὸς ὥραν εἴξαμεν τῇ ὑποταγῇ (perhaps = *yielded in subjection,*
i.e. *submissively*); Luke ii. 37 νηστείαις καὶ δεήσεσιν λατρεύουσα, *serving
with fastings and petitions* (which seems more like a Dat. of *accompaniment* than *instrumental*; cf. Phil. iv. 6 τῇ προσευχῇ καὶ τῇ δεήσει μετὰ
εὐχαριστίας τὰ αἰτήματα ὑμῶν γνωριζέσθω..., Col. iii. 16 ψαλμοῖς
ὕμνοις ᾠδαῖς πνευματικαῖς...ᾄδοντες); Acts xxiv. 4 ἀκοῦσαι...τῇ σῇ
ἐπιεικείᾳ, *to listen...with your clemency*; Acts ii. 8 ἀκούομεν...τῇ ἰδίᾳ
διαλέκτῳ; ii. 11 λαλούντων...ταῖς ἡμετέραις γλώσσαις; ii. 40 ἑτέροις
τε λόγοις πλείοσιν διεμαρτύρατο (cf. Luke iii. 18); perhaps Rom. viii. 24
τῇ...ἐλπίδι ἐσώθημεν (i.e. *proleptically—in hope though not in actuality*).
Extraordinary is the perhaps *causal* use in Gal. vi. 12 ἵνα τῷ σταυρῷ
τοῦ χριστοῦ μὴ διώκωνται (*to avoid persecution* for *the cross*...), and
(possibly) Phil. i. 14, πεποιθότας τοῖς δεσμοῖς μου (if this really can mean

---

[1] But in Plutarch the alternation of the Gen. Abs. with the Dat. quasi-Abs.
is said to be common (C. C. Tarelli).

[2] This is sometimes explained as a Dative depending upon a γεγραμμένον
implied in χειρόγραφον. But it remains problematic and unparalleled. The most
plausible suggestion known to me is the very ingenious one (J. A. T. Robinson,
The Body 43, n. 1) that 'What Paul is saying is now erased is our *subscription
to* the ordinances. (The dative is implied in the action of the verb.)' Too much
violence to word-order seems to be done by E. Percy's suggestion (*Die Probleme der Kolosser- und Epheserbriefe* 88–90) that the dative should be construed
with ὃ ἦν ὑπεναντίον ἡμῖν—*which, because of the decrees of God, was against us.*

having grown confident as a result of—encouraged by the witness of—*my imprisonment*).

Note that these uses often border on the *instrumental*, and can sometimes be best rendered in English by an adverb. Does οἱ πτωχοὶ τῷ πνεύματι (Matt. v. 3) mean *'the poor' used in its spiritual* (i.e. *religious) connotation* (while τοὺς πτωχοὺς τῷ κόσμῳ, Jas. ii. 5, means *the literally*, i.e. *materially, poor*)?† And does οἱ πνεύματι θεοῦ λατρεύοντες (Phil. iii. 3) mean *whose divine service is of a spiritual (and not of a material) sort*?† Clearly in Col. ii. 5 τῇ σαρκί (cf. I Pet. iv. 1 under i. (*b*) above, p. 44) means *physically*, as contrasted with τῷ πνεύματι, *spiritually*; cf. I Thess. ii. 17 προσώπῳ οὐ καρδίᾳ. Rom. xii. 10 τῇ φιλαδελφίᾳ...φιλόστοργοι also seems to be an adverbial use.

iii. Finally, there are uses which seem natural to a Latinist—such as would require a Dative in Latin also:

(*a*) After some words expressing speaking, adding, belonging, approaching, etc.: Mark v. 7, etc. τί ἐμοὶ καὶ σοί... (which, though a familiar idiom in Hebrew, is also found in Classical Greek: see D.-B. § 127, 3); Luke viii. 3 ἐκ τῶν ὑπαρχόντων αὐταῖς; Acts xxviii. 7 ὑπῆρχεν χωρία τῷ πρώτῳ τῆς νήσου.

(*b*) To express relations identical with or comparable to those expressed in Latin by the so-called *dativus commodi*, etc.: Rom. vi. 20 ἐλεύθεροι ἦτε τῇ δικαιοσύνῃ, *you were free with regard to righteousness* (not, I think, *free* from *righteousness*, although it might conceivably be argued that the Dative here is an 'ablatival' one); vi. 10 τῇ ἁμαρτίᾳ ἀπέθανεν ἐφάπαξ, *he died once for all in regard to sin*; I Pet. ii. 24 ἵνα ταῖς ἁμαρτίαις ἀπογενόμενοι τῇ δικαιοσύνῃ ζήσωμεν, *in order that, dead with regard to sins, we might live with regard to righteousness* (cf. the quasi-Biblical phrase which has become almost proverbial, *dead to the world*); I Cor. xiv. 11 ἔσομαι τῷ λαλοῦντι βάρβαρος, *I shall be, in the eyes of the speaker, a barbarian*. Rev. ii. 5, 16, ἔρχομαί σοι, is noted by Moulton (*Proleg.* 75) as a 'dative of disadvantage': *I am coming, to your cost*.

Note further: Rom. xiv. 1 ἀσθενοῦντα τῇ πίστει (tentatively classed under i. (*b*) above); Mark vii. 26 Συροφοινίκισσα τῷ γένει; Acts iv. 36 (cf. xviii. 24) Κύπριος τῷ γένει; ὀνόματι (Mark v. 22, Luke i. 61, etc.); Phil. iii. 5 περιτομῇ ὀκταήμερος (which may, literally, be *with regard to circumcision*...). It is, perhaps, arguable that all these are quasi-local, and therefore belong under i. (*b*) above.

Acts vii. 20 ἀστεῖος τῷ θεῷ and II Cor. x. 4 δυνατὰ τῷ θεῷ are possibly 'Semitisms' (*q.v.* p. 184).

Note. Quite anomalous, as it seems to me, are these two from Jude:†
v. 1 τοῖς ἐν θεῷ πατρὶ ἠγαπημένοις καὶ Ἰησοῦ χριστῷ τετηρημένοις
κλητοῖς, and *v*. 14 ἐπροφήτευσεν...τούτοις. In *v*. 1, the position of ἐν,
if it is intended to go with Ἰησοῦ χριστῷ as well as with θεῷ πατρί,
is extraordinary. Hort (W.-H.) favours the suggestion that it originally
stood before Ἰησοῦ only,[1] θεῷ then being a Dative of agent with the
Perfect Part. Passive. In *v*. 14, the anomaly vanishes if the sense is *he
prophesied* for *these* (so, for example, J. B. Mayor, *in loc.*); but the
context seems to require **with reference to** *these*, for which a plain
Dative is very odd and perhaps unparalleled. Contrast the περὶ ὑμῶν
of Matt. xv. 7, Mark vii. 6.

Incidentally, Jude 11 furnishes a curious study in the meanings of
the Dative: τῇ ὁδῷ τοῦ Κάϊν ἐπορεύθησαν [perhaps local], τῇ πλάνῃ
τοῦ Βαλαὰμ μισθοῦ ἐξεχύθησαν [?, cf. τῷ ἔθει τῷ Μωϋσέως under
ii. above], τῇ ἀντιλογίᾳ τοῦ Κορὲ ἀπώλοντο [perhaps instrumental—
because of a contradicting [*like that of*] *Korah*].

[1] *Select Readings*, Westcott and Hort, *N.T.* ii, 106.

VII

PREPOSITIONS

A preposition is an 'indeclinable word governing and normally placed before a noun or pronoun to show its relation to another word (e.g. *at*, *against*)'.[1] But the distinctive name is only a convenience: 'Between adverbs and prepositions no distinct line can be drawn.'[2] Note, too, the strongly adverbial quality of prepositions in compounds.

Of the N.T. prepositions, some are capable of being compounded with verbs, others are never so found; and the latter are technically (and, again, rather arbitrarily) styled 'improper' prepositions. There are some eighteen 'proper', as against about forty-two 'improper' prepositions.

It is believed that prepositions were originally adverbs, which, in turn, may have been nouns crystallized indeclinably in one particular case. Accordingly, some prepositions still bear traces of case-terminations: ἀντί and ἐπί are regarded as *Locatives* (cf. *instead of* =*in the stead* (i.e. *place*) *of*), and χάριν (an 'improper' preposition) is obviously merely the Accusative (perhaps the 'Accusative of Respect') of a still existing and declinable noun (cf. *thanks to*). Thus, prepositions may, at least in some instances, have been auxiliary nouns, used to help out the sense, exactly as the nouns *stead* and *thanks* are used in the English prepositional phrases just alluded to (although these, being indeclinable, require prepositions in addition, to indicate their 'case'). They do not really 'govern' cases, but are called in to help to clarify the meaning in which another word is used.

The κοινή period in the evolution of Greek shows a decline in the flexibility of the cases and a corresponding rise in the importance of prepositions.[3] J. S. Stewart writes: 'It was a dictum of Luther's that all religion lies in the pronouns....But Deissmann, going a step further..., has virtually declared that religion resides in the prepositions.'[4] This is the exordium to a consideration of Deissmann's famous work on the meaning of ἐν χριστῷ, and it is not intended to

[1] *Pocket Oxford Dictionary*.   [2] Giles in Rob. 554.
[3] See Rob. and Davis, § 339 (c); and Rad. 138, who points out that Hellenistic Greek tends in the direction of limiting prepositions to one case each, and shows a preference for the Accusative.
[4] *A Man in Christ*, 154, 155.

be taken too literally: indeed, it is now becoming more and more clearly recognized that it is a mistake to build exegetical conclusions on the notion that Classical accuracy in the use of prepositions was maintained in the κοινή period. An instance of the fluidity of usage is the uncertainty as to the cases governed by ἐπί (*q.v.*). But it is worth while to have some working generalizations in mind, if only to increase the accuracy with which one weighs each instance.

What follows, therefore, is a general review of the N.T. usages, in which the prepositions are classed, unscientifically perhaps, but with reasonable accessibility, according to the cases governed.

A. 'Proper' Prepositions

I. THOSE GOVERNING THREE CASES

1. **ἐπί.** The use of the cases after ἐπί is very fluid. C. C. Tarelli asks whether any grammarian has defined even the classical usage with any certainty: 'Herodotus has ἐπὶ τῶν ὄνων and ἐπὶ τοὺς ὄνους after ἐπιτίθημι in the same paragraph II. 121 (4), unless this is a scribal error.'[1] Similarly, Eph. i. 10 τὰ ἐπὶ τοῖς οὐρανοῖς καὶ τὰ ἐπὶ τῆς γῆς looks like a merely stylistic variation. Cf. Matt. xiv. 25 f., xxv. 21, 23, Acts xxvii. 44. The following effort to distinguish the uses is, therefore, only a makeshift from which to start.

i. *With the Accusative.* This primarily designates movement towards (i.e. it has a 'linear' sense): Luke xiv. 31 τῷ...ἐρχομένῳ ἐπ' αὐτόν, *the one who...is coming towards* [i.e. *against*] *him.* N.B. πιστεύω ἐπί, with Acc., is used in Matt. xxvii. 42, Acts ix. 42, xi. 17, xvi. 31, xxii. 19, Rom. iv. 24. This possibly retains a sense of movement, metaphorically.

In Acts xvi. 18 it is used *temporally*, and of *extent*: ἐπὶ πολλὰς ἡμέρας, *for many days* (though *movement towards* may even here be the underlying idea, if the phrase really means *for as much as* [i.e. *to the extent of*] *many days*). In I Pet. iii. 12 (as in LXX, Ps. xxxiii. 16, 17) ἐπί is used twice in quick succession, first to mean *towards* (favourably) and second to mean *against* (inimically).

But frequently it becomes 'punctiliar' rather than 'linear' and practically designates present *position* rather than ultimate *goal*: Mark iv. 38 ἐπὶ τὸ προσκεφάλαιον, *upon the cushion* (though D has ἐπὶ προσκεφαλαίου). So Matt. xiv. 25 has (according to the most

---

[1] *J.T.S.* xxxix (July 1938), 256.

probable reading) περιπατῶν ἐπὶ τὴν θάλασσαν, whereas Mark vi. 48, John vi. 19 use the Genitive in the same connexion. Cf. the usage with παρά (see below).

ii. *With the Genitive.* This primarily designates *position*: Mark ii. 10, etc. ἐπὶ τῆς γῆς, *upon the earth.* But, just as ἐπί with Acc. (i. above) can become 'punctiliar' rather than 'linear', so ἐπί with Gen. can become 'linear' despite its properly 'punctiliar' meaning: Mark iv. 26 βάλῃ τὸν σπόρον ἐπὶ τῆς γῆς, *throws the seed on to the ground* (note that our own *on* and *upon* are similarly ambiguous); cf. Acts x. 11 καθιέμενον ἐπὶ τῆς γῆς. Cf. again the usage with παρά (see below).

iii. *With the Dative.* (*a*) This primarily designates movement ending in a definite spot—as it were a line terminated by a given point: John iv. 6 ἐκαθέʒετο...ἐπὶ τῇ πηγῇ, *he sat at the well*; Matt. xvi. 18 ἐπὶ ταύτῃ τῇ πέτρᾳ οἰκοδομήσω, *I will build upon this rock* (D and Euseb. here have the Acc.; and the same verb is used in Matt. vii. 24 with Acc.—suggesting, perhaps, that motion is prominent in the associations of the verb; unless it is merely that the case-usage has become arbitrary. Cf. Tarelli quoted above); Gal. v. 13 ἐπ' ἐλευθερίᾳ ἐκλήθητε, *you were called to* (or *with a view to*) *freedom*; cf. I Thess. iv. 7, Eph. ii. 10.

(*b*) However, a more frequent use of ἐπί with Dat. is to designate what English expresses by *at*, both in local and transferred senses: ἐπὶ θύραις, ἐπὶ τῇ θύρᾳ, *at the door(s)* (Matt. xxiv. 33, Acts v. 9); Heb. ix. 26 ἐπὶ συντελείᾳ τῶν αἰώνων, *at the close of the ages*; Luke iv. 22 ἐθαύμαʒον ἐπὶ τοῖς λόγοις, *they marvelled at the words*; John iv. 27 ἐπὶ τούτῳ, *at this* (*juncture*); Rom. v. 12 ἐφ' ᾧ, *inasmuch as, because* (possibly also Phil. iii. 12—see S. and H. 349).

(*c*) Note Acts xiv. 3 παρρησιαʒόμενοι ἐπὶ τῷ κυρίῳ, perhaps *showing boldness in reliance upon the Lord*; cf. πιστεύειν ἐπί (with impersonal object only in Luke xxiv. 25; with personal object, Rom. ix. 33, I Pet. ii. 6, and Rom. x. 11 (all quotations), I Tim. i. 16); and see on ἐν, below (pp. 80 f.).

(*d*) On ἐπὶ τῷ ὀνόματι, see *Beg.* v, 123 n. 3 (contending that there is little or no difference in meaning between ἐν τῷ ὀνόματι, ἐπὶ τῷ ὀνόματι and εἰς τὸ ὄνομα).

2. παρά. i. *With the Accusative.* (*a*) This primarily designates *movement to a position alongside of* or *parallel with* (cf. παραβολή, a *parable* really being a *parallel* or *analogy*; παραθαλάσσιος, *by the sea*; and the

word *parallel* itself (παρ' ἄλληλα, *alongside of one another*)): Matt. xv. 29 ἦλθεν παρὰ τὴν θάλασσαν τῆς Γαλιλαίας, *He came to the shore of the Lake of Galilee*; Matt. xiii. 1 ἐξελθὼν ὁ Ἰησοῦς τῆς οἰκίας ἐκάθητο παρὰ τὴν θάλασσαν, *Jesus left the house and sat by the Lake*; Mark iv. 4 ὁ μὲν ἔπεσεν παρὰ τὴν ὁδόν (cf. ἐπὶ ii. above, p. 50), *some fell by the path.*

Note that it appears never to be used in the N.T. *in this sense* with a *personal* object in the *Acc.*, though παρὰ τοὺς πόδας τινός (e.g. Luke xvii. 16) is common enough (D.-B. § 236). παρὰ τὸν κτίσαντα in Rom. i. 25 has a different sense (see below). Contrast the reverse usage with the *Genitive* and, with one exception, with the *Dative*.

There are, however, other usages observable, e.g.:

(*b*) Of *rest* beside, apparently without any notion of *movement to*: Mark iv. 1 ἤρξατο διδάσκειν παρὰ τὴν θάλασσαν, *He began to teach by the Lake*; Mark x. 46 ἐκάθητο παρὰ τὴν ὁδόν. Cf. a scholiast on Aristoph. *Frogs*, 1114, καὶ φασκούσας οὐ 3ῆν: Ἔστι μὲν π α ρ ὰ τ ὰ ἐκ Φρίξου Εὐριπίδου Τίς οἶδεν... (noted by H. W. Moule).

(*c*) I Cor. xii. 15, 16 παρὰ τοῦτο, *on that score, for that reason* (perhaps cf. the colloquial *along of that*). See I Cor. iv. 4 ἐν τούτῳ, for another phrase with the same meaning.

(*d*) Gal. i. 8, cf. *v.* 9 ...εὐαγγελίσηται ὑμῖν παρ' ὃ εὐηγγελισάμεθα ὑμῖν, ...*preaches a good news to you other than the good news we* [*originally*] *preached to you*; Rom. i. 25 ἐλάτρευσαν τῇ κτίσει παρὰ τὸν κτίσαντα, *they worshipped the created rather than the Creator*. So Luke iii. 13 πλέον παρὰ τὸ διατεταγμένον, *more than the appointed amount*; cf. Luke xiii. 2, 4, Rom. xiv. 5, I Cor. iii. 11; similarly, II Cor. viii. 3 παρὰ δύναμιν, *beyond their power*, contrasted with κατὰ δύναμιν (there is a significant variant ὑπέρ for παρά here); Rom. xii. 3 μὴ ὑπερφρονεῖν παρ' ὃ δεῖ φρονεῖν points in the same direction.

(*e*) II Cor. xi. 24 τεσσεράκοντα παρὰ μίαν (*sc.* πληγήν) is hard to explain in view of the above meanings (cf. the reading of D in Luke v. 7, which inserts παρά τι, *all but*, i.e. *short of something*: see D.-B. § 236).

ii. *With the Genitive*. This primarily denotes *movement from beside*, *emanation from*: Luke i. 45 τοῖς λελαλημένοις...παρὰ κυρίου, *the things spoken by the Lord* (but, as D.-B. says, § 237, with the idea of indirect speech through the mediation of the Angel; i.e. it is not quite the same as the immediate ὑπό); Mark v. 26 δαπανήσασα τὰ παρ' αὐτῆς, *having spent all that she had* (lit. *the things from beside her*, with a suggestion, perhaps, of emphasis on the disastrous movement away of all her small savings), cf. Luke x. 7 τὰ παρ' αὐτῶν; Phil. iv. 18 δεξάμενος παρὰ Ἐπαφροδίτου τὰ παρ' ὑμῶν; Mark iii. 21 οἱ παρ' αὐτοῦ, *his relatives*.

Note that, unlike the *Accusative* usage, this *Genitive* usage is only with persons (D.-B. § 237).[1]

iii. *With the Dative*. This primarily denotes *rest with* or *in the presence of*. Its commonest use is in the metaphorical sense *in the sight of*—παρὰ τῷ θεῷ, Luke i. 30, Rom. ii. 11, I Cor. iii. 19, etc.; Rom. xii. 16 φρόνιμοι παρ' ἑαυτοῖς, *wise in their own eyes*; Acts xxvi. 8 τί ἄπιστον κρίνεται παρ' ὑμῖν...; *why is it judged incredible in your eyes...?*

But it is also used locally, always (with the exception of John xix. 25 παρὰ τῷ σταυρῷ, *beside the cross*) with a personal object: Luke ix. 47 ἔστησεν αὐτὸ παρ' ἑαυτῷ (D ἑαυτόν), *he stood him* [a child] *beside him*; John i. 39 παρ' αὐτῷ, *with him* (*chez lui*), etc.

3. **πρός.** i. *With the Accusative*. The use with Gen. or Dat. is so much less frequent that 'it is nearly a one-case preposition': there are 678 examples with Acc. in the N.T., and only eight with other cases[2]. Note, however, the frequency of the Dat. after *verbs* compounded with πρός.

(*a*) With the Accusative it usually denotes *motion to*: Matt. iii. 13 παραγίνεται ὁ Ἰησοῦς...πρὸς τὸν Ἰωάνην, etc. (It is questionable how far this can be distinguished from uses with ἐπί (see Matt. iii. 13 again) and εἰς.)

So, frequently, it is used, by transference, with verbs of saying: Luke ix. 3 εἶπεν πρὸς αὐτούς; Acts xxiii. 22 ἐνεφάνισας πρὸς ἐμέ (cf. the simple Dat. in *v*. 15, ἐμφανίσατε τῷ χιλιάρχῳ). (In *Beg*. II, 72 'πρός *used of speaking to*' comes in a list of words and phrases occurring at least five times in Luke and also at least twice as often in Luke as in the rest of the N.T. excluding Acts, and at least twenty-five times in the LXX.)

(*b*) But it also denotes *position*—i.e. it has a more 'punctiliar' sense as well: Matt. xiii. 56 (‖ Mark vi. 3) καὶ αἱ ἀδελφαὶ αὐτοῦ οὐχὶ πᾶσαι πρὸς ἡμᾶς εἰσιν; ...*all with us?*; Mark ix. 19 (‖ Luke ix. 41) ἕως πότε πρὸς ὑμᾶς ἔσομαι; Mark xiv. 49 καθ' ἡμέραν ἤμην πρὸς ὑμᾶς; Matt. xxvi. 18

---

[1] See further E.-B. Allo on I Cor. xi. 23, *Commentaire*, 313, discussing the shades of difference between ἀπό, ἐκ, and παρά. It is worth while to compare with the ἀπὸ τοῦ κυρίου of I Cor. xi. 23 the παρὰ τοῦ κυρίου Ἰησοῦ of Acts xx. 24.

[2] Rob. and Davis, § 369.

πρός σὲ ποιῶ τὸ πάσχα (cf. παρά with Dat. in the sense *chez*, above); John i. 1 ὁ λόγος ἦν πρὸς τὸν θεόν; I Thess. iii. 4 ὅτε πρὸς ὑμᾶς ἦμεν. So also I Cor. xvi. 6, 7, II Cor. v. 8, xi. 9, Gal. i. 18, iv. 18, 19, Phil. i. 26, II Thess. ii. 5, iii. 10, Philem. 13. Perhaps one should also include Mark ii. 2 τὰ πρὸς τὴν θύραν.[1]

In a perhaps 'pregnant' sense, seemingly combining 'linear' motion with 'punctiliar' rest on arrival, πρός with Acc. is found, for example, in Mark i. 33 ἐπισυνηγμένη πρὸς τὴν θύραν (though it is questionable whether this can be distinguished from Mark xi. 4 δεδεμένον πρὸς θύραν, or Mark xiii. 29 ἐπὶ θύραις); Matt. iii. 10 ἡ ἀξίνη πρὸς τὴν ῥίζαν τῶν δένδρων κεῖται; Acts v. 10 ἔπεσεν...πρὸς τοὺς πόδας αὐτοῦ...ἔθαψαν πρὸς τὸν ἄνδρα αὐτῆς, *she fell...at his feet...they buried her beside her husband*.

(*c*) With reference to *time*, it naturally means *towards*: Luke xxiv. 29 πρὸς ἑσπέραν ἐστίν.

Yet πρὸς καιρόν (Luke viii. 13, I Cor. vii. 5), πρὸς ὥραν (Gal. ii. 5) mean *for a time, hour*, denoting *duration*.

(*d*) In transferred senses, it means *tending towards, leading to, concerning, against, in view of*: Rom. viii. 31 τί οὖν ἐροῦμεν πρὸς ταῦτα; *what then shall we say in view of this?* I Cor. xii. 7 πρὸς τὸ συμφέρον, *for the common good*; Rom. xv. 2 πρὸς οἰκοδομήν, *making for upbuilding* (preceded by εἰς ἀγαθόν); Matt. xix. 8, Mark x. 5 πρὸς τὴν σκληροκαρδίαν ὑμῶν, *in view of your stubbornness*; Rom. viii. 18 οὐκ ἄξια τὰ παθήματα τοῦ νῦν καιροῦ πρὸς τὴν μέλλουσαν δόξαν ἀποκαλυφθῆναι, ...*are not worth comparing with*...(?); Gal. ii. 14 οὐκ ὀρθοποδοῦσιν πρὸς τὴν ἀλήθειαν, *their conduct does not square with the truth* (alternatively, *they do not advance towards the truth*);[2] II Cor. v. 10 πρὸς ἃ ἔπραξεν, *in proportion to his deeds*;[3] Mark xii. 12 πρὸς αὐτοὺς τὴν παραβολὴν εἶπεν, *he had spoken the parable with reference to* (perhaps almost *against*) *them*; Acts xxiii. 30 λέγειν πρὸς αὐτόν, *to accuse him*; I Cor. vi. 1 πρᾶγμα ἔχων πρὸς τὸν ἕτερον, *having a suit against his neighbour*; Eph. iv. 14 ἐν πανουργίᾳ πρὸς τὴν μεθοδίαν τῆς πλάνης, *by*

---

[1] For the rarity of this usage in the inscriptions and its absence from known papyri, see W. F. Howard, 'The Common Authorship of the Johannine Gospel and Epistles', *J.T.S.* xlviii (Jan.–April 1947), 15.

[2] See C. H. Roberts in *J.T.S.* xl (Jan. 1939), 55, J. G. Winter in *Harvard Theological Studies*, 34 (1941), 161, and G. D. Kilpatrick in *Neutestamentl. Studien für Bultmann*, 269–74.

[3] Cf. Ignatius, *Magn.* xii, where εἶναι πρός appears to mean *to be comparable* (see J. B. Lightfoot, *in loc.*). For εἰς in the same or a similar sense, see, for example, Gal. vi. 4, and see on εἰς, below

craftiness in accordance with the wiles of error (if that is the meaning of this obscure phrase. See J. A. Robinson, *in loc.*); Heb. iv. 13 πρὸς ὃν ἡμῖν ὁ λόγος, *with whom we have to reckon.*

Note. πιστεύω, which is used with εἰς and ἐν and ἐπί, is not found in the N.T. with πρός; but Philem. 5 comes near to it: τὴν πίστιν ἣν ἔχεις πρὸς† τὸν κύριον Ἰησοῦν, followed by καὶ εἰς πάντας τοὺς ἁγίους.

ii. *With the Genitive.* Of this there is only one instance in the N.T., Acts xxvii. 34 τοῦτο πρὸς τῆς ὑμετέρας σωτηρίας ὑπάρχει, *this is in the interests of your safety*; with which D.-B. § 240 compares Thuc. III. 59. 1 οὐ πρὸς τῆς ὑμετέρας δόξης τάδε. This usage occurs (*ibid.*) twenty-three times in the LXX.

iii. *With the Dative*, implying position. In the N.T. there are only six occurrences (for some of which there is a variant reading with Acc.), all, except the first, translatable by *at*: Mark v. 11 πρὸς τῷ ὄρει, *on the hill*; Luke xix. 37, John xviii. 16, xx. 11, 12, Rev. i. 13.

II. THOSE GOVERNING TWO CASES

1. **διά.** i. *With the Accusative.* This can usually be rendered *because of*, and the broad distinction 'διά with Accusative = *because of* (Latin *ob*), with Genitive = *through* (Latin *per*)' is a good working rule.

The principal meaning lying behind these senses may be *between* (cf. several instances of this meaning in compound verbs, below), and the word itself is supposed to be connected with δύο, *two*, and with *be-tween* itself.[1] If so, it is not difficult to imagine the sense *through* being evolved from the idea of duality or 'betweenness': you can talk about going *between* two people and then, thinking of many pairs *en masse*, speak of going *through* a crowd. The idea *because of* is harder to account for, though the vulgarism *along of* suggests that the idea of 'coextension' is somehow not far removed from the idea of causation, as indeed is the case with the word *through* itself.

From countless examples of διά with the Accusative, the following may be taken as representative: Acts xxviii. 2 διὰ τὸν ὑετὸν...καὶ διὰ τὸ ψῦχος, *because of the rain...and because of the cold*; Mark vi. 26 διὰ τοὺς ὅρκους καὶ τοὺς ἀνακειμένους, *because of the oaths and the guests*; Acts xviii. 2 διὰ τὸ διατεταχέναι Κλαύδιον, *because Claudius had issued an edict*. Of more particular interest are: Rom. iii. 25 διὰ τὴν πάρεσιν τῶν προγεγονότων ἁμαρτημάτων, where it makes a difference whether

[1] Rob. 580; see Rob. and Davis, § 359.

διά is taken strictly as = *because of*, or more loosely as almost = *by way of*, *involving*, or even *with a view to* (see commentators *in loc.*); Rom. iv. 25 ὃς παρεδόθη διὰ τὰ παραπτώματα ἡμῶν καὶ ἠγέρθη διὰ τὴν δικαίωσιν ἡμῶν, where again, in the case of the second διά, there is some doubt whether it should not be 'prospective', *with a view to*, *for the sake of*.[1] (See further 'Miscellaneous Notes on Style', ii. below, p. 194.) N.B. also Mark ii. 27 τὸ σάββατον διὰ τὸν ἄνθρωπον ἐγένετο, καὶ οὐχ ὁ ἄνθρωπος διὰ τὸ σάββατον, *the sabbath was made for man*, *and not man for the sabbath*, which certainly looks 'prospective'; and Rev. xii. 11, xiii. 14, where διά with the Accusative seems to be used in the sense of *through*.[2] In a strictly *local* sense it is only found in Luke xvii. 11 διὰ μέσον Σαμαρείας καὶ Γαλιλαίας, *between Samaria and Galilee* (?), where, however, the reading is uncertain (A *al.* διὰ μέσου, D μέσον simply, without διά).

In modern Greek the equivalent γιά with Accusative seems to have developed fully into a prospective and purposive preposition. Of the N.T. usage it may be said, then, that while the commonest sense is *because of* (consecutive), some steps are traceable towards the final or prospective sense, *for the sake of* or *with a view to*.[3]

ii. *With the Genitive.* (a) When used literally and spatially, this seems to denote *extension through*: Mark ix. 30 παρεπορεύοντο διὰ τῆς Γαλιλαίας, *they were journeying through Galilee*; cf. Matt. xii. 43, John iv. 4, Rom. xv. 28 (= *via*), Heb. xi. 29. But in this literal sense διελθεῖν with the Accusative frequently takes its place. Possibly we ought to place here the phrase from II Pet. iii. 5 γῆ ἐξ ὕδατος καὶ δι' ὕδατος συνεστῶσα, as though it meant *continuous land*, *rising out of and extending through water*; but the δι' ὕδατος may mean *between water*, and refer to the idea that there are waters above and below the earth.

[1] H. W. Moule notes the 'prospective' use in scholiasts; e.g. κόγχῃ δὲ τῷ κογχυλίῳ τῷ ἐπικειμένῳ ταῖς σφραγῖσι διὰ τὸ μὴ ἀφανίζεσθαι τοὺς τύπους αὐτῆς, schol. on Aristophanes, *Wasps*, 585.

[2] H. W. Moule notes an example of this use in Antiphon, *Murder of Herodes*, § 5 (Jebb's *Selections*, 6) οὐ γὰρ δίκαιον οὔτ' ἔργῳ ἁμαρτάνοντα διὰ ῥήματα σωθῆναι, οὔτ' ἔργῳ ὀρθῶς πράξαντα διὰ ῥήματα ἀπολέσθαι. He also quotes the following from a scholiast on Aristoph. *Pl.* 93 (Dindorf): διὰ τοὺς χρηστούς γε· Ἰστέον ὅτι ἡ διὰ πρόθεσις οὐ μόνον γενικῇ συντάσσεται, ὅταν δηλοῖ ἐνέργειαν, ἀλλὰ καὶ αἰτιατικῇ, ὡς ἐνταῦθα· εὑρήσεις δὲ τοῦτο καὶ ἐν πολλοῖς τῶν λογοποιῶν. καὶ μὴν ὅταν δηλοῖ αἰτίαν, αἰτιατικῇ μὲν ὡς ἐπὶ τὸ πολὺ συντάσσεται· ἀλλὰ καὶ πρὸς γενικὴν εὕρηται σπανίως. *Scholion recentissimum*, *quo carent R.V.*

[3] See summary by H. G. Meecham in *E.T.* L, no. 12 (Sept. 1939), 564.

(*b*) A similar sense is extended to expressions of time: Luke v. 5 δι' ὅλης νυκτός, *the whole night through*; Heb. ii. 15 διὰ παντὸς τοῦ ζῆν, *through the whole of life*. Acts i. 3 δι' ἡμερῶν τεσσεράκοντα ὀπτανόμενος is often taken (following Chrysostom) to mean *appearing at intervals during forty days*, but it has been pointed out that *at intervals* is derived not from the words but from independent knowledge of the traditions. In itself it simply means *during* or *in the course of*.... So Acts xvi. 9 διὰ νυκτός, *in the night* (cf. the absolute νυκτός, *by night*, in Matt. xxviii. 13, John xix. 39).

Less easy to explain are the phrases where διά seems = *after*: Matt. xxvi. 61 διὰ τριῶν ἡμερῶν οἰκοδομῆσαι (cf. John ii. 19 ἐν τρισὶν ἡμέραις); Acts xxiv. 17 δι' ἐτῶν πλειόνων; Gal. ii. 1 διὰ δεκατεσσάρων ἐτῶν; but these phrases are common in Greek authors; cf. Aristoph. *Pl.* 1045 διὰ πολλοῦ χρόνου, *after a long time* (evidently the same meaning as μετὰ δὲ πολὺν χρόνον, Matt. xxv. 19); Hdt. ii, 37 διὰ τρίτης ἡμέρας, *every other day* (Goodwin, § 1206 (*c*)). The same sense, but literally and spatially, meets us in Theophr. *De caus. plant.* lib. 3 (quoted in Stephanus' *Thesaurus*) διὰ πολλοῦ = *longis intervallis*). It is tempting, but purely conjectural, to suggest that in many such phrases διά is *adverbial*, and the Genitive is *absolute*; cf. the Latin idiom with *post* in such phrases as *tribus post annis, three years later*, where *post*, adverbial = *later*; as against the other possible construction *post tres annos, after three years*, where *post* is a true preposition.[1] But perhaps the truth may rather be that διά simply *takes the mind through the period*, and it depends on the *Aktionsart* of the verb (see ch. ii, above) whether the event in question is to be understood as falling during or after that period. That is why if, for independent reasons, an Aorist happens to be used, another and less ambiguous preposition is used: Acts xiii. 31 ὃς ὤφθη ἐπὶ ἡμέρας πλείους (referring to the same facts as in Acts i. 3 quoted above; see *Beg.* on Acts i. 3).

(*c*) Very common is the transferred sense, *by means of*. Just possibly I Tim. ii. 15 should be classed here—σωθήσεται δὲ διὰ τῆς τεκνογονίας (see commentaries for the interpretation *saved by means of her*, or *the*, *childbearing*; but why not *brought safely through childbirth*? cf. I Pet. iii. 20 διεσώθησαν δι' ὕδατος). The following, at any rate, are representative: Acts xiii. 38 διὰ τούτου ὑμῖν ἄφεσις ἁμαρτιῶν καταγγέλλεται, *remission of sins by means of him*... (?); II John 12 (cf. III John 13) γράφειν... διὰ χάρτου καὶ μέλανος,... *with paper and ink*; Col. i. 22 διὰ τοῦ θανάτου, *by means of his death*; Rom. iii. 25 διὰ

[1] G. G. Bradley's ed. of T. K. Arnold's *Latin Prose Composition*, § 322.

πίστεως; Heb. xiii. 15 δι' αὐτοῦ οὖν ἀναφέρωμεν θυσίαν (though it is difficult to tie down the sense here); Acts viii. 18 διὰ τῆς ἐπιθέσεως τῶν χειρῶν; Acts xxiv. 2 πολλῆς εἰρήνης τυγχάνοντες διὰ σοῦ καὶ διορθωμάτων γινομένων τῷ ἔθνει τούτῳ διὰ τῆς σῆς προνοίας; Gal. iii. 19 διαταγεὶς δι' ἀγγέλων; Heb. ii. 2 δι' ἀγγέλων λαληθείς; Heb. iii. 16 οἱ ἐξελθόντες ἐξ Αἰγύπτου διὰ Μωϋσέως; I Tim. iv. 5 ἁγιάζεται γὰρ διὰ λόγου θεοῦ καὶ ἐντεύξεως. Cf. διὰ στόματος, Acts i. 16, etc., διὰ τῶν χειρῶν, διὰ χειρός, Acts v. 12, xi. 30, etc. Note that the above uses are with both persons and things.†

(d) Possibly one should distinguish under a separate heading the use of διά with the Genitive to express *environment, attendant circumstances*, etc.: Heb. xiii. 22 διὰ βραχέων, *briefly*; Acts xv. 32 διὰ λόγου πολλοῦ, *at length (with much talk)*; II Cor. ii. 4 διὰ πολλῶν δακρύων, *with many tears*; Eph. vi. 18 διὰ πάσης προσευχῆς καὶ δεήσεως, *with all [possible] prayer and petition*; Heb. ix. 12 δι' αἵματος... διὰ δὲ τοῦ ἰδίου αἵματος, perhaps *with blood*, etc. (‖ ἐν αἵματι, *v.* 25); so, possibly, I John v. 6 δι' ὕδατος καὶ αἵματος (‖ ἐν τῷ ὕδατι κ.τ.λ.); I Cor. xvi. 3 δι' ἐπιστολῶν τούτους πέμψω, *I will send them with letters* (or perhaps *a letter*); I Tim. ii. 9, 10 κοσμεῖν ἑαυτὰς... δι' ἔργων ἀγαθῶν, *to adorn themselves...with good deeds* (‖ ἐν καταστολῇ; and cf. I Pet. iii. 4, using ἐν in a similar context); Rom. ii. 27 σὲ τὸν διὰ γράμματος καὶ περιτομῆς παραβάτην νόμου, *you, who with all your observances of the letter and your circumcision, still transgress the law*; Rom. iv. 11 τῶν πιστευόντων δι' ἀκροβυστίας, *who, in a state of uncircumcision, are yet believers* (cf. *v.* 13 διὰ νόμου). So, perhaps, I Tim. iv. 14 ἐδόθη σοι διὰ προφητείας, *was given to you with accompanying prophecy* (unless it means, instrumentally, *through the medium of prophecy*); II Tim. ii. 2 διὰ πολλῶν μαρτύρων, *in the presence of* (or perhaps *supported by*) *many witnesses*; I Thess. iv. 14 τοὺς κοιμηθέντας διὰ τοῦ Ἰησοῦ ἄξει σὺν αὐτῷ, *those who have fallen asleep* [i.e. *died*] *as Christians* (perhaps *in contact with Jesus*: ‖ οἱ νεκροὶ ἐν χριστῷ, *v.* 16)—but some commentators take the διά-phrase with ἄξει, *God will, by the instrumentality of Jesus, bring*....

But the dividing line between 'accompaniment' and 'instrumentality' is thin: Acts i. 2 διὰ πνεύματος ἁγίου, perhaps *by means of the Holy Spirit, in contact with the Holy Spirit* (cf. xxi. 4 διὰ τοῦ πνεύματος, perhaps *as a spiritual insight*); I Thess. iv. 2 τίνας παραγγελίας ἐδώκαμεν ὑμῖν διὰ τοῦ κυρίου Ἰησοῦ, *what injunctions we* [or perhaps *I*] *gave you in the name of the Lord Jesus* (‖ *v.l.* ἐν κυρίῳ Ἰησοῦ; or do both phrases mean *as those who are* [or *one who is*] *in contact with the*

Lord Jesus? Cf. Acts iv. 30, etc. διὰ τοῦ ὀνόματος, and Acts iii. 6, etc. ἐν τῷ ὀνόματι, which may provide a similar διά–ἐν analogy); Rom. xii. 1 παρακαλῶ οὖν ὑμᾶς... διὰ τῶν οἰκτιρμῶν τοῦ θεοῦ, *I appeal to you in God's mercies' name* (cf. II Cor. x. 1 παρακαλῶ ὑμᾶς διὰ τῆς πραΰτητος καὶ ἐπιεικείας τοῦ χριστοῦ); Rom. xii. 3 λέγω... διὰ τῆς χάριτος τῆς δοθείσης μοι, perhaps *in virtue of*....

This usage becomes all but adverbial or adjectival (cf. the Classical δι' ὀργῆς ἔχειν τινά, etc., e.g. Thuc. v. 46): Rom. viii. 25 δι' ὑπομονῆς, *with fortitude* (cf. Rom. ii. 7 καθ' ὑπομονὴν ἔργου ἀγαθοῦ, *by patiently doing good*, Rom. ii. 8 ἐξ ἐριθείας, *in a spirit of self-interest*); Rom. xiv. 20 τῷ διὰ προσκόμματος ἐσθίοντι, *he who eats in a way which causes stumbling*; II Cor. iii. 11 διὰ δόξης, practically =*glorious* (cf. *ibid.* ἐν δόξῃ); but in II Cor. vi. 7, διὰ τῶν ὅπλων might be instrumental, and διὰ δόξης in II Cor. vi. 8 might be local—*passing through*....

Does Acts iii. 16 ἡ πίστις ἡ δι' αὐτοῦ mean *faith which is caused by him* (*Christ*), or simply *Christian faith?* (See also under the 'Definite Article', p. 109.)

Note. The broad distinction already stated between διά with Acc. (=*because of*) and with Gen. (=*through, by means of*) may be illustrated by comparing the common phrase διὰ τοῦτο (e.g. Rom. v. 12), *therefore, because of this*, with διὰ τούτου, Acts xiii. 38, *through him* (i.e. Jesus). Heb. ii. 10 contains both constructions side by side.†

2. **κατά** The sense of this word seems originally to have been connected with the idea of 'down' (cf. the adverb κάτω, *down, down-wards*. So the adverb ἄνω, *up, upwards*, corresponds to the preposition ἀνά). This sense, however, is more obvious when κατά is used with the Genitive than with the Accusative.

i. *With the Accusative.* (*a*) Of *place* (literally or metaphorically), it denotes close connexion: Mark xiii. 8, etc. κατὰ τόπους, *in [certain] places*; Acts xxv. 14 τὰ κατὰ Παῦλον, *Paul's case*; Eph. i. 15 τὴν καθ' ὑμᾶς πίστιν; possibly Rom. i. 15 τὸ κατ' ἐμὲ πρόθυμον, if this simply means *my eagerness*; but more probably τὸ κατ' ἐμέ is a self-contained adverbial phrase, *as far as I am concerned* (cf. Rom. i. 3 κατὰ σάρκα— contrasted with κατὰ πνεῦμα ἁγιωσύνης, *v.* 4—Rom. ix. 5 τὸ κατὰ σάρκα, *as far as physical descent is concerned*). πρόθυμον will then be a slip, or a case of attraction, for πρόθυμος. (See D.-B. § 224.) Luke xv. 14 κατὰ τὴν χώραν ἐκείνην, *in* [perhaps *throughout*—Rob. and Davis § 364] *that land*; II Cor. x. 7 τὰ κατὰ πρόσωπον, *what is in front of you.*

(*b*) Of *time*, it can mean simply *at*: Acts xii. 1 κατ' ἐκεῖνον τὸν καιρόν, *at that time*; or it can be used distributively: Matt. xxvii. 15 κατὰ δὲ ἑορτήν, *at feast-time, at every feast*; so Luke xi. 3, Heb. vii. 27 καθ' ἡμέραν, Heb. ix. 25 κατ' ἐνιαυτόν.

(*c*) In *transferred senses*, it carries a variety of shades of meaning: *according to, by virtue of, in respect of*, etc. E.g. Κατὰ Ματθαῖον, etc., in the titles of the Gospels; I Cor. xv. 3, etc. κατὰ τὰς γραφάς, *in accordance with the scriptures*; Heb. ix. 9 καθ' ἥν, *in accordance with which*; Rom. xi. 21 κατὰ φύσιν, *natural, in accordance with nature*; II Cor. x. 3 κατὰ σάρκα, *in accordance with material standards* (to be distinguished in meaning from κατὰ σάρκα, Rom. i. 3, and τὸ κατὰ σάρκα, Rom. ix. 5, quoted above under (*a*)); Gal. iii. 15 κατὰ ἄνθρωπον λέγω, *I am using a human analogy, I am speaking like a man*; II Cor. vii. 9–11 ἐλυπήθητε...κατὰ θεόν...ἡ...κατὰ θεὸν λύπη... τὸ κατὰ θεὸν λυπηθῆναι, *you were grieved...in a godly way...godly grief...to be grieved in a godly way*. Rom. viii. 26, 27 τὸ πνεῦμα... κατὰ θεὸν ἐντυγχάνει, *the Spirit intercedes in accordance with the will of God*; Eph. iv. 24 τὸν καινὸν ἄνθρωπον τὸν κατὰ θεὸν κτισθέντα, *the new man who has been created in accordance with God* [*in God's image*, cf. Col. iii. 10]; I Pet. iv. 6 ἵνα κριθῶσι μὲν κατὰ ἀνθρώπους σαρκί, ζῶσι δὲ κατὰ θεὸν πνεύματι is difficult: perhaps *that they might be judged in the eyes of men* [*as men reckon judgment*] *physically, but might live as God lives spiritually* (see E. G. Selwyn *in loc.*); Heb. vii. 16 κατὰ νόμον...κατὰ δύναμιν..., *by virtue of a law...by virtue of a power*; Matt. xix. 3 κατὰ πᾶσαν αἰτίαν, *on the ground of any cause*; II Cor. viii. κατὰ δύναμιν, *to the utmost of their power* (cf. παρὰ δύναμιν, *contrary to* [i.e. *beyond*] *their power*, *ibid.*; and cf. καθὸ ἐὰν ἔχη, in the same context— II Cor. viii. 12—meaning καθ' ὃ ἐὰν ἔχη, *in proportion to what one has*); I Cor. vii. 6 κατὰ συγγνώμην, *by way of a concession*; Luke i. 18 κατὰ τί, *in view of what? whereby?*; Acts xxv. 23 σὺν...ἀνδράσιν τοῖς κατ' ἐξοχήν, *with the eminent men* (literally, *the men at prominence, in positions of eminence*)—κατ' ἐξοχήν commonly, e.g. in Strabo, means *par excellence*.

Distributively, κατά with Acc. is used, e.g. as follows: Mark vi. 40 κατὰ ἑκατὸν καὶ κατὰ πεντήκοντα (so אBD, see below). This is usually explained as meaning *in groups*, [*some*] *of a hundred and* [*some*] *of fifty*; but the context, with its πρασιαὶ πρασιαί, implies that they were seated *in rows*, and I suggest that they formed a great rectangle, *a hundred by fifty*; the κατά will then be equivalent to our *at* in the idiom: 'one side of the rectangle was reckoned *at* a hundred, the other *at* fifty.' This interpretation is not inconsistent with Luke ix. 14, if κλισία is a *rank* or *row* rather than a *group*.

So in Eph. v. 33 οἱ καθ' ἕνα = *individually*; in I Cor. xiv. 31 καθ' ἕνα = *one by one*; in Heb. ix. 5 κατὰ μέρος = *in detail*. Is Mark xiv. 19 εἷς κατὰ εἷς an *adverbial* use, or sheer bad grammar? (The textual variants are interesting.)[1]

N.B. curiously enough ἀνά, which might be expected to be the *reverse* of κατά, shares this distributive sense; and in Mark vi. 40 most of the MSS. except אBD[2] read ἀνά instead of κατά. See on ἀνά below.

ii. *With the Genitive.* The precise definition of the general sense *down* has to be determined by the context: Matt. viii. 32 ὥρμησεν... κατὰ τοῦ κρημνοῦ, *rushed down the cliff* (i.e. *down along*); Acts xxvii. 14 ἔβαλεν κατ' αὐτῆς ἄνεμος τυφωνικός, *a tornado struck down from it* (so *Beg. in loc.* and others. It is topography which here decides in favour of *down from Crete*, rather than the A.V. *against* (i.e. *down upon*) *it* (i.e. perhaps the ship—as though the feminine ναῦς had been used, as it actually is in *v.* 41)); Mark xiv. 55 κατὰ τοῦ Ἰησοῦ, against Jesus; I Cor. xi. 4 κατὰ κεφαλῆς ἔχων, *with [a covering?] on the head* (i.e. *down upon*; though Rob. 606-7 sees a reference to the veil hanging *down from* the head); II Cor. viii. 2 ἡ κατὰ βάθους πτωχεία αὐτῶν, *their profound* (perhaps = *down to the depths*) *poverty*.

Less obviously connected with *down* is the Lucan phrase, Luke iv. 14, καθ' ὅλης τῆς περιχώρου, *throughout the region round*, cf. Acts ix. 31, etc.

Note also the use to designate the guarantee of an oath: Heb. vi. 13 ὤμοσεν καθ' ἑαυτοῦ, *he swore by himself*; cf. Gen. xxii. 16 בִּי. But Matt. xxiii. 16 uses ἐν with the Dative in the same connexion. So Rev. x. 6.

3. **μετά.** i. *With the Accusative.* The meaning, however derived, is *after*, and, in the temporal sense, is common: Mark i. 14 μετὰ τὰ παραδοθῆναι τὸν Ἰωάνην, *after John had been committed to prison*, etc. So μετὰ τοῦτο, μετὰ ταῦτα, etc.

Only once does it occur in the N.T. in a spatial sense—Heb. ix. 3 μετὰ τὸ δεύτερον καταπέτασμα, *after [or beyond] the second veil*.

Note. It is debated whether Acts i. 5 οὐ μετὰ πολλὰς ταύτας ἡμέρας is a Latinism (cf. on διά with Gen. above, and πρό below), in which

---

[1] Cf. John viii. 9 ἐξήρχοντο εἷς καθεῖς, Rom. xii. 5 τὸ δὲ καθ' εἷς, Rev. xxi. 21 ἀνὰ εἷς ἕκαστος.

[2] The numerical phrase is lacking in 𝔓⁴⁵.

case μετά is used in an absolute, adverbial, sense; and, if so, whether it is a 'vulgar' Latinism, or (since it is used with a characteristically Lucan *litotes* or deliberate understatement—the only instance in the earlier chapters of Acts) something more deliberate; or, alternatively, is it an Aramaism?[1]

ii. *With the Genitive.* The meaning, broadly, is *with* (cf. perhaps μέσος,† German *mit* (cf. μετέωρος, *in mid air*), English *mid*(*st*); see Rob. 609), and it covers much the same variety of senses as the English word; e.g.:

(*a*) The idea of *association with*: Luke xxii. 37 μετὰ ἀνόμων ἐλογίσθη (Isa. liii. 12 LXX has ἐν τοῖς ἀνόμοις); Mark i. 13 ἦν μετὰ τῶν θηρίων; Mark x. 30 μετὰ διωγμῶν, *with* (i.e. *among* or *accompanied by*) *persecutions*; I Tim. iv. 14 μετὰ ἐπιθέσεως τῶν χειρῶν; Matt. xiv. 7 μεθ' ὅρκου, *with an oath*; Luke xxii. 52 ἐξήλθατε μετὰ μαχαιρῶν καὶ ξύλων.

(*b*) The idea of *communication with*: John xi. 56 ἔλεγον μετ' ἀλλήλων, *they were saying to one another*; John iv. 27 μετὰ γυναικὸς ἐλάλει, *he was conversing with a woman*. Note the change in English idiom from the now archaic *to speak* with *someone* to *to speak* to *someone*; but *to have a talk* with..., *to converse* with... is still idiomatic.

(*c*) The idea of *conflict with*: I Cor. vi 6 (cf. *v.* 7) ἀδελφὸς μετὰ ἀδελφοῦ κρίνεται, *brother* [i.e. *Christian*] *goes to law with brother*; Rev. ii. 16 πολεμήσω μετ' αὐτῶν, *I will do battle against them*.

Notes. (*a*) The idiom Luke i. 58, ἐμεγάλυνεν κύριος τὸ ἔλεος αὐτοῦ μετ' αὐτῆς (cf. Luke x. 37 ὁ ποιήσας τὸ ἔλεος μετ' αὐτοῦ), is noted under 'Semitisms' (below, pp. 183 f.). But Acts xiv. 27 ὅσα ἐποίησεν ὁ θεὸς μετ' αὐτῶν may well mean *all that God had done in fellowship* [or *co-operation*] *with them*—in which case it is plain Greek, and no 'Semitism'. So perhaps I John iv. 17 τετελείωται ἡ ἀγάπη μεθ' ἡμῶν, *love is perfected among us* (*in our community*). See Rob. 610–11.

(*b*) Whether it is possible to distinguish the meaning of μετά from that of σύν is a question.† That usage is partly, at least, merely a matter of style is suggested by the fact that in the Pastoral Epistles σύν (Pauline) is replaced by μετά.[2] Μετά is the commoner of the two in the N.T.; but σύν, not μετά, seems to be usual in composition with a verb, when the sense *with* is required, except in the case of μετέχω[3]

---

[1] See *Beg. in loc.* and II, 43 (de Zwaan).

[2] See, for example, Sir R. Falconer's commentary, p. 7; but see also on Σύν, below.

[3] In Eph. iii. 6 συμμέτοχος occurs in the sense *co-participant*, but in *v.* 7 it scarcely seems to mean more than *participant*.

(I Cor. ix. 12, x. 17, 21, 30, Heb. ii. 14, v. 13, vii. 13), μεταδίδωμι (Luke iii. 11, Rom. i. 11, xii. 8, Eph. iv. 28, I Thess. ii. 8), μεταλαμβάνω (Acts ii. 46, xxvii. 33 f., II Tim. ii. 6, Heb. vi. 7, xii. 10; Acts xxiv. 25 is different, though even here there may be a *partitive* sense). Note that ὁμο- is also a means of expressing a similar idea in compounds.

4. **περί.** Roughly speaking, this preposition, which means *about*[1] (cf. *perimeter, the measure round*), is used in the N.T. with Acc. when it is literally spatial (or temporal), and with either Acc. or Gen. when it is metaphorical. Thus:

i. *With the Accusative.* (*a*) *Spatial.* Luke xiii. 8 ἕως ὅτου σκάψω περὶ αὐτήν, *until I have dug round it*; Acts xxviii. 7 ἐν δὲ τοῖς περὶ τὸν τόπον ἐκεῖνον, *now in the neighbourhood of that place* (so *Beg. in loc.*); Mark iii. 8 περὶ Τύρον καὶ Σιδῶνα, *in the region of Tyre and Sidon*; Matt. iii. 4 περὶ τὴν ὀσφὺν αὐτοῦ, *round his loins*; Matt. xviii. 6 περὶ τὸν τράχηλον αὐτοῦ; Acts xxii. 6 περιαστράψαι...περὶ ἐμέ; Mark ix. 14 ὄχλον πολὺν περὶ αὐτούς; Acts xiii. 13 οἱ περὶ Παῦλον, *Paul and his companions* (a Classical idiom); but Luke xxii. 49 οἱ περὶ αὐτόν, *those who were round him*[2] (examples from Rob. 620).

(*b*) *Temporal.* Matt. xx. 3 περὶ τρίτην ὥραν, *at about the third hour* (so Matt. xxvii. 46, Mark vi. 48, Acts x. 9, xxii. 6). For this sense κατά (as in Acts xii. 1 κατ' ἐκεῖνον δὲ τὸν καιρόν) is perhaps commoner.

(*c*) *Metaphorical.* Phil. ii. 23 τὰ περὶ ἐμέ, *my affairs*; Luke x. 40 περιεσπᾶτο περὶ πολλὴν διακονίαν, *was distracted about much serving* (cf. *v.* 41); Acts xix. 25 τοὺς περὶ τοιαῦτα ἐργάτας, *the workmen connected with such things* (*in that line of business*, as one might say); I Tim. i. 19 περὶ τὴν πίστιν ἐναυάγησαν, *have been shipwrecked in respect of their* (or *the*) *faith* (cf. II Tim. ii. 18, iii. 8); Tit. ii. 7 περὶ πάντα, *in all respects*.[3]

ii. *With the Genitive* it is much commoner; but is only so used in metaphorical senses. These can be broadly comprehended within the sense *concerning*.

(*a*) Frequently with verbs of speaking, thinking, feeling, etc.: John vii. 13 ἐλάλει περὶ αὐτοῦ; ix. 17 τί σὺ λέγεις περὶ αὐτοῦ...; Matt. ix. 36 ἐσπλαγχνίσθη περὶ αὐτῶν, *he was moved with compassion*

---

[1] Note also its sense of περισσός, *excessive*, in some compounds.

[2] But D.-B. § 228 takes this also as *his disciples*.

[3] Note that 'περί with Acc. occurs six times in the Pastorals; in the ten Paulines only once' (Sir R. Falconer, *The Pastoral Epistles*, 8). Cf. on μετά, above.

for them; xx. 24 ἠγανάκτησαν περὶ τῶν δύο ἀδελφῶν, *they were indignant about*. . . ; I Pet. v. 7 αὐτῷ μέλει περὶ ὑμῶν, *he cares about you*; I Thess. v. 25 προσεύχεσθε περὶ ἡμῶν, *pray for us* (cf. Luke xxii. 32).

(*b*) In a virtually 'absolute' usage, like our *As for*. . . , I Cor. vii. 1 περὶ δὲ ὧν ἐγράψατε. . . , *as for the things you wrote about*. . . (cf. *v.* 25, viii. 1, xii. 1, xvi. 1). Cf. ὑπέρ ii. (*c*) below. Note the unusual use with ποιεῖν, Luke ii. 27 τοῦ ποιῆσαι. . . περὶ αὐτοῦ, *to do*. . . *in connexion with him* (*in respect of him*).

(*c*) In John xix. 24 it is used of casting lots: λάχωμεν περὶ αὐτοῦ (while the quotation from Ps. xxii. 18 (LXX xxi. 19) in the same verse runs ἐπὶ τὸν ἱματισμόν μου ἔβαλον κλῆρον).

(*d*) In Phil. ii. 20 τὰ περὶ ὑμῶν, *your affairs*, is exactly like the usage with Acc. in *v.* 23 (see above, i. (*c*)). So Luke xxiv. 27 τὰ περὶ ἑαυτοῦ, *what concerned himself* (cf. Acts xviii. 25 τὰ περὶ τοῦ ᾿Ιησοῦ).

(*e*) It is not certain whether περὶ ἁμαρτίας in Rom. viii. 3 is the technical LXX term = *sin-offering* (as in Heb. x. 6, cf. *v.* 26), or whether it is meant more generally as = *to deal with sin, in connexion with sin*; but in any case, even the technical sense is clearly derived from the more general one.

Again, there is debate over the famous use of περί in Matt. xxvi. 28, τὸ αἷμά μου τῆς διαθήκης τὸ περὶ πολλῶν ἐκχυννόμενον εἰς ἄφεσιν ἁμαρτιῶν (cf. I Thess. v. 10 τοῦ ἀποθανόντος περὶ ἡμῶν), where the parallels in Mark xiv. 24 and I Cor. xi. 24 and Luke xxii. 20 (in the longer text) have ὑπέρ. That περί and ὑπέρ may be synonymous is suggested by Eph. vi. 18, 19 δεήσει περὶ πάντων τῶν ἁγίων, καὶ ὑπὲρ ἐμοῦ, and by Heb. v. 1, 3 (ὑπέρ twice, then περί twice). In Polybius, the two are interchangeable.[1]

Note. In III John 2, περὶ πάντων is taken by many to mean simply *in all respects*.[2] The A.V. *above all things* might conceivably be justified by the περισσός associations (cf. above, p. 62 n. 1), but seems improbable unless clear parallels can be found.

5. **ὑπέρ.** This (see Rob. 629) is etymologically connected with *over* and *upper*.

It is not used locally at all in the N.T. (unless the reading of D* in Heb. ix. 5 be accepted); but, broadly speaking, it may be said that

---

[1] W. W. Capes, *History of the Achaean League*, xviii.
[2] See Brooke, *I.C.C. in loc.*; D-B. § 229, 2; Rob. 619; R.V., Moffatt's and Goodspeed's translations.

its use with the Accusative is more literal, and that with the Genitive more metaphorical.

i. *With the Accusative* it means *above, beyond* (cf. the *adverbial* use in II Cor. xi. 23 ὑπὲρ ἐγώ, *I am even more so*): Matt. x. 24 οὐκ ἔστιν μαθητὴς ὑπὲρ τὸν διδάσκαλον, *a disciple is not above his teacher*; Luke xvi. 8 φρονιμώτεροι ὑπὲρ τοὺς υἱοὺς τοῦ φωτός, *wiser than* [lit. *wiser beyond*] *the sons of light*; I Cor. iv. 6 μὴ ὑπὲρ ἃ γέγραπται, *not beyond what is written*. (But this may be a marginal gloss, in which the ὑπέρ was used in its rare local sense by a scribe, in reference to a MS. he had seen: '*the* μή *is written over the* α.')[1]

ii. *With the Genitive* it means *on behalf of, with a view to, concerning*— though the latter sense, identical with certain uses of περί (see περί, ii. (*b*), p. 63), is said to be almost confined to Paul in the N.T. (so D.-B. § 231, 1). The English *over* is still not far off from these senses.

Examples. (*a*) *On behalf of*: Mark ix. 40 ὃς γὰρ οὐκ ἔστιν καθ' ἡμῶν, ὑπὲρ ἡμῶν ἐστιν, *for he who is not against us is on our side*; I Cor. iv. 6 ἵνα μὴ εἷς ὑπὲρ τοῦ ἑνὸς φυσιοῦσθε κατὰ τοῦ ἑτέρου, *that you may not be inflated with pride each* (lit. *one*) *on behalf of the one* [*leader*] *against the other*.

Note. Rob. 630–2 discusses whether there is a distinction between ὑπέρ = *on behalf of* and ἀντί = *instead of*, and reaches the conclusion that it is inaccurate to draw too hard a line: 'In most cases one who acts on behalf of another takes his place' (Winer). See the following: Rom. v. 7, 8 μόλις γὰρ ὑπὲρ δικαίου τις ἀποθανεῖται· ὑπὲρ γὰρ τοῦ ἀγαθοῦ τάχα τις καὶ τολμᾷ ἀποθανεῖν. . . . χριστὸς ὑπὲρ ἡμῶν ἀπέθανεν; ix. 3 ἀνάθεμα εἶναι. . . ὑπὲρ τῶν ἀδελφῶν μου; II Cor. v. 15 ὑπὲρ πάντων ἀπέθανεν. . . τῷ ὑπὲρ αὐτῶν ἀποθανόντι; Gal. iii. 13 γενόμενος ὑπὲρ ἡμῶν κατάρα; I Tim. ii. 6 ἀντίλυτρον ὑπὲρ πάντων (where note the combination of ἀντί- and ὑπέρ); John xi. 50 ἵνα εἷς ἄνθρωπος ἀποθάνῃ ὑπὲρ τοῦ λαοῦ; Acts xxi. 26 ἕως οὗ προσηνέχθη ὑπὲρ ἑνὸς ἑκάστου αὐτῶν ἡ προσφορά; I Cor. xv. 29 οἱ βαπτιζόμενοι ὑπὲρ τῶν νεκρῶν; Philem. 13 ἵνα ὑπὲρ σοῦ μοι διακονῇ; Mark xiv. 24 τὸ αἷμα. . . τὸ ἐκχυννόμενον ὑπὲρ πολλῶν (cf. Luke xxii. 20, I Cor. xi. 24), side by side with Mark x. 45 λύτρον ἀντὶ πολλῶν. So Heb. x. 12 has ὑπὲρ ἁμαρτιῶν προσενέγκας θυσίαν, obviously in the same sense as περὶ ἁμαρτιῶν. . . θυσία in *v.* 26, etc.

[1] See W. F. Howard in *E.T.* xxxiii (July 1922), 479.

(b) *With a view to*: e.g. II Cor. i. 6 ὑπὲρ τῆς ὑμῶν παρακλήσεως καὶ σωτηρίας κ.τ.λ. [*it is*] *with a view to your encouragement and salvation*, etc.

But this sense is really very close to *for the sake of*, which, in its turn, is not easy to distinguish from meaning (a) above. Thus, in Phil. ii. 13, does θεὸς γάρ ἐστιν ὁ ἐνεργῶν ἐν ὑμῖν καὶ τὸ θέλειν καὶ τὸ ἐνεργεῖν ὑπὲρ τῆς εὐδοκίας mean ...*with a view to* [*performing*] *his good pleasure?* Or are we to connect ὑπὲρ τῆς εὐδοκίας with the following πάντα ποιεῖτε... and translate *for the sake of pleasing him*...? (see D.-B. § 231, 2). These senses are very close to each other.

(c) *Concerning, about*: e.g. Acts viii. 24 δεήθητε ὑμεῖς ὑπὲρ ἐμοῦ, *Do you pray for* (*about*) *me*; Rom. ix. 27 Ἡσαΐας κράζει ὑπὲρ τοῦ Ἰσραήλ...; II Cor. i. 8 ἀγνοεῖν...ὑπὲρ τῆς θλίψεως...; viii. 23 εἴτε ὑπὲρ Τίτου, *as for Titus*; xii. 8 ὑπὲρ τούτου τρὶς τὸν κύριον παρεκάλεσα, *about this I three times begged the Lord*; Phil. i. 7 τοῦτο φρονεῖν ὑπὲρ πάντων ὑμῶν, *to entertain these thoughts about all of you* (?); I Thess. iii. 2 παρακαλέσαι ὑπὲρ τῆς πίστεως ὑμῶν, *to encourage you about your faith*; II Thess. ii. 1 ὑπὲρ τῆς παρουσίας, *in connexion with the coming*; John i. 30 ὑπὲρ οὗ ἐγὼ εἶπον, *about whom I said*.... Cf. περί, p. 63, above.

6. **ὑπό.** Whatever its origin (perhaps *up from*; note an etymological connexion with *up*, according to Rob. 633), this preposition practically has only two meanings in the N.T.—*under* and *by* (denoting the agent of an action).

Strangely the sense *under*, even including that of *rest under* ('punctiliar') as well as the 'linear' one of *motion to beneath*, is confined to

i. *The use with the Accusative.* (a) *Motion to beneath*; e.g. Matt. v. 15 οὐδὲ καίουσιν λύχνον καὶ τιθέασιν αὐτὸν ὑπὸ τὸν μόδιον, *neither do they light a lamp and put it under the bushel*; viii. 8 οὐκ εἰμὶ ἱκανὸς ἵνα μου ὑπὸ τὴν στέγην εἰσέλθῃς, *I am not worthy that you should come under my roof*; Luke xiii. 34 ὃν τρόπον ὄρνις τὴν ἑαυτῆς νοσσιὰν ὑπὸ τὰς πτέρυγας, *as a hen* [*gathers*] *her brood under her wings*. Add, possibly, I Pet. v. 6 ταπεινώθητε οὖν ὑπὸ τὴν κραταιὰν χεῖρα τοῦ θεοῦ, if we interpret *humble yourselves therefore* [*to a position*] *beneath the strong hand of God* (otherwise it will = *humble yourselves, being, as you are, beneath...*, and will fall in (b) below).

(b) *Rest beneath*; e.g. Mark iv. 32 ὥστε δύνασθαι ὑπὸ τὴν σκιὰν αὐτοῦ τὰ πετεινὰ τοῦ οὐρανοῦ κατασκηνοῖν, *so that the birds of the sky could nest* (?) *under its shadow* (though it would be easy to see the idea of motion here, and remove this to (*a*) above); John i. 48 ὄντα ὑπὸ τὴν συκῆν, *when you were under the fig-tree* (but *v.* 50, ὑποκάτω τῆς συκῆς); Acts iv. 12 οὐδὲ γὰρ ὄνομά ἐστιν ἕτερον ὑπὸ τὸν οὐρανόν..., *for neither is there any other name under heaven*...; Rom. iii. 13, from Ps. cxl. 3 (LXX cxxxix. 4), ἰὸς ἀσπίδων ὑπὸ τὰ χείλη αὐτῶν, *the poison of asps is under their lips*; vi. 14, 15 ὑπὸ νόμον, *beneath law* (cf. Gal. iv. 4, 5, I Cor. ix. 20); Gal. iii. 25 οὐκέτι ὑπὸ παιδαγωγόν ἐσμεν, *we are no longer subject to a ' tutor-slave'*.

Note. Once in the N.T. ὑπό with the Acc. is used of time—Acts v. 21 ὑπὸ τὸν ὄρθρον, *at about dawn, close on dawn.*

ii. *With the Genitive* it always = *by*, and is generally used to denote the 'agent' of an act, as distinct from the 'instrument' which is often denoted by the Dative without a preposition (cf. the distinction in Latin between the Ablative with *a* or *ab* and the plain Ablative).

The use is so common that there is no need to illustrate it at length. But notice, with Rob. 636, the careful use of prepositions in Matt. i. 22 ἵνα πληρωθῇ τὸ ῥηθὲν ὑπὸ κυρίου διὰ τοῦ προφήτου (cf. ii. 15). In Rev. vi. 8 the 'instruments' *sword, famine*, and *death* are perhaps distinguished deliberately from the *beasts* which are more like 'agents': ἐν ῥομφαίᾳ κ.τ.λ., but ὑπὸ τῶν θηρίων (though here the variety may be due merely to the fact that the ἐν is from Ezekiel, while the ὑπό seems to fall outside the quotation). But note, with Rob. *loc. cit.*, that here ὑπὸ τῶν θηρίων actually follows an *Active* verb, ἀποκτεῖναι, so that in a sense the beasts are only the instrument wielded by the subject of that verb. Normally, of course, ὑπό is used of the agent after a Passive verb or its equivalent.

III. THOSE GOVERNING ONE CASE

Accusative

1. **ἀνά.** As has been suggested (see on κατά, above), ἀνά presumably has some connexion with the adverb ἄνω, *up*, as κατά with κάτω, *down*; but if so, the N.T. usage is not easy to connect with such a sense, except when ἀνά is compounded with verbs, or means *up to* some limit.

An adverbial use of ἀνά (though in a different sense from the true adverb ἄνω) may first be noted, namely the use as a *distributive particle*: Rev. iv. 8 ἔχων ἀνὰ πτέρυγας ἕξ (*six wings apiece*); cf. xxi. 21, and (probably) John ii. 6 χωροῦσαι ἀνὰ μετρητὰς δύο ἤ τρεῖς (*two or three* '*metretae*' *apiece*); so Matt. xx. 9 ἔλαβον ἀνὰ δηνάριον (*a denarius each*).

As a preposition proper, it has two main uses:

i. Distributive (obviously closely related to the adverbial use just noted); e.g.: perhaps Mark vi. 40 (according to all the Uncials except ℵBD, and virtually all the minuscules)[1] ἀνὰ ἑκατὸν καὶ ἀνὰ πεντήκοντα, [*in parties*] *a hundred strong and fifty strong* (i.e. *at a hundred each and at fifty each*) (but perhaps more probable is the same translation as that suggested under κατά, i. 'With the Accusative', i.e. '100 × 50'); Luke x. 1 ἀπέστειλεν αὐτοὺς ἀνὰ δύο (Mark vi. 7 δύο δύο, for which see under 'Semitisms'), *he sent them out in pairs*, i.e. perhaps *at the strength of, up to, two*.

The only reason for distinguishing these examples as prepositional from the others as adverbial is that, in the prepositional, ἀνά can be treated as 'governing' the numeral (which can be regarded as in the Accusative case), whereas, in the adverbial, the nouns are already 'governed' by the verbs.

ii. Meaning *in*, in the phrases ἀνὰ μέσον (with Gen.) *among* or *in the midst* and ἀνὰ μέρος, *in turn*: perhaps Mark vii. 31 ἀνὰ μέσον τῶν ὁρίων Δεκαπόλεως (problematic: does it mean *right through*?)[2]; Matt. xiii. 25, I Cor. xiv. 27 (though the latter might well be classed as distributive).

Note. Curiously enough, as has been noted above under κατά, practically all these senses of ἀνά can be matched by uses of κατά (which one would have expected to be *opposite*, not *parallel*, in meaning); and Mark vi. 40 is an instance of the MSS. being divided between ἀνά and κατά.

2. **εἰς.** This is such a frequent and versatile preposition that to catalogue all its uses here would take up too much space and be too complicated. For a detailed treatment see Rob. 591–6.

Two broad, general ideas may serve as a starting point: (*a*) etymologically (*op. cit.*) εἰς seems to be a variant of ἐν, originally written ἐνς (possibly on the analogy of ἐξ =ἐκς), and then, with the dropping of the ν, becoming either ἐς or εἰς. Thus εἰς and ἐν are related; and (*b*) in some respects, if ἐν is 'punctiliar', εἰς is the corresponding 'linear' word: where ἐν =*in*, εἰς would rather =*into*.

It may be added, as a very rough-and-ready distinction between the meanings of εἰς and πρός, that εἰς tends to include the idea of *entry*,

[1] See above under κατά i., *sub fin.*
[2] Cf. on Luke xvii. 11 διὰ μέσον, under διά, i. above, p. 55.

whereas πρός tends to stop short at going *up to* (without entering). Possibly, also, πρός tends to be used with a personal object and εἰς with an impersonal: II Cor. i. 15, 16 πρὸς ὑμᾶς (twice), but εἰς Μακεδονίαν...εἰς τὴν 'Ιουδαίαν; but this is anything but a rigid rule: Mark ii. 13 πρὸς αὐτόν, but iii. 7 πρὸς τὴν θάλασσαν (but see variant reading); John iv. 5 εἰς πόλιν τῆς Σαμαρίας λεγομένην Συχάρ, but viii. 26 λαλῶ εἰς τὸν κόσμον; Rom. xi. 36 εἰς αὐτόν (*sc.* θεόν): see D.-B. § 207. Philem. 5 πρὸς τὸν κύριον 'Ιησοῦν καὶ εἰς πάντας τοὺς ἁγίους looks like a purely stylistic variation of prepositions. See, too, II Tim. ii. 21 with iii. 17. Incidentally, John iv. 5 may itself be an exception to the tendency, just noted, for εἰς to mean *entering*, for here it seems to mean *going to* without entering.

This being said, the usage may be roughly classified into groups:

i. The typical, standard usage as = *into*; e.g.:

(*a*) *Locally*: Matt. ii. 11 ἐλθόντες εἰς τὴν οἰκίαν, *entering the house*, etc., *passim*.

(*b*) *Metaphorically*: Rom. i. 17 εἰς πίστιν, *leading to faith*; Mark iv. 8 εἰς τριάκοντα, *up to thirty* (if this is the correct reading; but see on ἐν, below). For this whole group compare the 'final' sense v. below, p. 70.

ii. What might be called the 'pregnant' use, apparently *combining* the ideas of motion and rest, the 'linear' and the 'punctiliar'—a line ending at a point, as it were, e.g.:

(*a*) *Locally*: Mark i. 9 ἐβαπτίσθη εἰς τὸν 'Ιορδάνην, perhaps *he came to the Jordan and was baptized in it*; Luke xi. 7 εἰς τὴν κοίτην, perhaps *they have got into bed* (D and some other MSS. do read ἐν); John xx. 7 τὸ σουδάριον...ἐντετυλιγμένον εἰς ἕνα τόπον;[1] John xx. 19, 26 ἔστη εἰς τὸ μέσον, *he came and stood among them*; Acts viii. 40 εὑρέθη εἰς Ἄζωτον (cf. Acts ii. 5 (but doubtful textually), vii. 4 (but perhaps by attraction), ix. 21, 28, xix. 22, xxv. 4, with Rob. 586); I Pet. iii. 20 εἰς ἦν (κιβωτόν), *in which* (*ark*), i.e. *by entering it*. Is εἰς μακράν, Acts ii. 39, to be so classed, or is it a 'Semitism'? (Isa. lvii. 19 LXX does *not* have this construction). In Acts ii. 27, 31 εἰς Ἅιδην clearly means nothing else than *in Hades*, whatever the original (Ps. xvi) may mean.

(*b*) *Metaphorically*: Luke i. 20 εἰς τὸν καιρὸν αὐτῶν, *at their proper time*; Luke xiii. 9 εἰς τὸ μέλλον, *in the future*; Acts xiii. 42 εἰς τὸ μεταξὺ

---

[1] Though this is taken, e.g. by Latham, *The Risen Master*, 90, to refer in an indirect and roundabout way to motion.

σάββατον, perhaps *on the next sabbath*; II Cor. xiii. 2 εἰς τὸ πάλιν, *again*, *for another visit*; Acts viii. 23 εἰς γὰρ χολὴν πικρίας...ὁρῶ σε ὄντα.[1]†

But some of these look uncommonly like synonyms for ἐν; and M.M. xiv call attention to 'the free interchange of εἰς and ἐν' in the Papyri; and say that, accordingly, John i. 18 εἰς τὸν κόλπον τοῦ πατρός must not be assumed to be subtly different in meaning from ἐν τῷ κ.τ.λ. D.-B. § 2, n. 1, shows, on the other hand, that whereas Luke does tend to confuse εἰς and ἐν, Rev. maintains the distinction between them.

iii. The use which seems equivalent to a pure Dative:† e.g. Matt. xxvi. 10 ἔργον γὰρ καλὸν ἠργάσατο εἰς ἐμέ; Mark xiii. 10 εἰς πάντα τὰ ἔθνη πρῶτον δεῖ κηρυχθῆναι τὸ εὐαγγέλιον (ἐν, D),† cf. Luke xxiv. 47, I Thess. ii. 9 (ℵ* ὑμῖν); John xv. 21 ταῦτα πάντα ποιήσουσιν εἰς ὑμᾶς (AD² *al.* ὑμῖν); I Pet. i. 25 τὸ ῥῆμα τὸ εὐαγγελισθὲν εἰς ὑμᾶς; Acts xxiv. 17 ἐλεημοσύνας ποιήσων εἰς τὸ ἔθνος μου; II Pet. i. 17 εἰς ὃν ἐγὼ εὐδόκησα (Matt. xvii. 5 has ἐν ᾧ εὐδόκησα; so Matt. iii. 17 and the parallels, Mark i. 11, Luke iii. 22; LXX differently).

For the difficult problems of πιστεύω, πίστις, πιστός with εἰς, ἐπί, ἐν, see under ἐν, p. 80 f.; but note meanwhile that πιστεύω εἰς (or ἐπί, or—though seldom used—ἐν) is regarded by Moulton, *Proleg.* 68, in contrast to Blass (*ibid.* 67), as bearing a meaning (*believe in, trust*) distinct from that of the plain Dative (*credit, believe*).[2] And note in particular I Pet. i. 8 εἰς ὃν...πιστεύοντες; *v.* 21 πιστοὺς εἰς θεόν; and Philem. 5 quoted above in the preliminary remarks to εἰς.[3]

It looks as though the sense of such phrases would need to be deduced from the context (if at all), when there is so bewildering a variety of usage. But the instances given above of εἰς with Acc. being equivalent to a simple Dative are enough to make one cautious about reading too much into it.[4]

[1] Classed by J. B. Lightfoot, *Apost. Fathers*, II, ii, 24 as meaning *destined for, reserved for*; but is he right?

[2] See also W. F. Howard, *Christianity according to St John*, 154 ff.; Burton, *Galatians*, 480, 481, who thinks that the novelty of this construction in the N.T. may be significant. But note Ecclus. xxxviii. 31 εἰς χεῖρας αὐτῶν ἐνεπίστευσαν.

[3] Bultmann, *Theologie des Neuen Testaments*, I *Lieferung* (1948), 90, 91, holds, curiously, that πιστεύω εἰς Ἰησοῦν was (at least in early days) only an abbreviation for πιστεύω ὅτι ὁ θεὸς αὐτὸν ἤγειρεν..., etc., not an expression of trust in Jesus.

[4] Ignatius, *Trall.* II πιστεύσαντες εἰς τὸν θάνατον αὐτοῦ (cf. μετάνοια εἰς, *Philad.* VIII) is regarded by Moffatt (*Harv. Theol. Rev.* XXIX (1936), 17) as an effort 'to bring out the idea of personal entry into truth of life'.

iv. Usages perhaps influenced by Semitic idiom: e.g. Mark v. 34 ὕπαγε εἰς εἰρήνην, which probably is not intended to suggest a *progressive* entering into peace, but departure in a state of peace (cf. Jas. ii. 16 ὑπάγετε ἐν εἰρήνῃ (see ἐν iii. (*c*) below); Acts vii. 53 εἰς διαταγὰς ἀγγέλων, perhaps *by angelic mediation* (which Rob. 482 regards as showing some Hebrew influence; *Beg*. II, 148 takes it as Aramaic). Note also, perhaps, Acts ii. 39 εἰς μακράν (see ii. above).

v. In the senses *with a view to*, or *resulting in*—i.e. final or consecutive: e.g. Matt. viii. 34 εἰς ὑπάντησιν τῷ ᾿Ιησοῦ (cf. xxv. 1); Rom. v. 18, a completely verbless sentence, ἄρα οὖν ὡς δι᾿ ἑνὸς παραπτώματος εἰς πάντας ἀνθρώπους εἰς κατάκριμα (i.e. the circumstances *led to condemnation, the result was condemnation*), οὕτως καὶ δι᾿ ἑνὸς δικαιώματος εἰς πάντας ἀνθρώπους εἰς δικαίωσιν ζωῆς (*the result was acquittal leading to life*); Rom. xii. 3 φρονεῖν εἰς τὸ σωφρονεῖν (perhaps *to adopt an outlook which tends to sobriety*); Phil. i. 19 εἰς σωτηρίαν (so Job xiii. 16 LXX), cf. Jas. v. 3 εἰς μαρτύριον ὑμῖν, and Luke xxi. 13; Col. iii. 10 ἀνακαινούμενον εἰς ἐπίγνωσιν (cf. Heb. vi. 6 πάλιν ἀνακαινίζειν εἰς μετάνοιαν); εἰς ἄφεσιν (τῶν) ἁμαρτιῶν, Mark i. 4, Acts ii. 38, etc.; Col. iii. 15 ἡ εἰρήνη τοῦ χριστοῦ . . . εἰς ἣν καὶ ἐκλήθητε; I Pet. ii. 21, iii. 9 εἰς τοῦτο γὰρ ἐκλήθητε; Rom. x. 1 ἡ. . .εὐδοκία τῆς ἐμῆς καρδίας καὶ ἡ δέησις. . .εἰς σωτηρίαν, perhaps *my heart's desire. . .has their salvation as its purpose*; *v.* 4 τέλος γὰρ νόμου χριστὸς εἰς δικαιοσύνην, perhaps *Christ is an end to legalism for the attainment of righteousness, as a means to righteousness*; *v.* 10 καρδίᾳ γὰρ πιστεύεται εἰς δικαιοσύνην, perhaps, i.e. *for with the heart one believes, and it results in righteousness*; xiii. 4 θεοῦ γὰρ διάκονός ἐστιν σοὶ εἰς τὸ ἀγαθόν, . . .*for your good*; I Cor. xiv. 22 εἰς σημεῖον, *intended as a sign*; I Thess. ii. 16 εἰς τέλος, *completely* (a phrase probably influenced by Hebrew); Gal. ii. 2 εἰς κενόν, *to no purpose*.

Under this head might fall the predicative use: e.g. Matt. xxi. 46 εἰς προφήτην αὐτὸν εἶχον, *they reckoned him as a prophet* (cf. our idiom *to take one for*. . ., and note that in *v.* 26 the phrase is ὡς προφήτην ἔχουσιν. . .); Acts xiii. 22 ἤγειρεν τὸν Δαυεὶδ αὐτοῖς εἰς βασιλέα, *he raised up David to be a king for them* (see Rob. 481, 482).†

Note also εἰς followed by the Articular Infinitive (see under 'Final and Consecutive Clauses').

vi. Note further the following phrases: Gal. vi. 4 τὸ δὲ ἔργον ἑαυτοῦ δοκιμαζέτω ἕκαστος, καὶ τότε εἰς ἑαυτὸν μόνον τὸ καύχημα ἕξει καὶ οὐκ εἰς τὸν ἕτερον (Moffatt has *on his own account. . .in com-*

parison with; cf. the use of πρός as meaning *compared with*, above);
II Cor. x. 13, 15, εἰς τὰ ἄμετρα καυχησόμεθα (καυχώμενοι), does this
mean *by reference to a standard which we have no right to use?* Or does
it simply mean *with reference to what lies outside our scope?*; cf. εἰς τὸ
ὄνομα, on which see *Beg.* v, 123, n. 3 and M.M. xiv. Cf. on ἐπί with
Dative above, and ἐν below.

Genitive

1. **ἀντί.** 'Αντί seems to have meant, originally, *facing, over against*
(cf. ἀντιπαρέρχεσθαι in Luke x. 31, 32); hence its prevailing sense of
instead of (cf. on ὑπέρ above); e.g.: Matt. xx. 28 = Mark x. 45 λύτρον
ἀντὶ πολλῶν; Matt. xvii. 27 ἐκεῖνον [*sc.* στατῆρα] λαβὼν δὸς αὐτοῖς
ἀντὶ ἐμοῦ καὶ σοῦ, *take it* [the coin] *and give it to them on behalf of
myself and you*; John i. 16 ... ἐλάβομεν ... χάριν ἀντὶ χάριτος, i.e. *we
have received one favour in place of another—a succession of favours*;
I Cor. xi. 15 ἡ κόμη ἀντὶ περιβολαίου δέδοται αὐτῇ, *her hair has been
given her as* [i.e. *instead of*] *a wrap*; Heb. xii. 16 ἀντὶ βρώσεως μιᾶς
ἀπέδετο τὰ πρωτοτόκια, *he sold his birthright for* (i.e. *in exchange for*)
one meal;† Jas. iv. 15 ἀντὶ τοῦ λέγειν ὑμᾶς..., *instead of your
saying*....

In Eph. v. 31 ἀντὶ τούτου means *because of this, therefore* (in Matt. xix. 5,
Mark x. 7, where the same LXX passage is referred to, the phrase,
as in the LXX itself, is ἕνεκεν (Matt. ἕνεκα) τούτου).

In Luke xii. 3 ἀνθ' ὧν = *and so, accordingly, therefore* (i.e. *in place of—
corresponding to—which things*). The same phrase, ἀνθ' ὧν *since* or
because, in Luke i. 20, xix. 44, Acts xii. 23, II Thess. ii. 10 (all with
reference to the nemesis on wrong); and the relative ὧν, which seems
grammatically illogical, is probably due to Semitic influence (תחת אשר;
see D.-B. § 208, 1).

In composition with verbs (ἀντιλέγειν, etc.) note its meaning *contra*;
but note also ἀντιπαρέρχεσθαι (Luke x. 31, 32—as above), and Col. i. 24
ἀνταναπληρῶ τὰ ὑστερήματα τῶν θλίψεων τοῦ χριστοῦ ἐν τῇ σαρκί
μου ὑπὲρ τοῦ σώματος αὐτοῦ, where the ἀντι- may merely imply that
fulness *replaces* lack, or may anticipate the force of the ὑπέρ which
follows. See commentators *in loc.*

2. **ἀπό** and **ἐκ (ἐξ).** These two prepositions are taken together
here, since ἀπό is in process of absorbing ἐκ† and the two frequently
overlap; and, where there does still remain any distinction, the contrast
is instructive.

A broad distinction has been attempted (cf. Rob. 577) on the lines that ἐκ means *from within*, while ἀπό indicates merely *the general starting-point*: a man will go ἐκ (ἐξ) a *house*, but ἀπό a *country*: thus (Mark i. 35) ἐξῆλθεν (*he left the house*) καὶ ἀπῆλθεν εἰς ἔρημον τόπον (*and went away to an uninhabited place*).

But even if this is consistently observed in Mark (which I doubt), it certainly does not hold good in the N.T. generally. Thus, Mark i. 34, δαιμόνια πολλὰ ἐξέβαλεν, compared with *v.* 42, ἀπῆλθεν ἀπ᾽ αὐτοῦ ἡ λέπρα, might (though very questionably) be taken to suggest that leprosy was regarded as *on* a man but evil spirits *in* him; but in Luke viii. 35 we find ἀφ᾽ οὗ τὰ δαιμόνια ἐ ξ ῆλθεν, and in Acts xii. 7 ἐξέπεσαν αὐτοῦ αἱ ἁλύσεις ἐκ τῶν χειρῶν (and chains are demonstrably *on*, not *in*, one's hands). Or, again, John xi. 1 is enough to reduce the systematizer to despair—ἀπὸ Βηθανίας, ἐκ τῆς κώμης Μαρίας καὶ Μάρθας. Note also Luke v. 8 ἔξελθε ἀπ᾽ ἐμοῦ.

However, it may be that *more often than not* the distinction holds;† and the following are a few specimens of conformity: Heb. xiii. 24 οἱ ἀπὸ τῆς Ἰταλίας; Rom. ix. 3 ἀνάθεμα...ἀπὸ τοῦ χριστοῦ (cf. II Thess. i. 9 ἀπὸ προσώπου τοῦ κυρίου καὶ ἀπὸ τῆς δόξης τῆς ἰσχύος αὐτοῦ; Rev. xii. 14 ὅπου τρέφεται...ἀπὸ προσώπου τοῦ ὄφεως).

Mark vii. 21 ἔσωθεν γὰρ ἐκ τῆς καρδίας τῶν ἀνθρώπων οἱ διαλογισμοὶ οἱ κακοὶ ἐκπορεύονται...; Rom. xi. 36 ὅτι ἐξ αὐτοῦ...τὰ πάντα; I Cor. i. 30 ἐξ αὐτοῦ δὲ ὑμεῖς ἐστε ἐν χριστῷ Ἰησοῦ; viii. 6 ἐξ οὗ τὰ πάντα; II Cor. v. 18 τὰ δὲ πάντα ἐκ τοῦ θεοῦ.

Note further: i. ἐκ seems to be usual in a *partitive* sense: John vii. 40 ἐκ τοῦ ὄχλου, *some of the crowd*; I John iv. 13 ἐκ τοῦ πνεύματος (cf. John i. 16 ἐκ τοῦ πληρώματος αὐτοῦ); Rev. xvii. 11 ἐκ τῶν ἑπτά ἐστιν. Possibly also Matt. xxiii. 25 γέμουσιν ἐξ ἁρπαγῆς καὶ ἀκρασίας is virtually partitive (as perhaps is its English equivalent 'full of').

ii. On I Cor. xi. 23 ἐγὼ γὰρ παρέλαβον ἀπὸ τοῦ κυρίου see the commentators, especially the exhaustive treatment by E.-B. Allo, *Commentaire, in loc.*, already cited under παρά, ii., p. 52 n. 1 above.

iii. Both prepositions are found in *Temporal* and in *Causal* or *Instrumental* senses. Thus:

(a) *Temporal*. ἀπ᾽ ἄρτι,[1] John xiii. 19, etc.; ἀπὸ τότε, Matt. xvi. 21, xxvi. 16, Luke xvi. 16;—yet, though ἐξ ἄρτι, ἐκ τότε are, admittedly, not found, ἐκ τούτου, John vi. 66, xix. 12, etc., is similar (unless it be

---

[1] But it is possible that in some places ἀπαρτί (*sic*) should be read and translated *precisely, expressly*. See D.-B. § 12.†

translated causatively, *because of this*, rather than temporally); Matt. xi. 12 ἀπὸ δὲ τῶν ἡμερῶν ᾽Ιωάνου τοῦ Βαπτιστοῦ; ἀπὸ καταβολῆς κόσμου (Matt. xxv. 34, Luke xi. 50, Heb. iv. 3, ix. 26, Rev. xiii. 8, xvii. 8)—yet Mark ix. 21 ἐκ παιδιόθεν (redundantly, since -θεν implies *from*); John ix. 1 ἐκ γενετῆς; Gal. i. 15 ἐκ κοιλίας μητρός μου (cf. Isa. xlix. 1 LXX); Acts xxiv. 10 ἐκ πολλῶν ἐτῶν ὄντα σε κριτήν; John ix. 32 ἐκ τοῦ αἰῶνος, perhaps *from time immemorial*.

Note. ἀπὸ τετάρτης ἡμέρας, Acts x. 30, is a peculiar idiom; cf. on πρό below.

(*b*) *Causal* or *Instrumental*: Luke vii. 35 καὶ ἐδικαιώθη ἡ σοφία ἀπὸ πάντων τῶν τέκνων αὐτῆς; Luke xxii. 45 εὗρεν κοιμωμένους αὐτούς ἀπὸ τῆς λύπης, *he found them sleeping because of grief*; Luke vi. 18 οἱ ἐνοχλούμενοι ἀπὸ πνευμάτων ἀκαθάρτων; Acts iv. 36 ὁ ἐπικληθεὶς Βαρνάβας ἀπὸ τῶν ἀποστόλων; Acts xv. 4 παρεδέχθησαν ἀπὸ τῆς ἐκκλησίας, *they were received by the Church*;[1] Acts xx. 9 κατενεχθεὶς ἀπὸ τοῦ ὕπνου, *borne down by sleep*. Yet—I John iv. 6, etc. ἐκ τούτου γινώσκομεν, *by this we know*; Gal. iii. 8 ἐκ πίστεως, perhaps *by means of faith* (but see below); Rev. xviii. 3 ἐκ τῆς δυνάμεως τοῦ στρήνους αὐτῆς ἐπλούτησαν, perhaps *grew rich on her enormous luxury*; Rev. xvi. 10 ἐμασῶντο τὰς γλώσσας αὐτῶν ἐκ τοῦ πόνου, *they gnawed their tongues for their pain* (cf. viii. 13 οὐαί...ἐκ..., *woe...for...*); Matt. xxvii. 7 ἡγόρασαν ἐξ αὐτῶν [*sc.* τῶν ἀργυρίων], *they purchased with them* [i.e. *the pieces of silver*].

Notes. 1. Is Rom. i. 4, ὁρισθέντος υἱοῦ θεοῦ...ἐξ ἀναστάσεως νεκρῶν, temporal (*from the time of...*) or causal (*on the ground of...*)? (S. and H. *in loc.* do not comment, but their paraphrase adopts the causal sense.)[2] So with Rom. i. 20: does ἀπὸ κτίσεως κόσμου mean (with Gifford) *from the created universe* (as the source of knowledge— the basis of a deduction), or (with S. and H.) *ever since...*?

2. In II Pet. i. 21 does ὑπὸ πνεύματος ἁγίου φερόμενοι ἐλάλησαν ἀπὸ θεοῦ ἄνθρωποι mean ...*spoke what was derived from God* (practically = τὰ ἀπὸ θεοῦ), or does ἀπὸ θεοῦ simply reinforce ὑπὸ πν. ἁγ. and mean *controlled by God*?

---

[1] Acts xv. 3 has προπεμφθέντες ὑπὸ τῆς ἐκκλησίας. See *Beg.* ii, 48–50 for remarks on this use of ἀπό.

[2] Acts xxvi. 23 εἰ πρῶτος ἐξ ἀναστάσεως νεκρῶν φῶς μέλλει καταγγέλλειν... invites comparison; but here it is just possible that ἐξ is not instrumental but quasi-local: *if he was destined to be the first* (*to come from*) *a rising from the dead and announce...*—as though Christ were pictured as coming from his act of resurrection. But *Beg.* translate as instrumental.

3. In Rev. xii. 6, τόπον ἡτοιμασμένον ἀπὸ τοῦ θεοῦ, is ἀπό purely instrumental, or does it carry the connotation *derived from God*?

4. Matt. xxiv. 17, ἄραι τὰ ἐκ τῆς οἰκίας αὐτοῦ, is an illustration of a 'pregnant' sense (to take *from* his house the things which are *in* it), comparable, in this respect, to the 'pregnant' sense of εἰς (see above, εἰς, ii.).

3. **πρό**. *Before* (cf. Latin *prae*. Latin *pro*, said to be etymologically identical with the Greek, has come to bear a different meaning).

Πρό only occurs forty-eight times in the N.T. and is almost confined to Matt., John, Luke and Paul (Rob. 621).

Three main uses can be distinguished:

i. *Local*. Acts xii. 6 πρὸ τῆς θύρας, *before the door*; cf. Jas. v. 9, Acts xii. 14, xiv. 13.

ii. *Temporal*. Matt. v. 12 τοὺς πρὸ ὑμῶν, *those who were before you*; Matt. viii. 29 πρὸ καιροῦ, *too soon*; John xi. 55 πρὸ τοῦ πάσχα, *before the Passover*; I Cor. ii. 7 πρὸ τῶν αἰώνων, *before the ages, before 'time'*; Luke ii. 21 πρὸ τοῦ συλλημφθῆναι αὐτόν, *before he was conceived*; Col. i. 17 πρὸ πάντων (?, see iii. below); πρὸ προσώπου (literally *before the face*) makes, in Acts xiii. 24, a composite phrase for *before* temporally, on a Semitic model.

Note. Much discussion revolves round the phrases πρὸ ἓξ ἡμερῶν in John xii. 1 and πρὸ ἐτῶν δεκατεσσάρων in II Cor. xii. 2. Evidently they mean, respectively, *six days before the Passover* and *fourteen years ago*; but what is the construction? Are ἓξ ἡμερῶν and ἐτῶν δεκατεσσάρων Genitives of time, leaving πρό in the one instance to govern τοῦ πάσχα and in the other to stand absolutely? And, if so, is the curious order a Latinism, parallel to the idiom *ante diem tertium Kalendas* (cf. on μετά with Acc. above)? Moulton, *Proleg.* 100ff., argues against this by quoting independent examples. Further, it is hard to see why the Genitive rather than an Accusative is used to denote a period of time, unless it be a Genitive to define quantity simply, comparable to a Genitive of price, with the 'linear' idea of extent scarcely visible. Rob. 622 suggests that while the Greek and Latin constructions may be independent, the Greek may have been increased in frequency by the Latin influence.

iii. *Metaphorical*. Jas. v. 12, I Pet. iv. 8 πρὸ πάντων, *above all*; perhaps Col. i. 17 (see ii. above).

Dative

1. ἐν. This 'maid of all work' (M.M. 209) is said to be the most frequent of all N.T. prepositions, and it will only be possible here to outline its main uses. It is probably even more versatile than the English *in*. It is further complicated by its overlapping with εἰς (see above *s.v.*), and sometimes with the use of the simple Dative. Most of the English prepositions, except such as *from* and *beside*, will have to be requisitioned at one time or another to translate it. What follows is therefore only a rough-and-ready classification of its chief and of its more remarkable uses.

Chiefly (and probably by origin) it carries a 'punctiliar', static sense— *in* or *within*. Note the following:

i. *Local*, constantly: Mark ii. 1 ἐν οἴκῳ; Matt. xi. 23 ἐν Σοδόμοις; Luke iv. 25 ἐν τῷ Ἰσραήλ; Luke viii. 7 ἐν μέσῳ; Acts ix. 17 ἐν τῇ ὁδῷ, *on the way*, etc. Is Rev. vii. 14, ἔπλυναν τὰς στολὰς αὐτῶν καὶ ἐλεύκαναν αὐτὰς ἐν τῷ αἵματι τοῦ ἀρνίου, local or instrumental? Are we to class as local such phrases as Col. iii. 11 πάντα καὶ ἐν πᾶσιν χριστός, I Cor. xv. 28 ἵνα ᾖ ὁ θεὸς πάντα ἐν πᾶσιν (as though the meaning were *in all persons* or *permeating the whole of things*)? Or is πάντα ἐν πᾶσιν a mere phrase of emphasis, such as its A.V. translation has become— *all in all*? (Cf. παντάπασι in Classical Greek, and Phil. iv. 12 ἐν παντὶ καὶ ἐν πᾶσιν μεμύημαι.) Local may be Acts xii. 11 ἐν ἑαυτῷ γενόμενος (the opposite condition to ἔκστασις. Cf. Luke xv. 17 εἰς ἑαυτὸν δὲ ἐλθών).

Notes. (*a*) It is sometimes difficult to decide whether ἐν = *within* (an individual) or *among* (a number of persons): Luke xxii. 24, ἐν αὐτοῖς, evidently (from the context) means *among them* (so Acts ii. 29 ἐν ἡμῖν); but Mark ii. 8, ἐν ἑαυτοῖς, is explained in *vv*. 6, 8 as = ἐν ταῖς καρδίαις αὐτῶν. Cf. the problematic ἐντὸς ὑμῶν of Luke xvii. 21 (see below *s.v.*). Col. iii. 16 ὁ λόγος τοῦ χριστοῦ ἐνοικείτω ἐν ὑμῖν πλουσίως is ambiguous; and cf. John viii. 37 ὁ λόγος ὁ ἐμὸς οὐ χωρεῖ ἐν ὑμῖν, etc.

(*b*) M.M. (209) produce some papyrus support for the R.V. translation of Luke ii. 49 ἐν τοῖς τοῦ πατρός μου as *in my Father's house*; though *a priori* the A.V. *about my Father's business* seems the more natural (cf. below, p. 106).

(*c*) For the overlapping of ἐν with εἰς, D.-B. § 218 quotes, among others, Rev. xi. 11 πνεῦμα ζωῆς...εἰσῆλθεν ἐν αὐτοῖς (A; but ℵ B and LXX of Ezek. xxxvii. 10, from which it is a quotation, have εἰς αὐτούς); John v. 4 (spurious verse) κατέβαινεν ἐν τῇ κολυμβήθρᾳ; John iii. 35 πάντα δέδωκεν ἐν τῇ χειρὶ αὐτοῦ; II Cor. i. 22 δούς...ἐν ταῖς καρδίαις (cf. viii. 16). So, too, Luke ix. 46 εἰσῆλθεν δὲ διαλογισμὸς ἐν αὐτοῖς; perhaps Acts iv. 12 τὸ δεδομένον ἐν ἀνθρώποις (om. ἐν D) (cf. II Cor. viii. 1). Perhaps the most remarkable instance, however, is Luke i. 17 ἐπιστρέψαι καρδίας πατέρων ἐπὶ τέκνα καὶ ἀπειθεῖς ἐν φρονήσει δικαίων—which is quite astonishing.†

(d) For the relations of ἐν and διά, see on διά, above pp. 57 f.

(e) For ἐν overlapping with the simple Dative, see on the *instrumental* usages (including *price*), below, and under iii. (d) 'Descriptive', below. But add also the relevant instances in (c) above (for εἰς with Acc. also overlaps with the simple Dat.), and the following: I Cor. xiv. 11 ἐν ἐμοὶ βάρβαρος [*sc*. ἔσται]; Matt. xvii. 12 ἐποίησαν ἐν αὐτῷ ὅσα ἠθέλησαν; perhaps Gal. i. 16 ἀποκαλύψαι τὸν υἱὸν αὐτοῦ ἐν ἐμοί;[1] Luke xxiii. 19 ἦν...βληθεὶς ἐν τῇ φυλακῇ; perhaps Eph. v. 18 πληροῦσθε ἐν πνεύματι (although here the simple case after πληροῦσθε would probably have been Gen. rather than Dat., despite the parallel μεθύσκεσθε οἴνῳ, earlier in the verse). For Acts xi. 16, see under iii. below.

ii. *Temporal*—again, constantly: Luke i. 5 ἐν ταῖς ἡμέραις Ἡρῴδου; Mark x. 30 ἐν τῷ καιρῷ τούτῳ...ἐν τῷ αἰῶνι τῷ ἐρχομένῳ; Luke x. 21 ἐν αὐτῇ τῇ ὥρᾳ; Luke i. 26 ἐν δὲ τῷ μηνὶ τῷ ἕκτῳ, etc.; John i. 1 ἐν ἀρχῇ; Eph. vi. 18 ἐν παντὶ καιρῷ; Luke xii. 1 ἐν οἷς (perhaps *meanwhile, at which juncture*—see under 'Relative Clauses', below, pp. 131 f.).

Note especially 'the characteristically Lucan usage' of ἐν τῷ with an infinitive (M.M. 210), which is to be classed no longer as a Hebraism but as 'possible but unidiomatic' Greek (*ibid.* and *Proleg.* 14, 215, 249). But even if it is true Greek, M.M. (*ibid.*, cf. *Proleg.* 249) note the lack of parallels for it in the sense *during*: Luke i. 8 ἐν τῷ ἱερατεύειν αὐτόν, *in the course of his performing his priestly duties* (but *v.* 21, ἐν τῷ χρονίζειν ...αὐτόν, is *at his tarrying*—not temporal, see below); Luke ii. 43 ἐν τῷ ὑποστρέφειν αὐτούς, *as they were returning*; Luke v. 1 ἐν τῷ τὸν ὄχλον ἐπικεῖσθαι αὐτῷ, *while the crowd was pressing on him*. So Luke ix. 51 ἐν τῷ συμπληροῦσθαι τὰς ἡμέρας may mean *while the days were being completed* (but see Acts ii. 1 and *Beg. in loc.*); Luke xix. 13 πραγματεύσασθε ἐν ᾧ ἔρχομαι presumably means ...*while I am coming* (i.e. *until I return*).

---

[1] Mr J. G. Bookless has suggested to me that the use of ἐν here may be due to the desire to make the phrase parallel with ἐν τοῖς ἔθνεσιν

This is not an exclusively Lucan use: Matt. xiii. 4 (|| Mark iv. 4),
Matt. xiii. 25, Heb. ii. 8, iii. 12, etc., are mentioned by Rob. 1073.
(M.M. *loc. cit.* quote from a papyrus ἐν τῶι λογίζεσθαι as = *in reason*;
this seems unparalleled in the N.T.)

iii. *Extended Uses.* (*a*) *Instrumental*, etc. Luke xxii. 49 εἰ πατάξομεν
ἐν μαχαίρῃ; *shall we strike with the sword?* Acts xi. 16 Ἰωάνης μὲν
ἐβάπτισεν ὕδατι, ὑμεῖς δὲ βαπτισθήσεσθε ἐν πνεύματι ἁγίῳ (where *Beg.*
suggests that Luke's consistent use of the plain Dative with ὕδατι
and of ἐν with πνεύματι ἁγίῳ is merely a matter of style and not
theologically significant; cf., however, Eph. v. 18 quoted under i. (*e*)
above); Matt. ix. 34 ἐν τῷ ἄρχοντι τῶν δαιμονίων ἐκβάλλει τὰ δαιμόνια,
by means of the prince of the demons . . . ; Acts xvii. 31 ἐν ἀνδρί, *by a man*;
Acts iv. 12 ἐν ἄλλῳ . . . ἐν ᾧ (|| *v.* 30 διὰ τοῦ ὀνόματος; note also *v.* 2,
καταγγέλλειν ἐν τῷ Ἰησοῦ τὴν ἀνάστασιν . . .); Phil. iv. 13 ἐν τῷ
ἐνδυναμοῦντί με (though this should possibly be classed with ἐν χριστῷ,
etc., see below); Matt. vi. 7 ἐν τῇ πολυλογίᾳ αὐτῶν, *by* (*means of*)
their many words; Mark iv. 11 ἐν παραβολαῖς, *by parables*; Rom. v. 9
δικαιωθέντες νῦν ἐν τῷ αἵματι αὐτοῦ, *acquitted now by his blood* (cf.
Rev. i. 5 τῷ λύσαντι ἡμᾶς . . . ἐν τῷ αἵματι αὐτοῦ); I John ii. 3, etc.
ἐν τούτῳ, *by this means*; Eph. vi. 16 ἐν ᾧ, *with which*; I Cor. iii. 13
ἐν πυρὶ ἀποκαλύπτεται (though this is ambiguous: it may go with
ἔργον as *instrumental*, or with ἡμέρα to express *accompaniment*).

A distinguishable extension† of the instrumental use is that of *price*:
Rev. v. 9 ἠγόρασας . . . ἐν τῷ αἵματί σου (which also illustrates, again,
the overlap with the simple Dative, for I Pet. i. 18, 19 has ἐλυτρώθητε . . .
τιμίῳ αἵματι). Possibly we should here include also the use with
numbers: Mark iv. 8 ἐν ἐξήκοντα καὶ ἐν ἑκατόν, i.e. perhaps *at the rate
of sixty and a hundred* [*to one*]. This, according to one reading, is
preceded by εἰς τριάκοντα, which may be an instance of the blurring
of the distinction between ἐν and εἰς, or may, conceivably, represent
a real shade of difference—*to the extent of thirty to one, and at the rate
of sixty*, etc.[1]

A further extension of the instrumental use might be called *exemplary*:
I Cor. iv. 6 ἵνα ἐν ἡμῖν μάθητε, perhaps *that, by considering our case,
you might learn*; I Tim. i. 16 ἵνα ἐν ἐμοὶ πρώτῳ, perhaps *that in my
case, as the foremost example* . . . ; I Cor. ix. 15 ἵνα οὕτως γένηται
ἐν ἐμοί, *that it might be so in my case.*

[1] See M.M. 209 *sub fin.* Contrast the meaning in Luke xiv. 31, below.

For ἐν χειρί meaning simply *by the agency of*, see under 'Semitisms', below, p. 184.

(*b*) *Adverbial*, a use so closely resembling the instrumental that it is hard to know where to draw the line of demarcation (e.g. ἐν παραβολαῖς above is virtually an adverb, *parabolically*, cf. Heb. xi. 19): II Cor. vi. 4, etc. ἐν παντί, *in every respect* (or is it temporal, *on every occasion* (cf. Eph. vi. 18 ἐν παντὶ καιρῷ)?); ἐν τάχει, *shortly* (Luke xviii. 8, Acts xxv. 4); Acts xxvi. 28, 29 ἐν ὀλίγῳ, perhaps *quickly, hastily*; Acts xvii. 31 ἐν δικαιοσύνῃ, *justly* (Ps. xcv. (Heb. xcvi) 13, etc.); Col. iii. 16 ἐν πάσῃ σοφίᾳ (adverbial if joined with the words which follow it: otherwise with a different shade of meaning—of *accompaniment*, as below); I Thess. iv. 4 ἐν ἁγιασμῷ καὶ τιμῇ (but what of *v.* 7 οὐ...ἐπὶ ἀκαθαρσίᾳ ἀλλ' ἐν ἁγιασμῷ? Is this a real distinction, or mere overlapping of prepositions? See Milligan's *Commentary in loc.*); Col. iii. 16 ἐν τῇ χάριτι, perhaps *gratefully*; I Thess. ii. 7 ἐν βάρει εἶναι, *to be burdensome*; Acts ii. 46 ἐν ἀγαλλιάσει καὶ ἀφελότητι, *with exultation and sincerity*. Examples could be further multiplied.

(*c*) *Of accompaniment, attendant circumstances* (cf. διά ii. (*d*) above)— again, a class which cannot be rigorously defined, but which shades off into others: Luke xiv. 31 ἐν δέκα χιλιάσιν (‖ μετὰ εἴκοσι χιλιάδων), *with ten thousand* (contrast the meaning in Mark iv. 8, (*a*) above); Eph. v. 26 ἐν ῥήματι, perhaps *accompanied by the formula* (or is it instrumental?); I Thess. i. 5 ἐν λόγῳ μόνον, *merely as so much talking*; I Thess. ii. 5 οὔτε...ἐν λόγῳ κολακίας ἐγενήθημεν, *we neither...used words of flattery* (cf. I Cor. ii. 4 in (*d*), below); I Thess. iv. 16 ἐν κελεύσματι, *at the word of command*; Phil. ii. 10 ἐν τῷ ὀνόματι Ἰησοῦ (here=*when the name of Jesus is spoken, at the name*...);† I Pet. iv. 16 δοξαζέτω δὲ τὸν θεὸν ἐν τῷ ὀνόματι τούτῳ ('possibly instrumental... but more probably connotes "the sphere in which"'; '*by virtue of bearing the name*'—from E. G. Selwyn *in loc.*; but cf. also 'Additional Note' (*a*), below); Rom. iii. 25 ἱλαστήριον...ἐν τῷ αὐτοῦ αἵματι, perhaps *to deal with sin...by his blood* (but there are other exegeses of this disputed passage); Luke xxii. 20 ἡ καινὴ διαθήκη ἐν τῷ αἵματί μου, perhaps *sealed, ratified, by my blood*; Heb. xiii. 20 ἐν αἵματι διαθήκης αἰωνίου (LXX Zech. ix. 11 has ἐν αἵματι διαθήκης), perhaps *with the blood*...; Eph. vi. 16 ἐν πᾶσιν, perhaps *in the midst of everything*, i.e. *in all circumstances*, and so *at all costs, above all* (A.V.), *withal* (R.V.); Rom. viii. 37 ἐν τούτοις πᾶσιν, perhaps *in the midst*, or *in spite, of all these things* (cf. Neh. x. (LXX xx) 1, etc.); Mark v. 25 ἐν ῥύσει αἵματος, *suffering from a haemorrhage*; Acts vii. 29

ἐν τῷ λόγῳ τούτῳ, *at these words*; Acts xxiv. 16 ἐν τούτῳ, perhaps *that being so*; Col. iii. 7 ἐν οἷς...περιεπατήσατέ ποτε, ὅτε ἐζῆτε ἐν τούτοις.

Instructive is II Cor. vi. 3–7 (and *v.* 8 merging into διά), showing the versatility of ἐν. Note, too, I Pet. i. 17 ἐν φόβῳ; I Cor. iv. 21 ἐν ῥάβδῳ ἔλθω πρὸς ὑμᾶς, ἢ ἐν ἀγάπῃ πνεύματί τε πραΰτητος; II Cor. xii. 9 καυχήσομαι ἐν ταῖς ἀσθενείαις, perhaps *boast about...* (but II Cor. xi. 30 has τὰ τῆς ἀσθενείας μου καυχήσομαι). In the phrase I Cor. vii. 15 ἐν δὲ εἰρήνῃ κέκληκεν ὑμᾶς ὁ θεός, the preposition may be used 'pregnantly': perhaps *God has called you* into *a peace* in *which he wishes you to live.* Note that one may write Luke vii. 50 πορεύου εἰς εἰρήνην (see under εἰς iv. above, p. 70), but also Acts xvi. 36 πορεύεσθε ἐν εἰρήνῃ and Jas. ii. 16 ὑπάγετε ἐν εἰρήνῃ.

(*d*) *Descriptive*—once more blending with or arising out of other shades of meaning: Eph. ii. 15 ἐν δόγμασιν, *consisting of decrees* (Col. ii. 14 has simple Dat. τοῖς δόγμασιν, but see p. 45 n. 2 above. In I Cor. xiv. 6, according to some MSS., a series of three words with ἐν is crowned by a fourth in the simple Dat.); I Cor. iv. 20 οὐ γὰρ ἐν λόγῳ ἡ βασιλεία τοῦ θεοῦ, ἀλλ' ἐν δυνάμει, *the kingdom of God is not a matter of words, but of power*; I Cor. ii. 7 ἐν μυστηρίῳ, perhaps *consisting of a mystery*; I Thess. iv. 15 ἐν λόγῳ κυρίου, *as a message from the Lord*; I Cor. ii. 4 ὁ λόγος μου καὶ τὸ κήρυγμά μου οὐκ ἐν πειθοῖς σοφίας λόγοις (but perhaps this belongs rather with I Thess. ii. 5 under (*c*) above); I Cor. xiv. 6 ἐὰν μή...λαλήσω ἢ ἐν ἀποκαλύψει ἢ ἐν γνώσει ἢ ἐν προφητείᾳ ἢ διδαχῇ (*v.l.* ἐν δ.); Acts vii. 14 ἐν ψυχαῖς ἑβδομήκοντα πέντε, *consisting of...*; Col. iii. 17 πᾶν ὅ τι ἐὰν ποιῆτε ἐν λόγῳ ἢ ἐν ἔργῳ, *whatever you do, whether it is a matter of words or actions*; I Pet. iii. 3, 4 ὧν ἔστω...κόσμος...ὁ κρυπτὸς τῆς καρδίας ἄνθρωπος ἐν τῷ ἀφθάρτῳ τοῦ πραέως καὶ ἡσυχίου πνεύματος, ...*the secret nature of the heart, consisting of*....

Additional notes. (*a*) On εἰς, ἐν and ἐπί with ὄνομα, see the important note in *Beg.* v, 123 n. 3 (cf. on ἐπί and εἰς, above, pp. 50, 71).

Note, over and above this, the use of ἐν ὀνόματι in the sense, virtually, of *on the ground* (*that*): Mark ix. 41 ἐν ὀνόματι, ὅτι χριστοῦ ἐστε (where Swete says that 'it is nearly equivalent to διὰ τὸ χριστοῦ εἶναι, on the score of your being Christ's—a use of ὀνόματι not unknown to Classical Greek, cf., for example, Thuc. IV, 60'); cf. Matt. x. 41, 42 εἰς ὄνομα προφήτου, δικαίου, μαθητοῦ, *because he is a prophet, a just man, a disciple.* Cf. I Pet. iv. 16 in (*c*) above, p. 78.

(*b*) ἐν χριστῷ. Much discussion has revolved round this and kindred phrases (ἐν κυρίῳ, ἐν πνεύματι, ἐν θεῷ, etc.). Very briefly, note the following points:

1. The use is prominent in Paul's writings, and, in contrast, is not found in the Synoptic Gospels, James, II Pet., Jude, or Hebrews.

2. It sometimes relates to spiritual incorporation in Christ, etc.[1] (|| in I Cor. xv. 22, with ἐν τῷ 'Αδάμ): contrast such prepositions as μετά and παρά, as used of ordinary contact with the physical presence of Jesus on earth. But note that even of spiritual union σύν is used by Paul (see 5 below); and verbs compounded with σύν are common in this connexion.

3. It is used not only of individuals but also of Churches (e.g. Gal. i. 22, I Thess. i. 1).

4. To interpret it in a quasi-material way, as though Christ were the 'atmosphere' or 'locality' in which believers are placed, seems to do less than justice to its deeply *personal* significance.[2]

5. Note a corresponding use of διά (I Thess. iv. 14, cf. 16) and σύν (I Thess. iv. 17, v. 10, Phil. i. 23, and cf. I Cor. xv. 10). And for διά as a parallel to ἐν, compare also I Tim. ii. 9, 10.[3]

(*c*) πιστεύω ἐν is rare in the LXX (Burton, *Gal.* 477, 478) and is used at most only twice in the N.T.,[4] Mark i. 15 πιστεύετε ἐν τῷ εὐαγγελίῳ, John iii. 15 ὁ πιστεύων ἐν αὐτῷ (*si vera l.*)—unless Eph. i. 13 is included, where ἐν ᾧ καὶ πιστεύσαντες ἐσφραγίσθητε is ambiguous: Moulton (*Proleg.* 67 and n. 2) holds that the sense is determined by ἐσφραγίσθητε, and agrees with Deissmann that in Mark i. 15 also πιστεύω is used absolutely. Curiously, he appears not to discuss

[1] This, however, is denied by the late Friedrich Büchsel in an important article '"In Christus" bei Paulus', completed in 1942, but published posthumously in the *Zeitschrift für neutestamentliche Wissenschaft*, XLII (1950), 141–58. He at least establishes that a large number of instances, which are modal, instrumental, etc., are irrelevant to any 'incorporation' idea. It is a question whether any of the non-Pauline instances are relevant, except the Johannine.

[2] For this point, see F. C. Porter, *The Mind of Christ in Paul*, especially 288, 298, 299.

[3] Deissmann's monograph, *Die neutestamentliche Formel in Christo Jesu* (Marburg, 1892) is a famous treatment of the subject (see S. and H. 161 for a summary and F. C. Porter, *op. cit.*, for a criticism).

[4] πιστεύω ἐπί also occurs in the N.T.: see p. 50 above. Note that in Ignatius, *Philad.* VIII, the sentence ἐὰν μὴ ἐν τοῖς ἀρχείοις (*v.l.* ἀρχαίοις) εὕρω, ἐν τῷ εὐαγγελίῳ οὐ πιστεύω seems to mean (see J. B. Lightfoot *in loc.*), *unless I find it* (the point at issue) *in the archives, I do not believe it* (*because it appears*) *in the Gospel.* Thus it is no parallel to the πιστεύω ἐν of Mark i. 15.†

John iii. 15, which might be explained similarly as meaning ἵνα. . .ὁ πιστεύων ζωὴν αἰώνιον ἐν αὐτῷ ἔχῃ.† For πιστεύω in the LXX with prepositions other than ἐν, see Isa. xxviii. 16, and Sap. xii. 2 (*Beg.* II, 64 n.). ἐν is, however, used after πίστις in Eph. i. 15, Col. i. 4, I Tim. iii. 13, II Tim. iii. 15, and possibly Rom. iii. 25. But in none of these passages is it certain that ἐν indicates the object so much as the sphere of faith (even when the article is repeated, as in I, II Timothy).[1]

2. **σύν.** Briefly, σύν means *with*; it is used less frequently in N.T. Greek than μετά, and, in fact, is mostly confined to Luke–Acts, being entirely absent from the Johannine Epistles, Rev., Heb., I Pet., II Thess., Philem., I, II Tim., Titus. See Rob. 627; and, when used, it does not seem to differ materially in meaning from μετά with Genitive (see above *s.v.*† Herein κοινή appears to differ from Attic usage: D.-B. § 221).

Examples. Matt. xxvi. 35 σὺν σοὶ ἀποθανεῖν; Acts xiv. 4 οἱ μὲν ἦσαν σὺν τοῖς ᾽Ιουδαίοις, οἱ δὲ σὺν τοῖς ἀποστόλοις (*with* in the sense of *on the side of*). Perhaps the most striking uses are: (i) Luke ix. 32 Πέτρος καὶ οἱ σὺν αὐτῷ, comparable to the idiom οἱ περί τινα (see above, περί, and Rob. 628). (ii) Luke xxiv. 21 ἀλλά γε καὶ σὺν πᾶσιν τούτοις, *yes, and besides all this*, or *yes, and what's more* (cf. ἐν iii. (c), above, p. 78).† (iii) σύν of *spiritual* contact with Christ, I Thess. iv. 17, v. 10, Phil. i. 23 (see ἐν, additional notes, above).

On σύν in compounds, see note under μετά above.

B. 'Improper' Prepositions

These are given alphabetically, with notes where necessary.

1. **ἅμα.** This is only used once in N.T. Greek as a preposition (with the Dative, meaning *simultaneously with*), Matt. xiii. 29 μή ποτε συλλέγοντες τὰ ζιζάνια ἐκριζώσητε ἅμα αὐτοῖς τὸν σῖτον. Otherwise as an adverb: see, for example, Rom. iii. 12 ἅμα ἠχρεώθησαν (=Ps. lii. 4

---

[1] For discussions on the translation of πιστεύω, πίστις with and without various prepositions, see Lightfoot on Col. i. 4 and Westcott on Heb. vi. 1; see also Moulton, *Proleg.* 68; *Beg.* II, 64; W. F. Howard, *Christianity according to St John*, 156–8; Moffatt in *Harv. Theol. Rev.* XXIX (1936) as cited above, p. 69 n. 4. For Col. i. 2 πιστοῖς ἀδελφοῖς ἐν χριστῷ as *faithful brothers who are in Christ* (not brothers who believe in Christ), see under 'The Definite Article', p. 108. For the influence of Semitic idiom on certain uses of ἐν, see under 'Semitisms', p. 183; and Moulton, *Proleg.* 68.

LXX); Philem. 22 ἅμα δὲ καὶ ἑτοίμαζέ μοι ξενίαν; I Tim. v. 13 ἅμα δὲ καὶ ἀργαὶ μανθάνουσιν; Col. iv. 3 προσευχόμενοι ἅμα καὶ περὶ ἡμῶν; Acts xxiv. 26 ἅμα καὶ ἐλπίζων. In I Thess. iv. 17, v. 10 ἅμα σύν with the Dative looks almost like a kind of compound preposition (see Rob. 638); but there is nothing to prove that ἅμα is there doing any of the duty of a preposition, any more than *simultaneously* in the phrase *simultaneously with*, above (cf. *together with*). Matt. xx. 1 ἅμα πρωΐ, *at dawn*, makes ἅμα practically equivalent to a preposition and πρωΐ practically equivalent to a noun.

Compare and contrast μετά, σύν (above) and ὁμοῦ (the latter appearing in N.T. Greek only as an adverb and never as a preposition).

2. ἄνευ. This occurs in the N.T. only three times (not counting the false reading ἄνευ χειρῶν of Mark xiii. 2), always with the Genitive and meaning *without*: Matt. x. 29 οὐ πεσεῖται ἐπὶ τὴν γῆν ἄνευ τοῦ πατρὸς ὑμῶν (i.e. perhaps *without the cognisance* or *permission of*); I Pet. iii. 1 ἄνευ λόγου; iv. 9 ἄνευ γογγυσμοῦ.

3. ἄντικρυς. Only once in the N.T., Acts xx. 15 ἄντικρυς Χίου, *opposite Chios*. The form ἄντικρυ is an inferior reading.

4. ἀντίπερα. Only once in the N.T., Luke viii. 26 ἀντίπερα τῆς Γαλιλαίας, where it apparently means *on the opposite side to Galilee*.

5. ἀπέναντι. With Gen. Apart from Matt. xxvii. 24, Mark xii. 41 where it is a doubtful variant in some MSS. for κατέναντι, it only occurs four times in the N.T., Matt. xxvii. 61, Acts iii. 16, xvii. 7, Rom. iii. 18 (quotation). The sense is *in the presence of, opposite, before*, or (in Acts xvii. 7) *contrary to*.

6. ἄτερ. With Gen. Only twice in the N.T., Luke xxii. 6, 35, *without*.

7. ἄχρι(ς). 'The meaning is "up to" and the case is the Genitive. It occurs with place (Acts xiii. 6), persons (Acts xi. 5), time (Acts xiii. 11)† and abstract ideas (Acts xxii. 4, 22). It occurs mainly in Acts, Paul's writings and Revelation' (Rob. 639). It is found thirty-five times (or thirty-two, if certain doubtful texts are omitted) in the N.T. (so *ibid.*). Cf. μέχρι and ἕως (for which, as variants for ἄχρι, see Matt. xiii. 30). ἄχρι οὗ (Rom. xi. 25, etc.) can be regarded strictly as prepositional = ἄχρις ἐκείνου χρόνου ἐν ᾧ....

8. **ἐγγύς.** Besides its use as an adverb, this word occurs in the N.T. as a preposition i. with Gen., e.g. John xi. 54 εἰς τὴν χώραν ἐγγὺς τῆς ἐρήμου (eight times, Rob. 640); ii. with Dat., e.g. Acts ix. 38 ἐγγὺς δὲ οὔσης Λύδδας τῇ 'Ιόππῃ (twice, and twice also with the indeclinable 'Ιερουσαλήμ—Rob. 640).

9. **ἐκτός.** This is used with the Genitive, e.g. I Cor. vi. 18 ἐκτὸς τοῦ σώματος; Acts xxvi. 22 ἐκτὸς...ὧν. In I Cor. xiv. 5 ἐκτὸς εἰ μὴ διερμηνεύῃ (so also I Cor. xv. 2, I Tim. v. 19), there is obviously a redundancy, but it may be presumed that, without the εἰ μή, ἐκτός would have been virtually a preposition even here; cf. the illiterate 'without he interpret'.

10. **ἔμπροσθεν.** This, with Gen., means *in the presence of*, e.g. Matt. x. 32 ἔμπροσθεν τῶν ἀνθρώπων...ἔμπροσθεν τοῦ πατρός μου; Matt. xxvii. 11 ἔμπροσθεν τοῦ ἡγεμόνος; or *in front of*, e.g. John x. 4 ἔμπροσθεν αὐτῶν πορεύεται; or *prior to*, John i. 15, 30, as though it were an adjective. It is also used adverbially.

11. **ἔναντι** and 12. **ἐναντίον** are both used with the Genitive, as prepositions meaning much the same as ἔμπροσθεν (which is, in fact, a variant reading in Mark ii. 12). Neither occurs in the N.T. as an adverb.

13. **ἕνεκα, ἕνεκεν,** or **εἵνεκεν,** also with Gen., means *for the sake of* or *on account of.* The majority of instances refer to persecution, privation, etc., *for the sake of* Christ (or his name or the kingdom). οὗ εἵνεκεν, Luke iv. 18 (quotation) = *because,* and τίνος ἕνεκα, Acts xix. 32 = *for what reason* (the only N.T. instances of this preposition *following* the word it 'governs'); and in II Cor. vii. 12 ἕνεκεν τοῦ φανερωθῆναι... is practically a final clause. It is not used in the N.T. as an adverb.

14. **ἐντός,** though occurring only twice in the N.T., has a special interest attaching to it. In Matt. xxiii. 26 it is probably adverbial, τὸ ἐντός meaning *that which is inside* (in contrast to τὸ ἐκτός). But in Luke xvii. 21 it is used as a preposition, with the Genitive: ἰδοὺ γὰρ ἡ βασιλεία τοῦ θεοῦ ἐντὸς ὑμῶν ἐστιν. Here commentators have long been divided between *within you* (i.e. in each individual's heart) and *among you* (i.e. present, in the Person of Jesus and his work, among those whom he was addressing). Those who argued for the

latter meaning did so mainly on the ground that the other meaning was unlikely and unparalleled, theologically speaking, in the Synoptic Gospels; but linguistic evidence seemed, if anything, slightly in favour of *within you*. In a careful review of the evidence up to that date, P. M. S. Allen[1] shows that the Xenophon passages usually quoted for *among* really support *within*; that the LXX evidence supports *within*; and that even a few examples from Symmachus which appear at first to support *among* are not valid as an argument since the words are such as to make the meanings interchangeable.† More recently a new turn has been given to the discussion by C. H. Roberts,[2] who argues for the sense *within one's power*, quoting an unpublished Oxyrhynchus Papyrus (A.D. 99/100) from a wine-merchant who complains that his partner's wife is defrauding him: ἡ δὲ ἔχουσ[α] τὸ φορτίον το[ῦ] οἴνου ἐντὸς αὐτῆς τὴν τιμὴν ἐνεβόλευσε πᾶσαν. But Harald Riesenfeld[3] points out the uncertainty of meaning in ἐνεβόλευσε, and, suggesting *she has laid an embargo upon, seized*, goes on to argue for the likelihood of ἐντὸς αὐτῆς meaning *at her house* rather than *in her power*, supporting this by another quotation made in C. H. Roberts's article: πέμψατέ μοι τὸ ἐραιοῦν κολώβειν (*l.* ἐρεοῦν κολώβιον [perhaps *woollen jacket*]) ἵνα ἐντός μου αὐτ[ὸ] εὕρω.[4]

15. **ἐνώπιον**, *in the presence of*, is used in the N.T. as a preposition only, and takes the Genitive. 'It appears sometimes with place...but usually with persons..., and especially of God' (Rob. 642). It is common in the LXX, and, though not unknown in earlier literature, it may owe its frequency to Semitic influence. Cf. p. 184 below. It does not occur in Matthew or Mark (*ibid.*).

16. **ἔξω**, *outside*, is used both as an adverb and as a preposition. As a preposition, it takes the Genitive and is used only with places (Rob. 642).

17. **ἔξωθεν** is a less common word with the same usage. The only unambiguously prepositional instances in the N.T. are Mark vii. 15, Rev. xi. 2, xiv. 20 (Rob. 642).

18. **ἐπάνω**, *upon*, *above* (spatially and metaphorically), is used both as an adverb and as a preposition with the Genitive.

---

[1] *E.T.* XLIX (July 1938) and L (Feb. 1939).
[2] In *Harv. Theol. Rev.* XLI (1948).
[3] In *Nuntius Sodalicii Neotestamentici Upsaliensis*, no. 2 (1949).
[4] P. Ross.-Georg. (ed. Zereteli and Jernstedt), vol. III (1930), no. 1 (A.D. 270).

19. ἐπέκεινα only once in N.T. (Acts vii. 43), and there as a preposition with Gen.

20. ἔσω is only found a few times at all in the N.T., and only once (Mark xv. 16) as a preposition, with the Genitive (Rob. 643).

21. ἕως seems essentially to be a conjunction meaning *while* or *until*. But it is also used as a preposition, with Gen., meaning *up to, as far as*, both spatially and metaphorically. It is also used, in a closely related way, with adverbs, e.g. ἕως πότε (e.g. Matt. xvii. 17). The phrase ἕως οὗ or ὅτου (=until) is, presumably, a prepositional use, being strictly equivalent to ἕως ἐκείνου τοῦ χρόνου ἐν ᾧ... *until such time as*... (cf. ἄχρις above).

ἕως also occurs reinforced by another preposition: Luke xxiv. 50 ἕως πρός; Acts xvii. 14 ἕως ἐπί; Acts xxi. 5 ἕως ἔξω; Acts xxvi. 11 ἕως καὶ εἰς. In Mark xiv. 54 ἕως ἔσω εἰς τὴν αὐλήν, εἰς τὴν αὐλήν may be an explanation of ἔσω, and ἔσω may be virtually equivalent to a noun: *as far as inside—that is, to the courtyard*....

22. **κατέναντι** is once adverbial and otherwise prepositional in the N.T., and is similar in meaning to ἀπέναντι, and is in fact sometimes a variant reading for it. See No. 5 'Απέναντι.

23. **κατενώπιον**, with Gen., means *in the presence of*. It is only prepositional in the N.T. (three times only).

24. **κυκλόθεν** is used as a preposition, with Gen., in Rev. iv. 3, 4 (κυκλόθεν τοῦ θρόνου), and as an adverb in Rev. iv. 8.

25. **κύκλῳ** is used as an adverb except in Rev. iv. 6, v. 11, vii. 11 (as κυκλόθεν).

26. **μέσον** occurs as a preposition with the Genitive in Phil. ii. 15 (μέσον γενεᾶς), Matt. xiv. 24 (in a variant reading, μέσον τῆς θαλάσσης), and Luke viii. 7, x. 3 (both in D).†

27. **μεταξύ** is found both as an adverb and as a preposition with the Genitive = *between*.

28. **μέχρι(ς)** is not found in the N.T. in a purely adverbial use. As a preposition, with Gen., it =*up to, as far as* (μέχρι τοῦ Ἰλλυρικοῦ, Rom. xv. 19). For μέχρις οὗ (Mark xiii. 30) cf. ἄχρις and ἕως above.

29. ὄπισθεν is used adverbially and (twice) as a preposition, with Gen. = *behind, after.*

30. ὀπίσω, with Gen., also = *after.* As an adverb only twice in the N.T. (Matt. xxiv. 18, Luke vii. 38).

31. ὀψέ may conceivably be prepositional in Matt. xxviii. 1 if ὀψὲ σαββάτων there means *after the sabbath*; but if it means *late on the sabbath* (cf. 'Genitive', ii. p. 39 above), this example disappears. It is used in both ways outside the N.T. (Rob. 645).

32. παραπλήσιον is used once only in the N.T. and then as a preposition, with the Dative = *near to* (Phil. ii. 27).

33. παρεκτός occurs in the N.T. once as an adverb (II Cor. xi. 28) and two or three times as a preposition, with Gen. = *apart from, except.*

34. πέραν is used both as an adverb and, with Gen., as a preposition = *beyond.*

35. πλήν (? = πλέον, *more*) is found as an adverb, as a conjunction, and, rarely, as a preposition, with Gen. = *except.*

36. πλησίον is used in John iv. 5, with Gen. as = *near.* Otherwise it is adverbial (ὁ πλησίον = *my neighbour—the one who is near*), and Rob. 646 seems right in counting Luke x. 29, 36 as no exception, since here (καὶ τίς ἐστίν μου πλησίον; etc.) it 'has more of the substantive idea ("neighbour")'.

37. ὑπεράνω is used only three times in the N.T. and all prepositionally, with Gen. = *above*: Eph. i. 21, iv. 10, Heb. ix. 5.

38. ὑπερέκεινα only occurs once in the N.T. (II Cor. x. 16) and then as a preposition with the Genitive = *beyond.*

39. ὑπερεκπερισσοῦ is used as a preposition with the Genitive = *very far in excess of*, in Eph. iii. 20. Otherwise it occurs in the N.T. only once or twice, and adverbially.

40. ὑποκάτω occurs in the N.T. only as a preposition, with Gen. = *beneath.*

41. χάριν, the Accusative of χάρις, *thanks*, is used as a preposition, with Gen. = *for the sake of*, and always follows the word it relates to except in I John iii. 12 (and, in the LXX, Ecclus. xxxv. 4).

42. χωρίς is common in the N.T. as a preposition with the Genitive = *without* (once following the word it relates to—οὗ χωρίς, Heb. xii. 14). It occurs only once (John xx. 7) as a pure adverb (Rob. 648).

For summary conclusions, see Rob. 648.

C. Prepositions Compounded with Verbs

All the 'proper' prepositions occurring in the N.T. are found as prefixes to verbs, and, in addition, ἀμφι-, which does not occur separately in the N.T.[1]

There follow some observations on prepositions compounded with verbs.

1. Prepositions compounded with verbs tend to retain their original *adverbial* nature ('prepositions when compounded are still the pure adverbs they were at the first', *Proleg.* 112, n. 1); and therefore it frequently happens that the so-called preposition, being in reality adverbial, 'governs' no object; e.g. in ἀναζωπυρέω (II Tim. i. 6), the verb ζωπυρέω 'governs' an object, but the ἀνα- simply denotes *afresh*; in περικυκλόω (Luke xix. 43), the περι- does not 'govern' an object but strengthens the idea of encirclement; further instances are: προϋπάρχω (προ- = *previously*), προσαπειλέω, προσοφείλω (προς- = *in addition*), συγχέω (συγ- = Latin *con*-, cf. our *mix* up), συμπίπτω (cf. *collapse*), ὑπερνικάω (Rom. viii. 37, where ὑπερ- = *exceedingly*).

2. Sometimes a verb is evidently constructed from a preposition governing a noun: ἀποστοματίζω (ἀπὸ στόματος), ἐνοχλέω (ἐν ὄχλῳ), ἐνταφιάζω (ἐν τάφῳ), ἐνυπνιάζομαι (ἐν ὕπνῳ with ἐνύπνιον as a connexion), ἐνωτίζομαι (ἐν ὠτί).† In such cases the preposition bears no direct relation to the noun governed by the composite verb itself.

3. Often a sense other than that of the separate preposition (as analysed in the foregoing pages) appears when the preposition is compounded; e.g.:

i. *Intensification*, simply: 'Από: ἀπαρνέομαι, ἀποδείκνυμι (cf. ἐπιδείκνυμι, ἐνδείκνυμαι), ἀποθνήσκω, ἀποκαταλλάσσω,[2] ἀποκτείνω, ἀπόλλυμι (note that there is no Aorist, in the N.T., of the simple

---

[1] Nor in Polybius (W. W. Capes, *History of the Achaean League*, xviii).
[2] See V. Taylor, *Forgiveness and Reconciliation*, 91 n., 131 n.

θνήσκω, nor any instance, in any tense, of the simple κτείνω or ὄλλυμι), ἀποτελέω, ἀποτολμάω. Ἐκ: ἐκδιηγέομαι, ἐκδικέω, ἐκζητέω (cf. ἀναζητέω), ἐκθαμβέομαι, ἐκλανθάνομαι (cf. ἐπιλανθάνομαι), ἐκπειράζω, ἐκταράσσω, ἐκτελέω, ἐκφοβέω, ἐξακολουθέω, ἐξαπατάω, ἐξαπορέω, ἐξελέγχω, ἐξετάζω (cf. ἀνετάζω), ἐξολοθρεύω (with all these cf. the intensive *ex-* in Latin *exaudio*, etc.; and such English prepositional phrases as *die off, kill off, finish off, follow out, try out, search out*). Ἀνά: ἀναζητέω (cf. *hunt up*; and ἐκζητέω above), ἀναθεωρέω (cf. ἐποπτεύω?), ἀνακρίνω, ἀναιρέω, ἀναλίσκω (cf. *use up*), ἀναλύω (does ἀνα- here carry something of its distributive sense? Grimm-Thayer suggest rather a parallel with ἀναπτύσσω, *roll up*; cf. διαλύω, ἐπιλύω), ἀναμένω, ἀναπείθω, ἀνασείω (cf. *beat up, shake up*; and διασείω); ἀνατρέπω (cf. *upset*). Διά: a large number of compounds with δια- are intensifications of the simple verb, but are perhaps in a different class from the present, since the meaning of the simple preposition (*through*) is itself the same word, virtually, as *thorough*: it is thus the most naturally and obviously intensive prefix in its own right, and scarcely calls for special notice: διακαθαρίζω is translated in the A.V. as *throughly purge*. Ἐπί: ἐπιδείκνυμι (cf. ἀποδείκνυμι, ἐνδείκνυμαι), ἐπιδιορθόω, ἐπιλανθάνομαι (cf. ἐκλανθάνομαι), ἐπιλείπω, ἐπιλύω (cf. ἀνα-, διαλύω), ἐπιποθέω, ἐπιστηρίζω, ἐπιτελέω, ἐποπτεύω (cf. ἀναθεωρέω). (Yet note that ἐπι-, like δια-, does tend to retain some trace of its prepositional, directional sense, which makes its intensifying quality easier to account for than is the case with some of the other prepositions; cf. Latin *aduro*.) Ἐν: ἐγκαινίζω, ἐγκαταλείπω, ? ἐμπίμπλημι (see Rom. xv. 24), ἐμπρήθω, ἐμφανίζω, ἐνδείκνυμαι (cf. ἀπο-, ἐπιδείκνυμι), ἐνδυναμόω, ἐνισχύω (Acts ix. 22, 19, with apparently no idea of *inwardness*, but only of *intensity*. Is the same true of Phil. iv. 13?), ἐννεύω (perhaps cf. Latin *induro*, etc.). Κατά: καθοπλίζω, καταδιώκω, κατακολουθέω, καταλαμβάνω, καταμανθάνω, καταναλίσκω, καταπίνω (English tends to say *drink up*, though *swallow down* as well as *up*), κατασκευάζω, καταφεύγω, καταφθείρω, καταφιλέω, καταχράομαι, κατεργάζομαι (cf. *run down* (active verb), *track down*), κατισχύω. Παρά: παραβιάζομαι, παρατηρέω, παροξύνω. Σύν: συλλυπέω (cf. Latin *contristo*; and περίλυπος (see below p. 90 n. 1)), συμπληρόω, συμπνίγω, συναρπάζω, συνθλάω, συνθρύπτω, συντελέω, συντέμνω, συντρίβω (cf. Latin *contundo*), συσπαράσσω (cf. *convulse*).

ii. *The (allegedly) original sense* of the preposition (lost or obscured in its separate use); e.g.: Διά, in its sense of *between* and associations with *duality* and an *interval* or *dividing-space* (see above, on διά as

a preposition): διαγίνομαι (of an interval elapsing, e.g. Acts xxv. 13),
διαλείπω, διαπρίω (perhaps lit. *saw in two*, Acts v. 33, vii. 54),
διαρρήγνυμι (cf. *disrupt*), διασκορπίζω, διασπάω, διασπείρω, διαστέλλομαι (perhaps with the connotation of detailed and *distinct* injunctions),
διαστρέφω (cf. *distort*), perhaps διατάσσω (cf. διαστέλλομαι), perhaps
διατίθημι (cf. διαστέλλομαι, and *dispose*), διαφέρω, διαχωρίζομαι,
διερωτάω (perhaps enquire into each separate item), διίστημι; and
'Ανά in its sense of *up* (see above, on ἀνά as a preposition): ἀναβαίνω,
ἀναβιβάζω, ἀναβλέπω, ἀνάγω, ἀνακαθίζω, ἀνακράζω.
Note. ἀναγινώσκω is usually taken to mean *read*, presumably in the
sense that the reader discerns *again* (ἀνά) what the writer originally
had in mind; but J. H. Kennedy argued interestingly, if not convincingly,
for interpreting the ἀνα- in II Cor. i. 13, iii. 2 as an intensive making,
the verb mean *admit* or *acknowledge*.[1]

iii. *A sense which defies exact explanation* (as is the case, apparently,
with many English verbal prepositions also). Note, for example, the
following: '**Από**: ἀπαλγέω (Eph. iv. 19 *to cease to feel*),† ἀποβαίνω
(in sense *turn out to be, eventuate*, Luke xxi. 13, Phil. i. 19), ἀπέχω,
ἀποδίδωμι, ἀποκαταλλάσσω, ἀπολαμβάνω (in which four instances,
as in certain others, the sense *duly* seems to be latent—perhaps
derived from the idea of getting *back from* its source what
one has already put in and is owed), ἀφικνέομαι (*arrive!*—but
ἄφιξις = *departure* in Acts xx. 29). '**Ανά**: ἀνακαλύπτω (cf. *uncover*),
ἀναπτύσσω (*unroll*), ἀνασκευάζω (possibly a similar '*un-*' connotation:
unfurnish, i.e. *unsettle*), ἀναχωρέω, ἀνήκω (perhaps to come *up* to
a thing = *to be suitable*). **Διά**: διαζωννύω (or -υμι). '**Εκ**: ἔξεστιν.
'**Εν**: ἐνέβλεπον (absolutely) in Acts xxii. 11 (but the *v.l.* in B, οὐδὲν
ἔβλεπον, seems more likely (cf. ix. 8); and אA read οὐκ ἔβλεπον);
ἐνδέχεται, ἐγκακέω, ἐντρέπομαι. '**Επί**: what is the force of Matt.
vii. 10 μὴ λίθον ἐπιδώσει αὐτῷ; ? **Κατά**: what is John viii. 3, ἐν
μοιχείᾳ κατειλημμένην, as compared with *v.* 9 καὶ κατελείφθη μόνος
ὁ Ἰησοῦς? **Μετά**: μεθερμηνεύω, μετακινέω, μεταλλάσσω, μεταμορφόω,
μετανοέω, μετασχηματίζω, μετοικίζω (in all of which μετα- = *trans-*).
Παρά: παρακαλέω (as = *exhort*), παραινέω, παραμυθέω (possibly all
carrying the prepositional idea of standing *beside*—to exhort, comfort,
etc.), παρακούω (see Matt. xviii. 17 and perhaps Mark v. 36, *si vera l.*),
παρασκευάζω. **Περί**: περιάπτω (of *lighting* a fire, Luke xxii. 55),
περιεργάζομαι, περιλείπω (both with the idea of *super-*; cf. περισσός,

[1] In *The Second and Third Epistles of St Paul to the Corinthians* (1900).

περισσεύω, περιούσιος), περιπείρω, περιποιέω, περιφρονέω.¹ **Πρός**: προσποιέω (Luke xxiv. 28). **Σύν**: συμβιβάζω (as = *deduce, prove*: is it from 'putting two and two together'?), συστρέφομαι (Matt. xvii. 22). **Ὑπό**: ὑπάγω, ὑπάρχω, ὑποδέχομαι (Luke xix. 6).

4. With regard to syntax, a compound verb sometimes dispenses with any further preposition, sometimes repeats the preposition with which it is compounded, and sometimes makes use of a different one; e.g.:

i. *Without further preposition*: Luke xiii. 12 ἀπολέλυσαι τῆς ἀσθενείας σου; II Pet. i. 4 ἀποφυγόντες τῆς...φθορᾶς (but ii. 18 *with Acc.*, see below); Luke xix. 4 ἐκείνης ἤμελλεν διέρχεσθαι (though here the Gen. might be an independent *gen. loci*); Gal. v. 4 τῆς χάριτος ἐξεπέσατε; Acts xiv. 22 ἐμμένειν τῇ πίστει; Gal. iii. 3 ἐναρξάμενοι πνεύματι (the force of which ἐν is sufficiently strong to be followed by another simple Dat. in conjunction with a *fresh* verb without a relevant preposition— νῦν σαρκὶ ἐπιτελεῖσθε;); Mark iii. 10 ἐπιπίπτειν αὐτῷ; Luke i. 35 δύναμις ὑψίστου ἐπισκιάσει σοι; Matt. ix. 24 κατεγέλων αὐτοῦ; Rom. xi. 18 μὴ κατακαυχῶ τῶν κλάδων; Matt. xvi. 18 πύλαι Ἅιδου οὐ κατισχύσουσιν αὐτῆς; Matt. xxvi. 62 τί οὗτοί σου καταμαρτυροῦσιν; Acts ix. 3 αὐτὸν περιήστραψεν φῶς (but also with περί *with Acc.*, Acts xxii. 6; see below); Mark vi. 55 περιέδραμον ὅλην τὴν χώραν ἐκείνην; Luke ii. 9 περιέλαμψεν αὐτούς; Matt. xxv. 36 περιεβάλετέ με (cf. *vv.* 38, 43; John xix. 2 with double Acc.); Acts vii. 40 θεοὺς οἳ προπορεύσονται ἡμῶν (in a quotation); Acts xiii. 2 τὸ ἔργον ὃ προσκέκλημαι αὐτούς; Acts ii. 42 ἦσαν δὲ προσκαρτεροῦντες τῇ διδαχῇ (where the προσ- at least *may* be directly responsible for the Dative); Matt. iv. 10 κύριον τὸν θεόν σου προσκυνήσεις (where, similarly, the προσ- is at least appropriate to the *Acc.*; but Heb. i. 6 has προσκυνησάτωσαν αὐτῷ (see Deut. xxxii. 43 LXX, and cf. Ps. xcvi. 7 LXX)); II Pet. ii. 13 συνευωχούμενοι ὑμῖν; Col. ii. 12 συνταφέντες αὐτῷ (so almost always—see below); Heb. x. 34 τοῖς δεσμίοις συνεπαθήσατε; I Cor. iv. 4 οὐδὲν γὰρ ἐμαυτῷ σύνοιδα; Luke xv. 6 συνχάρητέ μοι; Acts xvii. 30 τοὺς μὲν οὖν χρόνους τῆς ἀγνοίας ὑπεριδών (?); Jude 7 δίκην ὑπέχουσαι.

But here note also instances where the simple case is *not* one ever taken by the preposition when uncompounded (or not in the same sense); e.g. ἀνθίστημι, ἀνταποκρίνομαι, ἀντειπεῖν, ἀντίκειμαι, ἀντιλέγω, ἀντιπίπτω, ἀντιστρατεύομαι, all with *Dative*; ἀποστερέω, with *Acc.*

¹ Cf. also περίλυπος, although the *verb* is not found in the N.T.

of person and *Gen.* of thing (sometimes) (cf. ἀποφεύγω in II Pet. ii. 18, though with Gen in II Pet. i. 4 as above); ἀποτάσσομαι with *Dative*; διελθεῖν with *Accusative*; διαδίδωμι with *Dative* (Luke xviii. 22); διαιρέω with *Dative*; διαπορεύομαι with *Accusative* (Acts xvi. 4, where διά alone would require Gen. But this is the only instance so); Rev. iii. 18 ἐγχρῖσαι τοὺς ὀφθαλμούς σου; Heb. xii. 1 περικείμενον ἡμῖν νέφος; Matt. xxvii. 28 χλαμύδα κοκκίνην περιέθηκαν αὐτῷ; προάγω with *Accusative*.

ii. *Repeating the preposition* (ἀπό, ἐξ, εἰς, ἐν, ἐπί are the prepositions most often thus repeated—Rob. 559): **Ἀπό**: Luke xvi. 3 ἀφαιρεῖται τὴν οἰκονομίαν ἀπ’ ἐμοῦ (but Luke x. 42 with simple Gen.); Luke v. 2 ἀπ’ αὐτῶν ἀποβάντες; Luke xxiv. 2 τὸν λίθον ἀποκεκυλισμένον ἀπὸ τοῦ μνημείου (but followed by ἐκ in Mark xvi. 3); Acts ix. 18 ἀπέπεσαν ...ἀπὸ τῶν ὀφθαλμῶν; I Thess. ii. 17 ἀπορφανισθέντες ἀφ’ ὑμῶν; Luke xxii. 41 ἀπεσπάσθη ἀπ’ αὐτῶν; Rom. xi. 26 ἀποστρέψει ἀσεβείας ἀπὸ ’Ιακώβ (quotation). **Διά**: Matt. xii. 43 διέρχεται δι’ ἀνύδρων τόπων; Luke vi. 1 διαπορεύεσθαι...διὰ σπορίμων; I Pet. iii. 20 διεσώθησαν δι’ ὕδατος. **Ἐκ**: Acts xxvi. 17 ἐξαιρούμενός σε ἐκ τοῦ λαοῦ; Matt. xiii. 52 ἐκβάλλει ἐκ τοῦ θησαυροῦ; Rom. xi. 24 ἐκ τῆς κατὰ φύσιν ἐξεκόπης ἀγριελαίου; Acts xii. 7 ἐξέπεσαν...ἐκ τῶν χειρῶν. **Ἐν**: Matt. xxvi. 23 ἐμβάψας...ἐν τῷ τρυβλίῳ; II Cor. iii. 2 ἐγγεγραμμένη ἐν ταῖς καρδίαις (contrast Acts xvii. 23 ἐν ᾧ ἐπεγέγραπτο, below); Phil. ii. 13 ἐνεργῶν ἐν ὑμῖν; Heb. viii. 9 οὐκ ἐνέμειναν ἐν τῇ διαθήκῃ μου (quotation); Col. iii. 16 ἐνοικείτω ἐν ὑμῖν; II Pet. ii. 13 ἐντρυφῶντες ἐν ταῖς ἀπάταις (?) αὐτῶν. **Ἐπί**: Acts xix. 16 ἐφαλόμενος...ἐπ’ αὐτούς; Matt. xxi. 5 ἐπιβεβηκὼς ἐπὶ ὄνον (Zech. ix. 9 LXX ἐπιβ. ἐπὶ ὑποζύγιον); Luke i. 48 ἐπέβλεψεν ἐπὶ τὴν ταπείνωσιν τῆς δούλης αὐτοῦ (cf. I Sam. i. 11 LXX); Luke v. 36 ἐπίβλημα...ἐπιβάλλει ἐπὶ ἱμάτιον; Luke i. 35 πνεῦμα ἅγιον ἐπελεύσεται ἐπὶ σέ (cf. II Cor. xii. 9 ἵνα ἐπισκηνώσῃ ἐπ’ ἐμὲ ἡ δύναμις τοῦ χριστοῦ; but Luke i. 35 has δύναμις ὑψίστου ἐπισκιάσει σοι); Acts iv. 29 ἔπιδε ἐπὶ τὰς ἀπειλὰς αὐτῶν; I Pet. v. 7 πᾶσαν τὴν μέριμναν ὑμῶν ἐπιρίψαντες ἐπ’ αὐτόν. **Κατά**: Jas. iii. 14 μὴ κατακαυχᾶσθε καὶ ψεύδεσθε κατὰ τῆς ἀληθείας. **Παρά**: I Thess. iv. 1 παρελάβετε παρ’ ἡμῶν. **Περί**: Luke xvii. 2 περίκειται περὶ τὸν τράχηλον; Acts xxii. 6 περιαστράψαι...περὶ ἐμέ. **Πρός**: I Pet. ii. 4 πρὸς ὃν προσερχόμενοι; Eph. v. 31 προσκολληθήσεται πρὸς τὴν γυναῖκα αὐτοῦ (so Gen. ii. 24 LXX); Matt. iv. 6 μή ποτε προσκόψῃς πρὸς λίθον τὸν πόδα σου (so Ps. xc. 12 LXX); Mark vii. 25 προσέπεσεν πρὸς τοὺς πόδας αὐτοῦ. **Σύν**: Col. ii. 13 συνεζωοποίησεν ὑμᾶς σὺν αὐτῷ (the only N.T. instance of σύν repeated).

iii. *With a different preposition*: Mark i. 10 ἀναβαίνων ἐκ τοῦ ὕδατος; Matt. iii. 16 ἀνέβη ἀπὸ τοῦ ὕδατος; Heb. xii. 4 ἀντικατέστητε πρὸς τὴν ἁμαρτίαν ἀνταγωνιζόμενοι; Luke xiv. 6 ἀνταποκριθῆναι πρὸς ταῦτα; Acts xxiv. 7 ἐκ τῶν χειρῶν ἡμῶν ἀπήγαγε (*si vera l.*); Mark xvi. 3 τίς ἀποκυλίσει ἡμῖν τὸν λίθον ἐκ τῆς θύρας... (but Luke xxiv. 2 has ἀποκεκυλισμένον ἀπὸ τοῦ μνημείου); Matt. xiii. 49 ἀφοριοῦσιν τοὺς πονηροὺς ἐκ μέσου τῶν δικαίων (but Matt. xxv. 32 has ἀφορίσει αὐτοὺς ἀπ᾽ ἀλλήλων); John i. 6 ἀπεσταλμένος παρὰ θεοῦ; John i. 19 ἀπέστειλαν ...ἐξ Ἱεροσολύμων ἱερεῖς; I Cor. vi. 5 διακρῖναι ἀνὰ μέσον τοῦ ἀδελφοῦ αὐτοῦ; Acts xv. 9 οὐθὲν διέκρινεν μεταξὺ ἡμῶν τε καὶ αὐτῶν; Acts xvi. 40 εἰσῆλθον πρὸς τὴν Λυδίαν; Acts xxi. 18 εἰσῄει ὁ Παῦλος...πρὸς Ἰάκωβον; Luke xii. 11 ὅταν δὲ εἰσφέρωσιν ὑμᾶς ἐπὶ τὰς συναγωγάς; Matt. viii. 23 ἐμβάντι...εἰς τὸ πλοῖον; Luke xii. 5 ἐμβαλεῖν εἰς τὴν γέενναν; Mark xiv. 20 ὁ ἐμβαπτόμενος...εἰς τὸ τρύβλιον (cf. Matt. vi. 26, Rom. xi. 24, Luke x. 36, Matt. xxvi. 67—all ἐν- (ἐμ-)...εἰς); Luke ii. 1 ἐξῆλθεν δόγμα παρὰ Καίσαρος; I Pet. iii. 11 ἐκκλινάτω δὲ ἀπὸ κακοῦ (quotation); Matt. xx. 29 ἐκπορευομένων αὐτῶν ἀπὸ Ἱεριχώ (but ἐκ in Matt. xv. 18); John xv. 26 ὃ παρὰ τοῦ πατρὸς ἐκπορεύεται; Luke xviii. 13 τοὺς ὀφθαλμοὺς ἐπᾶραι εἰς τὸν οὐρανόν; Mark iv. 37 τὰ κύματα ἐπέβαλλεν εἰς τὸ πλοῖον; Acts xx. 18 ἐπέβην εἰς τὴν Ἀσίαν; Acts xvii. 23 ἐν ᾧ ἐπεγέγραπτο; II Cor. x. 14 ὡς μὴ ἐφικνούμενοι εἰς ὑμᾶς; κάθημαι is accompanied by ἐπί (with Acc.) in Matt. ix. 9, Mark ii. 14, Luke v. 27, John xii. 15 (quotation), (with Gen.) in Matt. xxiv. 3, xxvii. 19, (with Dat.) Acts iii. 10; by ἐν in Matt. xi. 16, xxvi. 69, Mark iv. 1, Col. iii. 1; by παρά (with Acc.) in Matt. xiii. 1 (indeed, it seems never to be found with κατά); Acts xx. 15 παρεβάλομεν εἰς Σάμον; Acts i. 25 ἀφ᾽ ἧς παρέβη; Luke vii. 4 οἱ δὲ παραγενόμενοι πρὸς τὸν Ἰησοῦν (cf. *v.* 20); Matt. v. 18 ἰῶτα ἓν...οὐ μὴ παρέλθῃ ἀπὸ τοῦ νόμου; I Cor. xi. 23 παρέλαβον ἀπὸ τοῦ κυρίου; Mark xiv. 36 παρένεγκε τὸ ποτήριον τοῦτο ἀπ᾽ ἐμοῦ; Matt. vi. 27 προσθεῖναι ἐπὶ τὴν ἡλικίαν; Acts i. 26 συνκατεψηφίσθη μετὰ τῶν ἕνδεκα ἀποστόλων; Matt. xvii. 3 συνλαλοῦντες μετ᾽ αὐτοῦ; II Cor. viii. 18 συνεπέμψαμεν δὲ μετ᾽ αὐτοῦ; Matt. xx. 2 συμφωνήσας δὲ μετὰ τῶν ἐργατῶν; II Thess. ii. 4 ὑπεραιρόμενος ἐπὶ πάντα λεγόμενον θεόν (part quotation); Rom. xii. 3 μὴ ὑπερφρονεῖν παρ᾽ ὃ δεῖ φρονεῖν.[1]

---

[1] It is an interesting fact that the force of idiom, apparently inexplicable, sometimes favoured the use of one particular compound verb, while another (more or less synonymous) verb was used when an uncompounded form was required. See, for example, G. D. Kilpatrick in *J.T.S.* xlviii (Jan.–April 1947), 61 ff., on πορεύεσθαι and its compounds.

VIII

THE ADJECTIVE

Precise definition of the adjective would, even if possible, not necessarily be very valuable. Instead, an attempt is here made to illustrate how adjectives resemble other parts of speech and differ from them.

I. ADJECTIVES AND PRONOUNS

i. αὐτός is a pronoun when it means *self* (αὐτὸς ὁ βασιλεύς, *the king himself*, αὐτὸς ἐγώ, *I myself*), but an adjective when it means *same* (ὁ αὐτὸς βασιλεύς, *the same king*).

This immediately points to a broad distinction between adjectives and pronouns: the pronoun stands 'for a noun' to the extent that it is not enclosed within the article-noun unit as a merely subsidiary idea: never could one say ὁ οὗτος βασιλεύς any more than one could say *the this king*.

Yet, even here, the strictness of idiomatic feeling seems to admit of exceptions. What is one to make of Luke x. 7 ἐν αὐτῇ δὲ τῇ οἰκίᾳ, x. 21, xii. 12, xiii. 31 ἐν αὐτῇ τῇ ὥρᾳ, xiii. 1 ἐν αὐτῷ τῷ καιρῷ, xxiv. 13 ἐν αὐτῇ τῇ ἡμέρᾳ, Acts xvi. 18, xxii. 13 αὐτῇ τῇ ὥρᾳ? All, or at least some, of these appear, from their context, to mean *in the same house*, etc., and not *in the house itself*, etc., and D.-B. § 288 call attention to some synoptic parallels where ἐκεῖνος is used instead of αὐτός, in a normal and correct way. It has been argued[1] that this is hardly Semitic (in view, at least, of the Acts instances); but M. Black suspects Aramaic influence.[2] In any case Luke seems to be the only N.T. writer who affects the construction. Cf. 'Pronouns', II. 1. below, p. 122.

ii. πᾶς has a duality of meaning comparable to that illustrated in αὐτός, though not identical with it.

When it means *all* or *every* it is not enclosed within the article-noun unit[3] (indeed, when it means *every* it is used with an anarthrous noun);

---

[1] E.g. by W. F. Howard in M.-H. II, 432.

[2] *An Aramaic Approach to the Gospels*, 72, and again in *J.T.S.* XLIX (July–Oct. 1948), 160 n. 2.

[3] Rom. xvi. 15 is a striking exception: τοὺς σὺν αὐτοῖς πάντας ἁγίους surely = πάντας τοὺς ἁγίους τοὺς σὺν αὐτοῖς.

but when it is a pure adjective, meaning *whole* or *entire*, it may be so enclosed: Acts xx. 18 τὸν πάντα χρόνον, I Tim. i. 16 τὴν ἅπασαν μακροθυμίαν, *his entire patience*. Acts xix. 7, οἱ πάντες ἄνδρες, seems to be the only N.T. instance of this in the plural.[1] For instances from elsewhere see T. F. Middleton, *The Doctrine of the Article* (ed. H. J. Rose, 1841), 102ff. But the fact that πᾶς may be outside the article-noun unit even when it means *entire* shows that the analogy with αὐτός is not exact: Matt. xxi. 10 πᾶσα ἡ πόλις.[2]

Specially problematic for the exegete are the instances of πᾶς with an anarthrous noun: does it invariably mean *every*, or can it mean *the whole, the entire?* It used to be claimed that it meant *every* and not *the whole*: Eph. iii. 15 πᾶσα πατριά was not to be translated (with A.V.) *the whole family*, but (with R.V.) *every family* (raising interesting speculations as to angelic or demonic *families* or *tribes* in 'heaven'). Lightfoot, on Ignatius *Eph.* XII ἐν πάσῃ ἐπιστολῇ, points out that Cicero's ambiguous *omne corpus* might stand for πᾶν τὸ σῶμα or πᾶν σῶμα, *the whole body* or *every body*—in other words, that Greek does not tolerate the ambiguity; and he thinks that in the other famous instance from Ephesians, namely ii. 21, πᾶσα οἰκοδομή does not mean *the whole building* but *every building*, adducing συνοικοδομεῖσθε to show that many οἰκοδομαί are required to make up one temple. In support of this commentators contrast such phrases as πᾶν τὸ σῶμα, in Ephesians itself (iv. 16, cf. Col. ii. 19), Matt. viii. 32 πᾶσα ἡ ἀγέλη, viii. 34 πᾶσα ἡ πόλις, xiii. 2, Mark iv. 1, πᾶς ὁ ὄχλος, Luke i. 10 πᾶν τὸ πλῆθος, vi. 19 πᾶς ὁ ὄχλος, xxi. 35 πάσης τῆς γῆς, Acts vi. 5 παντὸς τοῦ πλήθους, xiii. 44 πᾶσα ἡ πόλις, Rom. viii. 22 πᾶσα ἡ κτίσις. Moreover it is said that Matt. ii. 3, πᾶσα Ἱεροσόλυμα, Rom. xi. 26, πᾶς Ἰσραήλ, are not clear exceptions, since a proper name is unambiguous even without the article. I suppose that phrases like διὰ πάσης προσευχῆς καὶ δεήσεως and ἐν πάσῃ προσκαρτερήσει καὶ δεήσει (Eph. vi. 18) fit into the above canon as meaning, strictly, *with every possible prayer*, etc.

Yet one hesitates to accept this ruling, in view of the following—some of which may be explicable on the basis of the principles enunciated, but surely not all: Matt. iii. 15 πληρῶσαι πᾶσαν δικαιοσύνην, xxviii. 18 πᾶσα ἐξουσία, Acts i. 21 ἐν παντὶ χρόνῳ (where the context

---

[1] For instances from elsewhere, see T. F. Middleton, *The Doctrine of the Article*, 102.

[2] And, curiously enough, ὅλος, *whole, entire*, is never found in the N.T. between article and noun.

strongly suggests *during the whole time*, not *on every occasion*), ii. 36 πᾶς οἶκος Ἰσραήλ (though cf. πᾶς Ἰσραήλ above), vii. 22 πάσῃ σοφίᾳ Αἰγυπτίων, xvii. 26 παντὸς προσώπου τῆς γῆς, II Tim. iii. 16 πᾶσα γραφὴ θεόπνευστος (which is most unlikely to mean *every inspired scripture*, and much more probably means *the whole of scripture [is] inspired*),† Heb. ix. 19 πάσης ἐντολῆς. H. W. Moule notes, on Eph. iii. 15 πᾶσα πατριά: 'if the context requires "the *whole* family", this must be a Hebraism, as in Acts xvii. 26 (παντὸς προσώπου).... Cf. πᾶσαν σάρκα, Acts ii. 17; πᾶς οἶκος Ἰ., *ibid.* 36; πᾶσα οἰκοδομή, Eph. ii. 21.'† He also notes: 'כל המשפחה in Amos iii. 1 is πάσης φυλῆς in LXX, in spite of ה.' Similarly J. Y. Campbell, writing on 'ἐκκλησία',[1] notes κατὰ πρόσωπον πάσης ἐκκλησίας κυρίου in I Chron. xxviii. 8 as 'no doubt intended to mean, "in the sight of the whole (*not*, of every) assembly of the Lord"'. See Rob. 772 for a discussion.

iii. πολύς presents features comparable to the ones just discussed: it is sometimes virtually a pronoun—πολλοὶ ἐξ αὐτῶν, οἱ πολλοί, *the majority* or *the generality*—while at times it is a pure adjective—Luke vii. 47 αἱ ἁμαρτίαι αὐτῆς αἱ πολλαί.

In Matt. xi. 20 αἱ πλεῖσται δυνάμεις αὐτοῦ should, strictly, mean *his* very great *miracles* (the intensifying superlative, or 'elative' superlative, *Proleg.* 78, etc.), but the context makes it probable that the meaning is *the majority of his miracles*—as though it were αἱ πλεῖσται τῶν δυνάμεων αὐτοῦ, with πλεῖσται in a pronominal position.

In Acts xxvii. 12 the comparative is used pronominally, οἱ πλείονες, *the majority*.

II. ADJECTIVES AND PARTICIPLES

Any participle can act as an adjective, but few if any adjectives are capable of exerting all the verbal force which a participle may exert: II Tim. ii. 6, τὸν κοπιῶντα γεωργόν, perhaps means little more than *the industrious farmer*; but τὸν γεωργὸν κοπιῶντα would have meant *the farmer as he worked* (or *works*)—a sense which a mere adjective could not have conveyed (cf. *working men* and *men at work*). And further, few adjectives, if any, are strongly verbal enough to govern a direct Accusative.

Even a *passive* adjective like κλητός, *called*, is probably not exactly interchangeable with its corresponding Passive Participle, κεκλημένος. Commenting on I Cor. i. 2, κλητοῖς ἁγίοις, σὺν πᾶσιν τοῖς ἐπικαλουμένοις

[1] In *J.T.S.* XLIX (July–Oct. 1948), 134–5.

τὸ ὄνομα τοῦ κυρίου..., J. B. Lightfoot wrote: 'This clause [σὺν κ.τ.λ.] cannot be attached to κλητοῖς in the sense of "saints called together with all that invoke", etc. For though this construction would obviate considerable difficulty in interpreting what follows, it is grammatically harsh, if not untenable, and would require a participle for κλητοῖς, or at all events a different order of words.'[1] The fact is, I think, that κλητός means *a called [person]*, and is simply too noun-like to stand in precisely the same place as a participle.

NOTE. On the relation of adjective to article, see further under 'The Definite Article', pp. 106 ff.

III. ADJECTIVES AS NOUNS

This usage is easy enough to understand whenever a noun can be mentally supplied: e.g. χριστός, *an Anointed* Person, ἀγαθός, δίκαιος, μαλακός. Ἡ οἰκουμένη, an adjectival participle, probably means *the inhabited* world (supply γῆ); with ἡ περίχωρος supply perhaps γῆ or χώρα; so with ἡ ἔρημος, ἡ ὀρεινή (Luke i. 39, 65). With our sartorial idioms *wearing shorts, dressed in white, wearing flannels,* compare δύο ἀγγέλους ἐν λευκοῖς (John xx. 12), ἄνθρωπον ἐν μαλακοῖς ἠμφιεσμένον (Matt. xi. 8).

But on occasion there seems to be no implied noun, or at least it is hard to conceive of one: II Cor. viii. 8 τὸ γνήσιον; I Pet. i. 7, Jas. i. 3 τὸ δοκίμειον,† *test* or *tested* (i.e. *genuine*) *part* (see Deissmann, *B.S.* (E.T.) 259ff.); Rom. ix. 22 τὸ δυνατὸν αὐτοῦ; Phil. iv. 5 τὸ ἐπιεικές; I Cor. vii. 35 τὸ εὔσχημον καὶ εὐπάρεδρον; θεμέλιον (which 'is an adjective (*sc.* λίθον) but becomes a neuter substantive in late Greek'—Robertson and Plummer, *I.C.C.,* on I Cor. iii. 10); τὸ μαρτύριον (frequently); Rom. i. 15 τὸ πρόθυμον; I Cor. vii. 5 ἐκ συμφώνου; τὸ σωτήριον (Luke ii. 30, iii. 6, Acts xxviii. 28, Eph. vi. 17—all in O.T. references). In some of these instances it is not obvious why the corresponding noun (μαρτυρία, σωτηρία, etc.) is not used. Conversely, the participial term τὸ συνειδός is not found in the N.T., whereas the noun συνείδησις is.

The narrowness of the territory dividing adjectives from nouns is illustrated by δοῦλος which is commonly a normal noun like λόγος or any other, but which appears also in the feminine, δούλη (Luke

[1] *Notes on Epistles of St Paul,* 145.

i. 38, 48, Acts ii. 18; cf. Joel iii. 2 (Heb. ii. 29)), and in the neuter plural, Rom. vi. 19 παρεστήσατε τὰ μέλη ὑμῶν δοῦλα τῇ ἀκαθαρσίᾳ. Cf. ὅμηρα, *hostages* or *pledges*, neuter plural, in I Macc. xiii. 16 and in Classical Greek. Cf. νεκρός.

IV. COMPOUND ADJECTIVES

This is not the place to attempt a systematic analysis of these, but it is worth while to note the variety of relationships between the component parts. E.g.:

α-'privative' and noun—ἄπειρος, etc.

Noun governed by verb—ἀνθρωποκτόνος, etc.

αὐτός loosely connected with a verb or noun—αὐθαίρετος, αὐτόπτης, etc.

Verbal adjective governed by noun—θεοδίδακτος, etc.

Adjective with noun as though in Dative—ἰσάγγελος.

Adjective as though agreeing with noun—ἰσόψυχος.

Quasi-adverb, or adverb, with adjective or noun—εὔχρηστος, δυσβάστακτος, ὁμότεχνος, παντελής, πολυποίκιλος.

Many more varieties might be added.

V. COMPARATIVE AND SUPERLATIVE DEGREES

With regard to the Comparative and Superlative degrees, it is well known that N.T. Greek[1] shows a tendency to push the degrees down, as it were: positive tends to do duty for comparative, and comparative for superlative:[2] Luke v. 39, ὁ παλαιὸς χρηστός ἐστιν, should probably be translated *the old is* better. Compare, perhaps, John ii. 10 πᾶς ἄνθρωπος πρῶτον τὸν καλὸν οἶνον τίθησιν, καὶ ὅταν μεθυσθῶσιν τὸν ἐλάσσω· σὺ τετήρηκας τὸν καλὸν οἶνον ἕως ἄρτι—perhaps best in each case.

So, in Mark ix. 34, διελέχθησαν ἐν τῇ ὁδῷ τίς μείζων probably means ...*who was* greatest, though it might conceivably mean that they discussed their *relative* greatness—*who was* greater [*than another*]. Certainly Matt. xxii. 36 ποία ἐντολὴ μεγάλη (cf. Mark xii. 28 πρώτη

---

[1] In view of M.-H. II, 442, which claims it as a Semitic feature, we will not say κοινή as such.

[2] Cf. Richard Edwardes:

> When May is gone, of all the year
> The pleasant time is past,

which looks like positive for superlative.

πάντων) is significant (M.-H. ii, 442). Cf. Luke vii. 28 ὁ δὲ μικρότερος ἐν τῇ βασιλείᾳ τοῦ θεοῦ μείζων αὐτοῦ ἐστιν, where it looks as though the first comparative stands for a superlative, though the second is a genuine comparative. In the same chapter, *vv.* 42, 43, πλεῖον and τὸ πλεῖον are strictly correct—referring to *two* persons.

In I Cor. xiv. 27 we have a genuine superlative in δύο ἤ τὸ πλεῖστον τρεῖς; though often superlatives are merely used to intensify ('elative' use—*Proleg.* 78): so in Matt. xxi. 8, Mark iv. 1 (*si vera l.*) πλεῖστος is used of a crowd, ὄχλος, and means *huge*. On the other hand, in Matt. xi. 20 (see above, i. iii. p. 95) αἱ πλεῖσται δυνάμεις αὐτοῦ might be *the greater number* (*most*) *of his miracles*—a genuine superlative, despite the comparative in its idiomatic English counterpart. See also on οἱ πολλοί and οἱ πλείονες (above, *ibid.*).

The comparison is expressed by ἤ[1] or by the Genitive: Luke xi. 22 ἰσχυρότερος αὐτοῦ; vii. 28 μείζων ἐν γεννητοῖς γυναικῶν 'Ιωάνου οὐδείς ἐστιν; Matt. xi. 9 περισσότερον προφήτου; Matt. x. 15 ἀνεκτότερον ἔσται γῇ Σοδόμων...ἤ τῇ πόλει ἐκείνῃ; Matt. xix. 24 εὐκοπώτερόν ἐστιν κάμηλον...εἰσελθεῖν ἤ πλούσιον...; I Cor. i. 25 τὸ μωρὸν τοῦ θεοῦ σοφώτερον τῶν ἀνθρώπων ἐστίν...(where τῶν ἀνθρώπων, it is to be noted, is probably used loosely for τῆς σοφίας τῶν ἀνθρώπων—the abbreviation known technically as *comparatio compendiaria*).

Compound and redundant comparatives occur: Eph. iii. 8 ἐλαχιστότερος, well rendered in A.V. *less than the least*; Phil. i. 23 πολλῷ... μᾶλλον κρεῖσσον, lit. *much more better*; cf. vulgar English such as *more preferable*, and early English in which, at certain periods, even first-rate authors affected anomalies such as *most loveliest*. Note also the current usage *the lesser* (*of two evils*, etc.).

There are words, further, whose *sense* implies a comparison, even when they are in the positive: e.g. πρῶτος (cf. above under 'Some Observations on the Cases', 5. iv. (*b*)). It is possible that we may detect the converse when τὸ πρότερον means (if it does) *originally* rather than *formerly*. See commentators on Gal. iv. 13.

[1] Note, however, that ἤ is sometimes omitted without a Genitive of Comparison being introduced: for examples, see Rob. 666. See also notes under 'Some Observations on the Cases, Nom. and Gen.', above, pp. 31, 42.

IX

PARTICIPLES

The ruling consideration in interpreting participles is that they express something which is dependent on the main verb, or a pendant to it; and one is sometimes given a clue to the interpretation of a participle not by its own tense but by the main verb, or the context in general.

1. Thus, broadly speaking, following the 'linear'-'punctiliar' terms already adopted, one may say that the Present Participle represents 'linear' action and the Aorist represents 'punctiliar'.[1] But the time of these actions will be determined by the main verb. Thus, in John viii. 4, ἐπαυτοφώρῳ μοιχευομένη, *in the very act of committing adultery*, is connected with an Aorist indicative, κατελήφθη, *she was caught*; but a present or a future indicative would be equally easily attachable to the same participial phrase, according to the requirements of sense. Or again, in Luke xxii. 51, ἀψάμενος τοῦ ὠτίου, *by touching his ear*, is connected with an Aorist indicative, ἰάσατο αὐτόν, *he healed him*; but it would be equally possible (according to requirement) to say *he is healing him by a touch on the ear* (Pres. Indic., Aor. Part.) or *he will heal him by a touch on the ear* (Fut. Indic., Aor. Part.).

But it still remains to ask how the actions denoted by the participle are related in time-sequence to the main verb: granted that the main verb determines the time of the action as a whole, is it possible to distinguish, within that whole, a relative sequence of actions?

When the context positively demands a decision as to the sequence of the actions referred to in the participle and the main verb respectively, it often turns out that a Present Participle alludes to an action with which the action of the main verb coincides (at least in part), while an Aorist Participle refers to action previous to what is referred to in the main verb. Consequently, the 'schoolboy' translation of an Aorist Participle by *having done so-and-so*, though entirely false to the essential meaning of an Aorist as such, turns out to be a fair approximation to the sense in its context more often than it deserves to.

---

[1] However, Acts i. 21 presents a striking example of an *Aorist* Participle where one would have expected a durative ('linear') *Present*: τῶν συνελθόντων ἡμῖν ἀνδρῶν ἐν παντὶ χρόνῳ ᾧ... (which, indeed, is followed by the scarcely less striking Aorist indicatives, εἰσῆλθεν καὶ ἐξῆλθεν. Contrast Acts ix. 28).†

It 'works', in a rough-and-ready way, for a great many places where the time-sequence comes into account. For instance, one fears that in Acts xxiii. 27 Lysias is represented as deliberately taking credit for having rescued Paul *because* he had discovered that he was a Roman citizen: ...ἐξειλάμην, μαθὼν ὅτι ʽΡωμαῖός ἐστιν represents a diplomatic adjustment of the facts (see Acts xxi) which Lysias is all too likely to have made; and we are over-refining if we insist that the Aorist Participle is timeless in relation to the main verb, and that the sentence may equally well have meant *I rescued him and [subsequently] discovered that he was a Roman citizen.*

This brings us at once to the very few and extraordinarily problematic exceptions to this principle:

Acts xxv. 13, if the Aorist Participle is the right reading, is the most prominent exception: κατήντησαν εἰς Καισαρίαν ἀσπασάμενοι τὸν Φῆστον can, in the context, only mean *they went down...and greeted Festus*, but it is an abnormal way of saying so. καταντήσαντες... ἠσπάσαντο would be normal. The *v.l.* ἀσπασόμενοι (Fut. Part.) would make sense, *they went down...to greet*, but looks like a correction.†

So in Acts xvi. 6, Ramsay thinks that the geographical details require κωλυθέντες to be treated as referring to an event *after* the διῆλθον: *they went through the Phrygian and Galatian region and were [then] prevented....* But K. Lake (in *Beg.* v, 230) interprets the topography so as to make it *they went through...because they had been prevented...*, which removes this Aorist Participle from among the exceptions, and is certainly the natural translation of the Greek.

Are there other exceptions in the N.T.? I know of none.[1] This, if the facts have been fairly stated, suggests that the 'schoolboy' rule is even safer for N.T. Greek than for the Classical writers.[2]

Returning to the Present Participle and its relation to the main verb, an interesting series of examples may be drawn up to show that,

---

[1] Heb. ix. 12 εἰσῆλθεν ἐφάπαξ εἰς τὰ ἅγια, αἰωνίαν λύτρωσιν εὑράμενος, seems to me to yield tolerable sense if the action referred to in the participle is viewed as preceding that of the main verb. Acts xii. 25 would be an exception, if εἰς and not ἐξ were demonstrably the right reading.†

[2] For 'timeless' Aorists in Homer, Pindar, etc. (particularly ὦρνυτ' ἄρ' ἐξ εὐνῆφιν (or εὐνῆθεν ἀνίστατο), εἵματα ἑσσάμενος, Hom. β 2, δ 307, ν 124, which, on the 'schoolboy' interpretation, means that the warrior did not get up until after he had dressed), see Arthur Platt's entertaining article, 'Some Homeric Aorist Participles', in *J. Philol.* xxxv (1919), 128 ff. 'We grammarians', he writes, 'are always trying to bind the free growth of language in a strait waistcoat of necessity, but language laughs and eludes us' (129).

if the Present Participle usually alludes to an action with which the action of the main verb coincides (at least in part), there are exceptions both fore and aft:

i. Of what was taking place *before* what is referred to in the main verb: Luke ii. 42, 43,[1] ἀναβαινόντων αὐτῶν...ὑπέμεινεν (though possibly the ἀναβαινόντων refers to the *whole occasion*, rather than to the journey up to the feast as distinct from the return journey).†

Luke xxiii. 49 γυναῖκες αἱ συνακολουθοῦσαι αὐτῷ ἀπὸ τῆς Γαλιλαίας[2] (the setting is the Crucifixion. Contrast *v.* 55, referring to the same women, αἵτινες ἦσαν συνεληλυθυῖαι...; or Acts xiii. 31, referring to similar conditions with an Aorist Participle, συναναβᾶσιν αὐτῷ).

John v. 5 τριάκοντα καὶ ὀκτὼ ἔτη ἔχων ἐν τῇ ἀσθενείᾳ αὐτοῦ.

John ix. 25 τυφλὸς ὢν ἄρτι βλέπω (this and the next but one example may be attributable partly to the paucity of participles of the verb *to be*. Also, one must reckon, in both these, with the temporal idiom which, even when an indicative is used, would say τριάκοντα καὶ ὀκτὼ ἔτη ἔχω; cf. the corresponding idiom in French).

Acts xiv. 21[1] εὐαγγελιζόμενοί τε τὴν πόλιν...ὑπέστρεψαν.

Acts xxiv. 10 ἐκ πολλῶν ἐτῶν ὄντα σε κριτήν....

Acts xxvii. 7[1] ἐν ἱκαναῖς δὲ ἡμέραις βραδυπλοοῦντες...ὑπεπλεύσαμεν... (though here, again—cf. Luke ii. 42 above—βραδυπλοοῦντες may cover the whole episode: *in the course of*... rather than *after*...).

Acts xxviii. 6[1] ἐπὶ πολὺ δὲ αὐτῶν προσδοκώντων καὶ θεωρούντων μηδὲν ἄτοπον εἰς αὐτὸν γινόμενον, μεταβαλόμενοι ἔλεγον αὐτὸν εναιῖ θεόν.

Heb. x. 8, 9 ἀνώτερον λέγων...τότε εἴρηκεν.

II John 7 οἱ μὴ ὁμολογοῦντες Ἰησοῦν χριστὸν ἐρχόμενον ἐν σαρκί (K. and S. Lake[3] construe ἐρχόμενον in a future sense; but it appears from the context that it is past, *as having come*, equivalent, clearly, to the ἐληλυθότα of I John iv. 2; and cf. Polycarp, *Ep. ad Phil.* VII ὃς ἂν μὴ ὁμολογῇ Ἰησοῦν χριστὸν ἐν σαρκὶ ἐληλυθέναι...).†

ii. Of what was taking place *after* what is referred to by the main verb: Luke xxii. 66, 67 ἀπήγαγον αὐτὸν εἰς τὸ συνέδριον αὐτῶν, λέγοντες....

---

[1] N.B. In Luke ii. 42, Acts xiv. 21, xxvii. 7, xxviii. 6 the Pres. Part. is followed by an Aor. Part. before the main verb is introduced.

[2] A friend suggests to me, however, that γυναῖκες αἱ συνακολουθοῦσαι κ.τ.λ. may possibly be a general description: *women from Galilee who were in his entourage.*

[3] *An Introduction to the N.T.*, 170.

Acts xix. 9 ἀφώρισεν τοὺς μαθητάς, καθ' ἡμέραν διαλεγόμενος...
(i.e. *he separated...and* then *used to discourse...*).

Apart from such exceptions, the general working rule holds good:
Acts v. 4 οὐχὶ μένον σοὶ ἔμενεν; *while it remained, did it not remain yours?*
Mark i. 10 καὶ εὐθὺς ἀναβαίνων ἐκ τοῦ ὕδατος εἶδεν σχιζομένους τοὺς
οὐρανούς..., ...*as he came up..., he saw the sky parting...*†

2. Sometimes two participles are used in one sentence with reference
to two successive actions without a connecting καί: Luke iv. 20
καὶ πτύξας τὸ βιβλίον ἀποδοὺς τῷ ὑπηρέτῃ ἐκάθισεν, *he rolled up the
book and gave it back...and sat down.* On the whole, it is probably
true to say that the N.T. writers prefer the form with καί, e.g. Acts
xiv. 27 παραγενόμενοι δὲ καὶ συναγαγόντες τὴν ἐκκλησίαν, ἀνήγγελλον
ὅσα....

3. It is easy to see how the participle can also (as often in English)
express some relation to the main verb other than a time-relation.
Thus, in English one may say *Being no coward, I fight* (consecutive);
reduced to despair, he maintained his integrity (concessive = *though
reduced...*); *they came begging* (all but final = *to beg*). So in N.T.
Greek:

Concessive:† I Cor. ix. 19 ἐλεύθερος γὰρ ὢν ἐκ πάντων πᾶσιν ἐμαυτὸν
    ἐδούλωσα... (cf. *v.* 21 μὴ ὢν ἄνομος θεοῦ...);
    II Cor. x. 3 ἐν σαρκὶ...περιπατοῦντες...;
    Heb. v. 8 καίπερ ὢν υἱός;
    Philem. 8 πολλὴν...παρρησίαν ἔχων.

Note that *v.* 9 of the same Epistle presents an ambiguity: is it concessive or causal? Does τοιοῦτος ὢν ὡς Παῦλος πρεσβύτης... mean
though I am none other than... or *because I am...?* In other words
is the second παρακαλῶ still equivalent to *I only intreat* [*though I might
command*] (as in *v.* 8), or is it *I intreat* [*with all the more force because
I am*] *none other than...?*

The most notorious instance of the same ambiguity, as between
concessive and causal, is, of course, Gal. ii. 3 Ἕλλην ὢν: is it *although*
or *because he was a Greek?* (See the many discussions *in loc.*)

Causal: Luke x. 29 θέλων δικαιῶσαι ἑαυτόν, *because he wished...;*
    Acts xix. 36 ἀναντιρρήτων...ὄντων τούτων..., *as these
    things cannot be denied;*
    Acts xxiii. 18 ἔχοντά τι λαλῆσαί σοι (cf. *v.* 17), *for he has
    something to say to you;*

II Cor. xii. 16 ὑπάρχων πανοῦργος, *villain as I was*...;

I Thess. v. 8 ἡμεῖς δὲ ἡμέρας ὄντες..., *but we, since we belong to the day*....

Final: Acts viii. 27 ἐληλύθει προσκυνήσων, *he had come to worship* (cf. Acts xxii. 5, xxiv. 11, 17).

It is not easy to find a *Present* Participle certainly used in this sense, though Luke x. 25, ἀνέστη ἐκπειράζων αὐτόν, might possibly be claimed as an example (perhaps *stood up to test him*).†

Certainly in other than 'final' senses, the Present Participle sometimes stands for a future sense (just as does the Present Indicative): ὁ ἐρχόμενος, *the one who is to come* (or, in Rev. i. 4, perhaps *who is to exist for the time to come*); τὸ ἐκχυννόμενον, Mark xiv. 24 (but this latter, being in a sacramental setting in any case, may be a literal present).

4. Note that the definite article opens the door to a range of participial expressions from which Latin is debarred and which English will often prefer to turn otherwise, e.g. by the use of a relative clause: Acts xvii. 17 τοὺς παρατυγχάνοντας, *those who happened to be there* (or perhaps *those who, from time to time, came*); Rom. ii. 1 τὰ γὰρ αὐτὰ πράσσεις ὁ κρίνων, *for you who judge do the same yourself*; Matt. xvii. 27 τὸν ἀναβάντα πρῶτον ἰχθύν, *the first fish to rise*; Luke x. 37 ὁ ποιήσας τὸ ἔλεος, *the one who showed the mercy*; Luke xv. 12 τὸ ἐπιβάλλον μέρος τῆς οὐσίας, *the share of the property which falls to me*; Gal. iii. 21 νόμος ὁ δυνάμενος ζωοποιῆσαι, *a law such as could make alive*; Rom. viii. 34 τίς ὁ κατακρινῶν; *who is there to condemn* [*us*]? Matt. v. 32 πᾶς ὁ ἀπολύων τὴν γυναῖκα αὐτοῦ, *anyone who divorces his wife* (cf. *v.* 19 where the relative is used—ὃς ἐάν...λύσῃ); Rom. iii. 5 μὴ ἄδικος ὁ θεὸς ὁ ἐπιφέρων τὴν ὀργήν; *is God unjust when he brings the wrath to bear?*

In Acts iv. 12, οὐδὲ γὰρ ὄνομά ἐστιν ἕτερον...τὸ δεδομένον is a very odd usage, and some Semitic background has not unreasonably been suspected (possibly a misunderstanding of a Semitic participle). Incidentally, is Ps. cxv. 16 (LXX cxiii. 24) significant? If the participle must be translated as it stands, it presumably means *such as is given* (cf. Gal. iii. 21 above). See 'The Definite Article', 1. (p. 107 n. 1 below).

For the special problems of ἡ οὖσα and οἱ ὄντες in Acts v. 17, xxviii. 17, etc., see *Beg.* on Acts v. 17.

Sometimes the neuter participle with the article is virtually a noun (especially an abstract noun): τὸ συμφέρον, *your good, your welfare*, τὰ διαφέροντα (perhaps *different 'values'* or *the things which are superior, of value*), τὸ κατέχον, *the controlling* (or *restraining*) *factor*, τὸ ὑπερέχον, *the superiority*. Cf. the Stoic τὸ συνειδός, *conscience*, for which St Paul uses the abstract noun συνείδησις.

Note. As a rule the strict distinction may be maintained between the participle with the article and the participle without, in such contrasts as:

ὁ ὄχλος ὁ συνελθών, *the crowd which had assembled*,
and ὁ ὄχλος συνελθών..., *the crowd, when it had assembled....*

Yet, a passage like John xv. 2 makes one hesitate to dogmatize: is there really a distinction in this respect between πᾶν κλῆμα ἐν ἐμοὶ μὴ φέρον καρπόν and πᾶν τὸ καρπὸν φέρον? It is just conceivable that the first means *any branch*, if *it does not bear*, rather than *which does not bear*, while the second certainly means *which bears*; but it is a questionable distinction.[1]

A further *nuance* of meaning is discernible when a participle becomes virtually an adjective by being placed between the article and the noun. Thus τὸν κοπιῶντα γεωργόν, II Tim. ii. 6, practically means *the hard-working farmer*; whereas τὸν γεωργὸν κοπιῶντα would have meant (see above) *the farmer as he works* (or *worked*), and τὸν γεωργὸν τὸν κοπιῶντα would have meant *the farmer who works* (or *worked*).†
An anarthrous phrase, κοπιῶντα γεωργόν, would be ambiguous; it could mean *a farmer as he worked, a farmer who was working, a hard-working farmer* (or equivalents in other tenses, according to context). In other words, when noun and participle are both anarthrous, a participle may be adjectival or properly participial, according to context; e.g. ἀποθνήσκοντες ἄνθρωποι might mean *dying men*, or it might (as the context in Heb. vii. 8 clearly demands) be virtually adjectival and mean *mortal men, men who are to die*. In the same verse, μαρτυρούμενος ὅτι ζῇ is a bold and rather unusual way of saying (ἄνθρωπός τις) περὶ οὗ μαρτυρεῖται ὅτι ζῇ, *one of whom witness is*

---

[1] In John xiv. 10, however, the A.V. and R.V. translations are no doubt intended to represent different *texts* (not different *interpretations* of the same text): the A.V., *the Father that dwelleth in me, he doeth the works*, is ὁ δὲ πατὴρ ὁ ἐν ἐμοὶ μένων, αὐτὸς ποιεῖ...; the R.V., *the Father abiding in me doeth his works* is ὁ δὲ πατὴρ ἐν ἐμοὶ μένων ποιεῖ... (and the difference is made by the omission of the article, irrespective of the αὐτός).

borne that he is alive. Cf. Acts xix. 24, where Δημήτριος γάρ τις ὀνόματι, ἀργυροκόπος, ποιῶν ναοὺς ἀργυροῦς ᾿Αρτέμιδος παρείχετο τοῖς τεχνίταις οὐκ ὀλίγην ἐργασίαν might mean *D.,...a silversmith, a maker...brought the craftsmen no little trade,* or *D.,...a silversmith, brought the craftsmen no little trade by making....* The latter seems to be the more probable.

5. For the use of subordinated participles, instead of a series of short separate sentences with main verbs, as one mark of a more Greek than Semitic style, see under 'Semitisms', pp. 172 f., below; and for the use of participles instead of finite verbs or imperatives, see under 'Semitisms', pp. 179 f., below. Note also the 'hanging nominatives' (*nominativi pendentes*) in Eph. iii. 17, iv. 2, Col. ii. 2, iii. 16, which may also be partly due to Semitic influence.

6. The negative with a participle is usually μή, no matter how factual or confident the denial may be: Acts ix. 9 καὶ ἦν ἡμέρας τρεῖς μὴ βλέπων; Rom. iv. 19 μὴ ἀσθενήσας τῇ πίστει, *with no weakness in his faith,* etc. But οὐ is also used[1] (about twenty times in the N.T.).[2] See the series in II Cor. iv. 8, 9. It is difficult to account for the variations, but in some instances where οὐ is found, it seems to coalesce very closely with the participle, almost, it has been said, as though it were an *alpha privative*: John x. 12, ὁ μισθωτὸς καὶ οὐκ ὢν ποιμήν (contrast *v.* 1 ὁ μὴ εἰσερχόμενος), is tentatively explained by Abbott[3] as due either to μισθωτὸς-καὶ-οὐ-ποιμήν coalescing (but, if so, why is ὢν thus intruded?) or to οὐ ποιμήν being a sort of title, like τὴν οὐκ ἠγαπημένην in Rom. ix. 25 (and the Hosea passage behind it), but again the intrusion of the ὢν is strange. Note also Acts xix. 11 δυνάμεις τε οὐ τὰς τυχούσας (cf. xxviii. 2), *the miracles he worked were no ordinary ones.* Cf. Jas. i. 23 and iii. 2 under 'Conditional Clauses', p. 149, below. What of I Cor. ii. 1 ἦλθον οὐ καθ᾽ ὑπεροχὴν λόγου ἢ σοφίας καταγ- γέλλων...? Here the distance of the negative from the participle would make μή sound strange.† But Matt. xxii. 11 is a striking instance.

---

[1] Note the references to this in *Beg.* II, 40.

[2] W. D. Chamberlain, *An Exegetical Grammar of the New Testament* (Macmillan, 1941), 159.

[3] E. A. Abbott, *Johannine Grammar* (A. and C. Black, 1906), § [2704], 545, 546.

X

THE DEFINITE ARTICLE

The definite article, not found in Latin, provides, in Greek, a wide range of flexibility, not unattended, however, with ambiguities. An attempt is made here to state broad, general principles, and also to adduce some of the more interesting exceptions and ambiguities.

1. Not only does the article (i) do duty in simple definitions—βασιλεύς, a *king*, but ὁ βασιλεύς, the (*particular*) *king* (*in question*)—but (ii) it also offers (when used before a participle or adjective) a neat way of expressing what would otherwise have to be expressed by a relative clause: instead of ὃς ἔρχεται one may say ὁ ἐρχόμενος;[1] for ὃ περισσεύει one may say τὸ περισσεῦον. In Acts xiii. 9 we have Σαῦλος δέ, ὁ καὶ Παῦλος, where *who is also Paul* is expressed by the article conjoined with the name, without even a participle like ὤν or λεγόμενος. As an illustration of how the article with participle can be interchanged with a relative clause, take Rom. ii. 21–3 ὁ οὖν διδάσκων ἕτερον... ὁ κηρύσσων...ὁ λέγων...ὁ βδελυσσόμενος, followed by the relative clause ὃς ἐν νόμῳ καυχᾶσαι (which is clearly an exact parallel to the preceding clauses); or Matt. vii. 24, 26 πᾶς οὖν ὅστις ἀκούει...πᾶς ὁ ἀκούων. Again (iii) the article also serves to turn into virtual nouns words and phrases which are not nouns (Rad. 112): τὸ περισσόν (cf. ὁ περισσεύει and τὸ περισσεῦον above); ὁ πλησίον (*one's neighbour*—ὃς πλησίον ἐστίν); Acts xiii. 13 οἱ περὶ Παῦλον (a classical Greek expression—*Paul and his party*); Rom. xvi. 11 τοὺς ἐκ τῶν Ναρκίσσου (a double use); Matt. xxiii. 26 τὸ ἐντός (exactly like *the inside*); Luke xxiv. 27 τὰ περὶ ἑαυτοῦ, cf. Acts xviii. 25 τὰ περὶ τοῦ Ἰησοῦ; Luke xiv. 32 τὰ πρὸς εἰρήνην.

Note that a key to many uses of the article is the recognition that it often puts a word in apposition with another. Thus: ὁ βασιλεὺς

---

[1] A very idiomatic use of this sort is Col. ii. 8 (quoted by Rad. 117 as entirely in accord with Hellenistic idiom) βλέπετε μή τις ὑμᾶς ἔσται ὁ συλαγωγῶν, which one might render *Beware that there is nobody to despoil you* (or *to make spoil of you?*); cf. Gal. iii. 21 εἰ γὰρ ἐδόθη νόμος ὁ δυνάμενος ζωοποιῆσαι (...*a law which could make alive*). Rather curious is Gal. i. 7 εἰ μή τινές εἰσιν οἱ ταράσσοντες ὑμᾶς, where what is really required seems to be οἳ ταράσσουσιν (see Burton, *I.C.C. in loc.*, and also *M.T.* § 424). Perhaps Acts iv. 12 should here be noted (see 'Participles' 4, above, p. 103).

ἐρχόμενος (the participle *not* preceded by the article) means *the king as he comes* (or *came*); but ὁ βασιλεὺς ὁ ἐρχόμενος means *the king—* (*namely*) *the coming* (*one*), *the king who is coming*. The article, by changing the use of the participle from a verbal or adjectival to a substantival one, alters the meaning of the phrase.[1] Accordingly, it is possible without ambiguity to leave out the verb *to be* in a sentence such as ὁ βασιλεὺς μέγας, *the king* (*is*) *great*, because, strictly speaking, *the great king* must be ὁ βασιλεὺς ὁ μέγας.

Notes. (*a*) This canon is of the greatest importance when one is using pronouns—especially αὐτός which does duty also as an adjective: Gal. vi. 13 οὐδὲ γὰρ οἱ περιτεμνόμενοι αὐτοὶ νόμον φυλάσσουσιν means *for not even the very ones who get circumcised keep the law*, whereas, if the article had been omitted, the sense would have been *for not even* when they *get circumcised do they keep the law themselves*.

(*b*) The fact that the article followed by δέ or μέν or μὲν οὖν can be used as a personal pronoun (see below, 'Pronouns', II. 4. iv., p. 123) gives rise to an occasional ambiguity when a participle comes into the picture. Thus, in Acts ii. 41, does οἱ μὲν οὖν ἀποδεξάμενοι τὸν λόγον αὐτοῦ ἐβαπτίσθησαν mean *so those who had accepted...were baptized*, or *so they, having accepted...were baptized?*

(*c*) Returning to ὁ βασιλεὺς μέγας, it has to be admitted that there would be ambiguity if the article before βασιλεύς were omitted: βασιλεὺς μέγας might mean *a king is great, a great king*, or even (if the context favoured it) the *king is great*, or the *great king*. Admittedly, too, there are exceptions in the N.T. even where an article is present:

In Luke i. 35, τὸ γεννώμενον ἅγιον κληθήσεται υἱὸς θεοῦ may mean *the* [*child*] *which is to be born shall be called holy, the Son of God*, in which case no problem arises as to the article; but if the meaning is *the holy* [*child*] *which is to be born shall be called the Son of God*, then it is a distinctly irregular usage: τὸ ἅγιον τὸ γεννώμενον... would perhaps be the only clear way of saying it. But Mark xi. 10 ἡ ἐρχομένη βασιλεία might be adduced as a parallel to this position of an (adjectival) participle.

In John xii. 9, 12, ὁ ὄχλος πολύς evidently means *the great crowd* (*Proleg.* 84), although 'by the rules' it ought to have meant *the crowd is* (or *was*) *great*.

---

[1] Compare the similar potency of a *defining* word like πᾶς: Matt. iii. 10 πᾶν οὖν δένδρον μὴ ποιοῦν καρπὸν καλόν means (probably) *every tree that does not...* (rather than *every tree* when, or if, *it does not...*).

Conversely, Jas. ii. 8 νόμον τελεῖτε βασιλικόν is interesting: βασιλικός, by its very meaning (*royal* or *supreme*), practically implies definition, and one would accordingly expect τὸν νόμον τὸν βασιλικόν or τὸν β. νόμον. But Mayor (*in loc.*) is prepared to translate simply *you fulfil the royal law* (as though the article had been used). The strictly correct alternative,[1] *you fulfil the law* as *supreme*, is rendered less likely by the context.[2]

The use of the article with πολλοί and its cognates presents problems for the translator: does οἱ πολλοί mean *the many* as contrasted with *the few*, i.e. *the majority* (cf. οἱ πλείονες), or does it mean *the many*, i.e. *the large number* referred to on some previous occasion? Does τὰ πολλά (adverbial) in Rom. xv. 22 mean those *many times* (of which you are all aware), or *the majority of occasions, more often than not*? Certainly οἱ πλείονες is, in some instances, used for *the majority*, e.g. I Cor. x. 5 ἀλλ᾽ οὐκ ἐν τοῖς πλείοσιν αὐτῶν εὐδόκησεν ὁ θεός; but would Paul have equally readily used ἐν τοῖς πολλοῖς with such a meaning? What is the force of II Cor. iv. 15 ἡ χάρις πλεονάσασα διὰ τῶν πλειόνων τὴν εὐχαριστίαν περισσεύσῃ εἰς τὴν δόξαν τοῦ θεοῦ? πλεονάσασα and περισσεύσῃ suggest that τῶν πλ. here means *the increasing numbers*. In II Cor. ix. 2 τοὺς πλείονας perhaps means *the majority* (though not all). Cf. ii. 6.

For the article with πᾶς, see under 'The Adjective', pp. 93–5.

In Phil. i. 14 τῶν ἀδελφῶν ἐν κυρίῳ clearly means *the brothers who are in the Lord* (unless—which is extremely unlikely—the ἐν κυρίῳ goes with the πεποιθότας which follows); and it must thus be regarded as a loose way of expressing τῶν ἀδ. τῶν ἐν τῷ κυρίῳ. Similarly in Col. i. 2, τοῖς ἐν Κολοσσαῖς ἁγίοις καὶ πιστοῖς ἀδελφοῖς ἐν χριστῷ may be taken as equivalent to . . . τοῖς ἐν χριστῷ (instead of the unlikely and far-fetched alternative of taking ἐν χριστῷ as governed by πιστοῖς as = *believing*); cf. Eph. i. 1. Cf. on Eph. i. 15, Col. i. 4, etc., under 'Prepositions, ἐν, Add. Note (*c*)', p. 80.

But what of II Cor. i. 11 ἵνα ἐκ πολλῶν προσώπων τὸ εἰς ἡμᾶς χάρισμα διὰ πολλῶν εὐχαριστηθῇ . . .? If διὰ πολλῶν goes with εὐχαριστηθῇ as = *may be thanked for by many*, then ἐκ πολλῶν is redundant; but if διὰ πολλῶν goes with τὸ εἰς ἡμᾶς χάρισμα as = *the gift which reached us by the agency of many*, then strict grammar requires a second article—τὸ εἰς ἡμᾶς χάρισμα τὸ διὰ πολλῶν.

One may add, as a further instance of this phenomenon of the omitted article, Mark vi. 6 καὶ περιῆγεν τὰς κώμας κύκλῳ (as = τὰς κύκλῳ, rather

---

[1] *You fulfil a royal law* seems to be ruled out by the context.
[2] Cf. Tit. ii. 11 with Radermacher's comments (117).

than taking κύκλῳ with περιῆγεν as H. B. Swete, *in loc.*, wishes).[1]
See also the striking instances in Luke iv. 20, 28 referred to by Rad. 117
as scarcely permissible. Note too Luke xv. 22.

Conversely, there are many instances of what strikes the English
reader as an almost pedantic repetition of the article; e.g. such phrases
as I Cor. i. 18 ὁ λόγος γὰρ ὁ τοῦ σταυροῦ, Phil. iii. 11 τὴν ἐξανάστασιν
τὴν ἐκ νεκρῶν, Rom. iii. 24 τῆς ἀπολυτρώσεως τῆς ἐν χριστῷ Ἰησοῦ,
Acts iii. 16 ἡ πίστις ἡ δι' αὐτοῦ, xxvi. 18 πίστει τῇ εἰς ἐμέ, *v.* 22 ἐπι-
κουρίας...τῆς ἀπὸ τοῦ θεοῦ (where it would be very laboured to
translate *the story which is about the cross, the resurrection which is from
the dead*, and so forth). The Pastoral Epistles afford plentiful examples
of this repetition.[2]

(*d*) These anomalies must not be confused with perfectly correct
but rather subtly delicate usages such as Heb. vii. 24, ἀπαράβατον
ἔχει τὴν ἱερωσύνην, which probably does *not* =ἀπαράβατον ἔχει
ἱερωσύνην (*is possessed of an inalienable priesthood*), but means *has
a priesthood which is inalienable*, the article suggesting that we know
that he has a priesthood: it is ἡ ἱερωσύνη, *his* (*known, assumed*) *priesthood*; but we now add that he has it *as an inalienable one* (see Rob. 656).
Cf. Luke vi. 8 τῷ ἀνδρὶ τῷ ξηρὰν ἔχοντι τὴν χεῖρα.

2. Problems arise over the question whether or not one article, in
any given instance, is intended to apply to separate nouns.[3] Thus,
does Titus ii. 13, τῆς δόξης τοῦ μεγάλου θεοῦ καὶ σωτῆρος ἡμῶν χριστοῦ
Ἰησοῦ, mean *the glory of our great God-and-Saviour, Jesus Christ*, or
...*of the great God, and of our Saviour Jesus Christ* (a sense which would
be *guaranteed* if the article were repeated with σωτῆρος, but which is
possible in κοινή Greek even without the repetition)? In this particular
instance, there is the ingenious but highly improbable alternative[4]
of taking σωτῆρος κ.τ.λ. as in apposition with τῆς δόξης, and καί
as =*namely*. It would then mean: *the glory of our great God, namely
our Saviour Jesus Christ*. Similarly note II Pet. i. 1 τοῦ θεοῦ ἡμῶν καὶ

---

[1] Especially note Mark vi. 36 τοὺς κύκλῳ ἀγρούς. But κύκλῳ is, admittedly,
used with a verb in Rom. xv. 19.

[2] See Rad. 117 for valuable comments on the above. C. H. Dodd points out
to me that this usage is characteristic of the *ethos* of the Greek language.

[3] T. F. Middleton, *The Doctrine of the Greek Article* (ed. H. J. Rose, 1841), 63,
points out that in the idiom τὸν Ἀλέξανδρον καὶ Φίλιππον one article is
manifestly sufficient, since the two names are obviously not predicated of the
same person. Cf. Acts xv. 22, and note the curious Mark ix. 2.

[4] See Hort on Jas. ii. 1, and discussion in W. Lock, *I.C.C.* on Titus ii. 13.

σωτῆρος Ἰησοῦ χριστοῦ. It is probable that in both these instances the article has been correctly omitted and that τοῦ (μεγάλου) θεοῦ is intended to apply to Jesus. See *Proleg.* 84. B. S. Easton (*in loc.*) makes the point that '"God and Saviour" was a commonplace in the religion of the day' [i.e. according to him *c.* A.D. 95–105] 'and meant without exception one deity and not two'. The implications for the date and authorship are, of course, important.

Another instance of the same problem is in Eph. ii. 20, ἐπὶ τῷ θεμελίῳ τῶν ἀποστόλων καὶ προφητῶν, where interpretations include: (i) *the apostles and the [O.T.] prophets* (two separate groups); (ii) *the [N.T.] apostles and prophets* (one homogeneous group); (iii) *the apostles who are also prophets* (the one in apposition with the other). The last (Hort's suggestion in *The Christian Ecclesia,* 165) seems unlikely, considering the ambiguity of the Greek which it implies and the question whether the two were in fact identified. The other two are both possible, and I doubt if T. K. Abbott (*I.C.C. in loc.*) is right in saying that 'the absence of the article before προφητῶν is against' their being O.T. prophets.

As instances of 'comprehensive' single articles, note: Rom. xii. 2 τὸ θέλημα τοῦ θεοῦ, τὸ ἀγαθὸν καὶ εὐάρεστον καὶ τέλειον; and (with Rad. 115) Col. ii. 22 τὰ ἐντάλματα καὶ διδασκαλίας τῶν ἀνθρώπων; and cf. also the three forms of the apostolic decree in Acts xv. 20, 29, xxi. 25.

For the reverse phenomenon—an *intrusive* article—see Rom. iv. 12 τοῖς οὐκ ἐκ περιτομῆς μόνον ἀλλὰ καὶ τοῖς στοιχοῦσιν (which S. and H. *in loc.* take to be simply a mistake).

3. The neuter article provides, like inverted commas, a way of indicating that a whole clause is to be treated as a single entity—as a kind of composite noun—as when a sentence is quoted: Mark ix. 23 τὸ εἰ δύνῃ seems best treated as an exclamatory or questioning repetition by Jesus of the anxious father's words: '*If you can . . . !*' *Why, anything is possible . . .* (or '*If you can?*' *Do you ask such a question?*). So in Mark ix. 10 the disciples ask *what is meant by 'rising from the dead'*, τί ἐστιν τὸ ἐκ νεκρῶν ἀναστῆναι (unless here the article merely turns the infinitive into a noun). In Gal. vi. 9, τὸ δὲ καλὸν ποιοῦντες μὴ ἐνκακῶμεν, it is possible that the neuter article introduces a familiar proverbial phrase, and that the sentence means something like: *And [there is] the saying: 'Let us not grow tired . . .*'; alternatively, the article simply goes with καλόν in a 'generic' sense—τὸ καλόν, *what*

is good. However, it must be admitted that it may have been a sheer idiosyncrasy of Paul's to use the neuter article thus: see, particularly, Rom. viii. 26 τὸ γὰρ τί προσευξώμεθα καθὸ δεῖ οὐκ οἴδαμεν, with S. and H. *in loc.* (and see under 'Miscellaneous Notes on Style', p. 200, below).

The extraordinary phrase in I Cor. iv. 6, τὸ μὴ ὑπὲρ ἃ γέγραπται, has been plausibly emended;[1] but if an emendation is not resorted to, it is best taken as the quotation of some 'slogan' known to Paul and his readers: *the* [*well-known saying*]: '*Not beyond what is written.*'

Note, further, the neuter article in adverbial phrases such as Rom. ix. 5 τὸ κατὰ σάρκα, Rom. xii. 18 τὸ ἐξ ὑμῶν, etc. See below, ch. XXIII.

The articular infinitive is discussed separately, Ch. XII, below.

4. Occasionally, the article is practically equivalent to a demonstrative pronoun.[2] For example, in Acts xvi. 12 τῆς μερίδος Μακεδονίας (if that is the true reading—see *Beg. in loc.*) must mean *of that division of Macedonia* (i.e. *the relevant division, the division in question*). Sir W. Ramsay[3] has demonstrated that μερίς does not mean *province*, and we may not construe Μακεδονίας as in apposition to it—as though it meant *of the province Macedonia.* Again, Jas. ii. 14 μὴ δύναται ἡ πίστις σῶσαι αὐτόν; is sometimes claimed to mean *Can* such *faith save him?* But if αὐτόν is the emphatic word, then ἡ may (by a familiar idiom) mean *his: Can his faith save* him?

Sometimes the article, if not exactly demonstrative, may be described as 'deictic' (i.e. as pointing out some familiar type or *genus*): Rom. v. 7 μόλις γὰρ ὑπὲρ δικαίου τις ἀποθανεῖται· ὑπὲρ γὰρ τοῦ ἀγαθοῦ τάχα τις καὶ τολμᾷ ἀποθανεῖν, perhaps = …*for the good type of man*…, or, as colloquial English might put it, *for your good man.* Possibly I Cor. xv. 8 τῷ ἐκτρώματι may be an instance of the same, although it may be a perfectly normal use of the article, to mean *the abortion (of the apostolic family). I.C.C. in loc.* rejects τῷ (indefinite pronoun).

5. It is sometimes claimed[4] that an important theological issue is involved in the use or non-use of the article—e.g. with πνεῦμα; but each instance needs to be discussed on its own merits, and in some

---

[1] Joh. Weiss, Bousset, and Baljon all suggested, with slight variations, that a scribe's note had crept into the text. See W. F. Howard's summary in *E.T.* XXXIII (July 1922), 479.

[2] See J. B. Mayor, *St James*, clxxxix.

[3] Reference in *Beg. in loc.*

[4] E.g. recently by A. M. Perry in *J.B.L.* LXVIII (1949), 329 ff.

instances it is hard to avoid the impression that usage is arbitrary. Consider, for example, the following:

i. The use and non-use of the article with ἀλήθεια: one is not surprised to find it anarthrous in adverbial phrases such as ἐν ἀληθείᾳ, ἐπ᾽ ἀληθείας, κατ᾽ ἀλήθειαν, ἀληθείᾳ; but what is one to make of the following comparisons?

John viii. 44ᵃ ἐν τῇ ἀληθείᾳ οὐκ ἔστηκεν with viii. 44ᵇ ὅτι οὐκ ἔστιν ἀλήθεια ἐν αὐτῷ;

John xvii. 17ᵃ ἁγίασον αὐτοὺς ἐν τῇ ἀληθείᾳ with xvii. 17ᵇ ὁ λόγος ὁ σὸς ἀλήθεια ἐστιν;[1]

II Tim. ii. 25, iii. 7, Tit. i. 1 ἐπίγνωσις ἀληθείας with Heb. x. 26 ἡ ἐπίγνωσις τῆς ἀληθείας.[2] Note also III John 1, 3, 4, 12 for similar fluctuations.

Such apparent inconsistency makes one hesitate to build much on the presence of the article in so famous a sentence as John xiv. 6 ἐγώ εἰμι ἡ ὁδὸς καὶ ἡ ἀλήθεια καὶ ἡ ζωή. The definite article seems to be required (by the context) before ὁδός; but are the others merely examples of the Greek usage by which an abstract noun often has the article— or even mere accommodation to that first article? Is the English equivalent *I am the Way, I am Truth, I am Life*?† For a comparable list of abstract nouns, this time anarthrous, see Rom. xiv. 17 οὐ γάρ ἐστιν ἡ βασιλεία τοῦ θεοῦ βρῶσις καὶ πόσις, ἀλλὰ δικαιοσύνη καὶ εἰρήνη καὶ χαρὰ ἐν πνεύματι ἁγίῳ. Again, what is the meaning of the famous *crux*, Eph. iv. 21 καθώς ἐστιν ἀλήθεια ἐν τῷ Ἰησοῦ? Does it mean *just as Truth is (to be found) in Jesus* (as though it had been ἡ ἀλήθεια)? (II Cor. xi. 10 ἔστιν ἀλήθεια χριστοῦ ἐν ἐμοί, ὅτι... presumably means *I am speaking Christian truth when I say that...*: if so, it is a much smaller and more particularized sense of ἀλήθεια as associated with Christ.)

ii. The use and non-use of the article with πνεῦμα. This, again, is extremely difficult to reduce to consistency. Rom. xiv. 17 (just quoted) looks like an anarthrous use in the sense *the Holy Spirit*; and it seems to me rather forced to interpret the anarthrous uses

---

[1] Here Rob. 768 maintains that the article is omitted for a good reason— that ὁ λόγος and ἀλήθεια are *not convertible terms* (as the addition of the article would have made them). But is he right in maintaining that this rule holds good generally? But Colwell's rule (7. below) may here be relevant.

[2] But this is, of course, dependent in part on the canon of Apollonius referred to below.

(e.g. in the Gospels) as uniformly meaning something less than *God's Holy Spirit*. J. B. Mayor (*St James*, 87) speaks of ' ... the constantly recurring Πνεῦμα ἅγιον, which is used not only after a preposition, as in Matt. i. 18 εὑρέθη ἐν γαστρὶ ἔχουσα ἐκ Πνεύματος ἁγίου, but also without a preposition and even in the Nominative, e.g. Luke i. 15 Πνεύματος ἁγίου πλησθήσεται, *v.* 35 Πνεῦμα ἅγιον ἐπελεύσεται ἐπὶ σέ, *ibid.* ii. 25 Πνεῦμα ἦν ἅγιον ἐπ' αὐτόν. It is noticeable that, when there is no article, the words are always in this order, but, with the article, τὸ ἅγιον Πν. is not much less common than τὸ Πν. τὸ ἅγ.'

iii. Similarly, the use of νόμος and ὁ νόμος; for, although certain rules as to the N.T. usage have been formulated[1] they are certainly not deducible merely from the assumption that the article makes the concept definite, and the context is a surer guide to the meaning than is the use of the article.

iv. Eph. vi. 2, which is a well-known crux: does ἥτις ἐστὶν ἐντολὴ πρώτη ἐν ἐπαγγελίᾳ mean *which is* the *first commandment with a promise* (*attached to it*) (which is not literally true, and in which the omission of the article would be curious); or does it mean *which is* a *foremost commandment, and has a promise attached to it* (which is an unlikely sense for πρώτη in such a context)? The case for the former alternative is certainly strengthened by the omission of the article in Mark xii. 28, 29 ποία ἐστὶν ἐντολὴ πρώτη πάντων; ... πρώτη ἐστίν. ... †

v. An instance of an exegetical problem as to the article in Philem. 9: Παῦλος πρεσβύτης, νυνὶ δὲ καὶ δέσμιος χριστοῦ Ἰησοῦ: does this mean *Paul the aged, and now also a prisoner* ... (A.V.)? If so, the Greek might, with less ambiguity, have been Παῦλος ὁ πρεσβύτης, ὁ νυνὶ καὶ δέσμιος—the articles serving to place two qualifying concepts—'aged' and 'prisoner'—side by side.[2] Still more, if (with R.V. marg.) we take πρεσβύτης as = *ambassador* (for which the strict orthography seems to be πρεσβευτής—see Lightfoot and Vincent *in loc.*), the two concepts *ambassador* and *prisoner* are in (paradoxical) parallelism. Or does it, alternatively, mean simply *The aged Paul—who is now also a prisoner* ...?[3]

---

[1] See, for example, S. and H. on Rom. ii. 12, 13, or the exceedingly full and careful analysis by Burton in *I.C.C.* on Gal., 447–60.

[2] Middleton, *op. cit.* 398, seems to miss the point when he claims that the translation *the aged* would imply a distinction from other Pauls, and is not possible without the article.

[3] Cf. the English idiom in the familiar title *St Paul the Traveller and the Roman Citizen*.

vi. The following miscellaneous examples of articular behaviour: Rom. xii. 8 (for the omission in a perhaps *adverbial* use—cf. under i. above); Rom. xii. 10–13 (for a remarkable series of articles); Heb. xii. 18–24 (for an equally striking series of omissions); I Pet. i. 1 (for some more); and Acts vii. 51 (ἀπερίτμητοι καρδίαις καὶ τοῖς ὠσίν—unless καρδίας is the correct reading).

H. J. Rose, in his introduction to Middleton, *op. cit.* (xiii, xiv), discusses the liberties taken by English in anarthrous phrases such as *by sea, by land, day came,* etc. He might have added that the usage seems to vary partly with the preposition: we say *by sea, by land, by air,* but we tend to say *on the sea,* and *in the air. On shore,* of course, means something different from *on the shore.* Luke ii. 14 has ἐπὶ γῆς, but xxi. 25 ἐπὶ τῆς γῆς. Very interesting is II Cor. xii. 2, 3 εἴτε ἐν σώματι... εἴτε ἐκτὸς τοῦ σώματος... εἴτε ἐν σώματι... εἴτε χωρὶς τοῦ σώματος....†

On the other hand, examples are forthcoming in plenty of intelligible and significant uses; e.g. on Heb. i. 2, ἐλάλησεν ἡμῖν ἐν υἱῷ, Nairne (*Cambridge Greek Testament* 26) writes: '"His Son", A.V. and R.V., spoils the grandeur of the thought.... Yet R.V. mg., "Gr. *a Son*", is hardly correct. The Greeks, with their frequent omission of the article in the large tragic style, could express just what is wanted here, but there is no equivalent in English.... Hence Westcott's paraphrase (which he does not offer as adequate) "One who is Son". He carries us further by his remark that we should lose as much by omitting the article before προφήταις [in *v.* 1] as by inserting it here.'[1]

Similar is Westcott's note on Heb. iii. 12 ἀπὸ θεοῦ ζῶντος, 'which', he writes, 'is far more common than ὁ θ. ὁ ζῶν', and which 'always fixes attention upon the character as distinguished from the "Person" of God'.

Again, note (cf. Rad. 117) that in Titus ii. 11, if we read ἐπεφάνη γὰρ ἡ χάρις τοῦ θεοῦ σωτήριος, it means *God's favour has appeared with saving power,* whereas the reading ἡ σωτήριος would, of course, make σωτήριος into a merely qualifying adjective—*God's saving favour....*

6. *Apollonius' canon* (quoted by Middleton, *op. cit.* 36) is that 'Nouns in regimen [i.e. "the condition both of the governing and governed noun"—Middleton] must have articles prefixed to *both* of them or *neither*'. Apollonius notes βασιλεύς as an exception; and Middleton himself (37) adduces a few more; adding (37, 38) that Philo is the only

---

[1] Middleton, *op. cit.,* curiously omits this passage from his comments on the article in Hebrews (399).

prose writer known to him who violates the rule, Josephus, by contrast, observing it. (For examples, see Rad. 116.) But it has to be added, by way of modifying the canon, as Middleton himself recognizes, that the *governing* noun may be anarthrous without necessitating the omission of the article with the *governed*.

Thus, Apollonius' canon requires *either* ἐν λόγῳ ἀληθείας (II Cor. vi. 7) *or* ἐν τῷ λόγῳ τῆς ἀληθείας (Col. i. 5); but the modification is that, although ὁ λόγος ἀληθείας may be impossible, λόγος τῆς ἀληθείας (conversely) is possible. Thus Rom. iii. 25 has εἰς ἔνδειξιν τῆς δικαιοσύνης αὐτοῦ (though in *v.* 26 both nouns have the article); and Eph. i. 6 has εἰς ἔπαινον δόξης τῆς χάριτος αὐτοῦ.

A further modification has to be made in respect of proper names and national appellations (Middleton, 288), e.g. in Acts xix. 28, 34, 35, where we find Μεγάλη ἡ Ἄρτεμις Ἐφεσίων and τὴν Ἐφεσίων πόλιν. Middleton (207) regards Κύριος, as a title for God or Christ, as 'approaching more nearly to a proper name' than does θεός; and in this way he explains such usages as Acts ii. 20 (*v.l.*) τὴν ἡμέραν κυρίου, Jas. v. 11 τὸ τέλος κυρίου. Acts v. 9 τὸ πνεῦμα κυρίου is another instance (cf. II Cor. iii. 17, 18 τὸ πνεῦμα κυρίου, τὴν δόξαν κυρίου—Middleton, 208).[1]

On the article with θεός, see Middleton 206–9. His main conclusion is that the usage conforms to Apollonius' canon ('that law of Regimen which forbids an anarthrous Appellative to be governed by one having the Article prefixed'), so that 'such a phrase as ὁ υἱὸς θεοῦ is not to be found'. Contrast the observations above about κύριος.

7. Much more recently, E. C. Colwell has made important observations on the matter.[2] He formulates and supports with evidence a rule 'to describe the use of the article with definite predicate nouns in sentences in which the verb occurs. (1) Definite predicate nouns here regularly take the article. (2) The exceptions are for the most part due to a change in word-order: (*a*) definite predicate nouns which follow the verb (this is the usual order) usually take the article; (*b*) definite predicate nouns which precede the verb usually lack the article; (*c*) proper names regularly lack the article in the predicate; (*d*) predicate nominatives in relative clauses regularly follow the verb whether or not they have the article' (p. 20).

[1] On the article with Ἰησοῦς, κύριος, and χριστός, see H. J. Rose's appendix to his edition of Middleton, 486–96.

[2] In an article entitled 'A Definite Rule for the Use of the Article in the Greek New Testament' (*J.B.L.* LII (1933), 12 ff.).

The bearing of 2 (*b*) above on certain famous problems becomes immediately obvious; for instance (as Colwell himself points out) Matt. xxvii. 54 ἀληθῶς θεοῦ υἱὸς ἦν οὗτος may, after all, mean ...the *Son of God*, the omission of the article not necessitating the translation *a Son of God*. Similarly it may be the demands of this idiom, and not any intention to convey a distinction in meaning, which create a contrast such as that between Matt. xiii. 37 ὁ σπείρων...ἐστὶν ὁ υἱὸς τοῦ ἀνθρώπου and John v. 27 ὅτι υἱὸς ἀνθρώπου ἐστίν (cf. under 'Semitisms', II. vi. below, p. 177). More striking still is the application of this canon to the much debated John i. 1. Is the omission of the article in θεὸς ἦν ὁ λόγος nothing more than a matter of idiom? Middleton had already taken it as an instance of the article being omitted simply because θεός is 'the Predicate of a Proposition which does not reciprocate'.[1] Similarly, Stauffer in *T.W.N.T.* III, 106 speaks of the omission of the article as merely grammatically conditioned ('grammatisch bedingt'); and he notes John viii. 54 θεὸς ἡμῶν ἐστιν, II Cor. v. 19 θεὸς ἦν ἐν χριστῷ κόσμον καταλλάσσων ἑαυτῷ as examples of the predicative use of θεός without the article. Yet he says that in John i. 18 (reading μονογενὴς θεός) the omission of the article is striking, and reminds one of Philo's (anarthrous) δεύτερος θεός as applied to the λόγος.

On the other hand it needs to be recognized that the Fourth Evangelist need not have chosen this word-order, and that his choice of it, though creating some ambiguity, may in itself be an indication of his meaning; and Westcott's note (*in loc.*), although it may require the addition of some reference to idiom, does still, perhaps, represent the writer's theological intention: 'It is necessarily without the article (θεός not ὁ θεός) inasmuch as it describes the nature of the Word and does not identify His Person. It would be pure Sabellianism to say "the Word was ὁ θεός". No idea of inferiority of nature is suggested by the form of expression, which simply affirms the true deity of the Word. Compare the converse statement of the true humanity of Christ v. 27 (ὅτι υἱὸς ἀνθρώπου ἐστίν...).' With regard to the latter remark, however, Colwell's canon suggests that Westcott is putting too much weight upon the anarthrous condition of the noun.

In John xx. 28 Ὁ κύριός μου καὶ ὁ θεός μου, it is to be noted that a substantive in the Nominative case used in a vocative sense and followed by a possessive could not be anarthrous (see Hoskyns and Davey, *Commentary, in loc.*); the article before θεός may, therefore, not be significant.

[1] Cf. Rob.'s remarks, 768, quoted above, p. 112 n. 1, about 'convertible terms'.

8. It is worth while to note the rule which Middleton (32) refers to with the formula *Renewed mention*, whereby 'when a person or thing recently mentioned is spoken of again, the Article, as is well known, is inserted when the mention is renewed'. A good example is afforded by Rom. v. 3–5 ... ἐν ταῖς θλίψεσιν, εἰδότες ὅτι ἡ θλίψις ὑπομονὴν κατεργάζεται, ἡ δὲ ὑπομονὴ δοκιμήν, ἡ δὲ δοκιμὴ ἐλπίδα· ἡ δὲ ἐλπὶς . . . . (This borders on the demonstrative use alluded to above, 4. p. 111).

9. Finally, note that the use or non-use of the article may, in some cases, be due to the influence of Semitic idiom rather than deliberate desire to modify the sense. A noun in the *construct state* in Hebrew is never allowed to carry the article, and this may sometimes be sufficient to explain an anarthrous noun in a Greek equivalent phrase: ἄγγελος κυρίου might be a Hebraism for *the angel of the Lord*; so δόξα κυρίου. Conversely, the use of the article with a virtual *Vocative* (cf. John xx. 28 referred to above, and I Pet. ii. 18, Col. iii. 18ff.) may also be due to Semitic idiom.[1]

---

[1] See D. Daube's appended note in E. G. Selwyn's *I Peter*; and cf. under 'Semitisms', below, p. 177.

On the Article with the titles of Jesus, see N. A. Dahl in *Studia Paulina* (*Festschrift* for J. de Zwaan, Haarlem, 1953), 83 ff.

XI

PRONOUNS

For definitions (or cautions against their use) see under 'Adjectives'. What is more important than the definition of a pronoun is the definition of its use and the classification of its type.

The following are the chief *types* of pronoun:

I. PERSONAL PRONOUNS

1. *Simple*:

	Singular	Plural
1st pers.	ἐγώ	ἡμεῖς
2nd „	σύ	ὑμεῖς
3rd „	(αὐτός, see below)	(αὐτοί, see below)

Note. The so-called 'epistolary plural'. Just as in modern English (and modern Greek) it is customary to use the *plural* in the second person even when the singular is intended (*you* not *thou*, etc.), while in German the *third plural* is used for the *second singular*, so in κοινή Greek it was idiomatic, though by no means invariable, to use the *first person plural* (of the verb, whether or not with an expressed pronoun) with reference to the first person *singular*. It is a matter of considerable discussion exactly where in the Pauline Epistles the plural is intended literally and where it is idiomatically used for the singular.[1] Broadly, the conclusions are that (*a*) the epistolary plural is not frequent in papyrus letters, although its use is established in later Greek; (*b*) it is sufficiently established to make it necessary to take it into account in interpreting the N.T.: hence each passage must be tested on its own merits. Lofthouse (*E.T.* LVIII, no. 7 (April 1947), 179ff.)† argues for a significant distinction between singular and plural in the Pauline Epistles: '...when the sing. is used, St Paul is referring to his own life and personal experiences and convictions....When...he uses the pl., he is identifying himself with some or all of the group whom he mentions....'

[1] Moulton (*Proleg.* 86 n.) refers to K. Dick, *Der Schriftstellerische Plural bei Paulus*, 1900. See also the discussions in Milligan's edition of the Thessalonian Epistles (Note B, 131, 132) and in Dibelius's edition (Lietzmann's *Handbuch ʒ. N.T.*, 12–13); and in O. Roller, *Das Formular der Paulinischen Briefe*, 1933, 169 ff.

The problem is raised in an acute form at I Thess. ii. 18: does ἠθελήσαμεν...ἐγὼ μὲν Παῦλος mean *we* [*all*] *wanted*...[*at least,*] I *did?* or does it mean simply I *wanted* [*though others did not*]? In I Thess. iii. 1 ηὐδοκήσαμεν καταλειφθῆναι...μόνοι must (by the very meaning of μόνος) surely be 'epistolary'; and iii. 5 (ἔπεμψα) appears to be identical in meaning with iii. 2 (ἐπέμψαμεν). Moreover, in II Cor. xi. 6 there appears to be an obviously 'epistolary' plural participle: εἰ δὲ καὶ ἰδιώτης τῷ λόγῳ, ἀλλ᾽ οὐ τῇ γνώσει, ἀλλ᾽ ἐν παντὶ φανερώσαντες ἐν πᾶσιν εἰς ὑμᾶς.

On the other hand, in II Cor. i. 15–24 there appears to be a very careful distinction between singular and plural.

One may ask whether there is any significance in the distinction between singular and plural in I John, where, for example, one gets καὶ ταῦτα γράφομεν ἡμεῖς (i. 4) followed by ταῦτα γράφω (ii. 1). For discussions, see Hoskyns-Davey, *Fourth Gospel,* 86 ff.; Dodd, *Johannine Epistles,* 9–15. Note that Acts xxiv. 4 presents an example in Tertullus' speech: παρακαλῶ ἀκοῦσαί σε ἡμῶν....

2. *Reflexive*:

	Singular	Plural
1st pers.	ἐμαυτόν	ἡμᾶς αὐτούς
2nd „	σεαυτόν	ὑμᾶς αὐτούς
3rd „	ἑαυτόν / αὐτόν	ἑαυτούς

Notes. Third Person. Since breathings are seldom, if ever, put on by the earlier hands in MSS., it is a matter of conjecture when to read αὐτόν and when αὑτόν.† Instances where a reflexive (however written) is clearly required are Luke xxiii. 12 (...ἐν ἔχθρᾳ ὄντες πρὸς αυτους), xxiv. 12 (ἀπῆλθεν πρὸς αυτον) and John ii. 24 (οὐκ ἐπίστευσεν αυτον αὐτοῖς); in all ἑαυτούς, ἑαυτόν is a variant reading. In John xiii. 32 also the reflexive seems more natural, and again there is a *v.l.* accordingly. In Col. i. 20, δι᾽ αὐτοῦ ἀποκαταλλάξαι τὰ πάντα εἰς αὐτόν, it is surprising that there appears to be no variant ἑαυτόν and that editors do not print αὑτόν, which seems to be required by the sense in order to distinguish *Christ,* referred to in δι᾽ αὐτοῦ, from *God,* to whom (probably) the reconciliation is made.†

The Genitive αὑτοῦ is not clearly attested for the N.T.; and σαυτόν, the contracted 2nd person, only in variants in two passages.[1]

[1] See M.-H. II, 180, 181, and D.-B. § 64, for details. In Luke xii. 21 W.H. etc. print a contracted Dative.

In I Cor. vii. 38 τὴν ἑαυτοῦ παρθένον, the reflexive ἑαυτοῦ appears to have lost its reflexive force: τὴν παρθένον αὐτοῦ would appear to mean exactly the same, whether the passage is interpreted as referring to 'spiritual marriage' with '*virgines subintroductae*' or to a father's dealings with his daughter.

Third Person Plural. This tends to extend itself so as to do duty also for the 1st and 2nd plural—a use not unknown in the Classics: II Cor. xiii. 5 ἑαυτοὺς πειράζετε εἰ ἐστὲ ἐν τῇ πίστει, ἑαυτοὺς δοκιμάζετε. In Col. iii. 13 it seems to be used as a synonym for the reciprocal ἀλλήλους: ἀνεχόμενοι ἀλλήλων καὶ χαριζόμενοι ἑαυτοῖς. In I Cor. x. 29 the singular, ἑαυτοῦ, represents the English **one's own**.

3. *Reciprocal*: ἀλλήλους (of necessity not in the Nominative).

The same sense can be expressed by εἷς τὸν ἕνα, etc.; e.g. I Thess. v. 11 διὸ παρακαλεῖτε ἀλλήλους καὶ οἰκοδομεῖτε εἷς τὸν ἕνα. (Cf. I Cor. iv. 6.)

4. *Possessive*: 'Possessives' are often classified among pronouns; but they are actually indistinguishable, in respect of syntax, from adjectives: they can be used as pure adjectives, as in ἐμὸν βρῶμά ἐστιν... (John iv. 34); and when they stand alone it is in circumstances in which a genuine adjective might also stand for a noun: (οἱ) ὑμέτεροι, *your people* (which is no more 'pronominal' than οἱ ἀγαθοί); πάντα τὰ ἐμὰ σά ἐστιν... (Luke xv. 31, cf. John xvii. 10). In other words, there is not a distinctive possessive *pronoun* in N.T. Greek comparable to *mine* in modern English, as contrasted with the purely adjectival *my*.

Note that these possessive adjectives are not found for the 3rd person: we have ἐμός, *my* or *mine*, ἡμέτερος, *our* or *ours*, σός, *your* or *yours* (singular), and ὑμέτερος, *your* or *yours* (plural); but when it comes to the 3rd person, the Genitive of the personal pronoun is called in: ὁ υἱὸς αὐτοῦ (or ἑαυτοῦ), αὐτῶν: Rev. xi. 15 ἐγένετο ἡ βασιλεία τοῦ κόσμου τοῦ κυρίου ἡμῶν καὶ τοῦ χριστοῦ αὐτοῦ... (...*his Messiah*).

Note that a similar possessive Genitive (or Dative) of the personal pronoun can serve for the 1st and 2nd person possessive pronouns also: of the 1st person plural the last quotation provides an example; and for the 2nd singular there are phrases such as Luke v. 5 ἐπὶ δὲ τῷ ῥήματί σου. Whether σοί is Nom. pl. of the adjective or (possessive) Dat. of the singular personal pronoun in such phrases as Luke v. 33 οἱ δὲ σοί, John xvii. 6 σοὶ ἦσαν, is not clear. Certainly in Acts v. 4

the Dat. of the personal pronoun is used: οὐχὶ μένον σοὶ ἔμενεν; *as long as it remained, did it not remain your own?*[1]

Note that ἴδιος, *one's own*, is sometimes practically no more than a possessive adjective; e.g. in John i. 41, Matt. xxii. 5 it seems to be quite unemphatic (see D.-B. § 286). In the famous *crux* of Acts xx. 28, τοῦ ἰδίου is possibly used as a noun = *his own (Son)*; cf. John i. 11, xiii. 1, etc. For ἴδιος side by side with ἑαυτοῦ, see I Cor. vii. 2.

II. DEMONSTRATIVE PRONOUNS

(i.e. such as serve to *demonstrate* or *indicate* persons or things)

Note, first, the usage with regard to the following:

1. αὐτός (-ή, -ό), *he (she, it)* (see also under 1. 1. above).
2. οὗτος, αὕτη, τοῦτο, *this person (thing)*.
3. ἐκεῖνος, ἐκείνη, ἐκεῖνο, *that person (thing)*.

1. αὐτός in N.T. Greek can mean:

i. Simply *he* (unemphatic), as in Luke v. 1 αὐτὸς ἦν ἑστώς *he was standing* (where it adds little, if anything, to the implications of the verb). But such unemphatic use is commoner in the oblique cases: παραλαμβάνει αὐτόν, *he takes him*, where some object, it is true, is necessary to the sense, but where it is quite unemphatic: *takes* is the stressed word in the sentence, if there is any stress.†

Note. Luke xix. 2 (καὶ αὐτὸς ἦν ἀρχιτελώνης, καὶ αὐτὸς πλούσιος) and Jas. ii. 6 (οὐχ οἱ πλούσιοι καταδυναστεύουσιν ὑμῶν, καὶ αὐτοὶ ἕλκουσιν ὑμᾶς...;) are very curious: see under 'Semitisms', p. 176 below.

ii. *He* (emphatic) or *himself*: John ix. 21 αὐτὸς περὶ ἑαυτοῦ λαλήσει, *he himself shall speak for himself*; John xvi. 27 αὐτὸς γὰρ ὁ πατήρ..., *for the Father himself....*
In this sense αὐτός (cf. its use in 2nd as well as 3rd person plural *Reflexives*, and see 'Note. Third Person Plural', under 1. 2. above, p. 120) is not limited to the 3rd person, but does duty for *self* in the 1st and 2nd persons also: Luke xxiv. 39 ἐγώ εἰμι αὐτός, *it is I myself*; Luke xxii. 71 αὐτοὶ γὰρ ἠκούσαμεν, *for we ourselves have heard.*

Note. In John ix. 18, τοὺς γονεῖς αὐτοῦ τοῦ ἀναβλέψαντος, the αὐτοῦ is strange: the context seems to require *the parents themselves...*

[1] For the distribution of these pronouns in the different N.T. writers, see G. D. Kilpatrick in *J.T.S.* XLII (July–Oct. 1941), 184–6.

(τοὺς γονεῖς αὐτούς), not *the parents of the man himself*... (cf. 'The Order of Words', p. 168).

iii. *The same*, when it stands, exactly like an adjective, between the article and the noun: Matt. xxvi. 44 τὸν αὐτὸν λόγον εἰπών, *saying the same word* (i.e. *words*); or with a repeated article, as τὸν λόγον τὸν αὐτόν; or absolutely, with its own article but no noun: Matt. v. 46 οὐχὶ καὶ οἱ τελῶναι τὸ αὐτὸ ποιοῦσιν; *do not even the tax collectors do as much* (i.e. *the same thing*)?

Thus the Latin equivalent of αὐτός would be sometimes *is* (*he, that man*), sometimes *ipse* (*-self*, αὐτὸς ὁ ἄνθρωπος or ὁ ἄνθρωπος αὐτός), sometimes *idem* (*the same*, ὁ αὐτὸς ἄνθρωπος).

Note. There are some Lucan passages (see discussion under 'The Adjective', above, p. 93) which seem to be exceptions: Luke x. 7 ἐν αὐτῇ δὲ τῇ οἰκίᾳ (cf. x. 21, xii. 12 ἐν αὐτῇ τῇ ὥρᾳ) must mean *in that same house* (*hour*), as though it had been ἐν τῇ αὐτῇ οἰκίᾳ, etc. But see D.-B. § 288, *Proleg.* 91. M.-H. II, 432 adduces Acts xvi. 18, xxii. 13 as instances of this in clearly non-Semitic contexts, but M. Black[1] suspects Semitic influence behind the idiom.

2. οὗτος can mean:

i. A fairly emphatic *this one* (in contrast to ἐκεῖνος, *that one*, or similar expressions): Luke xxiii. 41 ...ἡμεῖς μὲν...οὗτος δὲ....

ii. A quite unemphatic *he*, almost exactly the same as αὐτός i. above: John xviii. 30 εἰ μὴ ἦν οὗτος κακὸν ποιῶν, *if he had not been a criminal*. Roughly the Latin equivalent would be *hic*.

3. ἐκεῖνος is the only one of these three which retains fairly uniformly the sense *that person* (in contrast to *this*), though, at its weakest, it becomes nearly as colourless as *he*. Cf. Latin *iste*.

Note that the position of οὗτος (when used attributively) in relation to its noun is a delicate and, it may be, significant matter. In St Matthew, St Mark, St Luke, the Acts, and St John, it occurs *after* more frequently than *before*. Possibly the comparatively few occurrences before may indicate some special intention. See H. Schürmann, 'Die Sprache des Christus' in *Biblische Zeitschrift*, n.F. 1 (1958), 65 and n. 91.

[1] *An Aramaic Approach to the Gospels* (O.U.P. 1946), 71, 72; and again in *J.T.S.* XLIX (July–Oct. 1948), 160, n. 2.

4. But now notice also   ὅδε, ἥδε, τόδε
and   ὁ δέ, ἡ δέ.
Of these it may be said:

i. That ὅδε, etc., is not common in the N.T., and only once occurs with a noun: Jas. iv. 13 τήνδε τὴν πόλιν.

ii. That ὅδε (ἥδε, τόδε) means, generally, *this man* (etc.) or *he* (*she*, *it*), and thus is a rough alternative for οὗτος, αὕτη, τοῦτο. Occasionally it gains a slight emphasis by context, and means *this one* in contrast to someone else; and one suspects that it was an eager and emphatic reader who, desirous of emphasizing it thus, caused the scribe in Luke xvi. 25 (best reading?) to write ὧδε (*here*), when an emphatic ὅδε (*he*, as opposed to σύ, *thou*) is obviously the sense required.†

iii. That the masc. or fem. article in the Nominative with δέ (accented and spaced as two separate words) provides a very common way of saying *and he* (*she*), or *but he* (*she*): ὁ δὲ ἔφη, *and he said*. But τὸ δέ, *and it*, does not seem to occur; and the oblique cases do not seem to be used thus. (In Acts xvii. 28 τοῦ for τούτου is in a quotation from Aratus.) In such cases the relative pronoun steps in.

iv. Note a similar use of the definite article with a particle, as the equivalent of a pronoun, in the idiom ὁ μέν...ὁ δέ, *the one...the other*; and ὁ μὲν οὖν, *so he*..., without necessarily any ὁ δέ to follow.
In Matt. xxvi. 57 οἱ δὲ κρατήσαντες τὸν Ἰησοῦν illustrates a slight ambiguity which arises as a result of this articular idiom: apart from its context, there is nothing to show whether this means *And they, seizing Jesus*... or *And those who had seized Jesus*.... See above, 'The Definite Article', 1. *Note* (*b*), p. 107.

III. RELATIVE PRONOUNS

1. At least in some classical writers, a distinction is discernible between ὅς, ἥ, ὅ as = *who, which*, and ὅστις, ἥτις, ὅτι as = something like *who is such that..., seeing that he...*, etc. (cf. Latin *quippe qui*), or (in other contexts) as = *whoever* (indefinite).
There is considerable discussion as to whether such a distinction still obtains in the N.T. Moulton (*Proleg.* 92) says that the distinction 'is not yet dead'. See also Rob. 67 (quoting Dieterich as including 'ὅστις for ὅς' as among the peculiarities of the κοινή of Asia Minor) and 726–8. There is an interesting discussion by H. J. Cadbury in

J.B.L. XLII (1923), 150 ff. Cadbury notes three considerations pointing to 'the complete extinction', in most N.T. writings, of any distinction, namely:

(*a*) 'The limitation of the forms [of ὅστις] used' (only Nom., except in ἕως ὅτου).

(*b*) 'The large degree to which the corresponding forms of the simple relative have been ousted by the compound.'†

(*c*) 'It is sometimes possible to compare within a single author instances of the use of the two pronouns where the very similarity in thought and form between the parallels shows that the distinction is merely a matter of declension, if one may say so, rather than of sense.'

For Luke, Cadbury maintains, the relatives had become a single pronoun declined as follows (with few exceptions):

ὅς, ἥτις, ὅ   οἵτινες, αἵτινες, ἅ
οὗ, ἧς, etc.   ὧν, etc.

The same holds, he says, for Hebrews; and for Paul, except that ἅτινα has nearly replaced ἅ.

The reason, he says, is not obvious. The avoidance of hiatus is not a convincing one, in view of the carelessness of N.T. writers about hiatus. Possibly it was to avoid confusion with the article, the avoided forms of the simple relative being (except for ἅ in Paul) the only ones which agree in all but accent with the corresponding forms of the article.

ὅσπερ, which would have seemed convenient, scarcely occurs in the N.T., if at all. It is a *v.l.* in Mark xv. 6, and ($\mathfrak{p}^{45}$) in John x. 16 (ἅπερ).[1]

Nevertheless, it is possible to argue that in the following passages a distinction certainly improves the sense and may have been intended: Acts x. 47, xvii. 11 (contrast *v.* 10), Rom. vi. 2, ix. 4, II Cor. viii. 10, Jas. iv. 14 (the latter seems to be used adversatively—*whereas actually...*). Moulton styles this usage 'essential', as meaning *which by its very nature....* In Matt. vii. 24 the pronoun appears to be indefinite (Moulton's 'generic', meaning *which, as other like things...*).

2. In Acts xiii. 25 (τί ἐμὲ ὑπονοεῖτε εἶναι, οὐκ εἰμὶ ἐγώ), τί is explained by some as equivalent to a *relative* (not an *interrogative*) pronoun: *I am not* that which *you suppose me to be*; but the grammar is saved and good sense is made by *What do you suppose me to be? I am not (the one)*.

---

[1] I have noticed this instance in a facsimile: I have not tested whether it recurs at all.

See further under 'Relative Clauses', p. 132.

3. Note that ὃς δέ and ὃς μέν are sometimes used (like ὁ δέ, etc., above) as demonstratives: Mark iv. 4, Rom. xiv. 5, etc.

IV. INDEFINITE PRONOUNS

(For ὅστις, etc., see under the previous section)

The nearest parallel to the Latin *quidam* etc., *a certain* (*person* or *thing*) is the enclitic τις (masc. and fem.), τι (neut.). This can stand by itself, or with a supporting noun: Acts xv. 1 καί τινες κατελθόντες ἀπὸ τῆς Ἰουδαίας ἐδίδασκον, Phil. i. 15 τινὲς μέν...τινὲς δέ (*some*...*others*); Luke x. 30 ἄνθρωπός τις..., Acts iii. 2 καί τις ἀνήρ. The tendency (as with other enclitic words) is not to place it first in the sentence, despite the exceptions, or partial exceptions, just quoted.

εἷς, *one*, is sometimes used in a similar sense: Matt. xix. 16 καὶ ἰδοὺ εἷς προσελθὼν αὐτῷ εἶπεν...; Mark x. 17 προσδραμὼν εἷς; Matt. viii. 19 προσελθὼν εἷς γραμματεύς; Matt. xxvi. 69 μία παιδίσκη. Note also εἷς τις, Luke xxii. 50, etc. See 'Semitisms', I. v. p. 176, below.

XII

OBSERVATIONS ON CERTAIN USES
OF THE INFINITIVE

For practical purposes the Infinitive is classed as a mood (*Proleg.* 202), although it is generally held[1] to be, in origin, the Locative or Dative case of a noun. Its substantival qualities appear, of course, most obviously in the Articular Infinitive.

The general remarks about *Aktionsart* (above, pp. 5, 6) apply to the Infinitive, and *Aktionsart* may often be studied more easily in the Infinitive than in other parts of the verb.

The chief uses of the Infinitive are discussed under various headings 'Final Clauses', etc.); but one or two less easily classified ones are here noted.

I. INFINITIVE FOR IMPERATIVE

At least a few passages in the N.T. exhibit Infinitives so independent of any verb of commanding or the like that one can only class them as Infinitives used in an imperatival sense: Rom. xii. 15, χαίρειν μετὰ χαιρόντων, κλαίειν μετὰ κλαιόντων, and Phil. iii. 16, πλὴν εἰς ὃ ἐφθάσαμεν, τῷ αὐτῷ στοιχεῖν, are usually adduced.[2] Less striking are instances of an Imperatival Infinitive following an Imperative, and, as it were, extending it: Luke ix. 3 Μηδὲν αἴρετε εἰς τὴν ὁδόν, μήτε ῥάβδον μήτε πήραν κ.τ.λ. ἔχειν; Acts xxiii. 23, 24 εἶπεν Ἑτοιμάσατε στρατιώτας... κτήνη τε παραστῆσαι (here I suspect that the preceding εἶπεν is influencing the thought of the writer); Tit. ii. 1–10 σὺ δὲ λάλει ἃ πρέπει τῇ ὑγιαινούσῃ διδασκαλίᾳ. πρεσβύτας νηφαλίους εἶναι... τοὺς νεωτέρους ὡσαύτως παρακάλει σωφρονεῖν (here, νηφαλίους εἶναι is perhaps a quite normal Accusative and Infinitive after λάλει).

The epistolary χαίρειν is perhaps to be regarded as one of the independent imperatival uses.[3]

---

[1] See, for example, Giles, *Manual*, § 525.

[2] See *Proleg.* 179; *M.T.* §§ 364, 365.

[3] But Burton (*M.T.* § 388) assumes an unexpressed verb of bidding; and Ignatius, *Magn., Inscr.*, has εὔχομαι... πλεῖστα χαίρειν, which supports Burton's view.

Whether the Hebrew 'Infinitive Absolute' has influenced the use at all it is hard to judge; but Homeric instances[1] make one cautious about detecting Semitic influence.

II. EPEXEGETIC INFINITIVE

This is a flexible and subtle use. One or two examples will serve to make a reader alert and a translator ready with the idiomatic equivalent.

Acts xv. 10 τί πειράζετε τὸν θεόν, ἐπιθεῖναι ζυγὸν κ.τ.λ., *why do you test God* by putting *a yoke...?* Heb. v. 5 ὁ χριστὸς οὐχ ἑαυτὸν ἐδόξασεν γενηθῆναι ἀρχιερέα, *Christ did not take for himself the honour of becoming high priest;* I Cor. vii. 25 ἠλεημένος...πιστὸς εἶναι, *pitied...enough to be trustworthy.* See also Luke i. 54, 72, 73, 79, and Eph. iv. 22 (for which see also 'Final Clauses', 4. p. 139).

It will be observed how thin the boundary wears here and there between epexegetic (that is, explanatory and extensive) Infinitives and consecutive Infinitives: the last instance might nearly be *pitied in such a way as to become....*

Note also that a ἵνα-clause can be used as an alternative for such epexegetic Infinitives (see under 'Remarks on ἵνα and ὥστε', pp. 145 f.).

III. ARTICULAR INFINITIVE

1. The Infinitive is believed to have originated as a noun, and is, in fact, often so used, with or without an article. As examples of its use as a noun but without an article, John iv. 7, δός μοι πεῖν, Matt. xiv. 16, δότε αὐτοῖς ὑμεῖς φαγεῖν, may perhaps be fairly quoted, although it is, perhaps, easier in these cases to understand τι, *something (to drink, to eat),* than to treat πεῖν and φαγεῖν as anarthrous nouns, *drink, food.* The use with an article is far commoner, and examples are here given, in various cases:

i. *Nominative:*
Phil. i. 24 τὸ δὲ ἐπιμένειν τῇ σαρκὶ ἀναγκαιότερον δι᾽ ὑμᾶς.

ii. *Accusative:*
Acts xxv. 11 οὐ παραιτοῦμαι τὸ ἀποθανεῖν.
Rom. xiv. 13 τοῦτο κρίνατε μᾶλλον, τὸ μὴ τιθέναι πρόσκομμα τῷ ἀδελφῷ.

---

[1] Monro, *Hom. Gramm.* 162 (cited by Rob. 943, n. 2).

iii. *Genitive:*

    Gal. ii. 12 πρὸ τοῦ γὰρ ἐλθεῖν τινας.

    Jas. iv. 15 ἀντὶ τοῦ λέγειν ὑμᾶς, if, which is not quite certain, it is to be construed as *instead of your saying*.

iv. *Dative:*

    Luke viii. 40 ἐν δὲ τῷ ὑποστρέφειν τὸν ᾿Ιησοῦν.

    Luke xii. 15 οὐκ ἐν τῷ περισσεύειν τινὶ ἡ ζωὴ αὐτοῦ ἐστιν.

Note. As one might expect, the subject of such an Infinitive is in the Accusative (see examples in iii. and iv. above, and note a rare exception under 2. iv. below, p. 129); and the negative is normally μή (see under example ii. above; wherever οὐ appears in the above examples, it is of course construed with the main verb, not with the Infinitive). Further, it is obviously normal that a subject should be actually expressed in a sentence such as those in iii. and the first in iv. above, where the Infinitive refers to the action of definite persons. An exception is Luke xi. 37 ἐν δὲ τῷ λαλῆσαι, where one would expect ἐν δὲ τῷ λαλῆσαι αὐτόν (so certain MSS.).

2. Certain peculiar uses of *the articular Infinitive with the article in the Genitive* will now be illustrated:

i. *Final.* Matt. ii. 13 μέλλει γὰρ ῾Ηρῴδης ζητεῖν τὸ παιδίον τοῦ ἀπολέσαι αὐτό. Here ἵνα ἀπολέσῃ would be equally exact, or the Infinitive without the article could be used. The same applies to, for example, Acts iii. 12 ὡς...πεποιηκόσιν τοῦ περιπατεῖν. Indeed, in Luke ii. 22, 24 the plain Infinitive and the Infinitive with τοῦ are used in identical senses:[1] παραστῆσαι...καὶ τοῦ δοῦναι...; and it has been pointed out[2] that this sequence, which occurs several times in the opening chapters of Luke, is practically unknown in the LXX (I Chron. xxix. 19 being not an exact parallel, for καί links the two more immediately), and may prove to be an index to the composition of these chapters.[3] For the distribution of this usage, see Rob. 990 (mostly confined to Matthew, Luke and Acts) and M.-H. II, 448 ('a decidedly Lucan characteristic'—Sir J. Hawkins).

ii. *Consecutive*, or either *Final* or *Consecutive*. Rom. vii. 3 ἐλευθέρα ἐστὶν ἀπὸ τοῦ νόμου, τοῦ μὴ εἶναι... (=ὥστε μὴ εἶναι...); Phil. iii. 10

[1] See H. P. V. Nunn, *A Syntax of N.T. Greek*, § 175.

[2] In an anonymous paper contributed to Professor Dodd's N.T. Seminar in October 1948.

[3] It is the more curious that Luke does not use this construction, as the LXX does, after προστιθέναι. See under 'Semitisms', II. vii, p. 177.

τοῦ γνῶναι αὐτόν (where it may be final, parallel to ἵνα...κερδήσω, or consecutive, expressing the result of the previous conditions (=ὥστε γνῶναι); or it may even fall into the next category).

iii. *Epexegetic*, i.e. explanatory or extensive of a preceding idea: Phil. iii. 21 κατὰ τὴν ἐνέργειαν τοῦ δύνασθαι αὐτόν..., i.e. *by virtue of the power by which he can...*, or *the power, namely his ability to...*; Acts xxi. 12 παρεκαλοῦμεν...τοῦ μὴ ἀναβαίνειν αὐτόν, *we begged him...not to go up*. Cf. Wisd. x. 8. This merges almost insensibly into—

iv. An *Appositional* use. The most extreme example, often quoted, is Rev. xii. 7 ἐγένετο πόλεμος ἐν τῷ οὐρανῷ, ὁ Μιχαὴλ καὶ οἱ ἄγγελοι αὐτοῦ τοῦ πολεμῆσαι μετὰ τοῦ δράκοντος, *there was war...Michael... fighting...*, where it is doubtful if any less barbarous Greek than that of Revelation would have tolerated the subjects of the Infinitive in the Nominative. Compare the following *subjective* uses: Luke xvii. 1 ἀνένδεκτόν ἐστιν τοῦ τὰ σκάνδαλα μὴ ἐλθεῖν, *that hindrances should not come is impossible*; Acts x. 25 ὡς δὲ ἐγένετο τοῦ εἰσελθεῖν τὸν Πέτρον, *when Peter's entry took place*;[1] xxvii. 1 ὡς δὲ ἐκρίθη τοῦ ἀποπλεῖν ἡμᾶς, *when our sailing away was determined*; I Cor. xvi. 4 ἐὰν δὲ ἄξιον ᾖ τοῦ κἀμὲ πορεύεσθαι, *if my going too is worth while* or *fitting*. There seems to be no logical reason whatever why these should be in the Genitive: they are strictly the subjects of their sentences. Compare further Acts xx. 3 ἐγένετο γνώμης[2] τοῦ ὑποστρέφειν, *he decided to return*, where the Genitive γνώμης is also curious. Is it a possessive use, perhaps to be compared with our phrase *of the opinion*?

With regard to these, *note*:

(*a*) The *Final* use had already been developed by Thucydides.

(*b*) The Hebrew 'Infinitive Construct', a noun-like type of Infinitive, in relations with other words partly corresponding to the genitive relationship in Greek, probably gave a fillip to the construction in Semitic Greek, especially the LXX.

(*c*) In the N.T. 'it is only in Luke (Gospel 23, Acts 21) and Paul (13) that τοῦ with the Inf. (without prepositions) is common' (Rob. 1067).[3]

---

[1] Only here, and in the reading of D in Acts ii. 1. *Beg. in loc.* quotes *Acta Barnabae* vii ὡς δὲ ἐγένετο τοῦ τελέσαι αὐτοὺς διδάσκοντας.

[2] Unless, indeed, ἐγένετο γνώμης means something more than *he decided*.

[3] See especially *Proleg.* 216, 217, Rob. 1066–8, D.-B. § 400.

XIII

RELATIVE CLAUSES

The simpler sorts of relative clause present no particular difficulties; and relative clauses concerned with time are, in any case, given a separate section below; but the following matters call for note:

1. As in Latin, there are in Greek plenty of instances of the attraction of a relative pronoun anomalously into the case of the antecedent: e.g. Acts xvii. 31 ἐν ἀνδρὶ ᾧ ὥρισεν (for ὃν ὥρισεν).[1]

2. This anomaly is carried a step further when the antecedent is omitted but its case still retained (allusively) by the relative pronoun; e.g. Acts xxiv. 13 οὐδὲ παραστῆσαι δύνανταί σοι περὶ ὧν νυνὶ κατηγοροῦσίν μου (for . . . ἐκεῖνα περὶ ὧν . . .); Acts xxvi. 22 οὐδὲν ἐκτὸς λέγων ὧν τε οἱ προφῆται ἐλάλησαν μελλόντων γίνεσθαι καὶ Μωϋσῆς (for οὐδὲν ἐκτὸς ἐκείνων ἅ . . .).

3. Whether or not the cases would be different if the sentence were written out in full, the omission of the antecedent is common enough: I Cor. x. 30 ὑπὲρ οὗ (for ὑπὲρ ἐκείνου ὑπὲρ οὗ); II Cor. ii. 10 ᾧ δέ τι χαρίζεσθε, κἀγώ (for ἐκείνῳ δὲ ᾧ χαρίζεσθέ τι καὶ ἐγὼ χαρίζομαι αὐτό); and, where necessary, the relevant noun is then placed *after* the relative pronoun: Matt. vii. 2 ἐν ᾧ μέτρῳ μετρεῖτε; Rom. ii. 16 ἐν ᾗ ἡμέρᾳ; Rom. iv. 17 κατέναντι οὗ ἐπίστευσεν θεοῦ; Rom. xvi. 2 ἐν ᾧ ἂν ὑμῶν χρήζῃ πράγματι.

4. Sometimes a neuter relative is used where strictly a masculine or feminine might have been expected—presumably with reference to the 'whole idea' of the preceding clause rather than to the single word which is the immediate antecedent of the relative:

Eph. v. 5 πᾶς πόρνος ἢ ἀκάθαρτος ἢ πλεονέκτης, ὅ [not ὅς, unless a variant reading is right] ἐστιν εἰδωλολάτρης. . . (cf. *id est*); contrast Col. iii. 5 καὶ τὴν πλεονεξίαν ἥτις ἐστὶν εἰδωλολατρεία.

I John ii. 8 is a possible parallel to Eph. v. 5: πάλιν ἐντολὴν καινὴν γράφω ὑμῖν, ὅ ἐστιν ἀληθὲς ἐν αὐτῷ καὶ ἐν ὑμῖν. . . (where R. Law,

---

[1] Conversely, in Acts xxi. 16 the noun is attracted into the case of the relative, ἄγοντες παρ᾽ ᾧ ξενισθῶμεν Μνάσωνί τινι Κυπρίῳ. . . (instead of ἄγοντες Μνάσωνά τινα Κύπριον. . .παρ᾽ ᾧ ξενισθῶμεν).

The Tests of Life, prefers so to construe it—'as a parenthetic clause in apposition', rather than taking ὅ ἐστιν ἀληθές 'as the direct object after γράφω, with ἐντολὴν καινήν as an Accusative of nearer definition: "I write to you, as a new commandment, what is true in Him..."' (p. 376). On p. 235 he paraphrases: 'This old commandment...is, nevertheless, a new, fresh, living commandment—a fact that is realized first in Christ and then in you...').

5. I Cor. iii. 17 is an instance of a very understandable *constructio ad sensum*: ὁ...ναὸς τοῦ θεοῦ...οἵτινές ἐστε ὑμεῖς.

6. Difficult to analyse or define with precision are *adverbial* relatives. Thus, Rom. vi. 10 ὃ γὰρ ἀπέθανεν, τῇ ἁμαρτίᾳ ἀπέθανεν ἐφάπαξ· ὃ δὲ ζῇ, ζῇ τῷ θεῷ, is, presumably, best rendered **whereas** *he died, he died to sin, once for all; and* **whereas** *he lives*..., rather than making ὃ a strictly cognate relative, as though it stood for τὸν θάνατον ὃν (or ᾧ) ἀπέθανεν...; in Gal. ii. 20 ὃ δὲ νῦν ζῶ ἐν σαρκί, ἐν πίστει ζῶ, the decision is less obvious: the A.V. and the R.V. take it as cognate— *the (that) life which I now live*; but it could be **whereas** *I now live, I live*...; in II Cor. xii. 13 τί γάρ ἐστιν ὃ ἡσσώθητε, the meaning must be *what is there* in regard to which *you came off worse...?* i.e. it is a genuine 'Accusative of respect' (see Rob. 479). So, apparently, in the famous 'Corban' sentence, Mark vii. 11 Κορβᾶν...ὃ ἐὰν ἐξ ἐμοῦ ὠφεληθῇς,[1] *anything* in regard to which *you would have received benefit.*

Still more intangible is the vague ἐν ᾧ or ἐν οἷς: Rom. viii. 3 τὸ γὰρ ἀδύνατον τοῦ νόμου, ἐν ᾧ ἠσθένει διὰ τῆς σαρκός, **since** (or **in that**) *it was weak*; but in *v.* 15 ἐλάβετε πνεῦμα υἱοθεσίας, ἐν ᾧ κράζομεν Ἀββᾶ ὁ πατήρ, perhaps means *a spirit...in* (or *by*) *which*...; Acts xxvi. 12 ἐν οἷς πορευόμενος εἰς τὴν Δαμασκόν..., where it is a question whether the relative refers strictly to what precedes, as though it meant *in the course of which activity*..., or whether it is a vague resumptive phrase, corresponding to our *and so, well then*. In I Peter the interpretation of ἐν ᾧ is of some exegetical moment, for in iii. 19 some commentators wish to refer it back strictly to its grammatical antecedent, πνεύματι, so that it means that Christ went *in spirit* [as opposed to *in flesh*] to the spirits in prison; whereas others maintain that here, as elsewhere in I Peter, it is a vague resumptive phrase—*and so*. Selwyn, *in loc.* and 315, 317, takes a middle course, preferring '"in which process", *in the course of which*'. In i.6 the same ambiguity appears: is it a genuine

[1] Better, ὠφελήθης.

relative, *in which circumstances you exult*, or simply *and so you exult?*[1] And in iv. 4 does it mean *and so they are surprised when you do not . . .*, or *at which they are surprised, namely when you do not . . .?* It is, perhaps, relevant that in Acts xxiv. 16 ἐν τούτῳ καὶ αὐτὸς ἀσκῶ ἀπρόσκοπον συνείδησιν ἔχειν . . . seems to represent a similarly vague reference, but in its direct, not relative, form.

ἐφ᾿ ᾧ in II Cor. v. 4 and Rom. v. 12 almost certainly means *inasmuch as* (the *in quo* interpretation of Rom. v. 12, closely connected with theories of Original Sin, is almost certainly wrong: see commentators *in loc.*); but it is harder to be sure about it in Phil. iv. 10: does it there also mean *inasmuch as*, or, more probably, *with regard to which* (i.e. τὸ ὑπὲρ ἐμοῦ φρονεῖν)? And is ἐφ᾿ οἷς in Rom. vi. 21 *at which things?* In Phil. iii. 12 εἰ καὶ καταλάβω, ἐφ᾿ ᾧ καὶ κατελήμφθην, it may be that καταλάβω is used absolutely (cf. I Cor. ix. 24), in which case ἐφ᾿ ᾧ again means *inasmuch as*, or, possibly, it implies an object for καταλάβω, *that I may grasp that [achievement] with a view to which I have been grasped.*

ὃν τρόπον (Luke xiii. 34, Acts i. 11, etc.) represents a compound adverbial phrase such as ἐκεῖνον τρόπον ὅν . . ., *in that manner in which*. Similarly, ἕως οὗ, ἄχρις οὗ (=*until*) are analysable into ἕως ἐκείνου τοῦ καιροῦ ἐν ᾧ, etc.

7. For the interrogative used as a relative, Acts xiii. 25 (as has been noted under 'Pronouns', p. 124) is sometimes quoted: τί ἐμὲ ὑπονοεῖτε εἶναι, οὐκ εἰμὶ ἐγώ, as though it meant *I am not* what (ὅτι or ὅ) *you suppose me to be*; but this could be divided into two sentences: *what do you suppose me to be? I am not [the one]*, whereby the τί would remain a true interrogative. See *Beg. in loc.* It is possible that the reverse phenomenon—relative as interrogative—is to be seen in Acts xi. 3 λέγοντες ὅτι εἰσῆλθες πρὸς ἄνδρας ἀκροβυστίαν ἔχοντας, as though it were Why *did you go in . . .?*; though this might also be merely an instance of ὅτι introducing direct speech: *they said You went in . . . .* See *Beg. in loc.*, and cf. Mark ix. 11. Cf. p. 159.†

8. For the redundant pronoun after the relative (ἧς εἶχεν τὸ θυγάτριον αὐτῆς . . ., Mark vii. 25, etc.), see under 'Semitisms', p. 176.

9. *Temporal Relative Clauses.* The reason for devoting a separate section to these is (i) that they present certain special features within the general framework of relative clauses, and (ii) that, in addition,

---

[1] Heb. vi. 17 presents a similar problem.

there are alternative ways of expressing the sense of a temporal relative clause—namely, by the Articular Infinitive preceded by an appropriate preposition, and by a Participle—which call for an extension of the general section on relative clauses.

i. Special features presented by *temporal*, as distinct from other, relative clauses are concerned chiefly with the moods. Thus:

(*a*) Temporal particles such as ὅτε, ὁπότε, ἕως, ὡς, or phrases equivalent to temporal particles such as ἐν ᾧ (when it =*while*) are, in certain circumstances, found with the indicative:

Matt. vii. 28 ὅτε ἐτέλεσεν ὁ Ἰησοῦς τοὺς λόγους τούτους.

Luke vi. 3 ὁπότε ἐπείνασεν (apparently merely = *when he was hungry*—not *whenever* . . .).

Luke xii. 58 ὡς γὰρ ὑπάγεις.

Luke xix. 13 ἐν ᾧ ἔρχομαι⟩ (Both virtually =*until I come back*, cf.
John xxi. 22 ἕως ἔρχομαι ⟩   *dum venio*.)

Mark ix. 21 πόσος χρόνος ἐστὶν ὡς (*v.l.* B 𝔭[45] ἕως) τοῦτο γέγονεν αὐτῷ; Here both ὡς and ἕως are unusual, and one would expect something like ἀφ' οὗ (the reading of several MSS.).[1]

(*b*) But a degree of indefiniteness or contingency often attaches to a temporal clause, and this is liable to affect the mood of the verb and to cause the addition of the particle ἄν. Thus:

In frequentative clauses (whose time is thus, by definition, indefinite): Mark xiii. 11 ὅταν ἄγωσιν ὑμᾶς (-αν and Subjunctive).

In indefinite clauses:

Luke ii. 26 πρὶν ἢ ἂν ἴδῃ τὸν χριστὸν κυρίου (ἄν and Subjunctive).

Acts xxv. 16 πρὶν ἢ ὁ κατηγορούμενος κατὰ πρόσωπον ἔχοι τοὺς κατηγόρους τόπον τε ἀπολογίας λάβοι (the Optatives representing, in indirect discourse, what would, in direct discourse, have been expressed by the Subjunctive with ἄν, as in the preceding instance. See *M.T.* § 333).

John xiii. 38 ἕως οὗ ἀρνήσῃ με. . . .

Rom. xv. 24 ὡς ἂν πορεύωμαι εἰς τὴν Σπανίαν.

I Cor. iv. 5 ἕως ἂν ἔλθῃ ὁ κύριος.

I Cor. xvi. 3 ὅταν δὲ παραγένωμαι.

II Thess. i. 10 ὅταν ἔλθῃ.

It is to be noted, however, that ὅταν with the *Indicative* does occur in Mark xi. 25, Rev. iv. 9 (ὅταν δώσουσιν—future!), and the Indicative is used also in certain non-temporal but equally *indefinite* clauses (see *M.T.* §§ 308, 309).

[1] See C. C. Tarelli in *J.T.S.* xxxix (July 1938), 258.

ii. The same sense as is expressed by a temporal particle and a verb in the Indicative, Subjunctive, or (rarely) Optative, may be expressed alternatively (*a*) by the Articular Infinitive preceded by an appropriate preposition, or (*b*) by a participle; e.g.:

(*a*) Mark i. 14 καὶ μετὰ τὸ παραδοθῆναι τὸν Ἰωάνην...; Luke ix. 18 καὶ ἐγένετο ἐν τῷ εἶναι αὐτὸν προσευχόμενον... (or *v*. 29 ἐν τῷ προσεύχεσθαι αὐτόν).[1]

(*b*) Acts xxiv. 27 διετίας δὲ πληρωθείσης; Acts xxv. 6 διατρίψας δὲ...ἡμέρας οὐ πλείους ὀκτὼ ἢ δέκα; Acts xxviii. 10 καὶ ἀναγομένοις [=*when we put to sea*] ἐπέθεντο τὰ πρὸς τὰς χρείας; Rom. xv. 29 οἶδα δὲ ὅτι ἐρχόμενος (=*when* or *if I come*).

The latter example shows how, for obvious reasons, conditional and temporal clauses overlap.

[1] For the possibility of Semitic influence on this apparently un-Attic use, see M.-H. II, 451, 464.

XIV

COMMANDS, PROHIBITIONS, WISHES

1. The Imperative is the most obvious vehicle of commands or prohibitions.

In general the Present Imperative commands (or, with μή, prohibits) *continued* or *habitual* action, the Aorist a *specific* action: Luke xvii. 8 ἑτοίμασον τί δειπνήσω (*get ready something for my dinner*—specific), καί... διακόνει μοι (*and... wait on me*—continued action).

But this is an extremely fluid rule, and often the tense appears to be determined more by the meaning of the verb or by some obscure habit than by the 'rules' of *Aktionsart*. Thus: in Matt. viii. 9 πορεύθητι... ποίησον τοῦτο (both Aorists) are according to rule, but between the two comes the present ἔρχου. Similarly in Acts xxii. 18 σπεῦσον καὶ ἔξελθε are followed by πορεύου (*v.* 21); in Luke xv the correctly Aorist Imperatives ἐξενέγκατε, ἐνδύσατε, δότε, θύσατε are interrupted (*v.* 23) by φέρετε; in John vii. 24 many MSS. at least read μὴ κρίνετε (Present) κατ' ὄψιν, ἀλλὰ τὴν δικαίαν κρίσιν κρίνατε (Aorist);[1] in Philem. 22 occurs an apparently inappropriate present ἑτοίμαζέ μοι ξενίαν.

Conversely, where one might expect the (frequentative) present, one sometimes finds the Aorist: Matt. xxiii. 8–10 ὑμεῖς δὲ μὴ κληθῆτε 'Ραββεί... πατέρα μὴ καλέσητε... μηδὲ κληθῆτε καθηγηταί (the Subjunctive is here equivalent to the Imperative). Very interesting are the Imperatives in the Lord's Prayer: both in Matt. vi. 9–13 and in Luke xi. 2–4 they are all Aorist except that Luke has the present δίδου where Matthew has the Aorist δός: ἁγιασθήτω... ἐλθάτω... γενηθήτω (Matthew only)... δός (Matthew) δίδου (Luke) ... μὴ εἰσενέγκῃς... ῥῦσαι (Matthew only). However, Luke's present is exactly right in his context which is a frequentative one, and Matthew's Aorist is right in the different context there provided.[2] Interesting, in the light of this, is the version of the Lord's Prayer in a Christian amulet[3] which has: [perhaps ἁγιασθήτω missing]...

[1] But here it is possible that a contrast is intended between frequentative and specific.

[2] I owe this observation to Dr W. F. Howard.

[3] Edited by Wilcken in *Archiv für Papyrusforschung*, 1, 431 ff., and assigned by him approximately to 6th cent. A.D. (Milligan, *Greek Papyri*, 132 ff.).

ἐλθ[ά]τω...γενηθήτω...δὸς (correct, with a context like that of Matthew)...ἄφες...καὶ [μὴ] ἄγε...ῥῦ[σαι]. Contrast a 3rd cent. A.D. Papyrus (Milligan, *Greek Papyri*, 106) which contains a series of injunctions running: γενοῦ πρὸς ἐμὲ (*come to me*) ...ἔνιγκον (i.e. ἔνεγκον, Aor. Imperat. from Indicative ἤνεγκα)...μ[ὴ] ἐνίγκῃς (Aor. Subj.) ...ἄφες...μὴ ἀμελήσῃς...μὴ σκύλῃς...ἔρχου (Present).

I suggest, as working rules, the following:

i. Where there could be any ambiguity, writers tended (more or less, according to their degree of accuracy and feeling for style) to distinguish between the Present and Aorist *Aktionsart*.

ii. Where there could be no ambiguity, the tense was determined by sheer chance, or euphony, or tradition, or availability of words.[1]

iii. The student will be well advised to observe the *Aktionsart* rules as precisely as possible when he is translating English into Greek, and to take special care, when translating Greek into English, to see what the writers themselves do.

2. Another way of expressing commands and prohibitions is by ἵνα or μή with the Subjunctive. See under 'Remarks on ἵνα and ὥστε', below, pp. 144 f.

3. The Subjunctive in the 1st pers. singular or plural may also be used to express an injunction or wish: Luke xv. 23 εὐφρανθῶμεν.

4. More rarely the Optative is employed to express a wish or a deprecation: there is the familiar μὴ γένοιτο; Optatives of prayerful expectation in I Thess. iii. 11, v. 23, II Thess. iii. 16; and, in Mark xi. 14 the most vehemently prohibitive of all the examples: μηκέτι...μηδεὶς καρπὸν φάγοι; and in Philem. 20 perhaps the most imperatival of all the examples: ναί, ἀδελφέ, ἐγώ σου ὀναίμην (Aorist Optative of ὀνίνημι) ἐν κυρίῳ, *yes, brother, let me have this benefit from you in the Lord* (followed by the Imperative ἀνάπαυσον).[2]

---

[1] φέρε seems more popular than ἔνεγκον, πορεύου than ἔλθον, no matter what the *Aktionsart*; and other examples could be collected where words are mostly used only in one tense. Cf. C. C. Tarelli in *J.T.S.* XLVII (July–Oct. 1946), 175 ff., referred to below ('Miscellaneous Notes on Style', p. 198).

[2] Cf. συνγνώμην δέ, κύριέ μου, σχοίης μοι [καὶ εὔνους] ἀποδέξει (*sic*) με..., *But pray, my lord, do you pardon me*..., 4th cent. A.D. papyrus (Milligan, *Greek Papyri*, 129).

5. The word ὄφελον, which is manifestly verbal in origin, has crystallized in the N.T. into a *particle* introducing a wish, and is followed by the Indic.—Aor. or Imperf.—if a wish for the past or present (I Cor. iv. 8, II Cor. xi. 1, Rev. iii. 15), Fut., if it is a wish for the future (Gal. v. 12). In all these instances it seems to express an unfulfilled or unattainable wish; for although in II Cor. xi. 1 the wish is, after all, realized, the ὄφελον clause itself regards it as unattainable; and Gal. v. 12 is surely unattainable (*pace M.T.* § 27, REM. 2). It serves the purpose of the classical εἴθε, εἰ γάρ, with the Optative. It is sometimes proposed to take εἰ ἤδη ἀνήφθη in Luke xii. 49 in this sense (*oh that it were already kindled!*); but both the construction and the meaning of this famous *crux* are far from established. See under 'Semitisms', v, p. 187.

6. Sometimes the Infinitive is used in an evidently imperative sense. For this, see under 'Observations on Certain Uses of the Infinitive', above, pp. 126 f.

7. For participles used imperatively, see under 'Semitisms', pp. 179 f.

8. For the simple Future Indicative used as a command, see under 'Semitisms', pp. 178 f.

XV

FINAL CLAUSES

It is proposed here to discuss and illustrate some ways of expressing *purpose* (strictly final clauses); then, under the heading *Consecutive Clauses* to do the same for *result*; but the remarks on ἵνα and ὥστε which follow that section will show that the distinction is sometimes a delicate one; and it is well to recognize this at once. In English idiom, likewise, it is easy to find not only strictly final and strictly consecutive clauses, but also hybrid and ambiguous sentences: strictly final is *He hit the ball hard in order to score*; strictly consecutive is *He hit the ball so hard that he scored*; but *He hit the ball hard so as to score* is grammatically hybrid and a trifle ambiguous in meaning, even if it is seen to be intended on the whole for a final clause. It is possible that such blending of types is due to both having originated alike from *parataxis*—i.e. the placing side by side of two simple sentences (see Rob. 980, 981).

Final Clauses may take the following forms:

1. ἵνα or (less commonly) ὅπως,[1] usually with the Subjunctive (even after a main verb in a past tense, where Classical Greek would use an Optative): Mark ii. 10 ἵνα δὲ εἰδῆτε, Acts ix. 24 ὅπως αὐτὸν ἀνέλωσιν, I Cor. i. 27–9 ἵνα καταισχύνῃ...ἵνα καταισχύνῃ...ἵνα...καταργήσῃ, ὅπως μὴ καυχήσηται..., II Cor. viii. 14 ἵνα...γένηται...ὅπως γένηται.

Very rarely ἄν is added; thus:

i. ὅπως ἄν, Rom. iii. 4 (O.T. quotation), Luke ii. 35, Acts iii. 20, xv. 17 (O.T. quotation), ix. 12 (if correct reading) (see Rob. 986).

ii. Twice only in the N.T. ἵνα κἄν is used in this type of clause, Mark vi. 56 ἵνα κἄν τοῦ κρασπέδου...ἅψωνται, Acts v. 15 ἵνα...κἄν ἡ σκιὰ ἐπισκιάσῃ; and in both instances an implied *conditional* clause may be detected lurking—*even if it were no more than the fringe, no more than the shadow*; so A.V. *if it were but the border, that at least the shadow*. But if a plain καί had been used, it is difficult to imagine that the ἄν would have been missed.

[1] In Acts xx. 24 ὡς, if correct (*v.l.* ὅπως), is the only N.T. instance of ὡς so used.

The negative is either μή alone (cf. Latin *ne*): Mark xiii. 36 μὴ ἐλθὼν ἐξαίφνης εὕρῃ ὑμᾶς καθεύδοντας; or μή with ἵνα, ὅπως: Matt. xvii. 27 ἵνα δὲ μὴ σκανδαλίσωμεν αὐτούς, Acts xx. 16 ὅπως μὴ γένηται; or μή πως (strictly *lest perhaps*) or μή ποτε (strictly *lest at any time*), II Cor. ix. 4 μή πως...καταισχυνθῶμεν, Matt. xxv. 9 μή ποτε οὐ μὴ ἀρκέσῃ ἡμῖν καὶ ὑμῖν. Occasionally ἵνα is followed by a Fut. *Indic.*; e.g. John vii. 3, Acts xxi. 24, I Cor. ix. 18 (Rob. 984), Gal. ii. 4 (but *v.l.* Subj.). The case for ὅπως with the Indic. is doubtful in the N.T. (Rob. 986). Perhaps the only N.T. instance of μή with this construction is Col. ii. 8 μή τις ἔσται (Rob. 995).

ἵνα τί; =*why?* is presumably an abbreviation for ἵνα τί γένηται or some such phrase. Possibly I Cor. i. 31 ἵνα...ὁ καυχώμενος... καυχάσθω should be understood to mean ἵνα γένηται, to introduce the O.T. quotation. For ἵνα introducing imperatival clauses, see under 'Remarks on ἵνα and ὥστε'.

2. A relative clause with Subj. or Fut. Indic.: Heb. viii. 3 ὅθεν ἀναγκαῖον ἔχειν τι καὶ τοῦτον ὃ προσενέγκῃ, ...*something to offer*; Luke xi. 6 ὃ παραθήσω αὐτῷ, *something to set before him*; Luke ix. 58 ὁ δὲ υἱὸς τοῦ ἀνθρώπου οὐκ ἔχει ποῦ τὴν κεφαλὴν κλίνῃ, ...*anywhere to lay....*

When a Fut. Indic. is used it is sometimes difficult to decide whether a final or a purely affirmative sense is intended: e.g. in Matt. xxi. 41 (see *M.T.* § 317) does οἵτινες ἀποδώσουσιν αὐτῷ τοὺς καρπούς mean *who shall render...?* or *so that they may render...?*. See above, 'Pronouns', III. 1. pp. 123 f.

3. A plain Subjunctive: Luke xxii. 9 ποῦ θέλεις ἑτοιμάσωμεν...; *where do you wish us to prepare...?* Matt. xiii. 28 θέλεις...συλλέξωμεν αὐτά; *do you want us to...collect them?*

4. A plain Infinitive (note that this is very rare in Latin). Mark x. 45 οὐκ ἦλθεν διακονηθῆναι ἀλλὰ διακονῆσαι καὶ δοῦναι.... This is particularly common in so-called 'object-clauses', where the main verb is followed by an Acc. and Infin. forming, virtually, the object: Acts xxv. 21 τοῦ δὲ Παύλου ἐπικαλεσαμένου τηρηθῆναι αὐτόν, *when Paul appealed that he might be kept* (or *to be kept*); Acts xxiii. 18 ἔχοντά τι λαλῆσαί σοι; Luke v. 3 ἠρώτησεν αὐτὸν ἀπὸ τῆς γῆς ἐπαναγαγεῖν ὀλίγον.

In Eph. iv. 22 ἀποθέσθαι is hard to classify, but it seems to represent the contents of the teaching referred to, and to be 'epexegetic' (see 'Observations on Certain Uses of the Infinitive', p. 127) rather than final.

5. Even ὥστε with Infin., which is properly *consecutive*, is occasionally used to express *purpose*: (perhaps) Matt. x. 1 ἔδωκεν αὐτοῖς ἐξουσίαν πνευμάτων ἀκαθάρτων ὥστε ἐκβάλλειν αὐτά; cf. Matt. xxvii. 1, Luke iv. 29, ix. 52 (*si vera l.*), xx. 20. I Cor. v. 1 πορνεία...τοιαύτη...ὥστε, seems to be more *epexegetic* than either consecutive or final, although the τοιαύτη may well have influenced the choice of ὥστε by casting the sentence into a consecutive *form*. See 'Remarks on ἵνα and ὥστε', 1. ii.

6. The Infinitive (with or without the article) preceded by a preposition expressing purpose: Matt. vi. 1 πρὸς τὸ θεαθῆναι αὐτοῖς, *in order to be seen by them*; Rom. i. 11 εἰς τὸ στηριχθῆναι ὑμᾶς (though it is arguable that this is consecutive); I Thess. iii. 5 ἔπεμψα εἰς τὸ γνῶναι; II Cor. vii. 12 ἔγραψα...ἕνεκεν τοῦ φανερωθῆναι.

Note. In I Thess. iii. 3 τὸ μηδένα σαίνεσθαι (which looks like the best reading) is an exception to the use of a preposition before the Articular Infinitive in this sense.

7. For the final use of the Genitive of the Articular Infinitive, see above, p. 128.

8. The Future Participle: Acts viii. 27 ὃς ἐληλύθει προσκυνήσων (cf. Matt. ii. 2, where the plain Infin. (as in 4. above) is used in precisely the same sense); Acts xxiv. 17 ἐλεημοσύνας ποιήσων. Contrast (*si vera l.*) the extraordinary Aorist Part. in Acts xxv. 13, where a *v.l.* is the Fut. (see under 'Participles', p. 100).

XVI

CONSECUTIVE CLAUSES

1. The regular method of expressing result is to use ὥστε followed by the Infinitive. Strictly speaking the Infinitive should indicate only the *potential* result, representing the inherent qualities of the situation and not necessarily the actual consequences; while the Indicative should be used for the actual consequences. But, as a fact, the Indicative is rare and the Infinitive serves for both potential and actual consequences. Two passages are adduced by Burton (*M.T.* § 236) as the only two clear instances 'in the New Testament of ὥστε with the Indicative so closely joined to what precedes as to constitute a subordinate clause'; John iii. 16 οὕτως γὰρ ἠγάπησεν...ὥστε...ἔδωκεν; Gal. ii. 13 ...ὥστε καὶ Βαρνάβας συναπήχθη....

Otherwise we have, for example, Matt. xv. 30, 31 καὶ ἐθεράπευσεν αὐτούς· ὥστε τὸν ὄχλον θαυμάσαι... (which is evidently a reference to actual consequences); or Matt. viii. 28 χαλεποὶ λίαν, ὥστε μὴ ἰσχύειν τινὰ παρελθεῖν (which might be potential rather than actual). A great many other examples could be added of this common construction.[1]

2. In II Cor. ix. 5 the simple Acc. and Infin. without ὥστε might be consecutive in meaning: ταύτην ἑτοίμην εἶναι. But it might equally well be final.

3. The Articular Infin. preceded by a suitable preposition may also be used: II Cor. viii. 6 εἰς τὸ παρακαλέσαι ἡμᾶς Τίτον, *with the result that*....

For the blending and overlapping of final and consecutive, see 'Remarks on ἵνα and ὥστε', pp. 142 ff.

[1] See *M.T.* § 235 for a clear analysis of why the infin. construction does double duty.

XVII

REMARKS ON 'ΙΝΑ AND 'ΩΣΤΕ

An attempt has been made to isolate and describe some of the usual methods of expressing *purpose* (Final Clauses), *consequence* (Consecutive Clauses), and *commands, prohibitions, and wishes* (which are often allied, syntactically, with Final Clauses). It remains to debate some of the elusive and fascinating anomalies, overlappings, and interrelationships of these groups of ideas.

1. First, be it noted that the Semitic mind was notoriously unwilling to draw a sharp dividing-line between purpose and consequence.[1] It may be for this reason (or, at least, Semitic influence may be a contributory cause) that ἵνα with Subj. sometimes occurs in contexts which seem to impose a *consecutive*, instead of *final*, sense upon it; and, conversely, that ὥστε with Infin. seems sometimes to approximate to a *final* meaning.

i. Thus (despite the opinion of some scholars of weight to the contrary)[2] it is still worth while to ask whether the following ἵνα-clauses are not logically *consecutive*: Luke ix. 45 ἦν παρακεκαλυμμένον ἀπ' αὐτῶν ἵνα μὴ αἴσθωνται αὐτό; Gal. v. 17 ταῦτα [*sc.* Flesh and Spirit] γὰρ ἀλλήλοις ἀντίκειται, ἵνα μὴ ἃ ἐὰν θέλητε ταῦτα ποιῆτε; I Thess. v. 4 οὐκ ἐστὲ ἐν σκότει, ἵνα ἡ ἡμέρα ὑμᾶς ὡς κλέπτης καταλάβῃ; I John i. 9 πιστός ἐστιν καὶ δίκαιος, ἵνα ἀφῇ ἡμῖν τὰς ἁμαρτίας; and the ἵνα-clause with ἄξιος, ἱκανός, etc. (see Rad. 193). A very impressive Septuagintal instance adduced is Gen. xxii. 14 ἐκάλεσεν Ἀβραὰμ τὸ ὄνομα τοῦ τόπου ἐκείνου κύριος εἶδεν, ἵνα εἴπωσιν σήμερον . . . (Heb. אֲשֶׁר יֵאָמֵר).

The most notorious problem in this connexion is, perhaps, the interpretation of such phrases as ἵνα πληρωθῇ (Matt. i. 22, etc.) and the famous Mark iv. 12 (parables are told) ἵνα . . . μὴ ἴδωσιν. Burton (§ 222) is convinced that ἵνα πληρωθῇ is final; but Kennett (*oj. cit.*) seems to me more convincing when he cuts the knot by making it plain that Biblical Greek must not be laid upon the Procrustean bed of Classical grammar. And the same applies, surely, to the much-debated passage

---

[1] There are some valuable remarks about the bearing of this upon Biblical syntax in R. H. Kennett's *In Our Tongues* (1907), Ch. 1.

[2] E.g. Burton, *M.T.* § 222 (in respect of Luke ix. 45 and Gal. v. 17).

about parables. As A. T. Robertson justly points out,[1] the μήποτε-clause (or its equivalent) still remains in all three Synoptics and in the LXX of Isa. vi, whatever is done about the ἵνα; and personally I find the radical view which interprets the whole phrase—ἵνα and μήποτε alike—as strictly final, so that parables are told *to prevent* any who are not predestined for salvation from hearing, too incongruous with any part of the N.T. period to be plausible. It is far more reasonable to take both ἵνα and μήποτε as instances of the Semitic blurring of purpose and result, so that Matthew's change of ἵνα to ὅτι is essentially true to the sense, while his illogical retention of the μήποτε is true to the Semitic idiom.[2]†

On the other hand, Rom. v. 20, 21, vi. 1 all seem to me to contain genuinely *final* ἵνα-clauses.

ii. Conversely, ὥστε with Infinitive seems, on rare occasions, to approximate to a *final* sense: D.-B. § 391, 3 quotes: ἵνα ἐπιλάβωνται αὐτοῦ λόγου, ὥστε παραδοῦναι αὐτὸν... (Luke xx. 20), though that might = *such words as would enable them to hand him over*...; also (D.-B. § 391, 5) δώσουσιν σημεῖα μεγάλα καὶ τέρατα, ὥστε πλανῆσαι (Matt. xxiv. 24), where, however, a similar *consecutive* train of thought may underlie the use.

What are we to think, further, of Rom. vii. 6, κατηργήθημεν ἀπὸ τοῦ νόμου...ὥστε δουλεύειν ἡμᾶς..., and of I Pet. i. 21 τοὺς δι' αὐτοῦ πιστοὺς εἰς θεὸν τὸν ἐγείραντα αὐτὸν ἐκ νεκρῶν καὶ δόξαν αὐτῷ δόντα, ὥστε τὴν πίστιν ὑμῶν καὶ ἐλπίδα εἶναι εἰς θεόν? Very vague, again, are the simple Infinitives in Acts xvii. 26, 27: do κατοικεῖν and ζητεῖν follow ἐποίησεν as *finals*, *consecutives*, or generally *descriptive* (*epexegetic*) Infinitives? Consider also (and this is relevant to the discussion of ἵνα in i. above) Matt. x. 35 ἦλθον γὰρ διχάσαι ἄνθρωπον κατὰ τοῦ πατρὸς αὐτοῦ κ.τ.λ.—which is perfectly represented by the plain Infinitive in English, and is equally ambiguous: is it a grim hyperbole, as though it meant *I came [in order] to...*? In any case its

---

[1] In *Studies in Early Christianity* (ed. S. J. Case, 1928). It is on this rock that T. W. Manson's ingenious theory (*The Teaching of Jesus*, 76 ff.) seems to me to founder (despite his attempt, p. 78, to meet the problem).

[2] Note that in II Cor. iv. 4 a real 'infatuation' such as prevents people seeing and accepting the truth is spoken of, and there a construction is used which is ambiguous, and might even, considered from the point of view of strict syntax, be either final or consecutive: ὁ θεὸς τοῦ αἰῶνος τούτου ἐτύφλωσεν τὰ νοήματα τῶν ἀπίστων εἰς τὸ μὴ αὐγάσαι τὸν φωτισμὸν τοῦ εὐαγγελίου τῆς δόξης τοῦ χριστοῦ.

basic, literal, meaning must actually be consecutive. Contrast the unambiguously *final* clause in John iii. 17 οὐ γὰρ ἀπέστειλεν ὁ θεὸς τὸν υἱὸν εἰς τὸν κόσμον ἵνα κρίνῃ τὸν κόσμον, ἀλλ᾽ ἵνα σωθῇ ὁ κόσμος.

It may here be added for convenience:

(*a*) That there seems to be a tendency, sometimes, to *ellipsis* in the use of ὥστε; e.g.: I Cor. xiii. 2 πᾶσαν τὴν πίστιν ὥστε [δύνασθαι] ὄρη μεθιστάναι (cf. Matt. x. 1); II Cor. ii. 6, 7 ἱκανὸν τῷ τοιούτῳ ἡ ἐπιτιμία αὕτη . . . ὥστε τοὐναντίον μᾶλλον ὑμᾶς [δεῖν] χαρίσασθαι . . . ; Heb. xiii. 6 ὥστε [δύνασθαι] θαρροῦντας ἡμᾶς λέγειν. . . .

(*b*) That ὥστε is also, in certain contexts, simply an *inferential particle* as if ὥς τε, meaning *and so, accordingly*, etc.; e.g.: Matt. xii. 12 ὥστε ἔξεστιν τοῖς σάββασιν καλῶς ποιεῖν, xix. 6, xxiii. 31, Mark ii. 28, x. 8, Rom. vii. 4, 12, xiii. 2, I Cor. iii. 7, 21 (with Imperative—ὥστε μηδεὶς καυχάσθω), iv. 5 (Imperat.), v. 8 (with Cohortative—ὥστε ἑορτάζωμεν), vii. 38, xi. 27, xiv. 22, II Cor. iv. 12, v. 16, 17, Gal. iii. 9, 24, iv. 7, 16, Phil. ii. 12 (Imperat.), iv. 1 (Imperat.), I Thess. iv. 18 (Imperat.), I Pet. iv. 19 (Imperat.).

2. An interesting extension of the *final* ἵνα is the well-known idiom whereby it becomes practically *imperative* in sense.[1]

i. Cadoux shows that, whereas one or two instances quoted from the Classical period are probably not genuine examples (Soph. *O.C.* 156–61 and Cic. *Epist. ad Att.* VI. v. 2 are both rejected), the new L. and S. gives two from 3rd cent. B.C. papyri, and from 1st cent. B.C. onwards the examples are numerous (e.g. II Macc. i. 9 (124 B.C.?) ἵνα ἄγητε τὰς ἡμέρας . . ., *see that ye keep* . . .).

ii. He refers to four widely recognized N.T. instances: Mark v. 23 ἵνα ἐλθὼν ἐπιθῇς, *do please come and lay* . . . ; II Cor. viii. 7 ἵνα καὶ ἐν ταύτῃ τῇ χάριτι περισσεύητε, *do please abound* . . . ; Eph. v. 33 ἡ δὲ γυνὴ ἵνα φοβῆται . . . , *and let the wife revere* . . . ; Gal. ii. 10 μόνον . . . ἵνα μνημονεύωμεν . . . , *only, we were to remember* . . . (Cadoux's translations, with one change in punctuation).

iii. He adds several instances in which the ἵνα-clause is often taken as subordinate, but in which, he suggests, it should be taken (like the above) as imperatival: Mark xiv. 49 ἵνα πληρωθῶσιν αἱ γραφαί, *the Scriptures have to be fulfilled*; John i. 8 ἵνα μαρτυρήσῃ, *he had to bear witness*; John xiv. 31 ἵνα γνῷ ὁ κόσμος, *the world needs to learn*;

[1] For discussions of this, see, besides the grammars, a useful series of articles in *J.T.S.*: C. J. Cadoux in XLII (July–Oct. 1941), 165 ff.; H. G. Meecham in XLIII (July–Oct. 1942), 179, 180; and A. R. George in XLV (Jan.–April 1944), 56 ff.

John xv. 25 ἵνα πληρωθῇ ὁ λόγος, *the word...had to be fulfilled*;
I John ii. 19 ἵνα φανερωθῶσιν, *they had to be shown up*. He notes
tentatively also: John ix. 3, xiii. 18, xviii. 9, 32, xix. 24, I Cor. vii. 5,
29, 30, II Cor. viii. 13; and compares the ἵνα-πληρωθῇ passages in
Matt. ii. 15, iv. 14, xii. 17–21 (cf. xiii. 35).[1]

Not all of these are likely to carry conviction. The criticism of
A. R. George (*loc. cit.*) is justified, that, whereas the origin of what may
truly be called the imperatival use lies in the omission of a word such
as θέλω [or, one might say, βλέπετε—II John 8 being a specimen of
the full phrase], we are very far from the mere omission of θέλω when
the sense requires one to supply some such word as ἔδει. Note further
that, if we accept Cadoux's position, we are logically committed to
carrying the process through with μή also. There are some indications
that it would be better in some cases to describe the ἵνα as 'denoting
content' rather than as imperatival: A. R. George adduces Eph. i. 16, 17,
iii. 15, 16. Note, further, Rom. xvi. 1, 2 συνίστημι δὲ ὑμῖν Φοίβην...ἵνα
αὐτὴν προσδέξησθε...καὶ παραστῆτε αὐτῇ; II Pet. i. 4 (?); II Cor. x. 9
ἵνα μὴ δόξω ὡς ἂν ἐκφοβεῖν ὑμᾶς; Philem. 19 ἵνα μὴ λέγω: all these can
plausibly be explained by an antecedent verb, stated or implied, of
saying, wishing, etc., and therefore permit the ἵνα to be more or less
consciously *final*.

But it is clear enough that in many cases the ἵνα is virtually imperatival: Col. ii. 4 seems to be a further example, for τοῦτο λέγω
ἵνα μηδεὶς παραλογίζηται makes much better sense as *What I mean is
this: Nobody is to talk you round*, than as *This I say in order to prevent
anybody....*[2]

It is harder to find a convincing N.T. instance of this in the 1st person,
but Mark x. 51 = Luke xviii. 41, ἵνα ἀναβλέψω, may be nearer to *Let me
recover my sight* than to *I want to recover....* Mark xii. 15 seems a much
less convincing case: A. R. George (*loc. cit.*) calls it 'probably final'.

3. ἵνα *denoting content* has been referred to. This is a very common idiom
in the Johannine writings,[3] and is profitably discussed by Kennett

---

[1] In Rev. xiv. 13 he suggests that ἵνα may mean *because*. But see above under
'The Subjunctive Mood', p. 23.

[2] See further an article by H. G. Meecham in *E.T.* LII, no. 11 (Aug. 1941), 437,
where he notes that θέλω ἵνα...δῷς in Mark vi. 25 is paralleled in Matt. xiv. 8
by δός.

[3] A possible instance in the Pauline writings is Phil. ii. 2 πληρώσατέ μου τὴν
χαρὰν ἵνα τὸ αὐτὸ φρονῆτε, perhaps *complete my joy by having the same outlook*
(the ἵνα-clause being perhaps descriptive of what the writer means by completing
his joy).

(*op. cit.*); e.g. John iv. 34 ἐμὸν βρῶμά ἐστιν ἵνα ποιῶ τὸ θέλημα τοῦ πέμψαντός με, *doing the will of him that sent me is my food*; viii. 56 *your father Abraham rejoiced to see* (ἵνα ἴδῃ) *my day*; xv. 8 ἵνα καρπὸν πολὺν φέρητε (*my Father is glorified*) *in your bearing much fruit*; and it has already been pointed out that it is sometimes difficult to decide whether the ἵνα is used with this or some other nuance of meaning.

XVIII

NOTES ON ὍΤΙ

It is worth observing not only that problems of exegesis sometimes arise in connexion with the question whether ὅτι means *because* or *that*, but also that the interpretation of a passage turns upon deciding *with which word the ὅτι is to be logically connected.*

Thus, take the famous passage, Luke vii. 47 οὗ χάριν λέγω σοι, ἀφέωνται αἱ ἁμαρτίαι αὐτῆς αἱ πολλαί, ὅτι ἠγάπησεν πολύ· ᾧ δὲ ὀλίγον ἀφίεται, ὀλίγον ἀγαπᾷ. Here complete consistency is reached if the ὅτι-clause is taken as depending, in respect of logical connexion, on λέγω σοι: 'I can say with confidence that her sins are forgiven, *because* her love is evidence of it.' But some commentators take it with ἀφέωνται, making her love the ground of her *forgiveness*, not of the *assurance* that she has been forgiven—a non-Christian conclusion which throws the sentence into complete opposition both to the preceding parable and to the second half of this very verse. Similar to the former alternative is Luke xiii. 2 δοκεῖτε ὅτι οἱ Γαλιλαῖοι οὗτοι ἁμαρτωλοὶ παρὰ πάντας τοὺς Γαλιλαίους ἐγένοντο, ὅτι ταῦτα πεπόνθασιν; Manifestly the Galileans were not pre-eminent *sinners* because they suffered; but they might (erroneously) have been *thought to be* pre-eminent sinners because of it (i.e. ὅτι logically depends on δοκεῖτε). This points to the true interpretation of Gal. iv. 6 ὅτι δέ ἐστε υἱοί, ἐξαπέστειλεν ὁ θεὸς τὸ πνεῦμα τοῦ υἱοῦ αὐτοῦ... : not because *you are sons, God sent...*, but [proof] that *you are sons* [*is the fact that*] *God sent....* The context clearly favours this sense.

In John xvi. 9–11 it is a nice point whether the ὅτι-clauses mean *in that...* (i.e. define the sin, the δικαιοσύνη, and the judgment) or are *consequential* (i.e. indicate that the sin, etc., are the *result of* the conditions in the ὅτι-clauses).[1]

---

[1] See the Commentaries of Westcott and Hoskyns *in loc.*

XIX

CONDITIONAL CLAUSES

The general formula 'Given certain conditions, certain results follow', which underlies Conditional Sentences, has to include a wide and flexible range of phrase in order to express the range of contingencies in varying conditions.

Simplifying in order to analyse, the following types may be broadly distinguished: 1. Past or present conditions, possible or actual. 2. Recurrent or future conditions, whether real or hypothetical. 3. Past or present conditions, only hypothetical. Thus:

1. Matt. vi. 23 εἰ οὖν τὸ φῶς τὸ ἐν σοὶ σκότος ἐστίν, τὸ σκότος πόσον. John xi. 12 εἰ κεκοίμηται, σωθήσεται.

I Cor. xv. 16 εἰ γὰρ νεκροὶ οὐκ ἐγείρονται, οὐδὲ χριστὸς ἐγήγερται. The construction is:

Protasis (if-clause): εἰ with Indic. in appropriate tense.

Apodosis (result-clause): another Indic. (or its equivalent) in appropriate tense.

The negative in the protasis is usually οὐ; I Tim. vi. 3, 4 is among the few exceptions: εἴ τις...μὴ προσέρχεται...τετύφωται.

2. Luke xii. 54 ὅταν ἴδητε νεφέλην ἀνατέλλουσαν ἐπὶ δυσμῶν, εὐθέως λέγετε ὅτι ὄμβρος ἔρχεται (this, though strictly *temporal*, is virtually a conditional clause).

Col. iv. 10 ἐὰν ἔλθῃ πρὸς ὑμᾶς, δέξασθε αὐτόν (the Imperative is equivalent to an Indicative here; cf. I Cor. xvi. 10).

I Cor. xvi. 4 ἐὰν δὲ ἄξιον ᾖ τοῦ κἀμὲ πορεύεσθαι, σὺν ἐμοὶ πορεύσονται. John viii. 55 κἂν εἴπω ὅτι οὐκ οἶδα αὐτόν, ἔσομαι...ψεύστης.

I John i. 10 ἐὰν εἴπωμεν ὅτι οὐχ ἡμαρτήκαμεν, ψεύστην ποιοῦμεν αὐτόν.

Notes. i. John xv. 6, ἐὰν μή τις μένῃ ἐν ἐμοί, ἐβλήθη ἔξω, is logically anomalous, requiring strictly a Pres. or Fut. in the apodosis.

ii. In I Cor. vii. 5, μὴ ἀποστερεῖτε ἀλλήλους, εἰ μήτι ἂν ἐκ συμφώνου..., a verb (ᾖ or the like) is implied.

The construction is:

Protasis: εἰ (or ὅτε, etc.) with ἄν (making ἐάν, ὅταν) with Subj. in appropriate tense.

Apodosis: Indic. (or its equivalent, cf. Col. iv. 10 above) in appropriate tense.

The negative in the protasis is usually μή. In Jas. i. 23 and iii. 2 the οὐ goes very closely with the noun and the verb respectively: see Mayor *in locc*.

Note. The difficulty of classifying is illustrated by sentences which belong by *meaning* in one class, but by *form* in another; e.g.: (1) in form, (2) in meaning: II Tim. ii. 12 εἰ ὑπομένομεν, καὶ συνβασιλεύσομεν; II John 10 εἴ τις ἔρχεται πρὸς ὑμᾶς καὶ ταύτην τὴν διδαχὴν οὐ φέρει, μὴ λαμβάνετε αὐτόν. Both these might well have had ἐάν with Subj. in the protasis. (1) in meaning, (2) in form: I Cor. ix. 16 ἐὰν γὰρ εὐαγγελίζωμαι, οὐκ ἔστιν μοι καύχημα (and note that in the next verse, 17, the parallel sentence is (1) in form also: εἰ γὰρ ἑκὼν τοῦτο πράσσω, μισθὸν ἔχω· εἰ δὲ ἄκων, οἰκονομίαν πεπίστευμαι. So John viii. 55).

3. Matt. xxiv. 43 εἰ ᾔδει ὁ οἰκοδεσπότης ποίᾳ φυλακῇ ὁ κλέπτης ἔρχεται, ἐγρηγόρησεν ἂν καὶ οὐκ ἂν εἴασεν διορυχθῆναι τὴν οἰκίαν αὐτοῦ.

Luke vii. 39 οὗτος εἰ ἦν προφήτης, ἐγίνωσκεν ἂν τίς καὶ ποταπὴ ἡ γυνή....

John viii. 42 εἰ ὁ θεὸς πατὴρ ὑμῶν ἦν, ἠγαπᾶτε ἂν ἐμέ.

John ix. 33 εἰ μὴ ἦν οὗτος παρὰ θεοῦ, οὐκ ἠδύνατο ποιεῖν οὐδέν.

John xi. 21 κύριε, εἰ ἦς ὧδε, οὐκ ἂν ἀπέθανεν ὁ ἀδελφός μου.

Acts xviii. 14 εἰ μὲν ἦν ἀδίκημά τι ἢ ῥᾳδιούργημα πονηρόν,...κατὰ λόγον ἂν ἀνεσχόμην ὑμῶν.

The construction is:

Protasis: εἰ with a past tense of the Indic.

Apodosis: a past (but not necessarily the same) tense of the Indic., usually with ἄν.

The negative in the protasis is μή (the only N.T. exception being apparently Matt. xxvi. 24 = Mark xiv. 21 εἰ οὐκ ἐγεννήθη).[1]

Note. ἄν is usually, if not always, omitted with verbs whose very sense implies *obligation, necessity, possibility*: Matt. xxiii. 23 ταῦτα ἔδει ποιῆσαι; Acts xxiv. 19 οὓς ἔδει...παρεῖναι; Heb. ix. 26 ἔδει αὐτὸν πολλάκις παθεῖν; Matt. xxvi. 9 ἐδύνατο τοῦτο πραθῆναι; I Cor. v. 10

---

[1] H. W. Moule pointed out that Matt. xviii. 16 (where, in fact, the words are ἐὰν δὲ μὴ ἀκούσῃ) is another place where one might well have tolerated an οὐ instead of a μή, on the ground that the negative goes closely with the verb: εἰ οὐ tends to mean *if not*, ἐὰν (εἰ) μή *unless*.

ὠφείλετε...ἐξελθεῖν. All these are related at least to *implied* protases, and form apodoses of the type 3, which would, if other verbs had been used, have carried the ἄν.

Thus the form of a conditional sentence is largely determined by two main factors—*time* (past, present, future) or *Aktionsart* (instantaneous, protracted, recurrent, etc.) and the degree of *reality* (impossible, improbable, possible, probable, actual).

Notes. i. The *protasis* is the only half in which the mood is variable. In the *apodosis* it is always Indic. (or its equivalent).

ii. The mood in the *protasis* is largely determined by the two factors referred to. Thus:

(*a*) Any *past* condition introduced by *if* must, in the nature of the case, be hypothetical, if not definitely unreal: otherwise there would be nothing *conditional* about the sentence. Therefore there appears to be no need to vary the mood, and it is regularly Indicative.

(*b*) But *present, future,* or *recurrent* conditions may vary widely in their degree of actuality: hence (perhaps) the variation in moods. In general, the Indic. represents certainty, while the Subj. represents something more hypothetical or uncertain: *Beg.* II, 39 (after Radermacher) notes Gamaliel's address in Acts v. 38, 39: ἐὰν ᾖ ἐξ ἀνθρώπων..., εἰ δὲ ἐκ θεοῦ ἐστιν....

The presence of ἄν in the protasis tends to reduce the degree of actuality.

In Classical Greek, a further degree of flexibility is introduced by the use of the Optative, but this has largely faded from N.T. conditional clauses: an instance of this rare use (falling in Group 2, above) is I Pet. iii. 14 ἀλλ᾽ εἰ καὶ πάσχοιτε διὰ δικαιοσύνην, μακάριοι. So possibly Acts xxiv. 19 εἴ τι ἔχοιεν πρὸς ἐμέ, *if they [really] had any complaint [which they have not]*...; perhaps cf. Acts xxvii. 39, and (below under note v. (*a*)), Acts xvii. 18, x. 17.

iii. Although the mood of the *apodosis* is invariably Indic. (or its equivalent), a considerable difference is made by the presence or absence of ἄν. Contrast Group 3 above with Groups 1 and 2; and note that in Group 2 the *protasis*, in Group 3 the *apodosis* usually requires ἄν.

iv. Besides the equivalents already noted to verbs in the *apodosis*, note that a *participle* (used in a concessive sense) may do duty for a verb in the *protasis*: I Cor. iv. 12 λοιδορούμενοι εὐλογοῦμεν (=ἐάν, or ὅταν, λοιδορώμεθα, εὐλογοῦμεν); cf. Acts xix. 36 (with a Gen. Abs.).

v. Often, in what is logically a conditional sentence, one half is not expressed but only implied; e.g.:

(a) *Implied protasis*: Mark vii. 11 ὃ ἐὰν ἐξ ἐμοῦ ὠφεληθῇς (or ὠφελήθης), *whatever benefit you would have derived from me* [*if the money had not been dedicated*] (cf., as above, p. 138, the elliptical κἄν in, for example, II Cor. xi. 16 κἂν ὡς ἄφρονα δέξασθέ με = δέξασθέ με, καὶ ἐὰν ᾖ μόνον ὡς ἄφρονα, *receive me, even if it be only as a fool*; cf. the English elliptical idiom with *if only*, in such a sentence as *he did it if only to show*...); Heb. x. 2 οὐκ ἂν ἐπαύσαντο προσφερόμεναι...; *would not* (*the offerings*) *have ceased to be offered* [, *if the law could have perfected its adherents*]? Possibly Acts xxvi. 29, εὐξαίμην ἂν τῷ θεῷ, is logically similar, since it strictly implies a protasis such as *if only it were possible*. Cf. Acts xvii. 18 τί ἂν θέλοι ὁ σπερμολόγος οὗτος λέγειν (cf. x. 17), which English could represent by *what might this cocksparrow*[1] *be trying to say?* Is the idiom ἐβουλόμην, *I should like*, in Acts xxv. 22 possibly a fossilized relic of a conditional clause also? If so, it has lost its ἄν (see also under 'The Tenses', p. 9).

(b) *Implied apodosis*: Luke xiii. 9 κἂν μὲν ποιήσῃ καρπὸν εἰς τὸ μέλλον, *and if it does bear fruit in future* [, *well and good*] (Exod. xxxii. 32 LXX supplies an apodosis to a sentence where the Hebrew leaves it to be implied); Rom. ix. 22 εἰ δὲ...ὁ θεὸς...ἤνεγκεν; [*what*] *if God has borne*...? (but this is a controverted passage: see commentators); II Thess. ii. 3 ἐὰν μὴ ἔλθῃ ἡ ἀποστασία..., *unless the apostasy comes* [*it cannot happen*]. Heb. iv. 3 (from LXX), εἰ εἰσελεύσονται εἰς τὴν κατάπαυσίν μου, and Mark viii. 12, εἰ δοθήσεται, are noted under 'Semitisms', p. 179.

vi. Distinguish from the *conditional* use, the use of εἰ in indirect (or even sometimes direct) *questions* as = *whether?* etc.: Luke xxii. 49 κύριε, εἰ πατάξομεν...; (*shall we strike?*); Acts xxvi. 8 εἰ ὁ θεὸς νεκροὺς ἐγείρει; xxvi. 23 εἰ παθητὸς ὁ χριστός. In Acts xxvii. 39 it is not absolutely clear in which sense εἰ is used: does ἐβουλεύοντο εἰ δύναιντο ἐξῶσαι mean *they were planning* whether *they could*..., or *they were planning* (*if they could*), *to*...? (see under 'Indirect Speech', p. 154).

vii. For εἰ καί and καὶ εἰ, see under 'Order of Words' 4, p. 167.

viii. Note that, in Group 2, the use of ἄν compounded with εἰ is all of a piece with the use of ἄν in senses corresponding with the English indefinite suffix -*ever*, in *whoever, whenever*, etc. There is a conditional clause latent in such words: Rom. x. 13 πᾶς...ὃς ἂν ἐπικαλέσηται, *whoever invokes*, is close in sense to *if anybody invokes*.

[1] For *cocksparrow*, see *Beg. in loc.*

This is illustrated by John xx. 23 ἄν τινων ἀφῆτε τὰς ἁμαρτίας...ἄν τινων κρατῆτε, where equally accurate renderings are (R.V.) *whose soever sins ye forgive* and (Moffatt) *if you remit the sins of any*. Sometimes ἐάν is written when ἄν would be correct: B has ὃς ἐάν...καὶ ὃς ἄν... in Luke ix. 48[1] (II Cor. x. 9, ἵνα μὴ δόξω ὡς ἄν ἐκφοβεῖν ὑμᾶς, looks like a conflation of ἵνα μὴ δόξω ἐκφοβεῖν ὑμᾶς and ἵνα μὴ δόξω ὡς ἐάν ἐκφοβεῖν ὑμᾶς βούλωμαι). Conversely, ἄν stands for ἐάν six times in John (and nowhere else in the N.T. except as a *v.l.* in Matt. xxviii. 14 (D) and Acts ix. 2 (א E)).[2]

ix. There are two instances in the N.T. of conditional clauses which are perfectly correct in grammatical form, but which are logically inconsequent, as it would seem: Gal. v. 15 εἰ δὲ ἀλλήλους δάκνετε καὶ κατεσθίετε, βλέπετε μὴ ὑπ᾽ ἀλλήλων ἀναλωθῆτε, and Jas. iii. 14 εἰ δὲ ζῆλον πικρὸν ἔχετε καὶ ἐριθείαν ἐν τῇ καρδίᾳ ὑμῶν, μὴ κατακαυχᾶσθε καὶ ψεύδεσθε κατὰ τῆς ἀληθείας. In both instances[3] the Imperative clause remains valid whether or not the condition in the protasis is fulfilled. Logically, the Imperative clauses should be Future Indicative clauses—*if you go on like this, you will....*

[1] See C. C. Tarelli in *J.T.S.* xxxix (July 1938), 257.
[2] See *Proleg.* 43 n. 2 and W. F. Howard in *J.T.S.* xlviii (Jan–April 1947), 21.
[3] For the sense of the James sentence is scarcely mended by putting a question mark at the end, since the μή would then make it a question expecting the answer 'No'. If only it could be a question expecting the answer 'Yes', it would make good sense: *If you have bitter rivalry...are you not exulting and lying against the truth?*

XX

INDIRECT SPEECH

It may be simplest to start from a comparison with Latin constructions. These are mainly of two sorts—either Accusative and Infinitive or Subjunctive clauses: *dixit eum venisse* or *dixit quod venisset*, etc.

In N.T. Greek, Accusative and Infinitive is also common; but, unlike Latin, a ὅτι-clause *with Indicative* is quite common. Examples follow.

I. ACCUSATIVE AND INFINITIVE

Luke xxiv. 23 λέγουσαι καὶ ὀπτασίαν ἀγγέλων ἑωρακέναι, [*women*] *saying that they had also seen a vision of angels*; Acts xxv. 4 ὁ μὲν οὖν Φῆστος ἀπεκρίθη τηρεῖσθαι τὸν Παῦλον...ἑαυτὸν[1] δὲ μέλλειν..., *Festus however answered that Paul was to be kept...and that he himself was going to...*; Rom. ii. 18 πέποιθάς τε σεαυτὸν ὁδηγὸν εἶναι τυφλῶν, *and you are confident that you are a guide to the blind*; Acts xxviii. 6 ἔλεγον αὐτὸν εἶναι θεόν, *they began to say that he was a god.*†

II. ΟΤΙ, ETC., WITH THE INDICATIVE

John vii. 42 οὐχ ἡ γραφὴ εἶπεν ὅτι ἐκ τοῦ σπέρματος Δαυείδ...ἔρχεται ὁ χριστός; *did not the scripture say that the Christ was to come of David's posterity?* John vi. 24 εἶδεν ὁ ὄχλος ὅτι Ἰησοῦς οὐκ ἔστιν ἐκεῖ, *the crowd saw that Jesus was not there*; Acts ix. 26 ἐφοβοῦντο...μὴ πιστεύοντες ὅτι ἐστὶν μαθητής, *they were afraid...not believing that he was a disciple*; Acts ix. 27 διηγήσατο αὐτοῖς πῶς...εἶδεν τὸν κύριον καὶ ὅτι ἐλάλησεν αὐτῷ, καὶ πῶς...ἐπαρρησιάσατο..., *he related to them how...he had seen the Lord, and that he had spoken to him, and how...he had spoken freely....*

The most noticeable thing here is that Greek, unlike Latin, tends *to retain the original tense* of the direct statement. Thus, in the above

---

[1] Note that Classical Greek, unlike Latin or this N.T. idiom, prefers to put a pronoun referring to the subject of the main verb in the *Nominative* in an instance like this. Note also the (perhaps sheer bad) grammar of I Cor. vii. 7 θέλω δὲ πάντας ἀνθρώπους εἶναι ὡς καὶ ἐμαυτόν. Presumably the preceding Accusative and Infinitive construction has influenced the writer.

examples, the Scripture said: *the Christ is to come...*; the crowd observed *Jesus is not here*; the Jerusalem Christians said *we don't believe that he is a disciple*; Barnabas related of Paul *he saw the Lord, the Lord spoke to him, Paul spoke freely* (all simple Aorists, not Pluperfects).

An extension of II. is constituted by *Indirect Questions*, which are mostly expressed by the Indicative with an appropriate introduction, although sometimes an Optative is used to give a more tentative and cautious tone: Acts xxv. 20 ἔλεγον εἰ βούλοιτο..., *I asked whether he would like...* (more loosely and idiomatically, *I said, would he like...?*); John ix. 25 εἰ ἁμαρτωλός ἐστιν οὐκ οἶδα, *whether he is a sinner or not, I do not know*; Acts x. 18 ἐπυνθάνοντο εἰ Σίμων... ἐνθάδε ξενίζεται, *they were enquiring whether Simon was lodging here* (but the fact that εἰ can be used to introduce a *direct* question and that ἐνθάδε, *here*, is strictly incorrect for an *indirect* question, which requires ἐκεῖ, *there*, may point to this not being intended to be indirect at all, but a direct quotation: *they were enquiring, Does Simon...lodge here?* see *Beg. in loc.*); Acts xxvii. 12 εἴ πως δύναιντο, [*hoping*] *that perhaps they might...* or [*wondering*] *whether*, etc. (cf. Acts viii. 22 εἰ ἄρα ἀφεθήσεται...). On Acts xxvii. 39 see 'Conditional Clauses', Note vi, p. 151.

Note. In I Cor. vii. 16, τί γὰρ οἶδας, γύναι, εἰ τὸν ἄνδρα σώσεις; ἢ τί οἶδας, ἄνερ, εἰ τὴν γυναῖκα σώσεις; it is uncertain whether the direct question implied is intended to expect the answer *yes* or *no*. See the commentators. In Mark xv. 44 ὁ δε Πειλᾶτος ἐθαύμασεν εἰ ἤδη τέθνηκεν, the sense is not *wondered whether...*, in the modern sense of *wonder* as = *speculate*; but rather, *expressed surprise that he was already dead, if he were*, i.e. Pilate's words might have been, *I shall be surprised if....*

III. A MIXED CONSTRUCTION
(with *direct object in the Accusative, followed by a* ὅτι-*clause, or its equivalent*)

Mark i. 24 οἶδά σε τίς εἶ, *I know who you are*; John ix. 29 τοῦτον δὲ οὐκ οἴδαμεν πόθεν ἐστίν (cf. Luke xiii. 25), *but we don't know where this man is from*; II Thess. ii. 4 ἀποδεικνύντα ἑαυτὸν ὅτι ἐστὶν θεός, *declaring that he is a god*. Note too Acts xxvii. 10 ὅτι...ἔσεσθαι, 'an understandable confusion paralleled in papyri and even in classical Greek'—H. G. Meecham, in *J.N.T. Studies*, I, no. 1 (Sept. 1954), 64.

XXI

SOME USES OF MH AND ΌΥ

The following are some miscellaneous observations about uses not covered in other sections.

1. Generally speaking *ne* is to *non* in Latin as μή is to οὐ: i.e. as a rule one finds οὐ associated with Indicatives and plain statements, μή with Subjunctives, Optatives, Imperatives, and more hypothetical or doubtful conceptions:

Rom. xiii. 13 ὡς ἐν ἡμέρᾳ εὐσχημόνως περιπατήσωμεν, μὴ κώμοις καὶ μέθαις, μὴ κοίταις καὶ ἀσελγείαις, μὴ ἔριδι καὶ 3ήλῳ.

II Cor. xii. 20 φοβοῦμαι...μή πως...εὕρω ὑμᾶς... (like *timeo ne*; φοβοῦμαι οὐ would be as unthinkable as *timeo non*).

Note, however, i. that N.T. Greek can easily (and apparently with no difference in meaning) use ἵνα μή...: I Cor. xvi. 2 ἵνα μὴ ὅταν ἔλθω τότε λογίαι γίνωνται. What can be rendered in English by *lest* must be μή alone; what can be rendered by *that...not* may be μή alone or ἵνα μή.

ii. Col. ii. 8 βλέπετε μή τις ἔσται is tolerated, as *videte ne erit* would not be tolerated. So Matt. xiii. 15 μή ποτε ἴδωσιν...καὶ... ἀκούσωσιν καὶ...συνῶσιν καὶ ἐπιστρέψωσιν, καὶ ἰάσομαι αὐτούς (and so the LXX of Isa. vi. 10).

iii. John iii. 18 ὅτι μὴ πεπίστευκεν is rather like *quod ne* credidit! (contrast I John v. 10 where οὐ is, correctly, used). Abbott (*Johannine Grammar* § [2253], p. 204), Moulton, *Proleg.* 171, and Chamberlain, *An Exegetical Grammar of the Greek N.T.*, 159, explain the μή as due to a hypothetical element: it states the ground of condemnation rather than the fact of disbelief. But all this could have been expressed grammatically instead of by this solecism. ὁ μὴ πιστεύων, however, just before makes it sound less harsh. Cf. I John iv. 3 πᾶν πνεῦμα ὃ μὴ ὁμολογεῖ, with R. Law's note *in loc.* (*The Tests of Life*, 396).

2. As a rule, μή is used with participles (see further under 'Participles' above, p. 105) and Infinitives, even when they are used in a virtually 'indicative' sense: II Cor. vi. 3 μηδεμίαν ἐν μηδενὶ διδόντες προσκοπήν; Tit. i. 6, 7 τέκνα ἔχων πιστά, μὴ ἐν κατηγορίᾳ ἀσωτίας...δεῖ γὰρ

τὸν ἐπίσκοπον ἀνέγκλητον εἶναι...μὴ αὐθάδη (which is virtually participial, since μὴ ὄντα κ.τ.λ. would give the meaning). Cf. Rom. xii. 11 τῇ σπουδῇ μὴ ὀκνηροί (cf. 'Semitisms', II. xii. below).

But John x. 12 ὁ μισθωτὸς καὶ οὐκ ὢν ποιμήν, is a famous exception; and in I Thess. ii. 17, ἀπορφανισθέντες...προσώπῳ οὐ καρδίᾳ, οὐ is, strictly, construed with the participle, though remote.[1]

So in I Cor. ii. 2, οὐ γὰρ ἔκρινα τί εἰδέναι evidently means what would normally have been expressed by ἔκρινα γὰρ μηδὲν εἰδέναι, and the use of οὐ instead of μή appears to be due to the displacement of the negative into juxtaposition with the Indicative (see under 'The Order of Words', pp. 167 f.).

3. In questions, *num* is to *nonne* as μή is to οὐ: i.e. μή expects the answer 'No'[2] and οὐ 'Yes': II Cor. xii. 18 μήτι ἐπλεονέκτησεν ὑμᾶς Τίτος; (answer 'No'); οὐ τῷ αὐτῷ πνεύματι περιεπατήσαμεν; (answer 'Yes'); so Rom. ix. 20, 21. At first sight I Cor. ix. 4, 5, μὴ οὐκ ἔχομεν ἐξουσίαν...; looks anomalous; but actually οὐκ-ἔχομεν is a closely-coalescing phrase, while the μή is a separate particle, introducing (correctly) a question expecting the answer 'No': *Are we without-the-right...?* So I Cor. xi. 22 μὴ γὰρ οἰκίας οὐκ-ἔχετε;

4. οὐ μή with the Aorist Subjunctive (or sometimes the Future Indicative) is a way of expressing emphatic denial for the future, a construction known in Classical Greek (see, for example, Goodwin, § 1360) and in the papyri.

In the N.T., it is frequent in the Gospels (in O.T. quotations and sayings of Jesus) and in Revelation; but otherwise is not common; and it is arguable that the contexts do not always justify the emphasis which it appears to carry.

Moulton, after a very interesting review of the evidence (*Proleg.* 187–92) concludes that 90 per cent of the N.T. instances are either from the O.T. or from sayings of Jesus, and writes 'one is tempted

---

[1] In connexion with οὐ coalescing closely with a noun or other word, it is relevant to adduce Winer's example from Lucian (III, 104 *Indoct.* § 5): καὶ ὁ κυβερνᾶν οὐκ εἰδὼς καὶ ἱππεύειν μὴ μεμελετηκώς, where he takes the οὐ as equivalent to 'α-privative': *absolutely ignorant of steering and not having given much pains to riding* (quoted by Abbott, *Johannine Grammar* § [2253 a], p. 203 n.).

[2] Luke xi. 11, 12 ...μὴ ἀντὶ ἰχθύος ὄφιν αὐτῷ ἐπιδώσει; ἢ καὶ αἰτήσει ᾠόν, ἐπιδώσει αὐτῷ σκορπίον; would be an interesting variant (with μή omitted in the second question) if it were the true reading: but there is considerable evidence for μή in the second question also.

to put it down to the same cause in both—a feeling that inspired language was fitly rendered by words of a peculiarly decisive tone'.

One instance of a particularly repetitive sort will serve to illustrate the construction with the Subjunctive: Matt. xxiv. 21 οὐδ' οὐ μὴ γένηται. For the use with the Future Indicative, see, for example, Matt. xvi. 22 οὐ μὴ ἔσται σοι τοῦτο.

5. Outside this construction, or in combination with it, one finds *negatives* which, judged by strict canons of Latin or English idiom, are *redundant*: Mark v. 3 καὶ οὐδὲ ἁλύσει οὐκέτι οὐδεὶς ἐδύνατο αὐτὸν δῆσαι; Luke xxiii. 53 οὗ οὐκ ἦν οὐδεὶς οὔπω κείμενος; John xv. 5 χωρὶς ἐμοῦ οὐ δύνασθε ποιεῖν οὐδέν; II Cor. xi. 9 οὐ κατενάρκησα οὐθενός; Heb. xiii. 5 οὐδ' οὐ μή σε ἐγκαταλίπω (which is more redundant than Deut. xxxi. 6 οὐ μή σε ἀνῇ οὔτε μή σε ἐγκαταλίπῃ, or *v.* 8 οὐκ ἀνήσει σε οὐδὲ μὴ ἐγκαταλίπῃ σε, which seem to be the sources of the quotation). All these passages are referred to by Rob. 1165. They show that the idiom is not confined to any one *stratum* of the N.T.[1]

6. μὴ followed by οὐ presents no difficulty grammatically, since οὐ simply negatives the verb; e.g.: II Cor. xii. 20 μή πως...οὐχ...εὕρω, *for fear that I fail-to-find*... (see Rob. 1174 and cf. 3 above).

7. A very problematic construction is II Tim. ii. 25 μή ποτε δῷη.... Does it mean *it may be that he will give*...? Cf. Philo, *Q.R.D.H.* § 63 (Wendland) μήποτ' οὖν ἐστι τοιοῦτον (*surely it is something of this kind*—Loeb); § 227 (*ibid.*) μήποτε δι' ἐκεῖνο (*probably*—Loeb); and *passim.*

[1] Note also redundant negative after verbs of hindering and denying: Acts x. 47, xiv. 18, I John ii. 22 (H. G. Meecham in *J.N.T. Studies*, i, no. 1 (Sept. 1954), 64).

XXII

QUESTIONS

The methods of asking questions in N.T. Greek are mostly obvious and logical enough. They may be illustrated under the following headings:

I. OPEN QUESTIONS

(i.e. those which give no indication of the answer expected)

Mark xiv. 61 Σὺ εἶ ὁ χριστὸς...; *Are you the Christ...?*

Matt. xiii. 28 θέλεις...συλλέξωμεν αὐτά; *would you like us...to collect them?*

Gal. iii. 2 ἐξ ἔργων νόμου τὸ πνεῦμα ἐλάβετε ἢ ἐξ ἀκοῆς πίστεως; *was it by performing the law that you received the Spirit, or by hearing and trusting?* (here the *context*, it is true, makes it clear enough what answer is expected, but not the form of the sentence itself; so with II Cor. iii. 1 ἀρχόμεθα πάλιν ἑαυτοὺς συνιστάνειν; *are we beginning to recommend ourselves again?*).

This type of question often has nothing but a question-mark to distinguish it as a question, and there are contexts which leave it doubtful what punctuation should be adopted. I Cor. i. 13 is cited by D.-B. § 440 as an instance.

It can, however, be introduced by an interrogative particle such as ἆρα or εἰ (=ἦ, see Rad. 44),[1] or by an interrogative pronoun (τίς, τί, ποῖος) or adverb (πῶς, ποῦ, πόθεν, διὰ τί (=*why*)):

Acts viii. 30 ἆρά γε γινώσκεις ἃ ἀναγινώσκεις; (though here the γε perhaps adds a sense of doubt: *Beg.* translates, *Do you after all know what you are reading?*).

Luke xxii. 49 κύριε, εἰ πατάξομεν ἐν μαχαίρῃ; *Lord, shall we strike with the sword?*

---

[1] Distinguish ἄρα (so accented) as an inferential particle (and also as a particle expressing an element of doubt: Acts viii. 22 εἰ ἄρα ἀφεθήσεται... *in the hope that perhaps...*), and εἰ as =*if*. Gal. ii. 17 is an instance where it is not clear whether we should accent ἆρα and read a question, or accent ἄρα and use some other punctuation. See below 'Some Observations on Adverbs and Adverbial Phrases', 6, p. 164, and 'Miscellaneous Notes on Style', 3, p. 196.

II. QUESTIONS EXPECTING THE ANSWER 'YES'[1]

These are normally introduced by οὐ (see under 'Some Uses of Μή and Οὐ', p. 156). In Matt. xxiv. 2 οὐ βλέπετε ταῦτα πάντα; English idiom would prefer an entirely open question—*do you see?* (not *do you not see...?*).

III. QUESTIONS EXPECTING THE ANSWER 'NO'

These are normally introduced by μή (see under 'Some Uses of Μή and Οὐ', p. 156).

IV. INDIRECT QUESTIONS. See under 'Indirect Speech', p. 154

Note. There are one or two places in the N.T. where it looks as though ὅτι may have been used as an interrogative adverb, *why*. Textual uncertainty and ambiguity complicate matters, but the following may at least be noted: Mark ix. 11, 28, Acts xi. 3, and possibly Mark ii. 16 (where אDW and the parallels in Matt. ix. 11, Luke v. 30 read διὰ τί). See the interesting note in *Beg.* on Acts xi. 3. Cf. p. 132.

[1] On I Cor. vii. 16 (whether expecting 'Yes' or 'No') see above, under 'Indirect Speech, II. Note', p. 154.

XXIII

SOME OBSERVATIONS ON ADVERBS AND ADVERBIAL PHRASES AND PARTICLES

Adverbs and particles are not generally treated together; but the two do in fact overlap to a considerable extent, λοιπόν being an instance; and the following notes may therefore conveniently be presented as a single section.

1. There are innumerable nouns or neuter adjectives employed as adverbs, which call for no special comment. But a few special phrases may here be noted as striking and idiomatic:

i. Acts xxiv. 25 τὸ νῦν ἔχον, *for the time being* (where the ἔχον is not very easy to explain). Cf. Tob. vii. 11, *Aristeas*, 198.

ii. Rom. xii. 18 τὸ ἐξ ὑμῶν, *so far as you are concerned, for your part* (possibly cf. Rom. i. 15, if τὸ κατ᾽ ἐμέ is to be separated from πρόθυμον in construing). See also under 'Some Observations on the Cases', 3. iii. above, pp. 33 f.

iii. Eph. i. 23 τὰ πάντα ἐν πᾶσιν appears to be simply an adverbial elative, *wholly and entirely, absolutely*, like παντάπασι in Classical Greek. But in I Cor. xv. 28 is ἵνα ᾖ ὁ θεὸς πάντα ἐν πᾶσιν to be interpreted similarly—*that God may be absolutely everything*—or is the ἐν πᾶσιν to be translated separately—*that God may be everything in all things*? Possibly the phrase in both instances may be influenced by a pantheistic cliché of Stoicism, but this is merely a guess. Yet what of Col. iii. 11 πάντα καὶ ἐν πᾶσιν χριστός? Here at least πάντα and ἐν πᾶσιν seem necessarily to stand for two distinguishable ideas; and I Cor. ix. 22, τοῖς πᾶσιν γέγονα πάντα, shows how close these phrases lie to quite ordinary terms of human conduct.

iv. II Cor. vi. 13 τὴν δὲ αὐτὴν ἀντιμισθίαν may be an instance of an adverbial phrase made up upon a basis other than that of a neuter noun: it looks like a subtle blend of τὸ δὲ αὐτό, *in the same way*, and κατ᾽ ἀντιμισθίαν, *by way of recompense*, and, on this showing, might be rendered *and accordingly, by way of response on your part*. But if it is rather an Accusative in apposition to the whole sentence which follows it, it should fall rather under that heading (see above, 'Some Observations on the Cases', 3. v, pp. 35 f.).

2. It is of interest to notice that, as in English idiom, adverbs tend to be used instead of adjectives of states of health; but whereas English uses the verb *to be*, the Greek idiom curiously uses ἔχω: καλῶς, κακῶς ἔχειν; κομψότερον ἔσχεν (John iv. 52). ἑτοίμως ἔχειν also occurs in Acts xxi. 13, II Cor. xii. 14, I Pet. iv. 5.

3. (τὸ) λοιπόν, τοῦ λοιποῦ are adverbial expressions which form a link with pure particles and which demand some care in exegesis. The meaning *finally* or (in a more vaguely resumptive sense) *and so* appears to be the commonest. But sometimes a definite time-significance, *henceforth* (or *thenceforth*), appears to be called for; and once or twice a metaphorical extension of this to mean *it follows that* seems to make good sense. The citations below, with suggested paraphrastic translations, will show the range of the expressions:

Matt. xxvi. 45 καθεύδετε λοιπόν... ⎫ *all that is left to do is to*
Mark xiv. 41 καθεύδετε τὸ λοιπόν...⎭ *sleep....*

Acts xxvii. 20 λοιπὸν περιῃρεῖτο ἐλπὶς πᾶσα, *at last all hope began to disappear....*

I Cor. i. 16 λοιπὸν οὐκ οἶδα εἴ τινα ἄλλον ἐβάπτισα, *I do not know that I baptized anybody else besides.*

I Cor. iv. 2 ὧδε λοιπὸν ζητεῖται ἐν τοῖς οἰκονόμοις ἵνα πιστός τις εὑρεθῇ, *on that showing* (ὧδε, referring back to the preceding verse where the apostles have been called stewards) *it follows that* (λοιπόν) *what is looked for in stewards is that....*

I Cor. vii. 29 τὸ λοιπὸν ἵνα..., *so that, for what remains,....†*

II Cor. xiii. 11 λοιπόν, ἀδελφοί, χαίρετε, *finally* (or *and so*), *brothers, rejoice* (or perhaps *farewell*).

Gal. vi. 17 τοῦ λοιποῦ, *henceforth.*

Eph. vi. 10 τοῦ λοιποῦ, ἐνδυναμοῦσθε..., *finally* (or *and so*)....

Phil. iii. 1 τὸ λοιπόν, ἀδελφοί μου, χαίρετε (as for II Cor. xiii. 11).

Phil. iv. 8 τὸ λοιπόν, ἀδελφοί, ὅσα ἐστὶν ἀληθῆ,..., *finally* (or *and so*), *all that is true,....*

I Thess. iv. 1 λοιπὸν οὖν, ἀδελφοί, ἐρωτῶμεν ὑμᾶς..., *finally, then* (or *and so*), *brothers, we beg you....*

II Thess. iii. 1 τὸ λοιπὸν προσεύχεσθε..., *finally* (or *and so*), *pray....*

II Tim. iv. 8 λοιπὸν ἀπόκειταί μοι..., *it remains that there is reserved for me....*

Heb. x. 13 τὸ λοιπὸν ἐκδεχόμενος..., *thenceforth awaiting....*

Note. For what remains thus appears to be the dominant or underlying meaning. Milligan on I Thess. iv. 1 cites Polyb. i. 15. 11 λοιπὸν ἀνάγκη συγχωρεῖν, τὰς ἀρχὰς καὶ τὰς ὑποθέσεις εἶναι ψευδεῖς, and Epict. *Diss.* i. 22. 15 ἄρχομαι λοιπὸν μισεῖν αὐτόν. He says that in Modern Greek λοιπόν has displaced οὖν; and it is interesting that in I Thess. iv. 1 λοιπόν alone, without οὖν, is read by B*, 1739*, some other MSS. and some versions.† ὧδε λοιπόν occurs in Epict. *Diss.* ii. 12. 24 (cited by M.M. *s.v.*), but certainly not in the sense suggested above in I Cor. iv. 2: ὧδε λοιπὸν ὁ κίνδυνος in Epict. *loc. cit.* seems to mean little more than *but here is the risk*. It is clear that in several of the above instances (e.g. II Cor. xiii. 11) the formula is exactly like the epistolary τὰ δ᾽ ἄλλα, which introduces the closing sentences (like our *Well,...*) in some of the papyri.[1]

4. μὲν οὖν is a primarily resumptive phrase;[2] but it evidently has other shades of meaning. The following is an attempt to classify them, but it would be ridiculous to pretend that they can be finally determined.

1 = purely resumptive or transitional;
2 = μέν distinct from οὖν, with οὖν = (*a*) resumptive, (*b*) inferential;
3 = antithetic, practically identical with a simple μέν;
4 = adversative (*however, nay rather*);

1	Mark xvi. 19 ὁ μὲν οὖν κύριος Ἰησοῦς....
1	Luke iii. 18 πολλὰ μὲν οὖν καὶ ἕτερα....
1	John xix. 24 οἱ μὲν οὖν στρατιῶται ταῦτα ἐποίησαν.
2 (*a*)	John xx. 30 πολλὰ μὲν οὖν... (*v.* 31 ταῦτα δὲ...).
1	Acts i. 18 οὗτος μὲν οὖν ἐκτήσατο χωρίον....
1	Acts ii. 41 οἱ μὲν οὖν ἀποδεξάμενοι....
1	Acts v. 41 οἱ μὲν οὖν ἐπορεύοντο....
1	Acts viii. 4 οἱ μὲν οὖν διασπαρέντες....
1	Acts viii. 25 οἱ μὲν οὖν διαμαρτυράμενοι....
1	Acts ix. 31 ἡ μὲν οὖν ἐκκλησία....
1 or ? 2 (*a*)	Acts xii. 5 ὁ μὲν οὖν Πέτρος ἐτηρεῖτο...προσευχὴ δὲ....
1	Acts xiii. 4 αὐτοὶ μὲν οὖν ἐκπεμφθέντες....
4†	Acts xiv. 3 ἱκανὸν μὲν οὖν χρόνον.
1	Acts xv. 3 οἱ μὲν οὖν πεμφθέντες....
1	Acts xv. 30 οἱ μὲν οὖν ἀπολυθέντες....
1	Acts xvii. 12 πολλοὶ μὲν οὖν ἐξ αὐτῶν ἐπίστευσαν....

[1] References in O. Roller, *Das Formular der Paulinischen Briefe* (Stuttgart, 1933), 66n.
[2] See J. D. Denniston, *The Greek Particles* (Oxford, 1934).

1 or ? 4   Acts xvii. 17 διελέγετο μὲν οὖν. . . .
1 or ? 2 (a) Acts xvii. 30 τοὺς μὲν οὖν χρόνους τῆς ἀγνοίας ὑπεριδὼν
         ὁ θεὸς τὰ νῦν. . . .
2 (a) Acts xviii. 14 εἰ μὲν ἦν ἀδίκημά τι. . . (ν.l. εἰ μὲν οὖν ἦν. . .).
2 (a) Acts xix. 38 εἰ μὲν οὖν Δημήτριος. . . (ν. 39 εἰ δέ τι
         περαιτέρω. . .).
1   Acts xxiii. 18 ὁ μὲν οὖν παραλαβὼν. . . .
1   Acts xxiii. 31 οἱ μὲν οὖν στρατιῶται. . . .
4   Acts xxv. 4 ὁ μὲν οὖν Φῆστος ἀπεκρίθη. . . .
1   Acts xxvi. 4 τὴν μὲν οὖν βίωσίν μου. . . .
?   Acts xxvi. 9 ἐγὼ μὲν οὖν ἔδοξα. . . .
4   Acts xxviii. 5 ὁ μὲν οὖν ἀποτινάξας. . . .
2 (b) I Cor. vi. 4 βιωτικὰ μὲν οὖν κριτήρια. . . .
?   I Cor. vi. 7 ἤδη μὲν οὖν. . . .
3   I Cor. ix. 25 ἐκεῖνοι μὲν οὖν. . . ἡμεῖς δὲ. . . .
1   Phil. ii. 23 τοῦτον μὲν οὖν ἐλπίζω πέμψαι. . . .
2 (b) Heb. vii. 11 εἰ μὲν οὖν τελείωσις. . . .†
1 or ? 4   Heb. ix. 1 εἴχε μὲν οὖν καὶ ἡ πρώτη. . . .

Notes. i. It will be observed that in the above list the use of μὲν οὖν as an affirmation (a Classical use) is absent.

ii. An adversative sense (*however*) appears to be required by the context in Acts xiv. 3, xvii. 17 (possibly), xxv. 4, xxviii. 5, and (perhaps) Heb. ix. 1. But this sense is not recognized by L. and S.⁹, and is questionable. See especially the note on Acts xiv. 3 in *Beg.*, and the remark that, in that passage, the transposition of *vv.* 2 and 3 would enable one to translate μὲν οὖν in the usual resumptive sense.

iii. In Acts xxvi. 9 and I Cor. vi. 7 μὲν οὖν appears to be equivalent to our colloquial *Why*,. . . : *Why, I myself thought*. . .; and *Why, it is a defect at the very outset*. . . .

iv. There are a few instances of μενοῦν (so printed) and μενοῦνγε at the beginning of a sentence or virtually at the beginning. In Luke xi. 28 its sense is the same as a frequent sense of μὲν οὖν (so printed, and not at the beginning) in Classical Greek, namely as an introduction to a new statement correcting or modifying a foregoing statement: Μενοῦν μακάριοι οἱ ἀκούοντες. . . (*ν.l.* μενοῦνγε), *Nay rather*. . . . In Rom. ix. 20, x. 18 it seems to be adversative: ὦ ἄνθρωπε, μενοῦνγε σὺ τίς εἶ. . .; *But who are you*. . .? Μενοῦνγε Εἰς πᾶσαν τὴν γῆν. . ., *On the contrary, 'Into all the earth*. . .'. In Phil. iii. 8 it follows ἀλλά and is printed in three words, but it appears to be closely akin to the 'modifying' usage of μενοῦνγε, in this case modifying in an affirmative direction instead of an adversative one: ἀλλὰ μὲν οὖν γε (*v.l. om.* γε)..., *Nay more*... or *In fact*....

L. and S.[9] note μενοῦν and μενοῦνγε at the beginning of a sentence as a N.T. usage. See below, 'The Order of Words', 3, p. 167.

5. ἀπαρτί (*sic*) as a particle meaning *precisely*, *expressly* is alluded to under 'Prepositions III, Genitive', 2. iii. *note*, above, p. 72 n. 1 *q.v.*

6. ἄρα and ἆρα. With either accent, this is an inferential particle; but the second accentuation is regarded as correct in an interrogative clause: Luke xviii. 8 ἆρα εὑρήσει τὴν πίστιν...; *is he, then, going to find faith...?* Acts viii. 30 ἆρά γε γινώσκεις...; *Now, do you understand...?* or *Do you, then, understand...?* For a discussion as to whether it is interrogative or not in Gal. ii. 17, see below, 'Miscellaneous Notes on Style', 3, p. 196.

Robertson and Plummer, *I.C.C.* on I Cor. xv. 18, say that 'in class. Gk. ἄρα rarely, if ever, stands first, as here'; and adduce II Cor. v. 15, Gal. ii. 21, v. 11 as further N.T. instances.

7. The particle γε is one whose exact force is difficult to define. Generally it appears to call attention and lend emphasis to the word or phrase to which it adheres. Thus εἴγε means *if, that is*, or *if, indeed*, and it depends upon the context whether or not such a strengthened *if* implies doubt or confident assumption.[1] Again, in Matt. vi. 1, εἰ δὲ μήγε, vii. 20 ἄραγε, I Cor. vi. 3 μήτιγε, the γε seems simply to strengthen the other words: *otherwise, mark you*..., *and so, mark you, not to mention, even*,....

8. διό and διότι. Of these two particles, διό means *and so* (cf. ἄρα) and διότι means *because, since*. See M.M. *s.vv.* But in Acts xx. 26, where the context certainly requires *and so*, there is considerable MS. support for διότι. διόπερ, with apparently much the same meaning as διό, but with perhaps a greater stress upon the logical connexion between the clauses it connects, occurs in I Cor. viii. 13, x. 14, and, in some MSS., xiv. 13.

9. εἰς τὸ διηνεκές, εἰς τὸ παντελές. Of these two expressions, the first occurs, in the N.T., only in Heb.—vii. 3, x. 1, 12, 14—and evidently means *uninterruptedly, continuously*. The second occurs in Luke xiii. 11,

---

[1] See a discussion in T. K. Abbott, *I.C.C.* on Ephesians and Colossians, pp. iv, v.

where it may mean *completely* (of the bent woman μὴ δυναμένη ἀνακύψαι εἰς τὸ παντελές), and in Heb. vii. 25 καὶ σώζειν εἰς τὸ παντελὲς δύναται. Here Westcott's comment is: '*completely, wholly, to the uttermost* ... the old commentators strangely explain it as if it were εἰς τὸ διηνεκές (so Latt. *in perpetuum*).' Yet M.M. *s.v.* support 'a temporal meaning..."to save finally"'; and Windisch[1] prints *für immer* as the translation.

Absolutely is certainly a sense which will fit both passages: the woman was *absolutely* unable to look up, could not look up *at all*; Christ is able to save *absolutely*; and this also fits the word etymologically. But if a temporal sense had come to attach itself to the phrase (as M.M.'s papyrus examples suggest) this might also be squared with both passages: the woman had been condemned by her disease *for good and all* not to look up; Christ saves *for good and all*. If so, *in perpetuum* might indeed serve as a translation alike for εἰς τὸ διηνεκές and εἰς τὸ παντελές, although the Greek phrases are not interchangeable.

10. καί is used idiomatically with several shades of meaning. For the displacement of the emphatic καί, see 'The Order of Words', 5. i. (*a*), p. 167.

Here it will be enough to note that, when the copula is sufficiently represented by δέ, a καί may be rendered by some such phrase as *Yes, and* or *Moreover*; thus I John i. 3[b] καὶ ἡ κοινωνία δὲ ἡ ἡμετέρα..., *yes, and our fellowship is*.... H. W. Moule compares Xen. *Sympos.* IV, 44 καὶ οὗτος δὲ οὐ...θαυμάζει, though O. J. Todd (Loeb ed., 433) translates *Like me, he does not*..., interpreting the καί as = *also*.

11. οὐκοῦν. This occurs only once in the N.T., in John xviii. 37 Οὐκοῦν βασιλεὺς εἶ σύ; Commentators vary in their interpretation: Westcott paraphrases 'So then, after all, thou art a king?' J. H. Bernard (*I.C.C. in loc.*) takes it merely as a resumptive particle 'Well, then, art thou...?' Grimm-Thayer, *Lexicon, s.v.*, prefer οὔκουν (*sic*): 'Art thou not a king, then?' or 'Thou art a king, art thou not?' But if it must be taken as οὐκοῦν (inferential), they prefer to take it as an exclamation rather than a question: 'Then thou art a king!' Westcott's paraphrase seems to me to make the best sense in the context, which seems to call for an inference from Christ's mention of his kingdom: 'So you *are* a king, are you?'

[1] In Lietzmann's *Handbuch z. N.T. in loc.*

XXIV

THE ORDER OF WORDS[1]

1. In Latin, one is taught, as a rough-and-ready rule, to put the verb at the end of the sentence. In Greek, the rule said to have been taught by Walter Headlam to his pupils is to *reverse the English order*, so that the emphatic word comes at or near the beginning of the sentence, whereas in English, it tends to gravitate to the end: *I can do* **anything** becomes πάντα ἰσχύω. An impressive example of bringing the emphatic words near the beginning of the sentence is afforded by Rom. v. 6 ἔτι γὰρ χριστὸς ὄντων ἡμῶν ἀσθενῶν ἔτι κατὰ καιρὸν ὑπὲρ ἀσεβῶν ἀπέθανεν. It is true that English itself by no means invariably casts its emphasis to the end: Matt. xxiii. 9 εἷς γάρ ἐστιν ὑμῶν ὁ πατὴρ ὁ οὐράνιος, might be rendered: *for, for you there is only* one *Father— the heavenly Father*.

But, as a rough-and-ready rule to start from, this 'reversing' one may serve.

2. The very great importance of the position of the *definite article* has been mentioned under that heading; see also under 'Participles' and 'Pronouns', pp. 103, 122. Note, for example, J. B. Mayor's remarks quoted under 'The Definite Article', p. 113, about πνεῦμα ἅγιον, τὸ ἅγιον πνεῦμα, and τὸ πνεῦμα τὸ ἅγιον. Here the following matters may also be noted:

i. N.T. usage appears to be variable as to phrases like ὁ τοῦ θεοῦ γὰρ υἱός (II Cor. i. 19) and ὁ υἱὸς τοῦ θεοῦ (John xx. 31). Possibly the 'sandwich' order, as in the first instance, would, in most instances, prove to be the more self-conscious and stylistically careful: II Pet. iii. 2, τῆς τῶν ἀποστόλων ὑμῶν ἐντολῆς, sounds a little stilted.

ii. II Pet. iii. 3 ἐπ' ἐσχάτων τῶν ἡμερῶν looks like a displacement for ἐπὶ τῶν ἐσχάτων ἡμερῶν; but D.-B. § 264. 5 takes it as an instance of the neuter plural ἔσχατα as a noun=אַחֲרִית.† In that case Jude 18 ἐπ' ἐσχάτου τοῦ χρόνου is either a deliberate displacement or a scribe's slip (*v.l.* ἐπ' ἐσχάτου χρόνου).

---

[1] For the study of word-order as a means of detecting 'translation' Greek, see J. M. Rife, 'The Mechanics of Translation Greek' (*J.B.L.* LII (1933), 244 ff.). See also M.-H. II, 416–18.

3. There are certain words which seldom or never begin a sentence: ἄν (particle), γάρ,[1] δέ, μέν, οὖν, and the enclitics (τις, ποτε, πως, etc.). But μενοῦν (so printed in W.H.) begins a sentence in Luke xi. 28 (or *v.l.* μενοῦνγε);[2] so does τοιγαροῦν in both its N.T. occurrences (I Thess. iv. 8, Heb. xii. 1); and Acts iii. 2, καί τις ἀνήρ..., is unusual for καὶ ἀνήρ τις or (Acts x. 1) ἀνὴρ δέ τις. (D.-B. § 473 provides one or two similar instances.)

4. It is worth while to consider εἰ καί and καὶ εἰ. εἰ καί is concessive (*even if, etsi*),[3] II Cor. vii. 8 (thrice), Heb. vi. 9; καὶ εἰ *may* be purely conditional (*and if*) or (especially in the form κἄν (=καὶ ἐάν)) *may* be concessive also. But the issue is complicated by the textual uncertainties.

5. The following are instances of apparent displacements:

i. *Of* καί. (*a*) Characteristic, it would seem, of St Paul is the displacement of a καί which ought logically to cohere closely with the verb: I Thess. ii. 13 καὶ διὰ τοῦτο καὶ ἡμεῖς εὐχαριστοῦμεν... (where the context points to εὐχαριστοῦμεν rather than ἡμεῖς as the proper 'focus'; *that is in fact* (καί) *why we give thanks*...); I Thess. iii. 5 διὰ τοῦτο κἀγώ...ἔπεμψα... (not *therefore I also sent*..., but *therefore I* actually *sent*..., or *that is in fact why I sent*...); Rom. iii. 7 τί ἔτι κἀγώ...κρίνομαι...; (not *why am I also*...? but *why am I* actually *judged*...? See Lietzmann, *Handbuch z. N.T. in loc.*). Is Phil. iv. 15, οἴδατε δὲ καὶ ὑμεῖς, another instance (for the ὑμεῖς does not seem to be emphatic)?

(*b*) Jude 14, ἐπροφήτευσεν δὲ καὶ τούτοις...'Ενώχ (where καὶ 'Ενώχ δὲ ἐπροφήτευσεν would seem more logical), is perhaps another (and slightly different type of) displacement of καί.

(*c*) In John xvii. 25, πατὴρ δίκαιε, καὶ ὁ κόσμος σε οὐκ ἔγνω, ἐγὼ δέ σε ἔγνων, καὶ οὗτοι ἔγνωσαν κ.τ.λ. is interpreted by E. A. Abbott (*Johannine Grammar* § [2164]) as meaning *both the world...and these*...; but the first καί does not seem so easily explicable.

ii. *Of* οὐ (or μή). Acts xxvi. 26 λανθάνειν γὰρ αὐτὸν τούτων οὐ πείθομαι οὐθέν (where the οὐ belongs not with πείθομαι but, as a double

---

[1] Though it is rare to find it so far from *second* place as in II Cor. i. 19 just quoted under 2. i.

[2] See above 'Some Observations on Adverbs, etc.' 4. Note iv, pp. 163 f.

[3] Accordingly J. Héring on I Cor. vii. 21 (*Commentaire in loc.*) associates himself with the exegesis which makes it an injunction to remain a slave 'even if' freedom is attainable. I prefer the opposite sense, taking the καί closely with δύνασαι: *but if you* can *secure your freedom, prefer to take the opportunity.*

negative, with λανθάνειν). In Rom. iii. 9, if the correct reading is
τί οὖν; προεχόμεθα; οὐ πάντως· προῃτιασάμεθα γὰρ Ἰουδαίους τε καὶ
Ἕλληνας κ.τ.λ., then οὐ πάντως must mean what would logically be
expressed by πάντως οὐ (*certainly not!*, rather than *not absolutely*).
But D.-B. § 433. 2 prefers the reading which omits οὐ and joins πάντως
with what follows. I Cor. ii. 2 οὐ γὰρ ἔκρινά τι εἰδέναι...εἰ μὴ...
looks as though it stood for ἔκρινα γὰρ μηδὲν εἰδέναι... (i.e. the
negative is displaced and changed from μή to οὐ accordingly); contrast
II Cor. ii. 1 ἔκρινα δὲ ἐμαυτῷ τοῦτο, τὸ μὴ πάλιν...ἐλθεῖν (which is
normal).[1] I Cor. xv. 51 πάντες οὐ κοιμηθησόμεθα seems to mean οὐ
πάντες κοιμηθησόμεθα, and the irregular order is possibly (see *I.C.C.
in loc.*) due to the desire to align it with the πάντες δὲ ἀλλαγησόμεθα
which follows. Heb. xi. 3 is very difficult: one of the results or
symptoms of faith (it says) is that we grasp (νοοῦμεν) that the worlds
(αἰῶνες) were made by the word of God, εἰς τὸ μὴ ἐκ φαινομένων τὸ
βλεπόμενον γεγονέναι—i.e. the reference seems to be to creation
ex nihilo, the *visible* having come into being out of the *invisible*; but,
if so, ἐκ μὴ φαινομένων is a much more natural phrase. But Westcott
and Nairne (Commentaries *in loc.*) both argue against the impropriety
of the order.† Cf. D.-B. § 433. 3, which quotes II Macc. vii. 28 (A)
ὅτι οὐκ ἐξ ὄντων ἐποίησεν αὐτὰ ὁ θεός, and also Acts i. 5 οὐ μετὰ πολλὰς
ταύτας ἡμέρας. On the strange οὐχὶ ἰδοὺ...; of Acts ii. 7, see *Beg.
in loc.*, where evidence is adduced to show that it may be not a Semitism
but a κοινή idiom replacing the classical ἆρ᾽ οὐ...; On the well-known
πᾶς...οὐ of I John iii. 9, etc., see under 'Semitisms', III. i, p. 182.

iii. *Of Pronouns.* Luke xxiv. 31 αὐτῶν δὲ διηνοίχθησαν οἱ ὀφθαλμοί
(where αὐτῶν does not seem to require so emphatic a position);†
Rom. ix. 24 οὓς καὶ ἐκάλεσεν ἡμᾶς (for ἡμᾶς, οὓς καὶ κ.τ.λ.); Col. ii. 8
βλέπετε μή τις ὑμᾶς ἔσται ὁ συλαγωγῶν (for μή τις ἔσται...); Heb. iv. 11
ἵνα μὴ ἐν τῷ αὐτῷ τις ὑποδείγματι πέσῃ τῆς ἀπειθείας (for ἵνα μή τις
πέσῃ ἐν τῷ αὐτῷ κ.τ.λ.); I Pet. v. 9 τῇ ἐν τῷ κόσμῳ ὑμῶν ἀδελφότητι
(which, as so much Greek, should mean *the brotherhood (brothers)
in your world*, instead of *your brothers in the world*); II Pet. iii. 1 διεγείρω
ὑμῶν ἐν ὑπομνήσει τὴν εἰλικρινῆ διάνοιαν (ὑμῶν displaced from τὴν
εἰλικρινῆ διάνοιαν).

iv. *Of Miscellaneous Words.* Luke xi. 27 (אBL) ἐπάρασά τις φωνὴν
γυνή is, if a serious reading, and not a mere slip, a very whimsical order.

---

[1] J. B. Lightfoot, *Notes on the Epistles of St Paul*, 171, on I Cor. ii. 2, argues,
on the contrary, that *I had no intent, no mind to know anything*... is the meaning.

John xiii. 2 τοῦ διαβόλου ἤδη βεβληκότος εἰς τὴν καρδίαν ἵνα παραδοῖ αὐτὸν Ἰούδας is a curious mixture (apparently) of two possible sentences.

Acts i. 2 ἐντειλάμενος τοῖς ἀποστόλοις διὰ πνεύματος ἁγίου οὓς ἐξελέξατο is notoriously problematic: see commentaries.

Acts iv. 25 is evidently corrupt or else influenced by an Aramaic original: see commentaries. It may even be a conflation of two or three alternative ways of expressing the meaning (so H. W. Moule, *E.T.* LI, no. 8 (May 1940)).

Acts iv. 33 καὶ δυνάμει μεγάλη ἀπεδίδουν τὸ μαρτύριον οἱ ἀπόστολοι τοῦ κυρίου Ἰησοῦ τῆς ἀναστάσεως is simply extraordinary: one would have expected either καὶ δυνάμει μεγάλη οἱ ἀπόστολοι τοῦ κυρίου Ἰησοῦ ἀπεδίδουν τὸ μαρτύριον τῆς ἀναστάσεως (*the apostles* of the Lord Jesus *rendered their witness* to the resurrection) or καὶ δυνάμει μεγάλη οἱ ἀπόστολοι ἀπεδίδουν τὸ μαρτύριον τῆς ἀναστάσεως τοῦ κυρίου Ἰησοῦ (*the apostles rendered their witness to the resurrection of the Lord Jesus*); as it stands, it is both ambiguous and awkward.† See *Beg.* III, cclix n. 2 for a variant order (B) τοῦ κυρίου Ἰησοῦ τῆς ἀναστάσεως. Cf. Acts xix. 20 οὕτως κατὰ κράτος τοῦ κυρίου ὁ λόγος ηὔξανεν..., for a similar apparent displacement of τοῦ κυρίου.

Acts xix. 4, ... Ἰωάνης ἐβάπτισεν βάπτισμα μετανοίας, τῷ λαῷ λέγων εἰς τὸν ἐρχόμενον μετ' αὐτὸν ἵνα πιστεύσωσιν..., is strange, considering how natural and easy it would have been to write λέγων τῷ λαῷ ἵνα πιστεύσωσιν εἰς τὸν....

Acts xxvi. 20 is an instance of a seemingly displaced τε: ἀλλὰ τοῖς ἐν Δαμασκῷ πρῶτόν τε καὶ Ἱεροσολύμοις πᾶσάν τε τὴν χώραν τῆς Ἰουδαίας... (so ℵAB 25. 61—Tischendorf). The passage is mended by the simple removal of the first τε (so other MSS.); or by transferring it so as to follow Δαμασκῷ. Is its position due purely to the familiar association of τε with πρῶτον? So in Acts xxvi. 22 also, there is a displaced τε: οὐδὲν ἐκτὸς λέγων ὧν τε οἱ προφῆται ἐλάλησαν μελλόντων γίνεσθαι καὶ Μωϋσῆς. A logical order would be ...οἵ τε προφῆται καὶ Μωϋσῆς.... The strictly correct position may be illustrated by, for example, Rom. ii. 9 Ἰουδαίου τε πρῶτον καὶ Ἕλληνος.

Gal. ii. 12 πρὸ τοῦ γὰρ ἐλθεῖν would more naturally, I think, have been πρὸ γὰρ τοῦ ἐλθεῖν. Cf. II Cor. i. 19 quoted under 2. i. above.

Rom. viii. 18 and Gal. iii. 23 both show a curious order in nearly identical clauses: πρὸς τὴν μέλλουσαν δόξαν ἀποκαλυφθῆναι and εἰς τὴν μέλλουσαν πίστιν ἀποκαλυφθῆναι, where one would expect

πρὸς }
εἰς } τὴν {δόξαν }
{πίστιν} τὴν μέλλουσαν ἀποκαλυφθῆναι (or, alternatively,

ἀπ. μελλ.); cf. I Pet. i. 5, εἰς σωτηρίαν ἑτοίμην ἀποκαλυφθῆναι, which is normal, and which, to cast it in a form parallel to the Pauline anomaly, would have to have been dislocated to εἰς ἑτοίμην σωτηρίαν ἀποκαλυφθῆναι. [Question: is there any other evidence in κοινή Greek for μέλλω exercising a disturbing influence?]

I Cor. xv. 19 εἰ ἐν τῇ ζωῇ ταύτῃ ἐν χριστῷ ἠλπικότες ἐσμὲν μόνον should, strictly, mean *if in this life we only have our* hopes *fixed in Christ* (as opposed to something securer than *hope*); but the N.T. use of ἐλπίζω and the context both call rather for the translation *if it is only in this life*..., εἰ μόνον ἐν τῇ ζωῇ ταύτῃ....

In Heb. xii. 23 commentators are divided as to how to translate κριτῇ θεῷ πάντων—whether *a God who is judge of all* or *a judge who is God of all*. If the former is right, the order can only be explained as a trick of style. It comes in a highly rhetorical passage.

XXV

'SEMITISMS'

This ugly and rather jargonistic word seems to have 'come to stay' as a term to describe features of Greek which are tinged more or less with either Aramaic or Hebrew. *Semiticism* would be a more accurate, if no less ugly, term, for a tendency to 'Semiticize'; but the commoner word is here accepted.

There is an extensive literature about the subject, and some attempt is made, at the end of this chapter, to name the most important works and, in some instances, to indicate their tendencies. It is a complex field of study for several reasons, among them being the following:

1. It is not always possible to determine where to draw the line between a clear, alien 'Semitism' and a term or idiom which is indeed reminiscent of a characteristically Semitic equivalent but which is none the less good or tolerable Greek, and which may, therefore, owe little or nothing to Semitic influence. Sometimes it is only the frequency of its occurrence, and not its actual existence, that a term or phrase owes to the alien influence.

Obviously, too, this problem is complicated by the question of how far the generally understood, secular κοινή had unconsciously absorbed and, so to speak, naturalized what were originally alien elements from Semitic populations.

2. There is the subtle problem of distinguishing between *direct* Semitisms (owing their existence to the direct impact of Hebrew or Aramaic upon the writer's own vocabulary) and *indirect* or *secondary* Semitisms mediated by the Septuagint or other translation Greek.

This problem is particularly prominent in the Lucan writings, for it looks uncommonly as though Luke were ignorant of Semitic languages himself, but could at will adopt a 'Septuagintal' style (just as a modern English writer may copy the style of the Authorized Version, including its Hebraic idioms, without himself knowing any Hebrew). Yet, there are indications that he may also have incorporated some Greek sources which were themselves direct translations from

Semitic originals and which contained, therefore, *direct*, not *secondary*, Semitisms.[1]

3. There are the problems arising from differences within the Semitic languages. Hebrew is not Aramaic; and Aramaic includes different dialects. Consequently, it is important to classify Semitisms, if the full value of their evidence is to be obtained. A demonstrable Aramaism (as distinct from a Hebraism) may point to contact with some source from primitive Palestinian Christianity or go back to the actual words of Jesus; a proved Hebraism will point only to contact, direct or secondary, with the Scriptures; while a Semitism such as might be either Aramaic or Hebrew will be correspondingly vague in evidential value.

It is instructive to study the impact of Semitic languages on our English versions.[2] The use of *of* in such phrases as *called of God* in modern theological or religious writers is a good example of *Biblicism*—i.e. of the language of the A.V. being projected into modern speech by association of ideas.

The following is a rough catalogue of clear or suspected Semitisms in the N.T., with examples and notes. It has not always proved possible to be definite as to their Aramaic, Hebraic, or other distinguishing qualities.

I. BROAD QUALITIES OF STYLE

i. It is well known that Hebrew was prone to what is usually called *parataxis* (that is, the placing side by side of complete sentences with main verbs, instead of the use of subordinate clauses). The Greek ethos was at least more ready to use subordinate clauses.[3] For example, Mark (which is particularly prone to parataxis) will say ἦν δὲ ὥρα τρίτη καὶ ἐσταύρωσαν αὐτόν (xv. 25), where a less Semitic style would probably have used a subordinate temporal clause (there happens to be no synoptic parallel to this). In sharp contrast is the highly

[1] For some interesting reflexions on this problem, see H. F. D. Sparks, 'The Semitisms of St Luke's Gospel', in *J.T.S.* XLIV (July–Oct. 1943), and 'The Semitisms of the Acts', *J.T.S.* (new series), 1 (April 1950), 16–28, and N. W. Lund, *Chiasmus in the New Testament* (Univ. of N. Carolina, 1942), 296, from which an excerpt is quoted under 'Miscellaneous Notes on Style', below, pp. 193 f.

[2] See the interesting observations by J. Isaacs in *The Bible in its Ancient and English Versions* (ed. H. W. Robinson, Oxford, 1940), 209 ff. Also *Proleg.* 98.

[3] But see M.-H. II, 422, 423; and Thumb, *Die griechische Sprache im Zeitalter des Hellenismus* (1901), 129, for Aristotle's proneness to parataxis.

'subordinating' style of the story of the coin in the fish's mouth, Matt. xvii. 24–7, which makes free use of the Greek participial constructions. One might, in fact, attempt a translation into a more Semitic style by way of contrast:

Matt.	Paratactic Style
ἐλθόντων δὲ αὐτῶν εἰς Καφαρναοὺμ προσῆλθον οἱ τὰ δίδραχμα λαμβάνοντες τῷ Πέτρῳ καὶ εἶπαν (here he has allowed himself a καί-clause) Ὁ διδάσκαλος ὑμῶν οὐ τελεῖ δίδραχμα; λέγει Ναί. καὶ ἐλθόντα εἰς τὴν οἰκίαν προέφθασεν αὐτὸν ὁ Ἰησοῦς λέγων Τί σοι δοκεῖ, Σίμων; ...	καὶ ἔρχονται εἰς Καφαρναοὺμ καὶ προσέρχονται τῷ Πέτρῳ οἱ τὰ δίδραχμα λαμβάνοντες καὶ λέγουσιν αὐτῷ Ὁ διδάσκαλος ὑμῶν οὐ τελεῖ δίδραχμα; λέγει Ναί. καὶ ἔρχεται εἰς τὴν οἰκίαν καὶ ὁ Ἰησοῦς προλαμβάνει (possibly—cf. Mark xiv. 8) αὐτὸν καὶ λέγει Τί σοι δοκεῖ, Σίμων; ...

E. Norden (*Antike Kunstprosa*, 491) adduces examples of Luke's tendency to subordinate, in contrast to Mark and Matthew (the above specimen of Matthaean subordination being far from typical of this writer):

Mark	Matt.	Luke
x. 17	xix. 16	xviii. 18
x. 28	xix. 27	xviii. 28
xi. 7	xxi. 7	xix. 35
xiv. 49	xxvi. 55	xxii. 53
	xxv. 29	xix. 26, etc.

But it needs to be said in all fairness that Luke (unless he is here faithfully copying a source) is capable of such *parataxis* as xix. 43 ἥξουσιν ἡμέραι ἐπὶ σὲ καὶ παρεμβαλοῦσιν οἱ ἐχθροί σου χάρακά σοι. And cf. Thumb, above, p. 172, n. 3.

ii. It is also true (cf. 'Remarks on ἵνα and ὥστε' above, p. 142) that the Semitic mind tended not to make a sharp distinction between final and consecutive—cause and effect; and this comes out in the blurring of ἵνα and ὥστε already noted.

iii. *Parallelism* is a well-known feature of Semitic poetical style. It would be dangerous to make it a rigid test (cf. M.-H. II, 418, 419); but it is natural to suspect Semitic influence in such a passage as Luke xii. 48:

παντὶ δὲ ᾧ ἐδόθη πολύ, | πολὺ ζητηθήσεται παρ' αὐτοῦ,
καὶ ᾧ παρέθεντο πολύ, | περισσότερον αἰτήσουσιν αὐτόν,

where note also the 'indefinite' 3rd plural (see II. xiv below) and the peculiar handling of the pronouns (see II. iv. (a) below).

iv. For 'Chiasmus' as a particularly Semitic feature of style, see N. W. Lund, Chiasmus in the New Testament, 33 (and see below, 'Miscellaneous Notes on Style', pp. 193 f.).

v. For possible 'Semitisms' in word order, see pp. 168 f. above.

II. PARTICULAR IDIOMS

The following idioms can at least be described as more Semitic than Greek, although the degree of the Semitic influence is, obviously, impossible to assess with exactitude:

i.[1] (καὶ) ἐγένετο introducing another verb in one form or another: Luke i. 8 ἐγένετο...ἔλαχε, it came about...that he received as his lot; so Luke i. 23 καὶ ἐγένετο...ἀπῆλθεν; xiv. 1 καὶ ἐγένετο...καὶ αὐτοὶ ἦσαν παρατηρούμενοι αὐτόν.

Acts x. 25 ὡς δὲ ἐγένετο τοῦ εἰσελθεῖν τὸν Πέτρον.

Acts xxi. 5 ὅτε δὲ ἐγένετο ἐξαρτίσαι ἡμᾶς τὰς ἡμέρας.

Notes. (a) M. Black, J.T.S. XLIX (July–Oct. 1948), reviewing material collected by the late A. J. Wensinck for the study of Palestinian Aramaic from the old Palestinian Targum, etc., notes that 'The "Hebraism" καὶ ἐγένετο is found also in the free Aramaic, Gen. iv. 16'.

(b) Of the above types, the LXX almost entirely excludes the constructions with the infinitive (M.-H. II, 425).†

ii. ἐν τῷ with Infin. in a temporal sense (as distinct from the sense consisting of) seems to be a Hebraism, especially frequent in Luke–Acts (M.-H. II, 451). This construction is often combined (as a subordinate clause) with the ἐγένετο-constructions of i. above.

iii. Adjectival Genitive. (a) The Semitic idiom whereby sons of light, of darkness, of life, of death, of belial, etc. means simply people worthy of, or associated with light, etc. Thus, in the N.T. we find: Mark ii. 19 οἱ υἱοὶ τοῦ νυμφῶνος, the bridal party; Luke xvi. 8 οἱ υἱοὶ τοῦ αἰῶνος τούτου...τοὺς υἱοὺς τοῦ φωτός; Matt. xxiii. 15 υἱὸν γεέννης; Eph. ii. 3 τέκνα φύσει ὀργῆς (perhaps = left to ourselves (φύσει) we are destined to suffer the consequences of sin); Eph. v. 8 τέκνα φωτός;

[1] See tables in M.-H. II, 426, 427.

I Thess. v. 5 υἱοὶ φωτός ἐστε καὶ υἱοὶ ἡμέρας; II Thess. ii. 3 ὁ ἄνθρωπος τῆς ἀνομίας, ὁ υἱὸς τῆς ἀπωλείας (so also John xvii. 12).

Is I Pet. i. 14 ὡς τέκνα ὑπακοῆς *obedient* people or literally *obedient children*? Note that the English versions themselves reproduce this 'Semitism' freely (*son of belial*, etc.).

(*b*) Even without the υἱός or τέκνον, the descriptive Genitive may well be due, in many instances, to Semitic influence: Luke ii. 14 ἐν ἀνθρώποις εὐδοκίας (*v.l.* εὐδοκία), probably *men on whom rests God's good will, men who are pleasing to God* (although one would, if so, expect (τῆς) εὐδοκίας αὐτοῦ); cf. Jer. xii. 10 (LXX) μερίδα ἐπιθυμητήν μου, חֶלְקַת חֶמְדָּתִי; II Cor. xi. 14 ἄγγελον φωτός perhaps = ἄγγελον φωτεινόν; Eph. i. 13 τῷ πνεύματι τῆς ἐπαγγελίας evidently = *the promised Spirit* (cf. M.-H. 11, 485); Eph. i. 19 τοῦ κράτους τῆς ἰσχύος αὐτοῦ probably = τοῦ ἰσχυροῦ κράτους αὐτοῦ; Col. i. 13 τοῦ υἱοῦ τῆς ἀγάπης αὐτοῦ (*not* υἱός in the sense of (*a*) above) probably = τοῦ ἀγαπητοῦ υἱοῦ αὐτοῦ; Heb. iv. 2 ὁ λόγος τῆς ἀκοῆς, *the word which they heard.*

(*c*) The following naturally associate themselves in one's mind with the above idiom, but exact Semitic parallels are difficult to find: Gal. iii. 2, 5 ἐξ ἀκοῆς πίστεως, which evidently = *hearing and believing*, i.e. *a sort of hearing which issues in belief*: cf. Heb. iv. 2 above; Jas. i. 25 ἀκροατὴς ἐπιλησμονῆς...ποιητὴς ἔργου (*forgetful hearer...active doer*); Jas. ii. 4 κριταὶ διαλογισμῶν πονηρῶν, *judges with wicked ideas*; Jude 9 κρίσιν...βλασφημίας, *a vituperative verdict.*

Are Eph. iii. 21 τοῦ αἰῶνος τῶν αἰώνων and cognate αἰών phrases essentially Semitic? See III. x, p. 185 below.

I Pet. ii. 12 ἐν ἡμέρᾳ ἐπισκοπῆς is an actual quotation (though Isa. x. 3 LXX has articles); cf. Luke xxi. 22 ἡμέραι ἐκδικήσεως.

(*d*) But it is a mistake to claim a Semitic Genitive where a good Greek Genitive makes better sense: it would be misplaced subtlety to translate Rom. viii. 21, τῆς δουλείας τῆς φθορᾶς, as *corrupting bondage*, when it obviously means *bondage to corruption* (or *mortality*); although in the same verse it seems more natural to translate τὴν ἐλευθερίαν τῆς δόξης 'semitically' as *glorious freedom* (rather than, for example, *freedom consisting in the glory*...).

Yet decision is not always easy. In Eph. iii. 16, does κατὰ τὸ πλοῦτος τῆς δόξης αὐτοῦ mean *his wealth of glory* (so Goodspeed's translation) or *his glorious wealth*? Further, note that a perfectly normal Greek *Genitive of definition* may sometimes best be rendered into English by an adjective or participle: Gal. iii. 14 τὴν ἐπαγγελίαν τοῦ πνεύματος has nothing distinctively Semitic about it, but it does fall into the category of genitival phrases equivalent to an English phrase such as *the promised Spirit* (and so, curiously enough, equivalent to the reverse phrase in Eph. i. 13 τῷ πνεύματι τῆς ἐπαγγελίας, classed ((*b*) above) as possibly Semitic).

iv. *Redundant Pronoun.* (*a*) Hebrew and Aramaic use an indeclinable and genderless relative followed by a pronoun indicating its case and gender; and this construction has probably left its stamp on the N.T. in the frequency of such turns of phrase as Mark vii. 25 ἧς εἶχεν τὸ θυγάτριον αὐτῆς, where the αὐτῆς is redundant. Luke xii. 48 (quoted under 1. iii. above) contains examples. M.-H. II, 435, cf. Mark xiii. 19 (contrast Matthew) οἷα οὐ γέγονεν τοιαύτη.[1] The difficulty of assessing the situation is illustrated by Moulton (*Proleg.* 94) from Mrs Gamp who 'will hardly be suspected of Hebraism' when she says 'which her name is Mrs Harris'.

(*b*) II Cor. xii. 17, μή τινα . . . δι᾽ αὐτοῦ ἐπλεονέκτησα, is a well-known anacolouthon, and may possibly be due to the same Semitic way of handling pronouns, as it were retrospectively; D.-B. § 466 adds, among other instances of such anacolouthon: Acts vii. 40 ὁ Μωϋσῆς οὗτος . . . οὐκ οἴδαμεν τί ἐγένετο αὐτῷ; I John ii. 27 καὶ ὑμεῖς τὸ χρῖσμα ὃ ἐλάβετε ἀπ᾽ αὐτοῦ μένει ἐν ὑμῖν (for which D.-B. cf. Gen. xxviii. 13 ἡ γῆ, ἐφ᾽ ἧς σὺ καθεύδεις ἐπ᾽ αὐτῆς, σοὶ δώσω αὐτήν).

(*c*) Note also redundant pronouns in other connexions, which may be due, at least in some instances, to Semitic influence: Mark v. 16 D αὐτῷ τῷ δαιμονιζομένῳ, vi. 17 αὐτὸς γὰρ ὁ Ἡρῴδης, John ix. 18 αὐτοῦ τοῦ ἀναβλέψαντος (but see also 'Pronouns', above, pp. 121 f.), adduced by M.-H. II, 431. There is also in some cases an un-Greek frequency in the use of the possessive αὐτοῦ, etc.; and a Semitic idiom is possibly behind the curious repetition of αὐτός in Luke xix. 2 καὶ αὐτὸς ἦν ἀρχιτελώνης, καὶ αὐτὸς πλούσιος, and Jas. ii. 6 οὐχ οἱ πλούσιοι καταδυναστεύουσιν ὑμῶν, καὶ αὐτοὶ ἕλκουσιν ὑμᾶς εἰς κριτήρια;

v. Εἷς = Τις. It is possible that the use of εἷς as an indefinite pronoun (examples under 'Pronouns' IV, above, p. 125) may be influenced by the idiom אִישׁ אֶחָד = *a certain man* (I Sam. i. 1, etc.).†

---

[1] For a minimizing of the Semitic influence in this respect, see *Proleg.* 94 (cf. M.-H. II, 435); and for a detailed examination of the idiom in Revelation, R. H. Charles (*I.C.C.*).

vi. *The Definite Article*. Sometimes it is possible that a Semitic idiom whereby the definite article is used in places where true Greek would probably omit it has impressed itself on the N.T. usage. M.-H. ii, 430 adduces Mark x. 25 διὰ τῆς τρυμαλιᾶς τῆς ῥαφίδος ('where Matthew and Luke have dropped the def. art. before each Genitive').

Conversely, certain omissions of the article in the N.T. may be traceable to the 'construct state' in Hebrew, which is a method of relating one noun to another (much as the Genitive relates one noun to another in Greek) such that the article is not permitted with the first of the two: Luke iv. 18 πνεῦμα κυρίου (=Isa. lxi. 1 LXX), the *Spirit of* the *Lord*; perhaps Matt. xii. 42, Luke xi. 31 βασίλισσα νότου. But see under 'The Definite Article', 6, pp. 114 f. In any case the very important ὁ υἱὸς τοῦ ἀνθρώπου needs careful consideration. In the LXX, while οἱ υἱοὶ τῶν ἀνθρώπων is fairly frequent (Pss., Isa., Jer., etc.), there are also the anarthrous singular and plural (Job, Pss., Isa., Jer., Eccles., Wisd., Ecclus., Tob., etc.); and there is Dan. vii. 13, ὡς υἱὸς ἀνθρώπου (for the Aramaic כְּבַר אֱנָשׁ: and so Θ also; and cf. Dan. iii. 92 Θ, ἡ ὅρασις τοῦ τετάρτου ὁμοία υἱῷ θεοῦ; x. 16 Θ, ὡς ὁμοίωσις υἱοῦ ἀνθρώπου); Ezek. ii. 1 and *passim* υἱὲ ἀνθρώπου (so too Dan. viii. 17); and other combinations (including Ecclus. xl. 1 υἱοὺς Ἀδάμ). But in the N.T. the anarthrous υἱὸς ἀνθρώπου occurs only in John v. 27, except in quotations from the O.T. (Heb. ii. 6, Rev. i. 13, xiv. 14).

See further under 'The Definite Article' (above), and, for the use or omission of the article with πᾶς, see 'The Adjective', 1. ii. pp. 93–5.

Incidentally, it is interesting that Radermacher, 16, quotes δῆμος Ῥωμαίων (from a Greek version of a Roman history) as an instance of omission of articles due to *Latin* influence.

vii. προστιθέναι *with Indicative or Infinitive* as = *do again*, or *do further*.

Luke xix. 11 προσθεὶς εἶπεν παραβολήν;

Luke xx. 11 καὶ προσέθετο ἕτερον πέμψαι δοῦλον;

Acts xii. 3 προσέθετο συλλαβεῖν καὶ Πέτρον; cf. Gen. iv. 2 καὶ προσέθηκεν τεκεῖν..., and *passim*.

It is interesting that the genitive Articular Infinitive after προστιθέναι, which is frequent in the LXX (e.g. Gen. viii. 12), is not reproduced by Luke: see above, 'Observations on Certain Uses of the Infinitive', iii, p. 128 n. 3.

viii. *The* 'ἐπιθυμίᾳ ἐπεθύμησα' *construction*. In Hebrew (but very rarely in pure Aramaic—M.-H. ii, 443) there is an idiom combining the 'infinitive absolute' of a verb with another part of the same verb so as to express emphasis or frequency. This idiom is reflected several times in the N.T. in quotations from the O.T., in the shape of a verb with a cognate participle or noun attached to it: Heb. vi. 14 εὐλογῶν εὐλογήσω σε καὶ πληθύνων πληθυνῶ σε; but it is rare in passages which are not O.T. quotations: Luke xxii. 15 ἐπιθυμίᾳ ἐπεθύμησα (perhaps = *I have* (or perhaps *had*) *earnestly desired*);[1] Acts v. 28 παραγγελίᾳ παρηγγείλαμεν ὑμῖν (perhaps = *we strictly enjoined upon you*); Acts xxiii. 14 ἀναθέματι ἀνεθεματίσαμεν ἑαυτούς (perhaps = *we have bound ourselves under a solemn oath*).[2]† All these are in settings where Luke may well be deliberately using Septuagintal style.† So Jas. v. 17 προσευχῇ προσηύξατο, with its O.T. allusion. Ought we to add Gal. v. 1 τῇ ἐλευθερίᾳ ἡμᾶς χριστὸς ἠλευθέρωσεν (unless the correct reading is τῇ ἐλευθερίᾳ οὖν ᾗ χριστὸς...)? It is tempting also to associate with this idiom II Pet. iii. 3 ἐμπαιγμονῇ ἐμπαῖκται, as though it were a compressed form of οἱ ἐμπαιγμονῇ ἐμπαίξουσιν. But M.-H. II, 420 includes it among possible *Aramaic* (not Hebraic) *pleonasms*. Cf. John iii. 29 χαρᾷ χαίρει, although this may only be a variant of the Cognate Accusative construction, Matt. ii. 10 ἐχάρησαν χαρὰν μεγάλην σφόδρα.

Note. H. W. Moule notes Plato, *Symp.* 195B φεύγων φυγῇ as evidence that one must not call the construction wholly un-Greek.

ix. *Adversative* καί. There are occasions when καί is used in a context which compels any modern English version to use an adversative particle such as *yet, for all that*. This is precisely one of the characteristics of the Hebrew[3] copula also, and it may, therefore, reflect Semitic influence: Luke vii. 35 καὶ ἐδικαιώθη ἡ σοφία, yet *wisdom...*; so, perhaps, in the problematic Luke xviii. 7 καὶ μακροθυμεῖ ἐπ' αὐτοῖς (perhaps = *despite his patience* or *deferring of judgment*).

x. *Commands and Prohibitions expressed by the Future Indicative.* This is a normal Hebrew construction, and is familiar to readers of the N.T. because of quotations from the LXX such as Luke iv. 8 προσκυνήσεις κύριον τὸν θεόν σου καὶ αὐτῷ μόνῳ λατρεύσεις. The negative is οὐ (naturally enough since the verb is in the Indicative—although the fact that the Hebrew has a special negative particle for

---

[1] But, though not a quotation, this is exactly paralleled by Gen. xxxi. 30 ἐπιθυμίᾳ γὰρ ἐπεθύμησας, as is Acts xxiii. 14 by Deut. xiii. 16, xx. 17.

[2] See Dalman, *The Words of Jesus (E.T.)*, 34.

[3] Perhaps not Aramaic.

such cases might have given rise to a Semitic μή with the Indicative in Prohibitions): Luke iv. 12 οὐκ ἐκπειράσεις. It is worth noting, however, that the Hebraic idiom is not always retained, even in similar contexts: Luke xviii. 20 μὴ μοιχεύσῃς, etc.

xi. *Emphatic Denial expressed by Aposiopesis.* In Mark viii. 12 εἰ δοθήσεται comes to mean *there certainly shall not be given*...; and in Heb. iii. 11 (=Ps. xcv. (LXX xciv) 11) εἰ εἰσελεύσονται comes to mean *they certainly shall not enter.*... This exactly corresponds to a familiar Hebrew[1] construction whereby the particle אִם (which commonly means *if*) followed by a verb expresses vigorous denial. The construction, whether rightly or not, is usually explained as *aposiopesis*—that is, the silencing or suppressing of a part of the sentence; it is claimed that the full sentence would take the form of such actual examples as: III Reg. xxi. 10 (Heb. I Kings xx. 10) τάδε ποιήσαι μοι ὁ θεὸς καὶ τάδε προσθείη, εἰ ἐκποιήσει..., *God do thus to me, and more besides, if*... (just as *I'm damned if I will = I certainly will not*). See under 'Conditional Clauses', p. 151.

xii. *Participles.* There are several examples in the N.T. of the use of the participle where normal[2] Greek would have used a finite verb or imperative.

Note, for example, Rom. v. 11 οὐ μόνον δέ, ἀλλὰ καὶ καυχώμενοι, where a finite verb (as in the Old Latin Version's *gloriabimur*) would have seemed natural; Phil. iii. 4 καίπερ ἐγὼ ἔχων..., where ἔχω (with a corresponding alternative to καίπερ) would have been strictly correct; II Cor. v. 12 οὐ...συνιστάνομεν..., ἀλλὰ...διδόντες; vii. 5 θλιβόμενοι; viii. 4 δεόμενοι; ix. 11 πλουτιζόμενοι; ix. 13 δοξάζοντες (perhaps imperatival).† For the last two, see also under 'Some Observations on the Cases: 1. Nominative', pp. 30f.

But specially notable is the long sequence of participles in Rom. xii. 9ff.; where the sense is evidently imperatival.

Now, in Biblical Hebrew the use of participles as finite verbs is well known (see D. Daube in E. G. Selwyn's *I Peter*, 471); and in certain Tannaitic writings they are used almost as imperatives in ethical injunctions, etc. (*ibid.* 472ff.). And since participles like the ones in Rom. xii also occur in the ethical injunctions of the *Didache*,

---

[1] Not Aramaic (M.-H. II, 469).
[2] Yet see W. Bauer in *Apost. Väter* (Lietzmann's *Handbuch z. N. T.*), 195, adducing evidence for this usage in pre-Christian κοινή.

a strong case can be made for tracing at least some of these participles to Semitic influence.[1]†

Note, further, how simple adjectives are sometimes imperatively used: Rom. xii. 10, 11 φιλόστοργοι...μὴ ὀκνηροί; cf. Ignatius, *Eph.* x, 2. This is a usage closely akin to the use of the participle just illustrated: see Daube, *loc. cit.* 476; and add Heb. xiii. 4, 5 (cited *ibid.* 482) where there are two adjectives and a participle.

Less frequent is an *Aorist* Participle in such a sense; but note II Cor. xi. 6 φανερώσαντες.

Note also the transition from a participle to a finite verb, which is known in Classical Greek but may have been increased in frequency by Hebrew influence. M.-H. II, 428, 429 adduces: John i. 32, v. 44, II John 2, Rev. i. 5, 6, etc., Col. i. 26, Heb. viii. 10, x. 16 (the last two in LXX quotations).

xiii. *Solecistic Changes in Person.* It is possible that a Semitic tendency to change from 2nd to 3rd person or from 3rd to 2nd may be behind Luke xiii. 34 Ἱερουσαλήμ...ἡ...λιθοβολοῦσα τοὺς ἀπεσταλμένους πρὸς αὐτήν, ποσάκις ἠθέλησα ἐπισυνάξαι τὰ τέκνα σου...καὶ οὐκ ἠθελήσατε. Note, too, the plural with which this apostrophe ends, although a plural verb with a collective singular noun is by no means distinctively Semitic.

xiv. *'Indefinite' Third Person.* Where English idiom (at least on more formal and correct occasions) takes the form *one does so-and-so* or *so-and-so is done*, and Greek might similarly use τις or a passive, there is a tendency in both Hebrew and Aramaic (M.-H. II, 447) to resort to a verb without any expressed subject[2] (cf. our informal idiom with *they*, referring quite vaguely to an undefined subject);

[1] See Daube, *loc. cit.*, and summary in W. D. Davies, *Paul and Rabbinic Judaism*, 329. It should be added that (had the material reached Dr Selwyn in time) Dr Daube would have expanded his remarks with a further footnote in which he said that in *Didache* v. 2 (*Ep. Barn.* xx) 'the unattached participles and nouns denoting persons might be construed as elliptic, exclamatory descriptions of what is to be seen on the Way of Death' (cf. *Derek Eres Zuta* quoted in his printed note); but that 'it does seem possible that the section from διῶκται stands in the same line of descent as the legislative Tannaitic participles here analysed'. In the latter case, the argument in favour of Semitic influence remains.

[2] A famous and pleasing instance is II Kings xix. 35 =Isa. xxxvii. 36, where R.V. has *and when men arose early in the morning, behold, they were all dead corpses*, but the Hebrew has no expressed subject, and LXX has in IV Reg. καὶ ὤρθρισαν τὸ πρωί, καὶ ἰδού..., and in Isaiah καὶ ἐξαναστάντες τὸ πρωὶ εὗρον....

and it is possible, though hardly demonstrable, that Semitic influence has made this trick more frequent in the N.T. than it would otherwise have been.† A good example is John xv. 6 καὶ συνάγουσιν αὐτὰ καὶ εἰς τὸ πῦρ βάλλουσιν... (A.V. men *gather them*...; R.V. they *gather them*...). See also under 'Impersonal Verbs', p. 28.

xv. *Abnormal Use of Tenses*. For possible instances of Semitic influence on the use of the Aorist, see above, 'The Tenses, 4. The Aorist', p. 11. But most possible Semitisms of tense seem to me to be too uncertain to be profitably discussed.

xvi. Ἄρχεσθαι. C. C. Torrey in *Harv. Theol. Studies*, I (1916), 25 ff. claims that certain peculiar uses of this verb point to an Aramaic idiom in which מִשְׁרֵא מִן really only amounts to *from*: 'in Aramaic the word is an accusative of state or condition, sometimes rather loosely connected, so that a faithful Greek rendering is likely to be awkward.' He traces to this origin the following: (*a*) Matt. xx. 8 ἀπόδος τὸν μισθόν, ἀρξάμενος ἀπὸ τῶν ἐσχάτων ἕως τῶν πρώτων; (*b*) Luke xxiii. 5 διδάσκων καθ' ὅλης τῆς 'Ιουδαίας, καὶ ἀρξάμενος ἀπὸ τῆς Γαλιλαίας ἕως ὧδε; (*c*) Luke xxiv. 27 καὶ ἀρξάμενος ἀπὸ Μωϋσέως καὶ ἀπὸ πάντων τῶν προφητῶν διερμήνευσεν αὐτοῖς...; (*d*) Acts i. 21, 22 δεῖ οὖν τῶν συνελθόντων ἡμῖν ἀνδρῶν ἐν παντὶ χρόνῳ ᾧ εἰσῆλθεν καὶ ἐξῆλθεν ἐφ' ἡμᾶς ὁ κύριος 'Ιησοῦς, ἀρξάμενος ἀπὸ τοῦ βαπτίσματος 'Ιωάνου ἕως τῆς ἡμέρας...μάρτυρα...γενέσθαι ἕνα τούτων; (*e*) Acts x. 37 οἴδατε τὸ γενόμενον ῥῆμα καθ' ὅλης τῆς 'Ιουδαίας, ἀρξάμενος ἀπὸ τῆς Γαλιλαίας..., 'Ιησοῦν. One might add (*f*) Luke xxiv. 47 κηρυχθῆναι...μετάνοιαν... ἀρξάμενοι ἀπὸ 'Ιερουσαλήμ. Of these (*a*), (*b*), and (*c*) are sufficiently grammatical to pass as normal Greek, although there is a peculiarity about (*c*) which will be noted shortly. But (*d*), (*e*), and (*f*) are quite astonishing, and certainly call for some explanation. Whether Torrey's is the right one or not is another matter.[1] Example (*c*) above, however, seems to me to be possibly a special case, comparable to the curious phrase in Acts i. 1 πάντων...ὧν ἤρξατο ὁ 'Ιησοῦς ποιεῖν τε καὶ διδάσκειν, ἄχρι ἧς ἡμέρας.... The feature common to both these passages is that ἄρχεσθαι does duty for some such sense as **from** *the beginning*: thus, in Luke xxiv. 27, the full meaning might be *he expounded to them from Moses* (*where he began*) *and then from all the prophets* (*with which he continued*)...; and in Acts i. 1, *all that Jesus did, from the beginning until*.... That is, ἄρχεσθαι is used in a comprehensive

[1] For a full discussion see J. W. Hunkin, '"Pleonastic" ἄρχομαι in the New Testament', *J.T.S.* xxv (July 1904), 390 ff., and *Beg.* on the Acts passages.

sense, embracing not only beginning but continuance and end.† I know of no indication that this is Semitically conditioned; but it is a curious usage worthy of note. In its employment of a finite verb to express an adverbial idea, it might be compared with vi. above (προστιθέναι, etc.), and, to some extent, with III. viii. below ('*Answered and said*'), p. 184.

III. LITERAL TRANSLATION

If the group of phenomena just surveyed represents Semitic influence upon Greek *idiom*, it may be convenient to mention, as a separate group, phenomena which appear, with more or less certainty, to be due to *literal translation* of Semitic words or phrases. But an exact distinction between the two groups is obviously not to be insisted upon.

i. πᾶς...οὐ *instead of* οὐδείς. This idiom is frequent in I John; e.g. ii. 21 πᾶν ψεῦδος ἐκ τῆς ἀληθείας οὐκ ἔστιν (instead of οὐδὲν ψεῦδος ἐκ τῆς ἀληθείας ἐστίν); ii. 23 πᾶς ὁ ἀρνούμενος τὸν υἱὸν οὐδὲ τὸν πατέρα ἔχει (although here, admittedly, it would be difficult to represent the force of the -δε in οὐδέ if the sentence were transposed); iv. 3 πᾶν πνεῦμα ὃ μὴ ὁμολογεῖ...ἐκ τοῦ θεοῦ οὐκ ἔστιν; etc. Note also (with M.-H. II, 433) Matt. x. 29 ἓν ἐξ αὐτῶν οὐ πεσεῖται.

This undoubtedly represents a normal and idiomatic construction in Hebrew; but it must be added that it is by no means un-Greek: see M.-H. II, 433, 4, and (especially) R. Law there quoted. Possibly it is a construction whose frequency may be traced to Semitic influence.

ii. *Multiples, etc., expressed by Simple Juxtaposition.*† Very natural in Semitic idiom are such expressions as Mark vi. 7 δύο δύο; vi. 39 συμπόσια συμπόσια; but Thumb[1] denies that even this is un-Greek; he compares Modern Greek δυὸ δυό and περιπατῶ τὸ γιαλὸ γιαλό; and adduces μίαν μίαν from a fragment of Sophocles. Note that P. Oxyr. 886 (a Magical Formula—see Milligan's *Selections from the Greek Papyri* (Cambridge, 1927), 111, 112) combines this idiom with the ordinary Greek distributive preposition in κατὰ δύο δύο.

iii. *Use of the Feminine.* (*a*) In Hebrew the feminine does duty for the neuter. Hence, no doubt, Mark xii. 11 (parallel to Matt. xxi. 42 = Ps. cxviii (LXX cxvii) 23) παρὰ κυρίου ἐγένετο αὕτη (*this* [*thing*] *came from the Lord*).†

[1] *Die griechische Sprache im Zeitalter des Hellenismus* (1901), 128.

(*b*) The curious τῇ βάαλ in Rom. xi. 4 is usually (and plausibly) accounted for by the Hebrew habit of *reading* a word meaning 'shame' or 'abomination' where the name of an alien deity (or some other abominable word) was *written*; hence, for 'Baal' one might read 'bosheth' (בשת), 'shameful thing'; and this, being a feminine (or neuter) word, would suggest a feminine article in the Greek (if not an actual feminine Greek word such as αἰσχύνη as in the LXX).[1]

iv. Ἰδού. Acts ix. 10, ἰδοὺ ἐγώ, is septuagintal for הנני; and the curious ἣν ἔδησεν ὁ Σατανᾶς ἰδοὺ δέκα καὶ ὀκτὼ ἔτη (Luke xiii. 16)† and οὐχὶ ἰδού (Acts ii. 7) may also be influenced by the Hebrew interjection corresponding to ἰδού;[2] and the frequency of ἰδού even in less startling positions in a sentence may plausibly be traced to septuagintal influence, although M.M., in their very interesting note (*s.v.*), show that it does occur in apparently un-Semitic writing also.

v. Ἀναβαίνειν ἐπὶ τὴν καρδίαν (*or* ἐν τῇ καρδίᾳ), Luke xxiv. 38, I Cor. ii. 9, Acts vii. 23 may be good Greek,† but looks like a literal translation of עלה על לב (לבב) (so LXX, e.g. IV Reg. xii. 5, Jer. iii. 16, xxviii. (Heb. li) 50).

vi. *Prepositional Phrases.* (*a*) Matt. xix. 5 (Mark x. 8), ἔσονται οἱ δύο εἰς σάρκα μίαν, is accepted by Thumb (*op. cit.* 132) as Hebraic.†

(*b*) The use of ἐν in certain phrases where it is not (so far as one can judge) wholly natural to κοινή may be due to the fact that the preposition roughly corresponding to it in Hebrew and Aramaic does not exactly correspond. The most familiar instance is ὁμολογέω ἐν as = simply *to acknowledge (someone)* (Matt. x. 32, Luke xii. 8), where the corresponding Aramaic (not Hebrew, M.-H. II, 463) is apparently as natural as the Greek is odd. ὀμνύναι ἐν or εἰς (Matt. v. 34–6, xxiii. 16, 18, 20–2, Rev. x. 6) is Hebraic (M.-H. II, 464). Col. ii. 18, θέλων ἐν ταπεινο-φροσύνῃ, looks as though it were better taken as a 'Semitism' (=*delighting in*...) than as though θέλων were used absolutely, separate from ἐν ταπεινοφροσύνῃ: cf., for example, Ps. cxii. (LXX cxi) 1 ἐν ταῖς ἐντολαῖς αὐτοῦ θελήσει σφόδρα, Heb. במצותיו חפץ מאד.

(*c*) μετά is used in Luke i. 58 in a phrase whose whole cast is Semitic— ἐμεγάλυνεν κύριος τὸ ἔλεος αὐτοῦ μετ' αὐτῆς—where plain κοινή would more naturally have used at least a plain Dative, if not a different verbal phrase altogether—ἠλέησεν αὐτὴν πολλά, perhaps; or at any rate ἐμεγάλυνεν αὐτῇ τὸ ἔλεος αὐτοῦ. The whole phrase represents an

---

[1] In Tob. i. 5 some MSS. have τῇ βάαλ τῇ δαμάλει.
[2] But see *Beg. in loc.* for contrary evidence.

entirely natural Hebrew expression, although, curiously enough, it appears not to occur in the Septuagint, except I Macc. x. 27, Tob. xii. 6 (M.-H. II, 466). It is questionable whether Acts xiv. 27, xv. 4, ὅσα ἐποίησεν ὁ θεὸς μετ' αὐτῶν (adduced by M.-H. II, 466) are examples of the same μετά.

(*d*) Note also ἀπό and ἐκ in constructions whose frequency, at least, is influenced by certain uses of מִן, the partly corresponding Hebrew preposition—φοβεῖσθαι, προσέχειν, φαγεῖν ἀπό, etc. (M.-H. II, 460).

(*e*) The phrase ἐν χειρί (Gal. iii. 19 ἐν χειρὶ μεσίτου) is a pure Hebraism for *by means of*, *by the agency of*, and should not be translated into English by any phrase containing the word *hand*. So Acts xi. 30 διὰ χειρός—although this latter is regarded by, for example, M.M. 145 as partly influenced also by vernacular Greek.

(*f*) Similarly literal translations of Hebrew prepositional phrases are ἀπὸ προσώπου, εἰς πρόσωπον, πρὸ προσώπου (cf. our *in front of*, and the 'frozen' quasi-prepositions ἐνώπιον, etc.) (see M.-H. II, 465–6).†

In translating ἐν προσώπῳ the problem arises when to take it literally: in II Cor. ii. 10 it seems only to mean *in the presence of*, but in II Cor. iv. 6 it may mean literally *in the face* (*countenance*) or *person*....

(*g*) Matt. xviii. 15 μεταξὺ σοῦ καὶ αὐτοῦ μόνου is claimed as an Aramaism by M.-H. II, 467.

vii. τῷ θεῷ *as an Intensive* is a well-known Hebraism. In Gen. x. 9, γίγας κυνηγὸς ἐναντίον κυρίου represents (probably) a merely intensive use of God's name; and even more clearly Jonah iii. 3 πόλις μεγάλη τῷ θεῷ means simply *a very great city*. Accordingly Acts vii. 20 ἀστεῖος τῷ θεῷ may well be a Semitism of the same sort. Cf. II Cor. x. 4 δυνατὰ τῷ θεῷ (although M.-H. II, 443 regards this as more probably a *dat. commodi*). Is II Cor. xi. 2 θεοῦ ζήλῳ to be interpreted as a *divine* (i.e. *supernaturally great*) *eagerness*, or is it nearer to the meaning *an eagerness which is God's own eagerness* (or *which springs from God Himself*)?

viii. '*Answered and said*', which Dalman[1] claimed as a Hebraism but not as a feature of 'genuine' Aramaic (as distinct from Biblical Aramaic and Aramaic of the Targums) is noted by M. Black[2] as among the idioms found in A. J. Wensinck's study of the old Palestinian Targum, etc. See also M.-H. II, 453.

---

[1] *The Words of Jesus* (*E.T.*), 24–25.
[2] *J.T.S.* XLIX (July–Oct. 1948), 159.

ix. Ψυχή *as* = '*Self*'. A common Hebrew method of expressing *himself* is *his* '*nephesh*' (נפשו); and since *nephesh* is commonly rendered by ψυχή it follows that in some instances, though not all, it is positively misleading to render ψυχή by *soul*. The rich fool is probably only apostrophizing *himself* when he says (Luke xii. 19) ψυχή, ἔχεις...; and in Matt. xvi. 26, ἀντάλλαγμα τῆς ψυχῆς αὐτοῦ is probably *in exchange for himself*. It is difficult to decide exactly when the word becomes more significant than this: in some passages it clearly does so; e.g. in I Pet. ii. 11, 25, Jas. i. 21, v. 20;[1] but in others it is clear that *soul* would be a far too theological rendering. In II Cor. i. 23, ἐγὼ δὲ μάρτυρα τὸν θεὸν ἐπικαλοῦμαι ἐπὶ τὴν ἐμὴν ψυχήν looks like ... *on my life*.

x. *Phrases with* αἰών may be assumed, unless evidence to the contrary is forthcoming, to owe their meaning to the Hebrew עולם, and sometimes also their very syntax to the Hebrew phrases made up round this word.

xi. *The Use of a Verb of Motion to give Progressive Force to another Verb*, as in I Chron. xi. 9 ἐπορεύετο Δαυιδ πορευόμενος καὶ μεγαλυνόμενος (= *David grew greater and greater*), which is a well-known Hebrew idiom, may conceivably have coloured Acts ix. 31 ἡ μὲν οὖν ἐκκλησία... εἶχεν εἰρήνην οἰκοδομουμένη καὶ πορευομένη τῷ φόβῳ τοῦ κυρίου, καὶ τῇ παρακλήσει τοῦ ἁγίου πνεύματος ἐπληθύνετο.†

IV. TRANSLITERATIONS

There are actual transliterations of Hebrew or Aramaic words; e.g. Ἀββᾶ, Ἀκελδαμάχ, ἀμήν, Βοανηργές, γαββαθᾶ, Γολγοθᾶ, Ἐλωΐ or Ἡλεί κ.τ.λ. (Matt. xxvii. 46, Mark xv. 34: on the variant readings and the question whether it is Hebrew or Aramaic, see the commentators), ἐφφαθά, Καναναῖος, κορβᾶν, κορβανᾶς, μαμωνᾶς, μαρὰν ἀθά, Μεσσίας, ῥαββεί, ῥαββουνεί, ῥακά, Ταβειθά, ταλιθὰ κούμ, ὡσαννά, etc.[2]

But more subtle is the question of the Greek words whose use, or at least frequency, may have been suggested by a certain (perhaps fortuitous) similarity of sound or spelling to certain Semitic words; e.g.: σκηνή, σκηνόω may be influenced by שׁכן;

[1] See E. de W. Burton, *Spirit, Soul, and Flesh* (Chicago, 1916), 204.
[2] The accents and the spelling are according to the 1904 Bible Society text (see Preface, p. viii, above).

ἀγάπη by אהב (see Kittel, *Lexicographia Sacra*, '*Theology*' *Occasional Papers*, no. 7, 19);

ἀγαλλίασις by גיל (see *T.W.N.T. s.v.*);

ῥιπή or ῥοπή ὀφθαλμοῦ (I Cor. xv. 52) by הֶרֶף עַיִן (derived from רפף by Jastrow, *Dictionary of the Targumim, etc.*, 386, col. ii. But possibly הרף itself=ῥιπή. For ῥ=הר, cf. ῥοδοδάφνη=הרדוף). I owe these suggestions to the late Mr H. Loewe and his son, Mr R. Loewe.†

One ought also to mention the collocation of βάρος and δόξα in II Cor. iv. 17, which may have been suggested by the fact that both *weight* and *glory* are expressed in Hebrew by the same consonants. It is possible that there are other 'puns' latent under the Greek: in Matt. xxiii. 24, κώνωπα and κάμηλον may, it has been hazarded, represent an Aramaic assonance between קַמְלָא and גַּמְלָא; and in Matt. iii. 9 λίθων and τέκνα might, it is said, have been אבניא and בניא respectively.

V. SHEER MISTAKES

Many scholars have attempted to explain difficulties in the N.T. by the assumption that they represent misunderstandings of Semitic originals. Here we are on very insecure ground, and each suggestion needs most careful testing by experts. Thus, such an apparently brilliant suggestion as Wellhausen's, that the Lucan form of the saying about the cleansing of the externals could be explained as a mistranslation, is open to serious doubt. Matt. xxiii. 26 has the straightforward form καθάρισον πρῶτον τὸ ἐντὸς τοῦ ποτηρίου, ἵνα γένηται καὶ τὸ ἐκτὸς αὐτοῦ καθαρόν; but Luke xi. 41 has the perplexing πλὴν τὰ ἐνόντα δότε ἐλεημοσύνην, καὶ ἰδοὺ πάντα καθαρὰ ὑμῖν ἐστιν, and Wellhausen [1] suggested a confusion between the Aramaic *dakkau* (*cleanse*) and *zakkau* (*give alms*)—a suggestion which M. Black (*An Aramaic Approach*, 2) describes as one which 'has survived criticism'. But in Professor Dodd's N.T. Seminar the matter was investigated, with the following results: (*a*) The √זכי (*zki*) appears itself to have been capable of meaning both *give alms* and *cleanse*; (*b*) it appears to be used of *moral* purity, as distinct from √דכה (*dkh*) =*physical* purity;† (*c*) in any case, the evidence for the currency of the word in Palestinian Aramaic seemed precarious. C. C. Torrey (*Our Translated Gospels*, 98, 99) suggested that the explanation might lie in a confusion between עֲבֵדוּ צִדְקָא, *make right*, and עֲבֵדוּ צִדְקָא, *give as alms*.

---

[1] *Einleitung in die drei ersten Evangelien*[2] (1911), 27.

Note, too, suggestions turning upon the Aramaic particle דְּ, which can be represented both by ἵνα *in order that*, and by a relative, and is genderless. Accordingly, T. W. Manson (*The Teaching of Jesus*, 77–78) tried to soften the apparent harshness of Mark iv. 12 by assuming that it was a mistranslation of the Targumic form of Isa. vi. 9, 10 in which דְּ should have been translated not as ἵνα but as οἱ. Similarly, M.-H. II, 436–7 adduces passages where a confusion of genders may have been caused by the same particle.

Three more specimens will serve to illustrate this distinctly hazardous method of easing difficulties: (*a*) In Mark iv. 8, 20 the anomalous εἰς...ἐν...ἐν has been tentatively explained as due to a literal translation of Aramaic חַד (literally *one*) as εἷς (*one*), whereas it should have been treated as a mere idiomatic use with multiples, as in Dan. iii. 19 (*one seven times*—A.V. itself Aramaizing) (M.-H. II, 439). (*b*) In Luke i. 39 the very odd εἰς πόλιν 'Ιούδα has been explained as due to the Hebrew מְדִינַת יְהוּדָה, where מדינת, *province*, is a word which later came to mean *city* (M.-H. II, 471). (*c*) The almost impossible Luke xii. 49 τί θέλω... is explained as due to the Hebrew מָה being equivalent to both *what* and *how!* (M.-H. II, 472). See under 'Commands, Prohibitions, Wishes', 5. p. 137.

VI. UNUSED 'SEMITISMS'

It is interesting to note obvious 'Semitisms' (including some which are extant in the LXX) which are *not* represented in the N.T., and to speculate why they are avoided; e.g.:

(*a*) ὁμολογεῖν ἐν has been noted above (III. vi. (*b*), p. 183), but no N.T. instance occurs of βούλεσθαι, ἐκλέγεσθαι, or αἱρετίζειν ἐν, which all occur in the LXX.

(*b*) τίς δώσει...; (or τίς δῴη...;) (מִי יִתֵּן) for *O that...!* is septuagintal[1] (e.g. Ps. xiii. 7, Num. xi. 29), but is not found in the N.T. Aug. *Conf.* I. 5. 5, *Quis mihi dabit acquiescere in te? Quis mihi dabit ut...?*, is a good example of it in ecclesiastical Latin.

---

[1] It is to be noted, however, that this idiom is closely allied to another which is not by any means exclusively or characteristically Semitic, namely that represented, for example, by II Reg. xxiii. 15 τίς ποτιεῖ...; *O that I might be given a drink...!*, Rom. vii. 24 τίς με ῥύσεται...; Vergil, *Georg.* II, 487–8 (but with Subj., not Fut.):

  '...o qui me gelidis in vallibus Haemi
  sistat, et ingenti ramorum protegat umbra!'

(c) The Hebraic use of *son of*... has been noted above (II. iii. (a)), but a comparable use of κύριος meaning *possessed of*... is not found in the N.T. nor (apparently) in the LXX, despite the frequency of the idiom in the Hebrew of the O.T. (בעל החלמות, *a dreamer*, בעל פיפיות, *double-edged*, etc.).

(d) The Hebraic repetition of בין, *between*, where Greek and English idiom would use the corresponding preposition only once, is reproduced (though not invariably) by the LXX (e.g. Gen. xiii. 3 ἀνὰ μέσον Βαιθηλ καὶ ἀνὰ μέσον Αγγαι), but not in the N.T.: Luke xi. 51 μεταξὺ τοῦ θυσιαστηρίου καὶ τοῦ οἴκου; I Cor. vi. 5 ἀνὰ μέσον τοῦ ἀδελφοῦ αὐτοῦ (a phrase which, so far from containing a redundancy, is logically defective).

(e) The use of הן, *behold*, to introduce a conditional clause (an idiom comparable to our *Suppose he does so-and-so*...) is familiar in Biblical Hebrew; but it is not reproduced by ἰδού in the LXX in any of the passages adduced under the idiom in Brown, Driver, and Briggs's Hebrew Lexicon (except in Isa. liv. 15, where the sense of the whole sentence is also changed); and it is not used in the N.T.—although the reading ἰδού in Jas. iii. 3 looks, at first sight, as though it might be so interpreted: *suppose we put bits in horses' mouths, then we can guide their whole body also*; but this is fallacious, for in the next verse ἰδού is undoubtedly used in its ordinary sense, *Look!*; and besides, it is not certain that we should not adopt the reading εἰ δέ in *v.* 3 (see commentators *in loc.*).†

VII. LITERATURE

The literature of this subject is enormous, and the following is an attempt (a) to select and comment on a few of the more important works, and (b) to give a list, which is confessedly arbitrary, of a wider selection.

(a) First, it should be remarked that Moulton and Deissmann represent a tendency to minimize the Semitic element in N.T. Greek. With their keen appreciation of the evidence from secular papyri, then recently made available, they were impressed by the number of words and idioms which, formerly asserted to be distinctively Biblical, were after all found to be current in genuine κοινή. Accordingly, their tendency was to do less than justice to the peculiarities of Biblical vocabulary and style (cf. 'The Language of the New Testament', above, pp. 3 f.).

C. C. Torrey, on the other hand, has almost certainly overstated the case for actual Aramaic sources; and some of the articles noted in the bibliography provide useful correctives. In particular, de Zwaan's very thorough discussion of Torrey's work on the Acts is a constructive and balanced critique easily accessible, reaching the conclusion that Torrey has made a good case for some but by no means all of his points. Professor Dodd (in conversation) has expressed the opinion that Torrey is wrong in imagining that a bilingual person uses the idioms of his second language rather than the vocabulary: the reverse, he holds, is the case.

M. Black has continued hopefully along the path blazed by Torrey. It is probably too early even for an expert in this particular field to estimate the value of his conclusions. Further material may be available if A. J. Wensinck's notes, reviewed by M. Black recently in the *J.T.S.*, are published.

Reverting to comparatively early studies in this field, Dalman's *The Words of Jesus* calls for special mention. Dalman aimed at discovering the actual words used by Jesus in speaking of the leading ideas of his message. He distinguished between Judaean and Galilean Aramaic, and conjectured that Jesus might have used both. To reconstruct the former, Dalman used mainly the Targum of Onkelos to the Pentateuch and that of Jonathan to the Prophets. For Galilean, he used mainly Talmudic sources. M. Black, however,[1] points out that Onkelos and Jonathan are themselves influenced both by Hebrew and by Babylonian Aramaic, and, therefore, are not reliable guides. Hence the importance of the late A. J. Wensinck's (unpublished) studies, in which the old Palestinian Pentateuch Targum, found in the Cairo Geniza, is used, 'together with its related *haggadic* portions preserved in the so-called Pseudo-Jonathan and Fragment Targums'.[2]

The most useful single work for anybody who needs an introduction to the subject and a handy reference book is probably W. F. Howard's invaluable appendix in Moulton and Howard's *Grammar*, vol. II (see below, under Moulton, J. H., and Howard, W. F.).

(*b*) Besides the sections on 'Semitism', etc., in such grammars (or kindred works) as Debrunner-Blass's and Radermacher's, the following books and articles may be noted:

Aytoun, R. A., 'The Ten Lucan Hymns of the Nativity in their Original Language', *J.T.S.* XVIII (1916–17), 274 ff.

---

[1] *An Aramaic Approach*, etc., 17, 18.
[2] *J.T.S.* XLIX, 195–6 (July–Oct. 1948), 157.

Barton, G. A., 'Torrey's Theory of the Aramaic Origin of the Gospels and the First Half of the Acts of the Apostles', *J.T.S.* xxxvi (1935), 357 ff.

Black, M., *An Aramaic Approach to the Gospels and Acts* (Oxford, 2nd. ed., 1954).

—— 'Unsolved New Testament Problems: the Problem of the Aramaic Element in the Gospels', *E.T.* lix, No. 7 (April 1948).

—— 'Aramaic Studies and the New Testament: the Unpublished Work of the late A. J. Wensinck of Leyden', *J.T.S.* xlix (July–Oct. 1948), 157 ff.

Burney, C. F., *The Aramaic Origin of the Fourth Gospel* (Oxford, 1922).

—— *The Poetry of Our Lord* (Oxford, 1925).

Burrows, M., 'Principles for Testing the Translation Hypothesis in the Gospels', *J.B.L.* liii (1934), 13 ff. (replying to Riddle, below).

Cadbury, H. J., 'Luke—Translator or Author?', *Amer. Journal of Theol.* xxiv (1920), 364 ff.

Charles, R. H., 'The Revelation of St John' (*I.C.C.*, 1920); especially vol. i, cxlii–clii (the standard analysis of Semitisms in the Apocalypse).

Clarke, W. K. L., 'The Use of the Septuagint in Acts', in *The Beginnings of Christianity* (ed. F. J. Foakes Jackson and K. Lake), ii (1922), 66 ff.

Connolly, R. H., 'Syriacisms in St Luke', *J.T.S.* xxxvii (1936), 374 ff.

Dalman, G., *The Words of Jesus* (English trans. by D. M. Kay; T. and T. Clark, 1909).

Daube, D., 'Participle and Imperative in I Peter' (appended note in E. G. Selwyn's *The First Epistle of St Peter*, Macmillan, 1946, pp. 467 ff.).

—— 'Concerning the Reconstruction of "the Aramaic Gospels"', *Ryl. Bull.* 29, No. 1 (July 1945).

de Zwaan, J., 'The Use of the Greek Language in Acts', in *The Beginnings of Christianity* (ed. F. J. Foakes Jackson and K. Lake), ii (1922), 30 ff.

Deissmann, G. A., *Bible Studies* (English trans., 2nd edit., by A. Grieve; T. and T. Clark, 1909).

—— *Light from the Ancient East* (English trans., 4th edit., by L. R. M. Strachan; Hodder and Stoughton, 1927).

Hunkin, J. W., '"Pleonastic" ἄρχομαι in the New Testament', *J.T.S.* xxv (1923–4), 390 ff.

Lund, N. W., *Chiasmus in the New Testament* (Univ. of N. Carolina, 1942).

Manson, T. W., *The Teaching of Jesus* (Cambridge, 1935).

Moulton, J. H., *A Grammar of New Testament Greek*, vol. i, *Prolegomena* (T. and T. Clark, 1908).

Moulton, J. H., and Howard, W. F., *ibid.* vol. ii (1929), Appendix on *Semitisms in the New Testament*, 412–85.

Nestle, E., *Philologica Sacra* (Berlin, 1896).

Riddle, R. W., 'The Logic of the Theory of Translation Greek', *J.B.L.* li (1932), 13 ff. (challenging the hypothesis of Semitic sources).

Schlatter, A. von, *Die Sprache und Heimat des vierten Evangelisten* (Gütersloh, 1902).

Sparks, H. F. D., 'The Semitisms of St Luke's Gospel', *J.T.S.* XLIV (July–Oct. 1943).

—— 'The Semitisms of the Acts', *J.T.S.* (new ser.), 1 (April 1950), 16–28.

Torrey, C. C., 'The Composition and Date of Acts', *Harvard Theol. Stud.* 1 (1916).

—— *The Four Gospels; a New Translation* (Harper, 1933).

—— *Our Translated Gospels; some of the Evidence* (Hodder and Stoughton, 1937).

Vergote, J., 'Grec biblique', in F. Vigouroux's *Dictionnaire de la Bible*, supplement, ed. L. Pirot, III (1938), 1320 ff. (especially important for the discussion of 'Copticisms').

Wellhausen, J., *Einleitung in die drei ersten Evangelien* (2nd edit., Berlin, 1911), 7–32.

XXVI

LATINISMS

On the analogy of the preceding chapter on 'Semitisms', a few words may here be added on words and phrases influenced by the Latin language. A quite long list of actual loan-words from Latin can be compiled, as the grammars and other books on the language of the N.T. testify; and a few specimens of these are given below. But even more interesting are the traces in the N.T. of idioms which are familiar in Latin but alien to Greek. Thus, grammarians note the following:

Luke xii. 58 δὸς ἐργασίαν, *da operam*;

Mark xv. 15 τὸ ἱκανὸν ποιῆσαι, *satisfacere*;

Acts xvii. 9 λαβόντες τὸ ἱκανόν, *cum satis accepissent*;

Matt. xii. 14, etc. συμβούλιον λαμβάνειν, *consilium capere*;

Luke vii. 4 ἄξιός ἐστιν ᾧ παρέξῃ τοῦτο, *dignus est cui hoc praestes*;

Mark xv. 19, Luke xxii. 41, Acts vii. 60, ix. 40, xx. 36, xxi. 5 τιθέναι τὰ γόνατα, *genua ponere*;

Mark xiv. 65 ῥαπίσμασιν αὐτὸν ἔλαβον, *verberibus eum acceperunt*;

Acts xix. 38 ἀγοραῖοι ἄγονται, *fora (conventus) aguntur*;

Matt. xix. 10 αἰτία = *causa*;

John viii. 55 (*v.l.*) ὅμοιος ὑμῶν, *vestri similis* (instead of Dat.).
(See D.-B. §§ 5, 3 and 182, 4.)

Among loan-words from Latin (which are numerous in the N.T.) may be mentioned such sheer transliterations as κεντυρίων, κοδράντης, λεγιών, μεμβράνα, ξέστης (*sextarius*—transliterated also into Rabbinic as קסט—H. B. Swete, on Mark vii. 4), σπεκουλάτωρ, φελόνης (φαιλόνης, φαινόλης, *paenula*)—there are many more; and also the more subtle Latinisms such as (possibly) συν- as an intensive in συλλυπεῖσθαι (Mark iii. 5), *contristari*.

The distribution of Latinisms would repay study. The Latinisms of Mark are often mentioned, but there are many in Luke-Acts, e.g. (besides the above) αὐστηρός, Luke xix. 21 f., σουδάριον, Luke xix. 20, Acts xix. 12 (also John xi. 44).

XXVII

MISCELLANEOUS NOTES ON STYLE

Any selection under this heading is necessarily arbitrary.† The following remarks are dictated by my personal interests and observation, and are merely offered for what they are worth.

1. *Chiasmus*. The well-known literary pattern *abba*, usually styled *chiasmus*, presumably because the letter *chi*, being a St Andrew's cross, symbolizes the cross-connexion of the members $\begin{smallmatrix} a & b \\ & \times \\ b & a \end{smallmatrix}$, may sometimes be a deliberate and conscious trick of style, or sometimes quite spontaneous. I Cor. vii. 3 presents a perfect example in a context which shows no signs of *literary* polish as such:

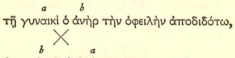

$$\begin{matrix} a & & b \\ \text{τῇ γυναικὶ ὁ ἀνὴρ} & \text{τὴν ὀφειλὴν ἀποδιδότω,} \end{matrix}$$

$$\begin{matrix} b & & a \\ \text{ὁμοίως δὲ καὶ ἡ γυνὴ} & \text{τῷ ἀνδρί:} \end{matrix}$$

not that the *words* γυνή and ἀνήρ change places in the two limbs, but *subject and (indirect) object* do.

In *Chiasmus in the New Testament*, by N. W. Lund (Univ. of N. Carolina Press, 1942), it is urged that chiastic structure is typical of Hebrew literature, and that St Paul's style, far from being rough or rugged, is the work of a mind steeped in the literature of the O.T. and exhibits on almost every page a highly developed literary pattern. A too cursory inspection of the book leaves me wondering whether chiasmus is so essentially Semitic (although this is indeed discussed on p. 33), and whether all the writer's examples are valid or significant; but it is undoubtedly interesting and may be important. A comment on the difference between Matthew and Luke in their use of a common source deserves quoting at length:

For our purpose it is not necessary to insist upon a source in the Aramaic language from which the Common Source is a translation. We only postulate an origin of the Common Source in a community in which the Hebrew cultural heritage and literary models of the Old Testament were still appreciated, whether in Jerusalem, in Galilee, or in Antioch. When the Aramaic specialists have determined what constitutes Aramaisms and have determined to what extent these exist in the Gospels, we shall know whether or not there was an underlying Aramaic gospel. That there was a Common Source in Greek the Q material [i.e. the non-Marcan material common to Matthew and Luke—p. 231] indicates; and that this source was produced in a community where Hebrew cultural influences prevailed the chiastic structures in the discourses of Matthew show clearly.

If, however, Luke was acquainted with these structures, why does he not preserve them? The answer is, that they were Hebrew and not Greek. However such structures might have appealed to a Jew, to a Greek they must have looked like unnecessary repetition. It is easily seen when we compare smaller sections of Matthew (where these forms are perfect) with parallel sections in Luke (where the forms break down) that some such motive of taste underlies the modifications. [p. 296.]

2. *Rhetorical Antithesis or Parallelism.* There are passages which, judged by their *words* rather than their *ideas*, contain antitheses or parallelisms, but which, judged by their *ideas*, appear less obviously balanced in structure; and it is possible that, in such cases, the antitheses or parallelisms may be for nothing more than rhetorical effect. Thus, in Rom. iv. 25,

$$\text{ὃς παρεδόθη διὰ τὰ παραπτώματα ἡμῶν}$$
$$\text{καὶ ἠγέρθη διὰ τὴν δικαίωσιν ἡμῶν,}$$

are we to understand a real distinction between the cause of the death and the cause of the resurrection—

> *it was owing to our sins that he was handed over,*
> *it was owing to*[1] *our acquittal that he was raised?*

Or is it a rhetorical way of saying that the *death-and-resurrection* (together) are connected inseparably with our *guilt-and-acquittal,* without any intention of separating the two pairs in thought? The latter is now fashionable exegesis—especially because of the difficulty of finding any logic in the separation of the terms and of squeezing the second διά into significance. Yet, it is worth while to notice that

---

[1] For διά *with Acc.* see under 'Prepositions', pp. 54f. This is a difficult passage in which to abide by the generally respected distinction between διά *with Acc.* and διά *with Gen.*; if we do abide by it (as in the above paraphrase) the *acquittal* in question will have to be interpreted proleptically: Christ's already achieved innocence (which was the survival-force leading to his resurrection) *implies* our (future) acquittal.

Rom. v. 10 curiously confirms (as it would seem) the presence of an antithesis latent in St Paul's actual thinking:

> we were *reconciled* by his *death*;
> we shall be *saved* by his *life*.

Possibly, too, there is something more than merely rhetorical in the parallelism of Rom. xiv. 9 εἰς τοῦτο γὰρ Χριστὸς ἀπέθανεν καὶ ἔζησεν, ἵνα καὶ νεκρῶν καὶ ζώντων κυριεύσῃ—as though his *death* were for the *dead*, his *life* for the *living*. But the distinction is, admittedly, strange to modern ears; and it must be confessed that Rom. v. 9 associates *acquittal* with Christ's *blood*, which is near to reversing the distinctions of the first-quoted passage, Rom. iv. 25. Finally, however, the balance of probability is tilted once more in the direction of a real distinction here, by one further passage in Romans, namely viii. 10 τὸ μὲν σῶμα νεκρὸν διὰ ἁμαρτίαν, τὸ δὲ πνεῦμα ζωὴ διὰ δικαιοσύνην; and it is impressive that, once again, there is the perplexing διὰ *with Acc.* in the second member, which (if it conforms to the regular usage in which διὰ *with Acc.* = *propter*) must mean *because of* [*the survival-force of* Christ's] *righteousness*.[1]

One is bound, however, to confess that it is difficult to detect a more than *rhetorical* antithesis in II Cor. v. 13:

> εἴτε γὰρ ἐξέστημεν, θεῷ·
> εἴτε σωφρονοῦμεν, ὑμῖν,

for what logic is there in saying that ecstasy is for God's sake, sanity for the sake of the Corinthians? (It is hardly possible to adduce I Cor. xiv. 2, 3 in answer: the situation is not really parallel.)

It is also to be noted that in Rom. iii. 30, εἷς ὁ θεὸς ὃς δικαιώσει περιτομὴν ἐκ πίστεως καὶ ἀκροβυστίαν διὰ τῆς πίστεως, one's credulity is strained by the attempt of Sanday and Headlam (*I.C.C. in loc.*) to draw a fine distinction between ἐκ πίστεως and διὰ πίστεως, as though it meant that the *Gentile* is justified ἐκ πίστεως, while the *Jew* is justified ἐκ πίστεως διὰ περιτομῆς.

In Rom. xi. 28 there is an apparent antithesis:

> κατὰ μὲν τὸ εὐαγγέλιον ἐχθροὶ δι' ὑμᾶς,
> κατὰ δὲ τὴν ἐκλογὴν ἀγαπητοὶ διὰ τοὺς πατέρας.

Lietzmann's dismissal of this 'als nur rhetorische Wortparallele' (*An die Römer, Handbuch z. N.T.* 106) is criticized by W. D. Davies, *Paul and Rabbinic Judaism*, 273, n. 1.

[1] Cf. W. L. Knox, *St Paul and the Church of the Gentiles*, 99 n. 5.

One may mention here the lure of catalogues and the mesmerism of lists. II Cor. vi. 4–10 is an impassioned and almost lyrical passage, where precision in the interpretation of the prepositions is probably impossible because the 'catalogue' has lured the writer into repeating a preposition in some instances where in sober prose it might have been unnatural. Cf. Ignatius' love of ἀξιο- compounds, which leads him into a series like ἀξιόθεος, ἀξιοπρεπής, ἀξιομακάριστος, ἀξιέπαινος, ἀξιοεπίτευκτος, ἀξίαγνος (*Rom.*, *Inscr.*), where Lightfoot writes: '. . . though symmetrical in composition, they are hardly so in meaning, but take their complexion from the other component element, "worthy *of* praise", "worthy *in* purity", etc.'

3. *Diatribe and Implied Dialogue.* It is a familiar fact that the Greek 'diatribe' style frequently resorted to a rhetorical question-and-answer, dialogue form. This is (as is well known) a feature of the Epistle of James.[1] But it is also recognized in polemical parts of the Pauline Epistles—notably in Rom. ii, where St Paul specifically addresses an imaginary interlocutor, and iii, where there is more or less sustained dialogue without any formal indication of the *dramatis personae*. It is this latter habit of breaking into dialogue, without (as it were) stage directions, which may lie behind certain notorious difficulties. Thus, in Gal. ii. 17, 18 I should propose to read ἄρα (not ἆρα) and a full stop (not a question-mark), and to assign μὴ γένοιτο to the (imagined) St Peter; St Paul will then continue to the effect: 'You may repudiate the position with a μὴ γένοιτο, but that is the position you logically place yourself in by your action; *for*, etc.'[2] Similarly it is conceivable that a *crux* in I Cor. vi is to be met by the dialogue expedient. Many commentators recognize that *v.* 12ᵃ may represent a 'libertine', antinomian slogan quoted by St Paul in order to be met by (his own) *v.* 12ᵇ, and that the case is similar with the two halves of *v.* 13; but it seems not to have been suggested that *v.* 18 may also be essentially a 'dialogue'. If it is *not*, then we are faced with the perplexity[3] that St Paul pronounces fornication to be *essentially* different (and not merely different in *degree*) from any other sort of sin—a position with which few modern Christians would agree. But if it is in dialogue form, we have:

18ᵃ (Corinthian 'libertine' slogan): πᾶν ἁμάρτημα ὃ ἐὰν ποιήσῃ ἄνθρωπος ἐκτὸς τοῦ σώματός ἐστιν (i.e. no sin can affect a man's true

[1] See, for example, a discussion in Ropes's (*I.C.C.*) Commentary.

[2] See my discussion, *E.T.* LVI, no. 8 (May 1945).

[3] Recognized clearly by some commentators, e.g. Lietzmann, Allo and Héring, *in loc.*

'body': physical lust cannot touch the secure 'personality' of the initiated).

18[b] (St Paul's retort): ὁ δὲ πορνεύων εἰς τὸ ἴδιον σῶμα ἁμαρτάνει (i.e. on the contrary: anyone who commits fornication *is* committing an offence against his very 'personality').

This more than corporeal sense for σῶμα is clearly required in some contexts; and although it may be thought improbable here (especially in view of II Cor. xii. 3, where it is demonstrably 'corporeal'), the logic of the passage is so difficult on the ordinary showing that this alternative is possibly worth considering.

4. *Mannerisms*. There are some turns of phrase which appear to have little significance for the sense, and are mere idiosyncrasies of the writer. The well-known εὐθύς (or εὐθέως) of Mark appears, in some of its occurrences, to be such, but not all of its about forty occurrences are otiose: nor is it evenly distributed over the Gospel. Possibly certain uses of the particle τε in the later chapters of Acts ought to be so classified also, e.g. Acts xxvi. 10 καὶ πολλούς τε τῶν ἁγίων . . . ;† and so (according to some) ought the ἐν ᾧ of I Peter (see under 'Relative Clauses', 6, pp. 131 f.); and to this might be added Acts xxiv. 16 ἐν τούτῳ, and xxvi. 12 ἐν οἷς, and, possibly, Luke xii. 1 ἐν οἷς—all of which may mean little more than *and so*, or some similar resumptive expression.

5. *Double Meanings*. Among matters of style may be classed the deliberate use of words or phrases with multiple meaning. Such, it is commonly held, is the ὑψόω of the Fourth Gospel, serving to drive home the paradox that Christ's *uplifting* on the shameful cross is itself his *exaltation* in glory. C. K. Barrett[1] illustrates and supports a similar suggestion about the famous κατέλαβεν of John i. 5, which Hoskyns (in Hoskyns-Davey, *in loc.*) had made—that it means both *to grasp with the mind* (*comprehend*) and *to grasp with the hand* (*overcome*). But in John xii. 35 it is unambiguously *overtake, overcome*. Similarly— to quote one other possible instance—the last words of Ephesians, ἐν ἀφθαρσίᾳ, may be intended to mean both *sincerely* (*in incorruption*) and *eternally* (*in incorruptibility*). Cf. Lightfoot on Ignatius, *Eph.* xvii, *Magn.* vi, where the same 'ambivalence' apparently attaches to ἀφθαρσίᾳ.

6. Conversely, *Synonyms* are to be watched for. It is a mistake to assume that whenever a writer changes his word he intends to change the sense: the change may be due to a desire for variety, or even because

[1] *E.T.* LIII, no. 9 (June 1942).

of usages which have arisen over certain tenses. On the whole modern exegetes are more ready to recognize this than those of, say, fifty years ago. Thus, whereas E. A. Abbott wrote ' . . . *there are no "synonyms" in John*, i.e. no words that convey precisely the same shade of meaning',[1] C. C. Tarelli, in an important article,[2] argues that, for example, *send* is ἀποστέλλω in the Perfect and Aorist Indicative and the Perfect Passive Participle, but πέμπω in the Aorist Active Participle, the Present, and the Future; and he deals similarly with βλέπω and θεωρέω, ἐρωτάω and αἰτέω. J. Moffatt, in his monograph *Love in the New Testament*, had already done the like for ἀγαπάω and φιλέω in John xxi; for which see also J. H. Bernard (*I.C.C. in loc.*). W. Temple[3] demurs to this, but (I believe) unconvincingly. Note, similarly, Acts xix. 15 (γινώσκω and ἐπίσταμαι).

It need hardly be said that this does not mean that distinctions are never observed: on the contrary, the safest principle is probably to assume a difference until one is driven to accept identity of meaning. But the fact remains that sheer variety, and the above-mentioned usages with certain tenses, have sometimes to be reckoned with among stylistic phenomena.†

7. *Connexions* with the preceding or succeeding clauses are, on occasion, problematic and a study of each individual's style may be the only clue to a decision. In Eph. iii. 1, 14 does τούτου χάριν refer *forward* or *backward*? In the Pastoral Epistles does πιστὸς ὁ λόγος refer to what *precedes* or to what *follows*? In I John, how often does ἐν τούτῳ refer *back*, and how often *forward*?

8. *Rhythm* is a complex subject, but one of great interest; and it may, on occasion, be a pointer to authorship. There are some useful remarks on the subject in J. Moffatt, *Introduction to the Literature of the N.T.*², 55–8; much material in E. Norden, *Die antike Kunstprosa* (Leipzig, 1898); and a study of the rhythms of Hebrews in Moffatt's (*I C.C.*) commentary, lvi–lix.

This note is concerned only with one or two arbitrarily chosen points:

(*a*) W. L. Knox[4] makes the very ingenious suggestion that in Stephen's speech in Acts vii. 43 the LXX (Amos v. 27) ἐπέκεινα

---

[1] *Johannine Grammar* (1906), 645.

[2] 'Johannine Synonyms', *J.T.S.* xlvii (July–Oct. 1946), 175 ff.

[3] *Readings in St John's Gospel*, 2nd ser., 404 n.1.

[4] *Some Hellenistic Elements in Primitive Christianity* (Schweich Lectures 1942, published 1944), 14, 15.

Δαμάσκου is changed to ἐπέκεινα Βαβυλῶνος purely on rhythmic grounds: Luke avoids 'the worst possible rhetorical ending, the end of a hexameter', in favour of 'the best possible...a cretic with the second long syllable resolved and a trochee, the famous *esse videatur* of Cicero'.

(*b*) There are plenty of specimens of Greek poetic metres in the N.T., apparently used unintentionally—quite apart from definite or suspected quotations. Thus, Matt. xxvi. 17, ποῦ θέλεις ἑτοιμάσωμέν σοι φαγεῖν τὸ πάσχα; ὁ δὲ... (cf. Luke xxii. 9), makes a trochaic tetrameter, and Heb. i. 6 (quoted from the LXX of Deut. xxxii, where, however, it is not metrical) another: (καὶ) προσκυνησάτωσαν αὐτῷ πάντες ἄγγελοι θεοῦ; and there are others; cf. also the sequence of trochees in Matt. v. 40. I Cor. x. 12, ὁ δοκῶν ἑστάναι βλεπέτω μὴ πέσῃ, is an anapaest and cretic twice repeated. Iambics (Heb. xii. 14 οὗ χωρὶς οὐδεὶς ὄψεται τὸν κύριον, and many others)[1] and anapaests (Acts x. 34 ἐπ' ἀληθείας καταλαμβάνομαι, etc.) and other classical metres are also common, especially, perhaps, in Hebrews, though they seem to be avoided by classical prose writers.

(*c*) Rhythms which are not reducible to Greek quantitative systems but are nevertheless stylistically significant provide, of course, an important range of study. Here will only be noted some passages which are frequently assumed (perhaps correctly) to be fragments of primitive hymns or other liturgical elements: Eph. v. 14, which has a certain 'lilt' about it, and a parallelism comparable to that of Hebrew poetry; I Tim. iii. 16, which consists of six brief sentences, with their verbs all in the 3rd sing. Aor. Passive and therefore rhyming, and with a noun in the Dative at the end of each; and the 'hymns' occurring frequently in Revelation.

9. The phenomena reviewed here, and countless others, may sometimes help to point the way to a decision on matters of authorship; but a high degree of inconclusiveness will remain as long as psychological factors continue to be elusive.

---

[1] One may here be singled out because it is just conceivable that it may not be unintentional, but may be a quotation from some unknown source (despite its violation of the 'law of the final Cretic'): Phil. iii. 1 ἐμοὶ μὲν οὐκ ὀκνηρόν, ὑμῖν δὲ ἀσφαλές. If this is a quotation, this may be the explanation of the apparent difficulty of fitting ὀκνηρόν and ἀσφαλές perfectly into their present context.† H. W. Moule, to whom some of the examples and part of the phrasing of paragraph (*b*) above are owed, notes that Thucydides has ἡμῖν μὲν ἴσην εἶναι, ὑμῖν δὲ ἀσφαλῆ, 'which of course is no parallel, though recalling the sound of Phil. iii. 1'.

Meanwhile, it is at least worth while to note differences of style, whatever deductions may be drawn from them; and one or two instances will serve to indicate the field.

(a) E. Norden, in *Die antike Kunstprosa*, 480ff., gives some specimens of the characteristic differences in style between the Synoptists, in his review of Luke's style. But what has been said under 'Semitisms', I. p. 173, is a warning against glib generalizations about Luke's superiority as a stylist. The fact remains, however, that, despite his extraordinary unevennesses (which are probably due to compilation from various sources or to the adoption of septuagintal style), his writings do contain, here and there, some specimens of more polished and rhetorical prose than can be found in Matthew, Mark, or John.

(b) The debate continues between those who affirm, and those who deny unity of authorship between the Fourth Gospel and I John (quite apart from subsidiary questions of the position with regard to II and III John). C. H. Dodd[1] denies unity of authorship; W. F. Howard[2] argues for it. See also W. G. Wilson.[3] H. Windisch[4] marshals the evidence, but is doubtful as to the conclusion. It is worth while to remember (with W. G. Wilson, *op. cit.*) that changing circumstances and intentions may cause differences in one and the same writer's style.

(c) Note the extremely interesting observation formulated by E. de W. Burton[5] that 'the instances of the Perfect in the sense of the Aorist are confined almost entirely to a few forms, ἔσχηκα, εἴληφα, ἑώρακα, εἴρηκα, and γέγονα, and the use of each of these forms in the sense of an Aorist mainly to one or more writers whose use of it is apparently almost a personal idiosyncrasy. Thus the aoristic use of γέγονα belongs to Matthew; of εἴληφα to John in Revelation; of ἔσχηκα to Paul; but see also Heb. vii. 13.' (See also under 'The Tenses: Perfect', above, p. 14.)

(d) Sanday and Headlam (*I.C.C.* on Rom. viii. 26) quote Gifford as noting that a use of the definite article in such a phrase as τὸ γὰρ τί προσευξώμεθα is characteristic of St Paul and St Luke.

---

[1] *The Johannine Epistles* (Moffatt Commentaries, 1946).
[2] 'The Common Authorship of the Johannine Gospel and Epistles', *J.T.S.* XLVIII, 189–90 (Jan.–April 1947), 12 ff.
[3] 'An Examination of the Linguistic Evidence adduced against the Unity of Authorship', etc., *J.T.S.* XLIX, 195–6 (July–Oct. 1948), 147 ff.
[4] In *Handbuch z. N.T.*, Commentary on the Johannine Epistles.
[5] *M.T.* § 88, p. 44.

(*e*) The problem of the authorship of Ephesians is still a matter of debate. There are clear features of style (e.g. the cumulative manner) which mark this Epistle as different from any of the acknowledged Paulines; but that does not prove that it is not St Paul's work.

There is in any case the very delicate problem of how any Epistle was written, and what part an amanuensis had in its composition.[1] J. A. Eschlinan[2] has brought together evidence for the slowness and difficulty of writing in the conditions of the time, which he uses to support the view that verbatim dictation would rarely be resorted to, but that a skilled friend would often be entrusted with putting the required sense into his own words. If this evidence is valid,[3] it raises the problem of how a distinctively Pauline style has ever come through—that it has can hardly be denied; but at the same time, the actual mechanics of writing may well have been given too little consideration by those who speak of Paul as though he poured out a fervid stream of words which were faithfully recorded verbatim. One instance of the problem is Eschlinan's suggestion that a difference in amanuenses lies behind the fact (noted by Allo in I Corinthians) that ἀγαθός (found in Romans) is absent from I Corinthians, where καλός is found.[4]

(*f*) For an estimate of Paul's rhetorical skill, see the very interesting excerpt from Augustine *de doctr. Christ.* IV, 7, 11 in Norden, *Antike Kunstprosa*, 502ff.; and a valuable survey of opinions of critics of style from the Fathers to Wilamowitz and Norden himself in N. W. Lund, *Chiasmus in the N.T.* 3–29.

---

[1] Otto Roller, *Das Formular der Paulinischen Briefe* (Stuttgart, 1933).

[2] *Revue Biblique*, LIII, 2, April 1946.

[3] But Roller (*op. cit.*), whom Eschlinan in large measure follows, has been challenged and severely criticised by Ernst Percy in *Die Probleme der Colosser- und Epheserbriefe* (Lund, 1946), p. 10 n. 1.

[4] Dr P. Katz notes that for the LXX καλός, Aquila uses the more literal ἀγαθός.

NOTES AND CORRECTIONS

The first edition contained two pages under this heading, representing chiefly material kindly furnished by Dr W. P. M. Katz (now Walters). To this is here added further material gathered from reviewers (especially the late Dr H. G. Meecham) and elsewhere.

page 3. For the preservation, however, of royal letters by 'publication' as inscriptions on stone, see C. Bradford Welles, *Royal Correspondence in the Hellenistic Period* (Yale University Press, 1934).

page 5. See the valuable criticism of this term, in favour of *aspect*, by J. P. Smith in *Verbum Domini*, XXXIII (1955), 54f.

page 7. See H. Schürmann, *Der Paschamahlbericht Lk. 22 (7-14), 15-18* (Münster, 1953), 83, for contrast with Luke; and see note, below, on *page 193*.

page 9. Add ἔδει, ἀνῆκεν, etc., D.-B. § 358; and ηὐδοκοῦμεν in I Thess. ii. 8.

page 10. 'Mark uses the imperfect perhaps four times as often as Matthew. It is important for the understanding of passages like the trial scene in Mark xiv to know whether the two evangelists are using the imperfect in just the same way or whether in Mark it is sometimes merely a general past tense'—G. D. Kilpatrick in *Theology* (S.P.C.K.), LVIII, no. 417 (March 1955), 105 ff.

page 13. H. G. Meecham, in *Journal of New Testament Studies* (C.U.P.), I, no. 1 (Sept. 1954), 62 ff., adds, as a further possible class, the Proleptic Aorist, for example, I Cor. vii. 28.

page 14. '...has the perfect in John the same force as it has in the other Gospels? [P.] Chantraine's discussion of the perfect in Hellenistic Greek in his *Histoire du Parfait Grec* [Paris, 1927] may be used to illuminate questions such as this'—G. D. Kilpatrick, *loc. cit.*

page 14. But *contra* J. B. Lightfoot on Col. i. 16, distinguishing between ἐγένετο...γέγονεν (John i. 3), ἐγενόμην...γέγονα (I Cor. ix. 22), ἀπέσταλκα...συναπέστειλα (II Cor. xii. 17f.), ἀπέσταλκεν...ἀπέστειλεν (I John iv. 9f.).

page 14. H. G. Meecham, *loc. cit.*, notes Rev. v. 7 εἴληφεν, *Aristeas* 173 ἀποδεδώκαμεν, Isa. liii. 5 μεμαλάκισται.

page 14. Perhaps this distinction does hold: there is a distinction between the death of Christ as a past event and as an abiding force. Cf. ἐσφαγμένος in Rev. v. 6. (So Dr Alfred Marshall, in a letter.)

page 15. Cf. D.-B. § 342. 5, taking the view that Gal. iv. 23 may = γέγραπται ὅτι ἐγεννήθη.

page 21. G. D. Kilpatrick, *loc. cit.*, refers to J. Wackernagel's *Vorlesungen über Syntax*, I (Basel, 1920), 212-16 for a clue.

page 22. But these forms are interchangeable in the LXX.

page 22. Dr W. P. M. Katz (Walters) in *Theologische Zeitschrift*, IX, 3 (Mai–Juni 1953), 228ff. notes that the LXX sometimes uses the Aorist Optative in a future sense, and that, in Deut. xxviii. 7–36 the Opt. is used when God is subject, the Fut. Indic. when men are. Is this relevant to the present idiom?

page 22. The passage is Gen. xxviii. 15 in the Bible common to Philo and the *auctor ad Hebraeos*. See P. Katz in *Biblica*, vol. 33 (1952), Fasc. 4, 523–5.

page 23. Cf. τεύξασθαι for τεύξεσθαι in II Macc. xv. 7, III Macc. ii. 33.

page 24. II Macc. xiv. 30 has συνεκρύπτετο τὸν Νικάνορα, *he concealed himself from N.* Perhaps the best example is δανίζειν = *lend*, δανίζεσθαι = *borrow* (for example, Deut. xv. 6, where the Hebrew, incidentally, uses the converse method, *cause to borrow* and *borrow*).

page 24. Meecham, *loc. cit.*, notes also the reciprocal use of the Middle, as in Matt. xxvi. 4, John xii. 10.

page 24. Meecham, *loc. cit.*, compares Gen. xxvi. 5, Lev. xx. 8 (ἐφύλαξεν, φυλάξεσθε respectively). Note the odd lack of reflexive in Acts xxvii. 43 ἀπορίψαντας.

page 26. See D.-B. § 101, *s.v.*

page 28. See J. Wackernagel, *Vorlesungen über Syntax*, I, 111; E. Schwyzer, *Griechische Grammatik*, II, 245, 620f. (cited by D. J. Georgacas in *Classical Philology*, LII, 3 (July 1957), 204ff.), for the occurrence of such a usage in non-Semitic contests. But the point is the intensifying of the usage.

page 31. Unless, of course, one construes ἡμέραι as the subject and supplies ἡμερῶν with δώδεκα. Cf. Acts xxv. 6.

page 33. See further C. Lindhagen, ΕΡΓΑΖΕΣΘΑΙ. *Apc. 18: 17. Hes. 48: 18. 19, usw.*, Uppsala and Leipzig (1950).

page 33. Meecham, *loc. cit.*, adds ὁρκίζω (Mark v. 7, etc.).

page 36. Cf. John v. 28 (Gen.), 37 (Acc.).

page 38. But see F. Spitta, *in loc.*, for doubts even here.

page 39. Add, with H. G. Meecham, *loc. cit.*, the considerable class of Genitives with verbs of filling, for example, Luke i. 15, 53, etc.

page 41. So also with Genitives after εὐαγγέλιον, πίστις, etc.; see D.-B. § 163, H. Conzelmann in *Theologische Zeitschrift*, XIII (1957), 65. For πίστις with Gen., see also T. F. Torrance in *E.T.* LXVIII (Jan. 1957), 111ff., (April 1957), 221f., and myself in *E.T.* LXVIII (Feb. 1957), 157, (April 1957), 222.

page 43. Note, with Meecham, *loc. cit.*, the occasional omission of the pronoun in the Genitive Absolute construction: Matt. xvii. 14, 26, Acts xxi. 31; and often in the papyri.

page 44. Perhaps add τῇ δεξιᾷ in Acts ii. 33, v. 31 (despite the citation of

Psalm cx in ii. 34). Elsewhere the local meaning is made clear by a preposition.

page 46. But perhaps Psalm xxxiii (Heb. xxxiv). 19, τοὺς ταπεινοὺς τῷ πνεύματι (דִּכְּאֵי רוּחַ), points in another direction.

page 46. This meaning becomes still easier if, with 𝔭⁴⁶, we omit θεοῦ. The *v.l.* θεῷ looks like a correction.

page 47. Perhaps add Luke xxiii. 15 πεπραγμένον αὐτῷ, 'unless the dative... may be otherwise explained (="in his case"?)'—Meecham, *loc. cit.*

page 54. If this reading is correct (see commentaries *in loc.*).

page 57. Meecham, *loc. cit.*, notes that with persons it sometimes comes very near to the sense of agency rather than mediation: Esther viii. 10, I Cor. i. 9, Heb. xiii. 11.

page 58. Heb. v. 14, διὰ τὴν ἕξιν, however, is an example of the Accusative where, on the whole, the Genitive seems at least as appropriate, if not more so.

page 61. Cf. the way in which compounds with μεσο- replace earlier compounds with μετα-.

page 61. *In addition to* is not expressed by μετά but can be expressed by σύν

page 69. Perhaps one ought to include here Matt. xii. 41, Luke xi. 32 εἰς τὸ κήρυγμα, *at the preaching*, Rom. iv. 20 εἰς...τὴν ἐπαγγελίαν, *at* (or *in view of*) *the promise*. See Bauer, and Arndt and Gingrich, *s.v.* εἰς.

page 69. G. D. Kilpatrick, *loc. cit.*, questions this: 'The instances quoted can, and probably should, be taken in a local sense with εἰς with accusative replacing ἐν with the dative. This is probably the explanation of διακονεῖν, διακονία εἰς, I Pet. iv. 10, Rom. xv. 31, cf. Acts xii. 25.'

page 69. On Mark xiii. 10 see further G. D. Kilpatrick in *Studies in the Gospels*, ed. D. E. Nineham (Blackwell, 1955), 145 ff.; and on Acts xii. 25, see below, note to *page* 100.

page 70. Add Wisd. ii. 16 εἰς κίβδηλον ἐλογίσθημεν αὐτῷ, and I Cor. xv. 45 ἐγένετο...εἰς. Dr G. S. Duncan suggests to me that conceivably Acts vii. 53 ἐλάβετε τὸν νόμον εἰς διαταγὰς ἀγγέλων might mean *received...as....* Similarly E. J. Goodspeed translates Acts viii. 23, εἰς γὰρ χολὴν πικρίας καὶ σύνδεσμον ἀδικίας ὁρῶ σε ὄντα, *For I see that you are a bitter poison and a bundle of iniquity. Contra Beg. in loc.*

page 71. More interesting still, and more important, is Heb. xii. 2 ...ὃς ἀντὶ τῆς προκειμένης αὐτῷ χαρᾶς ὑπέμεινεν σταυρὸν αἰσχύνης καταφρονήσας.... Does this mean that Jesus chose a cross instead of the joy he might have had (cf. Phil. ii. 6), or that he chose a cross for the sake of winning the joy which lay beyond and through it? For the latter meaning, cf. Heb. xii. 16 (cited, p. 71), and note also xi. 25 f. See commentators *in loc.* Gen. xliv. 33 where Judah offers to stay *in place of* Benjamin, παῖς ἀντὶ τοῦ παιδίου, is a clear example of a substitutionary sense.

page 71. For notes on their relative frequency, see B.-D. § 209.

page 72. For a carefully argued case for an important theological distinction between ἐκ τοῦ θεοῦ and ἀπ᾽ ἐμαυτοῦ in John viii. 42, see C. H. Dodd, *The Interpretation of the Fourth Gospel* (Cambridge, 1953), 259f.

page 72 n. 1. Add A. Debrunner in *Coniectanea Neotestamentica*, XI (1947), 45–9.

page 76. Mr W. J. Merrick, however (in a letter to me), is inclined to see here only one example of several where ἐν is used as εἰς; and he would adduce, besides Luke xxiii. 19 (cited on p. 76 (*e*)), Luke iv. 1, I Cor. vii. 15, I Thess. iv. 7, and possibly II Cor. x. 1. There is not one of these, however, which seems so inevitable as Luke i. 17.

page 77. But is it in fact distinguishable?—Meecham, *loc. cit.*

page 78. This is misleading. In the first place, the name in question is evidently not Jesus but the title κύριος which belongs to Jesus (that is, Ἰησοῦ is possessive, not appositional); and secondly, it may be that ἐν τῷ ὀνόματι = *to the name* (as object of worship). See LXX parallels provided by J. B. Lightfoot *in loc.*

page 80 n. 4. See further E. Molland in *Journal of Ecclesiastical History*, V, 1 (April 1954), 1ff. (arguing for *If I do not find it in the Old Testament, I do not believe in the Gospel*); and H. Köster, *Synoptische Überlieferung bei der apostolischen Vätern* (Berlin, 1957), 7ff.

page 81. Indeed, T. W. Manson defended the reading ἵνα πᾶς ὁ πιστεύων εἰς αὐτὸν ἐν αὐτῷ ἔχῃ... (deduced from the sub-Akhmimic text): *J.T.S.* XLVI (1945), 130 n. 1. Cf. John xx. 31 ...ἵνα πιστεύοντες ζωὴν ἔχητε ἐν τῷ ὀνόματι αὐτοῦ. Almost certainly the ἐν is not to be construed as 'an ἐν of object' in I Cor. ii. 5 ἵνα ἡ πίστις ὑμῶν μὴ ᾖ ἐν σοφίᾳ ἀνθρώπων ἀλλ᾽ ἐν δυνάμει θεοῦ. ἐλπίζω presents a similar problem in I Cor. xv. 19 ...ἐν χριστῷ ἠλπικότες..., Eph. i. 12...τοὺς προηλπικότας ἐν τῷ χριστῷ. Unequivocal examples of ἐλπίζω ἐν are very rare.

page 81. See note on p. 61 above.

page 81. This emphatic, amplifying use of σύν (Hebrew עם) is found only here in the N.T. Cf. ἐν πᾶσι τούτοις, Luke xvi. 26 (J. Jeremias, *The Eucharistic Words of Jesus*, E.T., Blackwell, 1955, 98).

page 82. The curious ἄχρι ἡμερῶν πέντε, *within five days*, of Acts xx. 6 is unique in the N.T., though cf. Heb. iii. 13.

page 84. See, however, A. Sledd, *E.T.* L (Feb. 1939), immediately following Allen's article with the remark that the interpretation of ὑμῶν must be taken into account; for if ἐντὸς ὑμῶν means *within your circle* (that is, *you* collectively, not singly), then it virtually means *among you.*

page 85. Perhaps ἀνὰ μέσον, διὰ μέσου, ἐν μέσῳ, and ἐκ μέσου deserve to be recognized as virtually prepositions also, with meanings more or less similar.

page 87. See A. Debrunner, *Griechische Wortbildungslehre* (Heidelberg,

1917), § 149, and D.-B. § 123. 2, referring to Hesychius' explanation of it as ἐν ὠτίοις δέχεσθαι.

page 89. Cf. Liddell and Scott's *Greek-English Lexicon*[9], ἀπό, D. 3.

page 95. But Schrenk, *T.W.N.T.* I, 753 takes it as *every passage in scripture.*

page 95. See J. A. Robinson, *Ephesians*, 70f., 164f.; E. G. Selwyn, *I Peter*, 289; but *contra* C. Masson, *Éphésiens* (1952), 170f.

page 96. For the orthography δοκιμεῖον, see Liddell and Scott *op. cit.*; also P. Chantraine, *La formation des noms* (Paris, 1933), p. 53.

page 99 n. 1. Luke x. 18 ἐθεώρουν τὸν Σατανᾶν...πεσόντα might perhaps mean *I have been seeing how Satan is overthrown*; Acts x. 3 εἶδεν...ἄγγελον ...εἰσελθόντα...καὶ εἰπόντα...presumably means *he saw...an angel... come in...and say.*

page 100. See further D.-B. § 339. 1; and M. Zerwick, *Graecitas biblica* (2nd ed., Rome, 1949), p. 61, *nota.* 3, where some reasons are adduced for interpreting ἀσπασάμενοι as *thus* or *thereby making a complimentary visit.*

page 100. n 1. There is a full discussion of the passage by J. Dupont in *Novum Testamentum*, I, 4 (1956), 275 ff. He would read εἰς, but would construe it with διακονίαν: *Barnabas and Saul returned* [to Antioch], *having fulfilled their ministry for* (or possibly *at*) *Jerusalem.* See note to p. 69 above.

page 101. So Zerwick, *op. cit.* p. 64, who makes ἀναβαινόντων αὐτῶν virtually equivalent to 'on the occasion of the pilgrimage'.

page 101. Other examples may be added (see Meecham, *loc. cit.*), mostly, I think, pointing to the conclusion that when the Present Participle refers to what preceded the main verb, it generally represents a frequentative or durative (a 'linear') sense: Matt. ii. 20, iv. 16, John ix. 8, xii. 17, Acts iv. 34 (contrast *v.* 37), x. 7, II Cor. xi. 9, Gal. i. 23, Eph. ii. 13, iv. 28, Col. i. 21, I Tim. i. 13, Rev. xx. 10. Many of these bear out the remark (p. 101 on John ix. 25) about the verb *to be.* Note also Matt. xxiii. 35 ὅπως ἔλθῃ ἐφ' ὑμᾶς πᾶν αἷμα δίκαιον ἐκχυννόμενον... (=*which has been poured out*).

page 102. The Present Participle in a 'gerundive' sense is another matter. It corresponds to the Present Indicative in a future sense (p. 7 above): ὁ ἐρχόμενος, perhaps τὸ ἐκχυννόμενον (Matt. xxvi. 28, etc.), etc.

page 102. Add (with Meecham, *loc. cit.*) *Conditional*, for example, Heb. ii. 3 ἀμελήσαντες, *if you neglect....* Cf. p. 104, on John xv. 2.

page 103. Meecham, *loc. cit.*, adds Acts xv. 27 ἀπαγγέλλοντας (*si vera l.*).

page 104. Denied by D. J. Georgacas (*loc. cit.*), citing *Class. Philol.* XLVIII (1953), 243 f., though his examples there do not in fact include any with Participles. See, however, Acts v. 22, οἱ δὲ παραγενόμενοι ὑπηρέται...

page 105. Deut. xxxii. 5 (*anonym.*) οὐχ υἱοὶ αὐτοῦ; Ps. xliii. 13 ('Α) ἐν οὐχ ὑπάρξει, (Σ) οὐχ ὑπάρξεως; II Macc. iv. 13 (a *Greek* book) τοῦ ἀσεβοῦς καὶ οὐκ ἀρχιερέως 'Ιάσονος; Philo *Cher.* 85 ἐν οὐ θνητῶν ἑορταῖς; and, with an Adjective, Ezek. xx. 25 προστάγματα οὐ καλά. Wackernagel, *Vorlesungen über Syntax* II (Basel, 1928), 263 f.,g ives examples from Euripides, etc.

page 112. Cf. the triplet in the doxology to the Lord's Prayer, Matt. vi. 13 (*v.l.*).

page 113. Perhaps in both cases the Article is dispensed with because of the sufficiently determinative force of what follows.

page 114. Dr Katz observes that the omission of the Article with *proper* Prepositions is good Greek; and he suggests that the determination of a noun by a Preposition only is a survival of a primitive stage before the use of the Article had become general.

page 118. Add *E.T.* LXIV, no. 8 (May 1953), 241 ff.

page 119. Except when a preceding οὐκ, οὐχ, etc. offers guidance.

page 119. See, however, J. B. Lightfoot on Col. i. 20. To the examples cited add I John v. 18 (where see commentators), Rev. xviii. 7.

page 121. It is a matter of some importance whether or not αὐτοῦ is emphatic in Rom. iii. 25. See L. L. Morris in *Journal of New Testament Studies* (C.U.P.) II, no. 1 (Sept. 1955), 38.

page 123. Cf. the way in which the early LXX idiom ὅδε ἐγώ is corrupted to ὧδε: Ex. viii. 29 (25), Lev. x. 16, original ὅδε with ὧδε as *falsa lectio*; Dan. iii. 92 (25) Θ ὅδε ἐγὼ ὁρῶ (B), ὧδε (Q), ἰδού (*rell.*): ἰδού is a different translation, ὧδε a corruption, of the original ὅδε; Num. xiv. 40 ἰδοὺ οἴδε ἡμεῖς (with variants ειδε, ιδε, ωδε, οιδα): ἰδοὺ οἴδε is an early doublet or conflation. See P. Katz, *Philo's Bible* (Cambridge, 1950), 75 ff., 153 f.

page 124. In the O.T. the Hexaplaric translations have ὅς for the LXX ὅστις as more literal.

page 132. Note also the use of πῶς (as though it were ὡς) in exclamations: Mark x. 23, Luke xii. 50, John xi. 36, and possibly Matt. xxi. 20.

page 143. Meecham, *loc. cit.*, asks 'Is it possible that ἵνα may [in Mark iv. 12] foreshadow the rare and later sense 'because' and thus correspond to Matthew's διὰ τοῦτο...ὅτι (xiii. 13)?' See D.-B. § 369, 2 for ἵνα in Rev. xiv. 13 (though there it is perhaps imperatival) and xxii. 14 ($\mathfrak{p}^{47}$ reads ὅτι in Rev. xiv. 13).

page 153. Note also Accusative and *Participle*, Acts vii. 12, Heb. xiii. 23.

page 161. Meecham, *loc. cit.*, wrote: '...we prefer the inferential sense, "therefore", as possibly in II Tim. iv. 8. This meaning is attested in Hellenistic Greek, both literary and vernacular.'

page 162. Cf. *Joseph and Asenath* (ed. P. Batiffol in *Studia Patristica*, Paris, 1889), XI (p. 54) λοιπὸν τολμήσω, *therefore*. . . .

page 162. Or ? 2 (*a*), with the relevant δέ in *v.* 5: *so, for some time...but when....*

page 163. Add ? 2 (*b*) Heb. viii. 4 (*v.l.* μὲν γάρ).

page 166. Cf. ἐπ' ἐσχάτων τῶν ἡμερῶν, *Test. XII, Dan i. 1* (*v.l. om.* τῶν)

page 168. See further A. Ehrhardt, *Creatio ex nihilo,* in *Studia Theologica,* IV (1950), 13–43.

page 168. Add John v. 14 ...ἵνα μὴ χεῖρόν σοί τι γένηται.

page 169. But *contra* J. Dupont in *Novum Testamentum* (Leiden), I, 4 (1956), 299.

page 174. On the formulae with καὶ ἐγένετο, see the exhaustive analysis by Martin Johannessohn, *Das biblische* ΚΑΙ ΕΓΕΝΕΤΟ *und seine Geschichte* (*Zeitschrift für vergleichende Sprachforschung,* Band 53, Heft 3–4, Göttingen, 1926).

page 176. But, for use outside Semitic influence, see E. Mayser, *Grammatik der griechischen Papyri aus der Ptolemäerzeit,* II (1926+), 2, 85; E. Schwyzer, *Griechische Grammatik,* II, 27—Georgacas, *loc. cit.*

page 178. Cf. Acts iv. 17, *v.l.* ἀπειλῇ ἀπειλησώμεθα.

page 178. Cf. *Corpus Hermeticum,* I, 18 ὁ θεὸς εὐθὺς εἶπεν ἁγίῳ λόγῳ· Αὐξάνεσθε ἐν αὐξήσει καὶ πληθύνεσθε ἐν πλήθει....

page 179. Possibly add (*si vera l.*) Mark iv. 31 ...ὃς ὅταν σπαρῇ... μικρότερον ὄν....

page 180. See, however, H. G. Meecham in *E.T.* LVIII (May 1947), 207 f.

page 181. It is, in particular, noteworthy that the indefinite third person was current in Jewish writings as a way of referring to God: see G. Dalman, *The Words of Jesus,* 224 f.; J. Jeremias, *The Parables of Jesus* (E.T., S.C.M., 1954), 12 and *passim.* On the other hand, see note to p. 28 above for caution against carelessly assuming 'Semitism'.

page 182. Cf. J. Jeremias, *The Parables of Jesus* (*ut supra*), 25.

page 182. Dr Katz notes that twice in Homer there is the comparable προπροκυλινδόμενος (*keep rolling*), imitated by Apollonius Rhodius and Oppian; but that the only strict parallel in secular Greek is μᾶλλον μᾶλλον, πλέον πλέον, Soph. fragment 201, according to an ancient grammarian. In the LXX, however, it is frequent: Gen. vi. 19 f., vii. 9 δύο δύο, vi. 14 (according to versions) νοσσιὰν νοσσιάν (i.e. *with nothing but small rooms*); Ex. viii. 10 θημωνιὰς θημωνιάς. But in the N.T. it is only found in Mark vi (where add *v.* 40 πρασιαὶ πρασιαί).

page 182. See further P. Katz, *Philo's Bible,* 24–6.

page 183. Perhaps cf. the French idiom with *voici: je l'ai vu voici trois ans.*

page 183. It seems to be the καρδία which makes it Semitic. For ἀναβαίνειν or ἐλθεῖν ἐπὶ νοῦν see Bauer, *s.v.* ἀναβαίνειν.

Note also the phrases with τιθέναι and καρδία or πνεῦμα in Luke i. 66,

xxi. 14, John xiii. 2 (βάλλω), Acts v. 4, xix. 21; and cf. (with F. F. Bruce on Acts v. 4), Dan. i. 8 (Θ), Haggai ii. 18.

Is John x. 24 τὴν ψυχὴν ἡμῶν αἴρεις a 'Semitism' for *raise our hopes*? There does not appear to be much evidence for *keep us in suspense*, whereas נשא נפש אל can mean *set one's hopes on* (Pi. *desire*, *long*), and LXX sometimes has ἐλπίζειν, etc. in such contexts. See C. K. Barrett, *in loc.*, who, however, is inclined to follow Pallis in suggesting 'trouble', 'annoy', etc.

page 183. ὁ τόπος εἰς ἀγορὰν γίγνεται (Polybius), and instances in Rad. p. 21 and n. 1 show that this can be regarded as a Semitic exaggeration of genuine Greek.

page 184. Add κατὰ πρόσωπον, μετὰ προσώπου. But such locutions are not unattested in non-Semitic Greek: see Bauer *s.v.* Note also πρόσωπον λαμβάνειν, Luke xx. 21, Gal. ii. 6 (with Lev. xix. 15, Job xlii. 8, Mal. ii. 9, etc.), and the (non-Septuagintal) προσωπολημψία, προσωπολήμπτης, προσωπολημπτῶ—apparently coined by Christian writers on the analogy of the LXX phrase; also Jude 16 θαυμάζοντες πρόσωπα (with Gen. xix. 21, etc.).

page 185. Is it possible that Luke viii. 14 πορευόμενοι συνπνίγονται is similar, and even that Jas. i. 11 ἐν ταῖς πορείαις αὐτοῦ μαρανθήσεται might have arisen from a misunderstanding of a Semitic saying in the form πορευόμενος μαρανθήσεται?

page 186. Add κηρύσσειν and κράζειν, both used for קרא—C. H. Dodd, *The Interpretation of the Fourth Gospel* (Cambridge, 1953), 382, n. 1 (citing H. St J. Thackeray).

page 186. Dr Katz adds that, since ז (Z) and ד (D) are sometimes interchanged, there may be a case here of homonymy: either word, may have been patient of both meanings.

page 188. Perhaps add (*f*) The *pluralis majestatis*, אלהים for *God*, etc.

page 193. G. D. Kilpatrick, *loc. cit.*, alludes to an important realm of investigation not treated of here: 'It is also important to observe the standards of taste. For example, in the first century the historic present was used at one extreme by the atticists in their imitation of the ancient models and at the other by writers of little or no literary pretensions, like the author of Mark (cf. the G recension of the *Life of Aesop*). Midway between them, writers of good *Koine* Greek in general avoid the idiom (cf. Eriksson, *Das Präsens Historicum in der nachklassischen griechischen Historiographie*).'

A very valuable index to Lucan usage is provided in H. Schürmann's studies on Luke xxii; see the third volume, *Jesu Abschiedsrede* (Münster, Westf., 1957), indices. See also C. H. Turner's famous articles on Marcan usage in *J.T.S.* xxv–xxix, and G. D. Kilpatrick's notes on Marcan usage in *The Bible Translator* (British and Foreign Bible Society), VII, no. 1 (Jan. 1956), 2ff., no. 2 (April 1956), 51ff.

page 197. A teasing example is in Acts xxvi. 20. See Dr A. Marshall's article on these particles in *The Bible Translator*, v, no. 4 (Oct. 1954), 182 f.

page 198. Similarly Dr A. Marshall questions whether εἰμι and ὑπάρχω can be differentiated; and J. B. Lightfoot, on Col. ii. 20 wrote (of ἀποθνήσκειν and θνήσκειν) 'when the aorist is wanted, the compound verb...is used; when the perfect, the simple verb.... This rule holds universally in the Greek Testament'.

page 199, n. 1. Another notorious problem is the meaning of Gal. iv. 17 f. Since ζηλοῦσιν ὑμᾶς οὐ καλῶς, ἀλλ' ἐκκλεῖσαι ὑμᾶς θέλουσιν comprises a scazon and a piece of another line, is it conceivable that this, too, may be an allusion?

I. INDEX OF PASSAGES

(a) THE NEW TESTAMENT

(b) OLD TESTAMENT

(c) OTHER WRITERS

II. INDEX OF GREEK WORDS

III. INDEX OF PERSONS AND SUBJECTS